WHATEVER HAPPENED TO THE QUIZ KIDS?

WHATEVER HAPPENED TO THE QUIZ KIDS?

Perils and Profits of Growing Up Gifted

by Ruth Duskin Feldman

Chicago Review Press • 213 West Institute Place • Chicago IL 60610

Library of Congress Cataloging in Publication Data

Feldman, Ruth Duskin.
  Whatever happened to the Quiz Kids?

  Includes index.
  1. Gifted children—Longitudinal studies.
2. Quiz kids (Radio program) I. Title.
BF723.G5F44   1982   155.4'55   82-14589
ISBN 0-914091-17-4

All photographs, unless otherwise credited, are reproduced by permission of
Quiz Kids, Inc.

Acknowledgment is made for permission to quote from the following: *The
Quiz Kids* © 1947 by Eliza Merrill Hickok, published by Houghton Mifflin;
Working © 1972 by Studs Terkel, published by Pantheon Books; *The Frugal
Chariot* © 1970 by Rita Duskin, published by Windfall Press; *In My Father's
House* by Vanessa Brown in the archives of the Yivo Institute, New York,
New York; and "The Chief Quizzer" © 1947 by Lawson C. Lunde.
Book design and typography by Siemens Communications Graphics.

First Edition
Published by Chicago Review Press, 213 West Institute Place, Chicago,
  Illinois 60610
ISBN 0-914091-17-4

To my mother and father
Rita and Boris Duskin
and to every parent of a gifted child
and every child someone thinks is gifted

Table of Contents

Foreword

Sundays in the 1940s.

We spent a lot of time in the living room.

A red, oriental-style rug (with fringe all around) covered the floor. Against one wall was a long, brown mohair sofa. Next to it was a matching brown mohair easy chair. On the arms and the back of the sofa and easy chair were little lace doilies—antimacassars—held in place by straight pins (which never did the job). Between the chair and the sofa stood a large floor lamp with a giant lampshade resting on a brass-type stem supported at the bottom by a green onyx base.

Opposite the lamp, in the other corner of the living room, stood the most important piece of furniture in our house—the radio: a Zenith console radio with an illuminated dial and a flickering green eye.

Mom sat at one end of the sofa, paging through the latest issue of *Good Housekeeping*. Dad, in the easy chair, read the Sunday edition of the *Chicago Tribune*. My brother was playing with toy soldiers on and around the floor lamp and I was on the floor in front of the Zenith, working on a jigsaw puzzle.

And we were all listening to the radio.

There were some great shows on the air on Sundays in those days. After dinner we tuned in to Jack Benny, Fred Allen, Charlie McCarthy, the Fitch Bandwagon, the Manhattan Merry-Go-Round, and Take It Or

Leave It. Before dinner, in the afternoon, we listened to The Shadow, Nick Carter, True Detective Mysteries, Quick As A Flash and the Quiz Kids.

The Quiz Kids.

At the time, I didn't think they were so great. In fact, I hated it when the Quiz Kids came on. For me, it was like being in school and not knowing the answers. The Quiz Kids gave me an inferiority complex.

Naturally, my folks always enjoyed the broadcasts. They would make sure we tuned in every week and would always comment on how smart those youngsters were and how proud their parents must be. And then they would give me "that" look. A look that said, "So how come *you're* not a Quiz Kid?"

"Nuts," I thought. "Who wants to be a Quiz Kid? They probably have to study from early morning to late at night . . . never have time for fun, never have time to play with the other kids. And what do they get out of it? A war bond to use for their future education. More school! Not me. I don't want to be a Quiz Kid. I want to be a newspaper copy boy like Jimmy Olson and work at the Daily Planet and cover stories with Clark Kent and Lois Lane, that's what I want to be. Not a Quiz Kid. Not on your life!"

But secretly, I did admire Joel and Ruthie and Pat and Lonny and the others. They may not have been my intellectual equal, but they did represent the Kids of America and if grown-ups were surprised that any kids could know so much and be so smart, well, score one for our side.

So, I listened every Sunday with my family and the rest of the country. I will even admit, begrudgingly, that I enjoyed the program . . . especially on those rare occasions when one of those smart alecks missed a question!

THOSE were the days.

—Chuck Schaden
Host of "Those Were the Days"
radio program

Acknowledgments

Many people made this book possible.

The first glimmer of the idea came from a newspaper article sent me by Minna Novick. My husband, Gilbert Feldman, and my daughter, Laurie Feldman, urged me to undertake the project, helped with every step of the planning and execution, provided moral support, and served as "first readers" for all the innumerable drafts. My agent and publicist, Carol Dechant, provided invaluable editorial and practical advice. Betty Nudelman helped me delineate the questions to be addressed. Initial leads to the whereabouts of the former Quiz Kids came from Eliza Hickok Kesler, Rachel Stevenson, and Joan Bishop Barber. My son, Steven Feldman, transcribed many of the interviews; my daughter, Heidi Feldman, helped with correspondence; both read and criticized the manuscript, as did my mother, Rita Duskin, and my sister-in-law, Rhoda Feldman (who also helped with transcription). The following people read parts of the book and offered helpful advice: my sister, Bunny Shuch, my brother-in-law, Dr. Sidney Feldman, Daniel Feldman, Broudy Simons, Joan Fickinger, Peter Tarpey, Dorinda Hoarty, Eunice Joffe, George Crenshaw, and Laurel Crandus, a teacher of the gifted in Woodridge, Illinois. However, I am solely responsible for the content.

I received special cooperation and resource materials from Chuck Schaden (host of "Those Were the Days"), Studs Terkel, Geoffrey

Cowan, Peter Reich, Betty Swanson Upjohn, Elinor Tanin and Ron Staley of the UCLA Radio Archives, Catharine Heinz of Broadcast Pioneers Library in Washington, D.C., Professor Julian C. Stanley of Johns Hopkins University, Alice Schlessinger of the University of Chicago Laboratory School Alumni Office, Henrietta Wexler, Barbara and Michael Rosen, Elise Barack, Lawrence Solomon, Judy Peres and Harriet Spiesman and Margaret Becicka, teachers of the gifted program at Edgewood School, Highland Park, Illinois.

Much of the material on the history of the Quiz Kids program and the Quiz Kids themselves came from Eliza Merrill Hickok's book, *The Quiz Kids* (Houghton Mifflin, 1947) and from scrapbooks and clippings made available by "Roby" Hickok Kesler; the Rev. John Lucal, S.J.; Joan Bishop Barber; Harve Bennett; Claude Brenner; Vanessa Brown; Lon Lunde; Marcella and Sheila Conlon; the late Rose Cooks; Lucille Dytch; Gino Stockero; Joe Darrow; Clara Williams; and my mother, Rita Duskin. Pictures were supplied by the foregoing and by Dorothy Merrick, Rachel Stevenson, Harvey Dytch, Margaret Merrick Scheffelin, Sally Wilhelm Fullerton, and Robert Easton.

I wish to thank my editors, Linda Matthews and Mary Munro, for their patient and wise guidance and my publisher, Curt Matthews, for his faith in this project. Finally, my deep appreciation to all my former Quiz Kid colleagues, their families and friends, and the original staff members, who responded to my questions with openness, sincerity, and good humor.

Ruth Duskin Feldman
Highland Park, Illinois
October, 1982

Introduction

"I predict for the Quiz Kids life success far beyond the average," wrote Professor Lewis M. Terman, America's foremost authority on gifted children, shortly after World War II.

Terman's prophecy held more than casual interest for me. The Quiz Kids were at a peak of popularity, and I, Ruth Duskin, was one of them. Broadcasting from Chicago on nationwide radio and later on television, our "panel of embryonic Einsteins" amazed up to twenty million home folks each week, answering questions about nuclear physics or Wagnerian operas at an age when most youngsters were reading about Dick and Jane, Nancy Drew and the Hardy Boys.

In many American homes in the early 1940s, tuning in the Quiz Kids was nearly as habitual as turning on the evening news to hear how our boys were doing overseas. The press followed our feats almost as closely as the troop maneuvers in Europe and the Pacific. The term *quiz kid* had become part of the vernacular and some of our names, household words.

The complete Quiz Kids roster is lost, so it is impossible to say how many youngsters competed during the show's thirteen-year span. The most reliable estimate is six hundred. A few dozen, at most, were recalled repeatedly until our sixteenth birthdays.

A small corps of regulars toured with our "Chief Quizzer himself," Joe Kelly. We raised millions of dollars in war bonds; entertained soldiers, sailors and WAACs; trounced university professors, United States senators, army generals, and business executives in question-and-answer bouts; did guest spots with Fred Allen, Jack Benny, Bob Hope, Arthur Godfrey, Milton Berle, and other beloved personalities; visited Paul Revere's house and the White House; launched a ship and clambered inside a B-29 bomber; made movies, records, and constant front-page headlines.

We were turned into cartoons, follow-the-dot and cutout books. (Imagine playing with a paper doll of yourself? I did.) We sold oceans of Alka-Seltzer and mountains of One-A-Day vitamins. We signed autographs until our hands were numb.

Children all over the country read *Quiz Kids Magazine,* played with Quiz Kids toys and games, and wore Quiz Kids club badges on their Quiz Kids sweatshirts. They looked up words in the *Quiz Kids Dictionary*, read our favorite stories and poems in a Quiz Kids anthology, and tried to "Beat the Quiz Kids" by topping our scores in a syndicated quiz column.

In 1947, the show's assistant director, Eliza Merrill Hickok (affectionately known as Roby) wrote a best-selling book about us, *The Quiz Kids* (Houghton Mifflin, 1947). "The Quiz Kids," she assured her readers, "are typical American school children. The tremendous acclaim they have won . . . is the acclaim for all children who are bright, modest, and ambitious."

Our nation was just beginning to discover its untapped vein of gifted youth. Juvenile intelligence had been, as a rule, discounted. Children were to be seen but not heard. "Precocious" was virtually equivalent to "freak" or "brat." Genius was thought to be one step removed from lunacy.

In the decades to follow, after the Soviets shook up America with their 1957 Sputnik launch, articles such as "Gifted Children, Our Nation's Greatest Resource" and "Are We Wasting Tomorrow's Leaders?" would appear with growing frequency in national magazines. But back in 1940, when Chicago producer Louis G. Cowan began to peddle his idea for a new kind of quiz show featuring bright youngsters, a dozen sponsors turned him down. "Nobody wants to listen to smart-alecks," they said. "Smart kids make other kids look dumb."

Cowan finally got his chance, and the show clicked. We Quiz Kids were an enigma. Touted as prodigies, we bore a refreshing resemblance to the boy or girl next door. Interviewers expecting pale, bespectacled bookworms or overbearing little monsters were surprised to find us "just kids." We were living testimonials to the joy of learning.

Skeptics charged the program was rehearsed. "Everyone knows children couldn't possibly know so much," sputtered one indignant letter writer. Another insisted we Kids actually were adults. I was accused of being a midget posing as a little girl. Eldon Roark, one of a succession of journalists to test the program's authenticity, sequestered four of us in a Memphis hotel room and bombarded us with questions for half an hour before admitting we knew our stuff.

Some of the doubts focused on our future. The conventional wisdom of an egalitarian America was that prodigies fizzle. Knowing heads wagged, "Early ripe, early rot."

The image of the child wonder doomed to misery was buttressed by the highly publicized case of William Sidis, who died in 1944 in obscure poverty at the age of forty-six. The son of a psychopathologist father who set out to prove he could raise a genius, the boy learned to read and spell at two, was familiar with three languages at four, and passed a Harvard anatomy exam at eight. He entered Harvard at eleven, lectured mathematics professors on four-dimensional bodies, and graduated cum laude at sixteen. But Sidis, subjected to a merciless barrage of publicity, gave up a teaching position at Rice University at nineteen and became a recluse. Reacting against the intellectualism his father had forced on him, he spurned his mathematical skill and drifted from one menial job to another. living in shabby rooms and priding himself on his facility with an adding machine. The final output of his tormented mind was a book, published at his own expense, on his childhood hobby: collecting streetcar transfers.

"Perhaps our Quiz Kids would come to that unhappy ending, too, if they had parents who wanted to make freaks out of them," wrote Roby Hickok. Dedicating her book to the proposition that we Quiz Kids were Perfectly Normal Children, she seized upon Professor Terman's optimistic prognosis.

Terman had dedicated himself to exploding the myth that early brilliance fades. In a now-classic study, he had followed for more than twenty years the progress of fifteen hundred California schoolchildren with high I.Q.'s and had found most of them unusually successful and well-adjusted adults. After examining Quiz Kids graduates, he expected they would be too. His pioneering research, and similar studies by Professor Paul Witty of Northwestern University, debunked the notion that smart kids are physical weaklings or bookish misfits.

Witty credited us Quiz Kids with correcting the public's misconception of young achievers as peculiar eccentrics. He praised the show for offering outstanding boys and girls a challenge often lacking at home and at school.

We Quiz Kids had "glamorized learning," according to Roby Hickok. "They have proved to countless other school children . . . that it is no longer 'sissy' to get good grades."

One of those children, a girl too tall and gawky to be a cheerleader, wrote four decades later about the program's effect on her:

> I don't know where the Quiz Kids came from, or where they went. For a while they were important in my life. A "girl" could be a Quiz Kid. . . . Sitting by the radio, on the floor of my bedroom, I would hear the applause, and when I knew the answer, sometimes even before a Quiz Kid knew it, I'd clap for myself.
> —Dorothy Storck, *Chicago Tribune,* June 7, 1981
>   (Knight-Ridder Newspapers)

Some of our contemporaries to whom our accomplishments were held up as examples had a different reaction. Said one of Joel Kupperman's classmates, recalling how teachers would put the "smirking" little math whiz through his paces before his dutifully applauding peers: "I hope they all turned out to be garbage collectors."

Did time prove Professor Terman right? We Quiz Kids are at an age when our achievements can be measured against the expectations we aroused.

The hazards that await child stars have been abundantly documented: the early washouts, the struggles with drugs, the failed marriages. Work, wedlock, and parenting can pose uncommon challenges for those who reach the pinnacle by puberty, and the midlife crisis can hold particular poignancy.

What is different about us Quiz Kids is that we were celebrated for our mental endowments. We were known and loved for ourselves, not for playing someone else. Today we are a set of people shaped to varying degrees by that shared experience.

For those who appeared only once or even a few times, the effect may have been no more than that of being "Queen for a Day" or singing on the "Ted Mack Amateur Hour." But for those of us who were regulars in our formative years, the show and all that went with it could have been expected to make an imprint on our personalities.

Studs Terkel, in *Working*, drew a disturbing portrait of "Bruce Fletcher" (not his real name), one of the first and most famous Quiz Kids. Proclaimed a prodigy at seven, he was at thirty-nine a refugee, content with an undemanding job tending roses. He told Terkel:

Peace and quiet and privacy have meant a great deal to me in the years since I made my escape. I didn't feel free as one of the Quiz Kids. Reporters and photographers poking you and knocking you around and asking ridiculous questions. As a child you can't cope with these things. I was exploited. I can't forgive those who exploited me.

. . . Had I grown up as others did, I would have come out a much better person. In school, if I would fail to answer a question, the teacher would lean forward and say in front of the class, "All right! Just because you were one of the Quiz Kids doesn't mean that you're a smart pupil in my class." I wish it had never happened.

(Softly) But we were unique at the time. The Depression was over. America was the haven and all good things were here. And I was the youngest of the Quiz Kids. Of course, I'm a has-been. The Quiz Kids itself has been a has-been. But . . . it achieved history, and that is where I'm proud to have been a part of it. (Laughs) Ah, the time of retirement has come and I'm in it! I'm in it!*

Reading "Bruce's" painful words, I winced as I recognized their source. I was uncomfortable to see the label, "The Quiz Kid," attached to the one Kid who, by his own admission, had become "pretty obnoxious" by eleven and had been retired nearly five years early. As if he were a member of my family, his self-pity seemed to reflect on me. I was sorry but not entirely surprised to learn what had become of him.

"Why doesn't somebody write about the Quiz Kids who came out all right?" I protested, wondering how many of us had.

I had followed the careers of very few of my former colleagues. The most highly publicized, stage and screen actress Vanessa Brown, had starred in *The Seven Year Itch* on Broadway and in "My Favorite Husband" on television in 1955. James Watson (whom I did not remember) had won the Nobel Prize for Medicine in 1962 for the discovery of the structure of DNA, the key to propagation of life.

Harve Bennett Fischman had dropped his last name and become a Hollywood television producer. In 1974, on a family trip, I looked him up. My three children were thrilled to sit in on the shooting of his hit show, "The Six Million Dollar Man." At lunch, Harve regaled us with inside stories but brushed aside the children's questions about our "olden

*Studs Terkel, *Working,* Pantheon Books, New York, 1972, p. 516.

days.'' On our arrival, he had introduced me to his secretary as ''someone from an earlier chapter of my life.'' We did not reopen it.

Six years later, I got my first hint of how Harve felt about that chapter. He and Geoffrey Cowan, son of the originator of Quiz Kids, were airing a television revival. The *New York Times* asked Harve about his transition from Quiz Kidhood to adulthood.

''Over the long run,'' he replied, ''the fame and success, I believe, had a totally positive effect on me. But I went through a period of several years after leaving the show when I suppose I was experiencing a classic letdown, like a lot of child actors, who have achieved too much, too soon.''

What did happen to the Quiz Kids?

In a broader sense, the question is: what happens to gifted children?

In our day, the smartest kids often became troublemakers out of boredom; teachers, not knowing what else to do, left them to their own devices or double-promoted them in self-defense. Now the gifted are coming into their own. In many places, schools enrich their education and put them on the fast track. For us, there were only two routes: skipping a grade or getting on the Quiz Kids show. Some of us did both.

Criteria for identifying the gifted are far more sophisticated today. But according to the usual indices—high I.Q., early and avid reading, large vocabulary, rapid educational progress, strong curiosity and concentration, multiple interests and talents—many, if not most Quiz Kids undoubtedly would have qualified. What the show displayed primarily (and what was stressed in school) was memory; but most of us also showed evidence of reasoning, imagination, and musical or dramatic ability. Perhaps as much to the point, we were *perceived* as gifted, with all the attendant attitudes and expectations.

Professor James J. Gallagher of the University of North Carolina, a leading advocate for the gifted, has remarked on America's ''love-hate relationship'' with those who are ''told by their elders that they are the future of the nation.'' A telling parable by Kurt Vonnegut, Jr., was published in 1950, about the time the Quiz Kids went on television:

> The year was 2081, and everybody was finally equal. . . . Nobody was smarter than anybody else. Nobody was better looking than anybody else. . . .
>
> George, while his intelligence was way above normal, had a little metal handicap radio in his ear. He was required by law to wear it at all times. He was tuned into a government transmitter.

Every twenty seconds or so, the transmitter would send out some
noise to keep people like George from taking unfair advantage of
their brains.
—"Harrison Bergeron," *Welcome to the Monkey House*
(New York: Dell, 1950), p. 7.

Despite the burgeoning interest in the gifted, the American ethos still
resonates with the old overtones. Our democracy remains ambivalent
about its intellectual standouts, though not its athletic ones. An
unusually bright child may be resented as a know-it-all by peers uncomfortable with those who know too much. The top of the class can be a
lonely place.

Certainly few gifted or talented children today are singled out to the
extent we Quiz Kids were, or subjected to such acclaim and scrutiny.
Nevertheless, marked out they are, whether in special programs, at public
performances, or informally among their peers. Thus our experience can
be seen as a paradigm of what the gifted youngster goes through . . . of
some perils and profits that come with the territory.

Much still is unclear about the nurture of the gifted and how they view
themselves. Parents and teachers wonder why some children seem to
fulfill their potential, while others do not. Our stories, seen through the
retrospective eye of maturity, may hold some insights.

The fate of the Quiz Kid women is a special question. Thirty or forty
years ago, girls with enough nerve and knowledge to compete on the air
(or elsewhere) were rare. The Quiz Kids staff, as Roby Hickok wrote,
would "pray for girls as farmers pray for rain." What, then, became of
the exceptional few who made it as Quiz Kids? Did we follow the usual
feminine paths or move into fields traditionally reserved for men?—
and how do we feel about the choices we made?

The Quiz Kids era is gone, but its values are ingrained in our cultural
fabric. For us Quiz Kids, our early show business initiation opened our
youthful eyes to the games our society plays, giving us special perspec-
tives on the changes that affected America as we matured. Changes,
among other things, in the accepted meaning of success. What does it take
to get there, and what happens to those who do—or do not?

Perhaps we who were Quiz Kids can offer some answers. That was our
specialty, wasn't it?

WHATEVER HAPPENED TO THE QUIZ KIDS?

Part One:
The Quiz Kids Story—and Mine

A Backward Look

When I was a child, I spoke as a child
. . . but when I became a man, I put away
childish things.
> —I Corinthians 13:11

A little more than three decades ago, when I turned sixteen, I graduated from both high school and the Quiz Kids program. While most other June graduates were donning cap and gown for the first time, those trappings were familiar to me. I had worn them regularly for almost nine years on network broadcasts.

My Quiz Kids tenure ran from 1941, a year and a half after the show began, to 1950, shortly after our classroom of the air came to television. As of that time, I was the top female contestant, with 146 radio and 11 television appearances.

On tour, I sat in Queen Elizabeth's chair and Chico Marx's lap. I met Maurice Evans backstage and Henry Ford at his Willow Run plant. On my tenth birthday, Louisiana Governor Jimmie Davis (composer of "You Are My Sunshine") and fifteen thousand fans sang "Happy Birthday" to me as I blew out the candles on a tremendous three-tiered cake.

At thirteen, turning the tables, I became emcee of the *Chicago Sun-Times'* radio Quizdown, an assignment I inherited from Quiz Kid Harve Bennett Fischman and passed on to Quiz Kids Jack Rooney and Patrick Conlon. Each Saturday morning I fed brainteasers to teams of public and parochial school students not much younger than I. That same year my first book, *Chemi the Magician,* came out. Max Siegel's book store and Carson's State Street emporium threw autograph parties.

Despite all this attention, mine was (as my parents kept telling me) a normal childhood. As normal as it could be under the circumstances. To the kids at school and down the block, I was an oddity. From the age of seven on, I found myself a target for teasing and ''can-I-touch-you?'' awe. When I went out to play, bullies would chase me, trying to snap my picture. In a culture that prized conformity, I stuck out. Longing to blend chameleon-like into the gang, I was branded ''the Quiz Kid.''

My solution, not wholly successful, was to compartmentalize my life. For half an hour a week, I was a Quiz Kid and thrived on it. The rest of the time I tried to pretend it didn't exist.

When I took off my cap and gown at sixteen, I wrote ''A Quiz Kid Grows Up'' for *This Week*, a national Sunday newspaper supplement. Taking the passage from Corinthians as my theme, I declaimed with the solemnity of inexperience:

> We are modern youth, rapidly growing to adulthood in a strife-
> torn world. We must launch ourselves in careers and jobs, marry
> and raise families, and assume countless other responsibilities. The
> effects of two wars, a depression and postwar readjustments give
> special urgency to our problem of growing up. Now is the time
> when we must ''put away childish things.''

And so I did. Along with my Quiz Kids mortarboard, I put away both the glamor and burden of stardom. I married and relaxed into the anonymity of a new name. I was part of the silent fifties; the liberated sixties and seventies were far ahead. I was no longer little Ruthie Duskin but grown-up Ruth Feldman, and proud of it.

The Quiz Kids business lay shoved out of sight like the huge box in my parents' basement, full of press notices, fan mail, glossy photos, Quiz Kids postcards, and other relics. Years later, my mother brought me a shopping bag crammed with what she had been able to salvage from cellar mildew. I consigned the unopened bag to a closet cubbyhole, where it remained almost forgotten. With three children to raise, volunteer work, and eventually a writing, teaching, and photography career, I had more important things to do than to go through that old stuff. ''Live in the moment,'' my mother had taught me, and I did.

My elder daughter recalls that ''Quiz Kids'' was virtually a taboo topic in our home. Afraid the children might feel overshadowed, I kept them in the dark. ''Every once in a while,'' says my son, ''some bit of information would slip out that would astound me—that you'd sung with Bing Crosby, met Judy Garland, traveled all over, been famous, signed autographs. All those stories seemed incoherent in terms of the person you presented yourself as. You made it seem irrelevant.''

When someone would ask me what it was like being a Quiz Kid, I would shrug, ''That was a long time ago,'' inwardly groaning: *Why dredge up ancient history?*—yet also secretly pleased at being remembered. Almost invariably the next question would be, ''Whatever happened to Joel Kupperman (or one of the others)?'' My sketchy answers were gleaned from the grapevine.

Then, after thirty years, I decided to seek out the old bunch and see what directions their lives had taken. My search was prompted more by curiosity than by the tug of old acquaintance. I had known them only as Quiz Kids. Like me, each must have had a private side that I had scarcely glimpsed.

Over a period of a little more than a year, in 1981 and early 1982, I interviewed about a dozen, as well as their parents, siblings, and acquaintances, and sent questionnaires to as many others as I could locate. All but one of those I interviewed in depth had been prominent regulars; Vanessa Brown was included because of her sustained notoriety as a former Quiz Kid in her movie buildup.

In large part, my urge, and ultimately my satisfaction, was to confront my own Quiz Kid identity. The initial stimulus was my children's growing fascination with the ''skeleton'' in my closet. When one of their friends asked to interview me for a class assignment, we rummaged through the bag of clues to a past buried almost beyond recall.

The crumbling clippings reminded me that my fame had extended abroad. Soldiers had seen me in Paramount movie shorts and put up my pin-up picture in their barracks. Australians had heard me on record, and French and British schoolchildren had read of me in their newspapers as an ''internationally famous child.''

Out came the brittle 78 r.p.m. discs that preserved fragments of my radio days. My husband, a Jack Benny fan, delighted in the hilariously-rigged triumph the Benny Kids (Mary Livingstone, Dennis Day, Phil Harris, and Don Wilson) had scored over us Quiz Kids. My musical off-spring chuckled to hear their mother break up in bashful giggles while trying to sing ''Ah! Sweet Mystery of Life!'' with Bing Crosby.

I dug out my engraved QK key from the back of the bureau drawer, where it had rested for years in a small cardboard box beside my college sorority pin, my Phi Beta Kappa key, and the ID bracelet my husband had given me when we were going steady. With mild regret, I remembered bestowing the gold ring I had received from Jack Benny (whose generosity belied his carefully crafted image) on my high school boyfriend, to ease the pain of postgraduation parting. I paged through autograph books filled with signatures of those I had considered *real* celebrities. Page after page smeared with lip prints of movie queens like Hedy Lamarr, Veronica Lake and Susan Hayward.

And I marveled at the innocence of a nation that had lapped it all up so long ago.

School Days, School Days

. . . Dear old golden rule days . . .

It was starting to rain as I ran home from school. Housewives hurried from the butcher shop with chickens wrapped in brown paper and patiently singed off the feathers over match-lit gas burners.

No one was thinking of dinner in the Duskin household. In just a few hours, I was to become a Quiz Kid.

One week before, I had heard my name announced and then received a confirming letter:

> Dear Ruth:
>
> As you probably heard on the radio last night, you are to be one of the new contestants on the QUIZ KIDS program on Wednesday, November 19, 1941. . . .
>
> Kindly arrange to be in Studio E on the nineteenth floor of the Merchandise Mart at 5:45 . . .

Punctuality was not one of my mother's virtues. By the time she had us all ready, it was getting late. In those post-Depression days, we— like four out of five Americans—had no car. The elevated train was a long walk from our west side Chicago flat, and we would have to transfer. My father decided to splurge and hail a taxi.

But on that rainy evening, there were none to be had. In a panic, my dad prevailed upon our landlord's son to drive us downtown. The studio audience already had assembled when we finally arrived, shortly before air time.

"Quiz Kids Introduce a 7-Year-Old Charmer," read the next day's headline in *PM.* The story predicted that I would give Gerard Darrow, until then the Quiz Kid baby, "a good stiff tussle for individual popularity." I was the seventy-eighth Quiz Kid, the youngest (a title I soon lost to Joel Kupperman), and the first little girl.

Two and a half weeks later, the skies rained Japanese bombs. The day after Pearl Harbor, the *Chicago Tribune* carried an item about me. I had been on Quiz Kids three times and was on my way to becoming a regular. Both the country and I were launched on irreversibly transforming courses.

The Japanese attack came as a jolt to ordinary people like my family, whose most earth-shaking worry had been about where our next meal was coming from. During the Depression, my father, like other Chicago schoolteachers, had been paid in scrip, a currency with no value unless shopkeepers chose to honor it. My mother had managed to feed four mouths on a dollar a day. By 1941, things still were tight.

To families like mine, the box radio on the kitchen shelf was the most affordable source of entertainment. Radio was the national pastime. Americans laughed at the homespun humor of Lum'n'Abner, Fibber McGee and Mollie, and Charlie McCarthy; waited, breathless, to learn what the Shadow knew; and rooted for Gang Busters, America's "crusade against crime." Fathers followed the Max Schmeling-Joe Lewis bouts. Mothers admired the way Portia faced life, wept with Helen Trent, and were reassured that Life Can Be Beautiful. Children dropped their hopscotch and marbles games to run inside and thrill to the latest adventures of the Lone Ranger, Tom Mix, and Jack Armstrong, the All-American Boy. All the shows were live. Each had a single sponsor whose product became identified with the program.

Values were clear and loyalties unquestioned. In 1941, "God Bless America" was third on the Hit Parade, and President Franklin Delano Roosevelt was sworn in for an unprecedented third term. FDR's fireside chats had pulled a desperate nation with him step by step of the rocky climb out of the economic depths. Now, in the grim wake of Pearl Harbor, his fellow-Americans listened as he condemned the "day of infamy" and declared war on the Axis.

Later there would be exposes of FDR's alleged complicity in manipulating America into the war. But in December, 1941, and for what was called, simply, ''the duration,'' there were no protests at the Pentagon, no pickets at draft board offices. Our President had spoken, and his country supported him.

The power of radio was enormous. In Jack Benny's words, ''Radio was do-it-yourself television. . . . You saw the performers in your own mind. You were not restricted by the boundaries of a 21-inch tube, but instead painted your own big-as-life version of each moment with that loving creative brush we call 'imagination'.''

Transporting us beyond our narrow environment, radio shaped our view of the wider world. In a time of struggle and despair, radio gave us happy endings. The boy always got the girl, and the good guys always won. You could save your boxtops to send in for a magic ring, and you really believed it would work.

Radio pandered to the American Dream of easy money and instant success. The brass ring dangling within reach at the next turn of the merry-go-round had been transmogrified into a wheel of fortune that might spin you a $1000 Pot o' Gold if your telephone number came up.

My mother was forever entering contests. In April, 1941, she hit the jackpot when she wrote to the Quiz Kids office suggesting me for the panel. The program had been on the air less than a year.

The quiz show was a new genre. Families long had enjoyed playing competitive parlor games like Twenty Questions and testing each other on quiz books. But it was not until the late thirties that the American passion for Q-and-A was exploited on radio. People in Denver, Dayton, and Dubuque flocked to broadcasts that originated from their local movie houses, hoping for a chance to win ten silver dollars for answering Dr. I.Q.'s puzzlers. Sponsors liked quiz shows because the talent came cheap.

Unlike today's daytime television game shows, the quiz program in its heyday was prime-time entertainment. Millions of listeners held their breath while a contestant decided whether to stake all his winnings on the sixty-four-dollar question. (''You'll be sorr-ee-ee!'') To a Depression-weary people, the quiz show offered a symbolic way out.

''Information Please'' introduced a new twist: audience members sent in rather than answered the questions. The challenge and reward lay in stumping a panel of experts. Hosted by Clifton Fadiman, book editor of the *New Yorker,* the program showcased erudite wits like John Kieran, Franklin P. Adams, and Oscar Levant.

''Quiz Kids'' was what Fred Allen called '' 'Information Please' in short pants.'' Five ''youthful experts'' fielded questions submitted by listeners.

If the Kids answered correctly, as we did nine out of ten times, the person who had sent in the question got a Zenith radio; if we missed, a radio-phonograph (later a television set). For each appearance, we received a $100 U.S. savings bond. The top three scorers (four or five in case of a tie) returned the next week.

Louis G. Cowan, the man who originated Quiz Kids, has been called "the quiet innovator." A six-foot-three University of Chicago graduate with the proverbial rich uncle and a wife who was a Spiegel mail order heir, Cowan had a fervent belief in the power of broadcasting to educate and inform. He started out as a publicist with a weakness for worthy causes, helped Kay Kyser develop his enormously popular "Kollege of Musical Knowledge," and produced three minor quiz shows, "Musico," "Who Said It?" and "Play Broadcast."

In the spring of 1940, twenty-nine-year-old Lou Cowan was casting about for another idea. Then expecting his first child, he mulled the dearth of opportunities for bright youngsters. Shirley Temple was the rage, and mothers all over America were dragging their children to singing and tap-dancing lessons. Cowan felt there should be a place in radio for smart kids to shine. Why not a juvenile quiz show—a radio schoolroom?

As with "Information Please," the panelists would be the key. They must be not just a budding brain trust but an interesting mix of winsome personalities. "Everyone said it was impossible—you can't get the kids," Cowan would reflect later. To his way of thinking, that proved he was on to something. With the right young contestants, he felt, the show could be a blockbuster.

Pence James of the *Chicago Daily News* pulled three names from his feature files: Gerard Darrow, seven-year-old bird savant; thirteen-year-old Joan Bishop, who had been a piano soloist with the Chicago Symphony Orchestra; and thirteen-year-old Van Dyke Tiers, who at two had appeared in newsreels, naming state capitals and spelling words like Czechoslovakia. Another find was fourteen-year-old Cynthia Cline, who composed music, wrote poetry, and played the flute. These four made the audition record that Cowan took to advertising agencies.

One after another, sponsors declined. Children with grown-up minds would have no adult appeal. Besides, no one would believe the show was on the level.

Finally, the Wade agency, which handled Miles Laboratories, (makers of Alka-Seltzer and One-A-Day vitamins) agreed to test the show for ten Friday nights on a coast-to-coast NBC hookup as a summer replacement for Alec Templeton, a blind pianist.

The big stumbling-block was finding a quizmaster. At least fifteen candidates flunked out: writers, lecturers, college professors; news commentator Clifton Utley; radio announcers Norman Ross, Harlow Wilcox, Durward Kirby, and Fort Pearson (who became the show's first announcer); and Sidney James, *Time-Life*'s Chicago bureau chief (who served for a while as question editor). Most were either stuffy, pedantic, or overwhelmed by the children's knowledge, or wanted to display their own. The kids, in turn, clammed up.

Walter Wade, the agency president, hit upon an unlikely prospect: Joe Kelly, Hoosier emcee of Alka-Seltzer's "National Barn Dance," a knee-thumping hillbilly romp. Kelly had begun singing in theaters at six and had quit school after third grade to go on the road as "the Irish Nightingale." He joined a minstrel show, and, then, when his voice changed, taught himself to play the piano by watching dime store demonstrations and pounded the ivories for his own dance band, Kelly's Klowns. Later he sold pianos and men's clothing and ran a railroad warehouse in Benton Harbor, Michigan, before returning to show business as a WLS announcer. As "Jolly Joe," he read the funnies to Chicago kiddies each morning and coaxed them to wash behind their ears.

Now it was Joe Kelly who had to be coaxed to try out for quizmaster. He feared he would make a fool of himself; but his humble, easy manner proved to be exactly what was needed. He was the perfect foil for smart kids; his befuddlement humanized them and highlighted their intelligence. He himself was a grown-up kid, unburdened with highfalutin' knowledge. He used down-home expressions like "swell" and "dandy" and "yessirree." "Now, put on your thinking caps," he would say. He could bring out a shy child and tone down a mike-hogger or wild guesser. He liked kids, and kids liked him.

So the man in overalls who rang the cowbell on "Barn Dance" slipped on a cap and gown to sound the schoolbell on "Quiz Kids." Stout, balding Joe Kelly stayed with the Chicago show throughout its thirteen years; as of 1944, his salary was upwards of $600 a week. Called "the magnificent ignoramus" and "the living question mark," he was named the nation's best quizmaster at least twice running in *Radio Mirror* listeners' polls and won a Silver Mike award from *Radio Best.* Occasional fill-ins like Ralph Edwards, Victor Borge, and Fran Allison merely served to demonstrate how much the show's success owed to Joe Kelly's common touch.

Quiz Kids Joel Kupperman and Rinny Templeton once wrote, "Mr. Kelly is like a kindly stepfather to every Quiz Kid. . . . He doesn't *dare* you to answer a question correctly, like some grownups do. He acts like he expects you to know." As ex-Quiz Kid Vanessa Brown says, "When he asked you something, you wanted to tell him something back.''

Before the broadcasts, he delighted in teasing us Kids. ''Do you want to have a look at the questions?'' he would smile, flipping his pack of three-by-five cards in front of our faces, but showing us only the blank sides. ''Oh, sorry,'' he would add—''these are last week's.'' During the warmup period before we went on the air, he would tell corny jokes and play bouncy tunes on the piano. As ex-Quiz Kid Robert Easton recalls, ''his infectious goodwill permeated the studio.''

But no one foresaw all of that when the program first went on the air June 28, 1940, a week after the fall of France. The sweating ''schoolmaster'' with the third-grade education was only a little more nervous than the producers and sponsor. Joe Kelly's opening question was ''What would I be carrying home if I brought an antimacassar, a dinghy, a sarong, and an apteryx?''

''Well-l-l-l,'' began little Gerard, as all concerned held their breath, ''an apteryx—that's a small bird with hardly any wings at all, and it has no tail, and it lives in New Zealand . . . ''

There were rough moments on that premiere night. At times Kelly hadn't the foggiest notion whether the answers the Kids came up with were right or not, because the information on his cards was too sketchy. ''Sakes alive, am I ever dumb!'' he exclaimed at one point. Staff members shuddered when he pronounced Sophocles ''So-PHOC-o-les.''

For a while, his job was in jeopardy. After three months, Roby Hickok, a sprightly Junior Leaguer and feature writer from Cedar Rapids, Iowa, who had just gotten her master's degree from Northwestern's journalism school, was hired to research all conceivable answers and coach the quivering quizmaster in advance. Still, the Kids argued with their good-natured Chief Quizzer, and the ''judges'' (staff members at his elbow) had to correct his gaffes. When Gerard and Van got into a dispute over whether the dodo is prehistoric or extinct, Kelly threw up his hands: ''I guess there isn't much difference, eh?'' In Richmond, as the group toured the Jefferson Davis house, Roby drilled her overgrown pupil on Confederate history. Then, just before the show went on the air, he leaned over to her and asked, ''Say, who *did* win the Civil War?''

Despite the shaky start, the new show's first week had brought 2,600 letters, 250 Quiz Kid prospects, rave reviews in *Variety, Billboard,* and elsewhere, and inquiries from sponsors who initially had turned Cowan down. He stuck with Miles Laboratories and soon had a five-year contract.

The Quiz Kids were the talk of the nation.

On the air barely a month, the five bright youngsters . . . have amazed their elders with their popularity, quickness on the uptake, their encyclopedic knowledge.
—*Life,* August 5, 1940

Quiz Kids is ringing the bell with a resounding clang. . . . the sensation of the hour. . . . They are clean-cut and likable as well as intelligent kids . . . who may lead in shaping the society of tomorrow.
—*Radio Guide*, August 31-September 6, 1940

The term *quiz kid* was fast becoming synonymous with "one who knows all the answers." The Quiz Kids were America's "whiz kids," a variation later adopted by the 1942 University of Illinois basketball team.

Cowan insisted most of his proteges were just bright kids with interesting hobbies, who liked to read encyclopedias rather than comic books. (Eleven Quiz Kid regulars failed to identify Superman as Clark Kent.) But awed reporters exuded superlatives: "Chicagoland's master minds," "Brain-trustlings," "Vest-pocket prodigies."

"Have you ever been embarrassed by a Quiz Kid?" gushed Ann Marsters in the *Chicago Herald-American.* "Have you ever been surrounded by half a dozen bright young things popping bewildering questions at you? Surely these children couldn't answer such difficult questions on the spur of the moment—questions which the average adult finds beyond his store of knowledge. But they can and they do . . . "

On the early broadcasts, a psychology professor or other eminent guest observer" would assure listeners that the program was on the up-and-up. One was artist Grant Wood, who said, "I've always known that some youngsters could ask impossible questions, but here are some who answer the impossible." When Norman Siegel of the *Cleveland Press* charged that the show was rehearsed, Lou Cowan brought him to Chicago to see for himself. Siegel came, saw, and recanted.

"The hit show of 1940," Quiz Kids after ten months had been hailed as best new program and best children's show and, according to a newspaper account, it "probably had garnered more unsolicited nationwide publicity than any radio program in history over a comparable period," including five magazine spreads in one week. Already the show was firmly established in the Hooper ratings, hard behind "Information Please," with roughly one out of ten households tuning in NBC's Blue Network each Wednesday night and, later, on Sunday evenings and afternoons. Though never in the same league as Jack Benny, Fibber McGee and Molly, Bob Hope, and Red Skelton, who commanded thirty to forty percent of the national audience, the Quiz Kids maintained a faithful following estimated at ten to twenty million.

Correspondence mounted, levelling off at twenty thousand letters and fifty applications per week. Potential Quiz Kids usually came recommended by teachers, parents, friends, or relatives, though some were uncovered by staff members or initiated the inquiry themselves. (One girl who did so pretended for years that someone else had written the letter: "I felt that there was something shameful about putting myself forward, perhaps a show of conceit.")

Staffing this smash hit was a bright bunch, all about thirty, without broadcast experience. Sons and daughters of farmers, ministers, professors and missionaries, they hailed from small towns in Wyoming, Texas, Indiana and Iowa. "The power behind Joe Kelly's throne" was executive producer John Lewellen, a gentle, soft-spoken math and science whiz who had finished less than two years of college and had been plucked by Cowan from the *Time-Life* staff. Lewellen's assistant until 1947 (when she left to get married) was warm-hearted Roby Hickok, whose duties quickly expanded from coaching Joe Kelly to writing press releases, running auditions, making trip arrangements, and acting as mother hen; she modestly called herself "low man on the factotem pole." When Roby became too overworked, Rachel Waples Stevenson was hired as chief researcher. Mild, dainty Rachel, a professor's wife with an English degree from Rice University, had done a little public relations work and produced some university shows and was looking for a "fun" job.

A staff of eighteen combed the mail for good questions; Rachel and Roby often rewrote them, adding a clever hook. For instance: "What would a musical automobilist do if he approached highway signs that read a) andante, b) a tempo, c) finale?"*

Questions were chosen with a careful ear to pace and balance. Often staff members would sit up late at night, kicking around questions. They had a post-mortem after each show, listening to the records to see what worked and what dragged. The questions had to be hard enough to show off the Kids' knowledge but not totally beyond the audience's ken. After all, half the fun was in trying to beat the Kids to the answers. "To outsmart a Quiz Kid is a triumph that rings sweetly in the ears for months," wrote John K. Hutchens in *New York Times Magazine*. "Even to score a tie in that fast company leaves a certain glow."

---

* a) slow down, b) resume regular speed, c) stop—end of road.

The Kids knew what famous person in French history disguised himself as a valet (Louis XVI) and that a book called *Arachnida,* which "follows the fortunes of thirty American families," was about spiders. They explained what makes torpedoes go and knew how far a phonograph needle travels while paying a ten-inch record (2½ inches—the needle travels across the record, not around it).

No matter how carefully the questions were prepared, the Kids would come up with the unexpected. Take this question: "Multiply the number of the famous Dionne children by the length of time it took to create the world; subtract the result from "when life begins"; add the time it took Phileas Fogg to go around the world. What is the final figure?" The answer 85 was judged correct. But one of the girls pointed out that the world was created in six days, not seven, the seventh being a day of rest.

To counteract the impression that Quiz Kids were mere memory machines, there were discussion questions on national and world affairs. The National Opinion Research Center reported that the Kids were "considerably better informed than the average adult" (which wasn't saying much) because they knew what the Bill of Rights was and could name both of Illinois' U.S. senators.

During the show's maiden year, the Kids journeyed to New York to make the first of seven Paramount movie shorts (for which they got $300 apiece) and on to Washington. "You're all so learned, you frighten me," Eleanor Roosevelt confessed as she showed them around the White House. The First Lady confided that her children had enjoyed trying to catch their father on tough questions at the dinner table. Just the other day, she went on, she had asked him about a treaty with Spain—"and I stumped him!" Roosevelt himself, four years later, told Lou Cowan, then chief of the Office of War Information, "I listen to those youngsters and I love them!"

In Atlantic City, the Kids did a program for 12,000 school administrators; gray-haired pedagogues lined up for their autographs. And then came Hollywood.

> Envy of every U.S. kid (were radio's Quiz Kids) . . . not for their dazzling braininess, not for their sizeable winnings in U.S. defense bonds, but for their trek across the country to take Hollywood by storm in a round of parties, film-making dates, and guest broadcasts.
> —*Movie-Radio Guide,* June 7-13, 1941

The announcement that the Quiz Kids were to go to Hollywood as Jack

Benny's guests was what impelled my mother, fearing the change of location might soon become permanent, to write her letter:

> We have a daughter who will be seven in June. She has been reading and writing since four years of age, and already has about forty poems to her credit. . . .
>
> At school, we have had to prevent them from advancing her too fast. . . . At the request of her teacher, she went up to the eighth grade and read the eighth grade material. . . . She recently won a contest for the best poem in the school.
>
> A few weeks ago, the Board of Education gave her an intelligence test and . . . told me she has a "genius rating," that she is absolutely "tops."

The return mail brought a detailed questionnaire, which I laboriously completed all by myself. There were questions about school activities, hobbies, ambitions, and favorite books (I listed thirty). I also had to submit a 250-word essay on why I should be a Quiz Kid.

"I love to play guessing games, do riddles and answer questions," I wrote. "I have an excellent memory, a very good vocabulary, and I am at ease in front of strangers. I love knowledge, and when I begin working at something I will not stop until I have finished."

Joe Bailey, general manager of the Cowan office, liked my questionnaire enough to interview me. He asked me riddles; I asked him some. To his surprise, I knew that the youngest President was Theodore Roosevelt. He was even more surprised when he asked me how old Roosevelt had been at the time, and I replied, "I think he was sixteen."

The real test was a formal audition, a simulation of the show. Brainpower and book-learning did not assure acceptance. Poise, quickness, originality, humor, modesty, and mike sense were more important than profundity. It helped to be young and/or small—the ability to wow the audience bore an inverse relation to size and depth of voice. Sportsminded boys were in demand as an antidote to the egghead image.

Showmanship was crucial. At Margaret Merrick's audition, she recalls, "there were kids who clearly knew something and couldn't say it, kids who were wild guessers, kids who froze, kids who giggled, kids I'd never put in a school play. You've got to be able to *act* a little!" Quiz Kids had to be wholesome and unspoiled. Showoffs and smart-alecks were crossed off at once. Pushy parents were the kiss of death. "Don't you feel like a Hollywood mother?" gushed one mama to mine. Her child did not make it.

Of the thousands of Chicago area schoolchildren who paraded through the weekly auditions, one in twenty was chosen, and most of those lasted only once or twice. I could imagine them tuning in week after week, hoping to hear their names announced for the following broadcast.

"I felt sorry for kids who would be on the show for the first time, absolutely silent, contributing nothing," says Lon Lunde, who himself appeared only sporadically at first. "Some of the smartest kids bombed because no particular area caused them to stand out."

Those with the most staying power had a fund of general information plus a specific interest or talent. The classic case was Richard Williams, who could acquit himself well in almost any subject and could work complex math problems in his head—a stunt little Joel Kupperman repeated. Harve Bennett Fischman knew oddities about American Presidents, like the fact that William Howard Taft weighed 332 pounds and got stuck in the White House bathtub. Joan Bishop and Lonny Lunde had perfect pitch, a natural for radio: they could identify musical notes or sing them on demand. Claude Brenner knew airplanes. Gerard Darrow knew everything hardly anyone wants to know about birds. My specialties were literature and chemistry, the latter interest picked up from my father, a high school chemistry teacher, not long before tiny Patrick Conlon came along to challenge me on the Shakespearian and Biblical fronts. But most of the girls stuck to the humanities, while boys also delved into social studies and science.

A diversified portfolio paid off. Joel and Pat, who as they grew older branched into history, sports, and current events, were tops in longevity. For most of us, moving onto each other's turf was a law of survival; but Dick Williams, whose territory was so vast that he took first place week after week, usually refrained from raiding. People with exotic fields, like Gerard's birds, were relatively invasion-proof.

Some of us spent a fair amount of time reviewing; others little or none. *Time* was required reading for those in the know. "That was a third of the questions right there," laughs Dick. "Those other kids were wondering how we knew so much!"

Helpful assets were a test-taking knack, a venturesome spirit, and the ability to think on one's feet. Lonny was fast at raising his hand, figuring out where a question was headed before Joe Kelly finished asking it: "On the easy questions that every Quiz Kid knew," says Lon, "I was the one that pulled the trigger the quickest."

Kelly was supposed to call on the first Kid with a hand up. But the calls often were close; and try as he might to be fair, predictably complaints of favoritism circulated among some of the mothers, each anxious that her offspring outdo the rest. (More than one mother got so carried away as to mouth answers from the front row of the audience.) Staff members had to keep disgruntled mamas at bay and deal with letters objecting that So-and-So was being called on too much.

Guessing was discouraged but not penalized, so some of us played our hunches. Margaret Merrick would deduce from other people's errors. "Clean-up hitter," she called herself—"If they went down a blind alley, I would pick up the pieces."

Pat recalls identifying the creator of a certain painting as Homer. "It was a one-in-a-million shot, and it happened to be right. I remembered from somewhere that Homer, the Greek writer, had also been an artist. It turned out the answer was Winslow Homer, the American painter. Talk about an educated guess! I didn't even know there *was* a Winslow Homer."

I.Q.'s ranged as high as 200 or more (Richard's, Joel's, Lonny's and mine). Ex-Quiz Kids responding to my survey—those who knew their scores—almost all fell between 135 and 180. But Lou Cowan told the staff to ignore applicants' I.Q.'s, which he felt were not indicative of creativity or originality.

"A child doesn't have to have a fantastically high I.Q. to be on the program," Rachel Stevenson (who in later years became co-producer and handled the talent search) told the *Chicago Tribune*. "Personality, voice, manners—those count a great deal. Our Quiz Kids are certainly bright. . . . But they're a well-rounded, normal bunch of youngsters—not a roster of long-haired geniuses."

It was a statement the producers were forced to reiterate endlessly as debate raged over the question "Is it good for the Quiz Kids?"

"Would You Want Your Child To Be a Quiz Kid?" demanded George W. Lyon in the December, 1941 *Journal of Education:*

> . . . Would you want to prostitute your child's mind to the selfish and material ends of some advertiser? . . . . Growing minds, like growing bodies, need normal development. . . . Education is no sideshow. . . . When there is too much *positive acceleration* in the learning process very often a *mental plateau* is reached where further learning slows down or slumps.

The Quiz Kids' peers, Lyons warned, would treat them like "teacher's pets":

. . . The child . . . may become self-conscious, introspective, and
even depressed . . . by the constant "kidding" of his companions.
Or he may . . . become an insufferable little snob. . . . Prodigies
and geniuses do not, as a rule, grow old gracefully. . . . It is not
pleasant to live on an intellectual plane too far above one's
fellows.

In a follow-up survey, however, Quiz Kids' parents and teachers over-
whelmingly reported that the experience was beneficial for us: it gave us
poise and confidence, provided intellectual stimulation and self-
expression, expanded our horizons, and earned us the admiration of our
schoolmates. When three thousand Chicago youngsters were questioned,
more than two-thirds said they listened to the program and enjoyed it,
and half evinced a desire to be on it. Why? "It shows people that boys
and girls are intelligent." Said *Movie-Radio Guide*: "Quiz Kids teaches
parents to respect their children."

Dorothy Hayes, a University of Chicago instructor writing in *Parents'
Magazine,* described the Kids' "happy, eager faces as they don their caps
and gowns." They seemed, she marveled, calm, wholesome, natural, and
unconcerned with the audience—in fact, to be "having the time of their
lives."

But Hayes also quoted authorities who expressed reservations about
constantly calling attention to children's superiority and who warned that
the program might be discouraging to average youngsters and lead their
parents to expect too much of them. "If it motivates," said one educator,
"it very likely motivates the wrong kind of learning. It is somewhat
amazing to hear a child locate Timbuktu in the French Sudan and indicate
that it may be approached through French Guinea or Rio de Oro, but
from an educational standpoint the performance has little value."

Certainly, Hayes concluded, "the Quiz Kids are a group of superior,
outstanding children. Whether they will remain so and become leaders . . .
will probably depend largely on careful planning for their development.
The Quiz Kids . . . are children who have especial need for level-
headed parents!"

The homes we Quiz Kids came from were financially poor-to-middling
but culturally rich. One father was a janitor, another a street worker,
another a railroad conductor. One was on relief. One family's sole
earnings were from the mother's homemade candy. Most of the mothers
stayed home with their children and did their own housework; many were

not even college graduates. To such families, the show and all that went with it—the college nest egg, the chance to travel, the honor and glory—seemed a golden opportunity. The Quiz Kids were "tots in clover." Many of us had ethnic roots, and our story was an American saga in the rags-to-riches tradition.

It was an opportunity affluent parents were more likely to pass up. Roby Hickok Kesler remembers the son of a steel company president, a boy who was so obsessed with "Quiz Kids" that he was constantly working up questions to stump his family and even ran his own quiz show at an elegant resort. But he never tried out for the program. "The family probably didn't want the publicity," Roby says.

As the scion of a wealthy clan puts it, "The last thing a WASP family that had made it would want to do was to put a kid out there to be subjected to that kind of pressure. They didn't have to prove anything." A similar attitude prevailed, my husband tells me, in his upper-middle-class Jewish neighborhood: "My mother felt it wasn't healthy for a youngster to have all that attention. There were certain molds you followed. Our rewards were within our own subculture, and they were quite sufficient."

With the chastening example of the Our Gang kids, whose parents and guardians had exploited their earnings, we Quiz Kids were given contracts safeguarding our amateur status, and the regulars' bonds were put in trust for our future education. I gave little thought to the money. A $100 bond was an unimaginable prize to a seven-year-old who thought of nickel ice cream as a rare treat and made doll houses from discarded orange crates. The program to me was simply an exciting thing to do, a welcome supplement to a dull school diet that offered little mental nourishment compared with what I got at home.

Vanessa Brown's mother, a psychologist, used to say that it was the Quiz Kid mothers who really were responsible for the show's success. The families we Kids came from were solid, stable and affectionate; of the first 419 Quiz Kids, it was reported, only one (Robert Easton Burke) came from what was then called a broken home. Quite a few Quiz Kids were the only children in their families and most of us had just one brother or sister (who generally also got a chance to be on the show). Arthur Gordon, writing in *Guideposts,* said an investigation of Quiz Kids' backgrounds had shown that in each case there was at least one parent "who shared enthusiasms with the child, who watched for areas of interest, who gave encouragement and praise for achievement, who made a game of searching out the answers to questions, who went out of his way to supply the tools of learning.

"No doubt," he added, "the capacity for outstanding performance was already there, but it took the love and interest and companionship of a parent to bring it out. . . . Children are naturally inquisitive and love to try new things. But they cannot find these things by themselves; someone must offer them the choices."

"There are thousands of special children, but they are lost in the shuffle for lack of special parents," wrote Margaret Lukes Wise and Clara Belle Thompson. The authors listed "rules for making a quiz kid":

1. Banish for all time the thought that the two-year-old chip off the block rates nothing but baby talk.

2. If three-year-old Johnny is always making a run for his father's fine coin collection, don't think you've done your part by slapping his hands.

3. There's not a mother or father who has not heard *What's that?* The stock answer is, "You're too little to understand." Maybe he is not too little to understand. . . .

My mother got calls from strangers seeking child-raising advice. The secrets were deceptively simple. At a time when adult and child worlds were sharply demarcated, Quiz Kids' moms and dads fed us generous helpings of attention with our oatmeal and spinach, "exposed" us to the classics, played word games with us, and treated us like people, not pests.

At the same time, the public was assured, our parents avoided pushing or spoiling us, let us follow our own bent at our own pace, and professed to be as baffled as anyone by our accomplishments. The papers ran pictures of Quiz Kids turned over parents' knees. ("Yes, children, the Quiz Kids get spanked even as you," ran one caption. "But they probably are smart enough to get out of it most of the time," added another.)

"They were always posing us doing things we never did," laughs Joan Bishop. Joan putting a cake in the oven. Jack Lucal painting a picket fence. Gerard Darrow washing his dog in the laundry tub. Cynthia Cline scrubbing floors "like girls her age are supposed to do."

When asked how it felt to be the mother of a Quiz Kid, Kitty Fischman blushed, "It's like being the parent of any other child." Her son Harve told a Buffalo reporter, "I guess some people expect us to be dressed in Lord Fauntleroy suits and use six-syllable words. They just can't believe that I play football and basketball and Dick is a whiz at tennis. Joel can kick a football like nobody's business, and Ruthie plays games with the kids in her neighborhood just like any other girl."

Once a woman approached Pat Conlon before a New York broadcast and asked him, "Tell me the truth—are you children normal?" My mother was accused of having stood over my crib, teaching me.

People seemed to imagine some sort of invisible balance, on which extra mental chips automatically shortweighted the social and emotional side. Arthur Gordon, in *Reader's Digest*, stood that assumption on its head:

> They are not ordinary children. They are extraordinary, not only in terms of mental development but in categories where very bright children are popularly (and erroneously) supposed to be deficient: leadership, friendliness, generosity, good humor, good manners and general emotional balance. They are, in fact, such well-rounded and superior human beings that anyone who observes them is bound to ask: How did they get that way? Are they made, or are they born?
>
> The answer is, almost certainly, *both*. Heredity is the seed, environment the soil in which an exceptional child must grow. . . . When good heredity and favorable environment meet in one small individual, the results can be truly astonishing.

Certainly we Quiz Kids did show signs of being different. Many of us were heavier than average at birth, walked and talked sooner, and read early and widely without being taught—all signs of giftedness, according to Professor Terman's study. The typical Quiz Kid had a near-photographic memory, an adult vocabulary, a vivid imagination, lots of hobbies and collections, and an insatiable curiosity about just about everything. At the White House, Eleanor Roosevelt found Van Dyke Tiers in the East Room inspecting George Washington's portrait to see whether the Father of Our Country was wearing the false teeth Paul Revere had made him. Jack Lucal and Dick Williams could be overheard arguing, while traveling, about the exact population of a state or the latitude and longitude of its capital.

On tour, as on the broadcasts, boys predominated. The paucity of strong female contenders was a continual headache for the staff. Lou Cowan observed that boys tended to concentrate deeply on a few areas, while girls' knowledge was more diffuse. Dick Williams explains, "There were lots of boys in those days who memorized all the baseball cards. Girls were less likely to do that. The boys on the show, instead of getting passionately interested in baseball cards, happened to have a different turn of mind and got passionately interested in another subject.'' If girls were passionately interested in anything, it usually was boys. Smart girls were expected to play dumb; brains did not go with a petticoat personality. ''We were supposed to be sweet young June Allysons with squeaky clean hair, dependent and not too bright,'' recalls ex-Quiz Kid Joan Moy Smith. ''Boys would tell us things we already knew, and we'd say, 'Oh, really?' or 'Hmmm,' acting very impressed. It was depressing.''

True, girls often outdid boys scholastically. The public schools to which most Quiz Kids went rewarded regular attendance and painstaking work on assigned tasks, rather than ''masculine'' traits like initiative, intensity, and independence. Richard Williams lost out to a pair of girls for high school valedictorian because he missed gym classes during Quiz Kids trips. Jack Lucal finished behind three girls. Pat Conlon was number six; the first five were girls who ''took typing and steno and stuff like that.'' The valedictorian, he says, ''would study hard and get good grades. But many people had much better minds. They would really be interested in things and search out and have ideas. She was into the score, and she got it.'' Whatever it took to score as a Quiz Kid, boys had in greater abundance.

Soon after I came on the program, I found myself the lone female in the usual traveling brigade. Except for Gerard, the original older crew had been supplanted by a younger team: Richard, Harve, Joel, and me. The four of us made pleasing counterpoint . . . Dick's genteel gravity, Harve's sly wit, Joel's irrepressible energy, my girlish simplicity. With the occasional substitution of Margaret, Pat, Bob Easton Burke, and others, we toured coast-to-coast, raising $118 million for the war effort, a feat for which we received a Treasury Department medal. In Philadelphia, we sat in Gimbel's store window, vying to sell the most bonds. I won, dispensing sixteen hundred dollars' worth in a single hour.

At the height of our wartime popularity, we were on the road for weeks on end, each accompanied by a parent or guardian, usually our mothers. ''A trip to Boston and New York is worth two months in school,'' Harve's principal averred. We took homework along; Margaret complained that when she got back, she usually found her classmates had done less than she.

Entering a city, we would get red-carpet treatment. The Philadelphia city fathers declared Quiz Kids Week. Each of us rode in a personal jeep (mine in the lead) with our names on the sides and our own private chauffeurs. A specially assigned U.S. Treasury Department guide showed us the sights. We touched the crack in the Liberty Bell and sat in Benjamin Franklin's pew at Christ Church. At Valley Forge, the chaplain unlocked George Washington's study for us. I visited the nearby Farm School my father had attended and asked to see his grades.

When we got off the train in Houston, we were greeted with a gift of horned toads. We rode through the center of town waving at the crowds from a fire engine preceded by sirens and a police escort, and the sheriff swore us in as deputies.

In Portland, a Meier and Frank department store window had been turned into a wax museum with lifesize models of each of us. From Seattle, we crossed the border to British Columbia, where we were presented with handmade Indian sweaters. We dined in the lieutenant-governor's mansion, sitting in chairs previously occupied by Winston Churchill, Franklin Roosevelt, King George the Sixth, and her Majesty, the Queen.

In Boston, Harve swung the lanterns that had burned in the belfry of the Old North Church the night of Paul Revere's ride; the organist gave us a rendition of "America," so stirring we felt compelled to join in and sing. We lunched at Paul Revere's house with all his living descendants.

In Baton Rouge, Louisiana's songster-governor, Jimmie Davis, entertained us in a vast mirrored banquet room with endlessly reflected crystal chandeliers; he and his seven-piece band serenaded us with "Home on the Range." We toured the Standard Oil laboratories, tested the elasticity of synthetic rubber, and took home samples.

One of our first stops in New Orleans was Antoine's. The maitre d' proudly reeled off a long list of exquisite concoctions, in French, of course. As he waited expectantly, our plebeian party looked at each other uncomfortably. Finally I blurted out, "Don't you have any lamb chops?"

"Of course, madame," said the headwaiter, disconcerted. He became even more so when every last person in our group ordered lamb chops too.

In Salt Lake City, we went sleigh riding in the mountains and nearly tipped over. At the Borden farm, we sat on Elsie the cow. In Hollywood, where we spent a glorious three weeks, we went behind the scenes to watch Joe Kelly in the filming of a Barn Dance picture; lunched with Fred Allen at Sardi's and in the studio canteen with Donald O'Connor, Peggy Ryan, and George Raft; had a swim and barbecue at cowboy star Smiley Burnett's fabulous ranch; sat in Shirley Temple's playroom; and met dozens of other celebrities. Nigel Bruce (Dr. Watson) saluted me:

"As one artist to another, I shall kiss your cheek." And he did.

As we traveled, youngsters throughout the country got the chance to become Quiz-Kid-for-a-day. The lucky children were chosen in city-wide contests; in Los Angeles, twenty-five thousand contended, and the finals were held in the Hollywood Bowl. But no matter how smart these neophytes were, only rarely could they match us seasoned veterans.

Monopoly, chess, and gin rummy games occupied us on the days-long Pullman train rides. Gerard would get off at every stop to catch butter-flies; his Aunt Bessie, who accompanied him, was forever worrying that he'd get left behind.

Once, when we were piling into taxis, headed for a show at Philadel-phia's Stage Door Canteen, Gerard slipped out of his cab unnoticed and ran back into the hotel for a sweater. When we arrived Gerardless, Tallulah Bankhead, guest emcee, struck a dramatic pose, hand to forehead, and intoned, "Oh, my God, we've lost a Quiz Kid!"

Gerard was not the only one to cause a near-panic. At Niagara Falls, I disappeared. Everyone was frantic, certain I'd fallen in. Suddenly I jumped out from behind a tree and smiled, "Did I scare you?"

We were children, after all, and we acted as such, playing musical chairs on movie sets and chasing each other around hotel lobbies. Our every word and escapade, it seemed, was page one news in city after city.

A light-hearted show like "Quiz Kids" was a tonic to a nation depressed by food rationing and casualty lists. We Kids exhorted our peers to plant victory gardens, collect scrap, and buy war stamps. When guest artist Larry Adler aired a request for harmonicas for the boys overseas, more than four thousand of our fans obliged. When actress Gertrude Lawrence appealed for radios for wounded soldiers, 1,320 piled in.

We got thousands of letters. Our correspondents ranged from San Quentin prison inmates to children asking for help with homework and lists of books to read. But most of the mail came from elderly folk, the backbone of our audience. Richard's mother answered all of his, signing his name. For years she corresponded with a Grandma Rosen of St. Louis, whose letters began, "My darling baby boy . . . " Then Grandma Rosen came to Chicago to see the show, and Dick had to pretend his hand was injured, lest he be asked to sign a telltale autograph.

There were gifts: a rare Bible for Dick, a model ship for Joel, history books for Harve, a Bulgarian doll for me, and alligators for Gerard, who mentioned on the air that he was saving for one.

Opening Gerard's mail, the Quiz Kids staff had to hold their noses. Like as not, a dead lizard might fall out. When the horned toad he had been given in Houston met an untimely end, the office soon was hopping with dozens of replacements sent in by sympathetic listeners.

In Detroit, a Hudson Department Store executive offered me my pick of the toy department. My mother, worried about having let me go off alone with this strange man, was dumbfounded when I returned with a costly, satin-clad bride doll, complete with trousseau.

Babies were named for us. When a pair of Minnesota twins were christened Richard and William, Dick's mother knitted them booties, and listeners stocked their layette. When Dick and Harve reached their teens, they began getting love letters. One admirer came to see Dick in Los Angeles; she turned out to be (he moaned) short, fat, and buck-toothed.

After the war, the tie-in for the trips shifted to charitable causes like Red Cross, Community Chest, and March of Dimes; and with the switch to air transport, the travel shrunk to occasional weekends. Once more, a replacement team had been brought up. Richard, Harve and Margaret had graduated, Gerard had fallen by the wayside, and I had given up the touring circuit. Joel and Pat were joined by Lonny, little Naomi Cooks (my replacement), and others.

They visited the Roosevelt home in Warm Springs, Georgia, where FDR had breathed his last. In Denver, the Kids launched a drive to rehabilitate war-torn France, climbed Cheyenne Mountain, and had a peek at Pike's Peak. At an infantile paralysis benefit broadcast from Miami's Orange Bowl, more than one hundred cured polio patients paraded around the field before the Kids emerged from the fifty-yard line tunnel and tossed a football to kick off the show.

By 1948, the Quiz Kids had traveled a total of seventy-two thousand miles to nearly forty cities and sixty military bases and hospitals. The show, named best quiz program, was heard on 142 NBC stations and had been shortwaved abroad. A newspaper in Claude Brenner's Johannesburg called us "the seventh wonder," and an Australian edition of Quiz Kids was the most popular show on that continent. In American cities and towns, local clones of the Chicago show produced winners who, if they survived regional eliminations, would be flown in for a network shot.

But although the full effects were not immediately perceptible, the atomic bomb and the war's end had signalled an explosion of industrial power, affluence, and knowledge. The age of innocent austerity was over. Smart children were no longer a novelty. On "Juvenile Jury," a set of sassy younguns debated questions like "When should a girl start wearing lipstick?"

Big-money game shows proliferated; a quickly jaded public required ever higher stakes. A new gold rush was on. Millions of dollars in money and merchandise lured listeners away from their old favorites. In 1947, "Stop the Music," a Louis Cowan invention, began telephoning people to "name that tune" for $20,000, $30,000 and more. Families sat home awaiting the call. Fred Allen, who was in an opposing time slot and always had been a bit highbrow for mass taste, plummeted to thirty-eighth in the Hooper ratings and retired.

Overshadowed by flashy giveaways, "Information Please" faded. "Quiz Kids" held on longer, its producers reshaping the show to fit an altered America. By the time the Nielsen ratings had slid to four percent, the Quiz Kids had jumped on the television bandwagon.

Radio lost its preeminence, as the small square screen brought Mr. and Mrs. America's beloved idols right into the living room. The award-winning televised Quiz Kids show that began in 1949 soon eclipsed its radio counterpart, recapturing a 10.5 percent Nielsen rating and a 29 percent audience share by 1952, and winding up as one of the 100 longest-running series in TV history.

The move to television overcame a persistent bugaboo: the image of the "bespectacled little monster isolated from the mischief and fun of a normal childhood," as Radio-TV Mirror put it. Naturally, the most photogenic children were assigned to the television pool. But television also cut the Kids down to size. As Lon Lunde observes, "the aura of five bright kids with unseen faces disappeared."

The infant television venture, at first a shoestring operation, covering only four Midwestern cities, soon hooked up with four more on the east coast. By 1951, twenty-eight stations carried the show; forty-eight by 1952. Some of us remember, from those pioneer days, crews crawling on the floor to get cables out of the way of dollying cameras. The lights were so hot that we sweltered under our heavy gowns, and the slates in front of our desks, bearing our names and ages, were too hot to touch.

Jay Sheridan, a twenty-three-year-old Irish bit actor with a little directing experience, was brought in to work with John Lewellen and Rachel Stevenson on the low-budget video production.* At his instigation, the format was changed, eliminating competition and scoring in favor of pure entertainment.

---

* After about three years, he left to become associate producer and director of "Robert Montgomery Presents," and then executive director and producer of ZIV Productions, working with such series as "Bat Masterson," "Highway Patrol," and "Sea Hunt."

Even on the radio, there had been breaks in the question-answer routine. Lonny would play and sing his compositions, Pat wrote skits for the other Kids to act out, Naomi did imitations, and we all made up impromptu poems. Ex-Quiz Kid Marlene Richman remembers one stunt in which the Kids held squealing baby pigs and raced to see who could feed them fastest: "Mine kept biting."

On television, visual gimmicks, often centered on guest celebrities, took priority. Once a hyponotist tried to put the youngsters under. Another time cartoonist Ham Fischer offered a prize to the Kid who could draw the most perfect likeness of his Joe Palooka. (Joel won.) The show became a circus, with animal trainer acts, clown Emmett Kelly demonstrating speed reading, and Naomi riding a horse on camera. The Kids dressed in costume on Hallowe'en . . . boarded one of the original merry Oldsmobiles . . . joined guitarist Tito Guizar in a south-of-the-border jam session. Once little Melvin Miles was shown arriving for the broadcast in a helicopter, atop the Merchandise Mart. The questions were visualized, too. Joe Kelly dressed as a swami, with turban and crystal ball, to portray the opera *The Medium*. In one of my last appearances before my 1950 graduation, I performed an explosive chemical experiment.

That year "Quiz Kids," cited as best TV show, reached its five hundredth broadcast, with telegrams from nearly one hundred illustrious friends who had been our guests. Gridiron giant Red Grange. Actors John Garfield and Roy Rogers. Politicos Harold Stassen and Earl Warren. Admiral Richard Byrd. Atomic scientist Glenn T. Seaborg (who had chosen his Quiz Kids appearance to announce the discovery of two new elements, americium and curium).

The same year, Milton Berle did a hilarious gig as guest quizmaster. Seven years earlier, when Berle ran into our party in a Philadelphia hotel lobby, he had been just another failed radio comedian and had asked my mother enviously about the Quiz Kids' doings. Now he was Mr. Television, king of the tube. The show opened with Berle boning up for his encounter with the Quiz Kids by practicing how to spell C-A-T. He strode into the "schoolroom" in boxing gloves, spoiling for a fight and trailed by two aides staggering under piles of reference books. Throwing away the prepared questions, he pulled out his own, which all turned out to be from a "Mrs. B." ("She needs a TV set.")

Berle did what the Quiz Kids staff always had cautioned guests not to do: upstage the Kids. He stole the show with his fast-paced clowning, leaving them open-mouthed.

For a decade, the Quiz Kids producers had milked the joke of the adult intimidated by brainy small fry . . . the phenomenon Roby called "child fright." In her book, *The Quiz Kids,* she recalled Bob Hope's panic before going on as emcee. "I'm just a little boy from Cleveland," he whined, "who only went through the eighth grade. I just heard yesterday that Shakespeare was dead." Groucho Marx, when the first batch of Quiz Kids came to see him on the MGM set, yelled, "The Quiz Kids! Get them out of here—they know too much!"

Actually, we Kids had served as straight men for comics (including Joe Kelly) who were smarter than they pretended to be . . . smart enough to identify with the hayseed out there who didn't know a parallelogram from a paramecium. "Jack Benny will probably be willing to admit that I.Q. in his case means 'I Quit' by the time he gets through his guest appearance as one of the . . . Quiz Kids," said *Movie-Radio Guide* in 1941. Introducing himself on the show, Quiz Kid-style, the comedian piped, "I'm Jackie Benny, I'm thirty-seven years old, and I was born in Waukegan, Illinois in 1894. I went to Waukegan High School for twelve years. Believe me, I wish I was home." As little Joel plunged into one of his run-on mathematical dissertations, Jack remarked, "It wasn't my fault I didn't read a book when I was young. I wanted to, but the front steps of the Waukegan library were so high."

Fred Allen got in his licks at us Quiz Kids too: "If their I.Q.'s were their temperatures, they would have been dead long ago." His own I.Q., he added, was "so low it has roots on it."

By the 1950s, the gag was becoming a cliche. The audience had smartened up, and the show had run its cycle. Being a Quiz Kid was losing some of its allure. Smart youngsters no longer seemed so formidable. Nor so profitable. "At a certain point," says Pat Conlon, "people said, 'So what?' and flipped the channel to 'I Love Lucy.' "

Miles Laboratories, perhaps seeing the handwriting on the screen, withdrew in fall of 1951, convinced the Quiz Kids audience had reached its saturation point. After a brief hiatus, the program resumed, sponsored by Cat's Paw Soles, and in the fall of 1952 moved to CBS-TV, in shifting weekend time slots. "The show had so many false endings, it was like a Haydn symphony," laughs Pat. Meanwhile the sponsorless radio version limped along, the contestants performing in an empty theater, their compensation cut to fifty-dollar bonds.

The age level dropped during the television years, for the same reason it did in 1941 when the movies and tours began. "It was one thing," Dick Williams observes, "to hear young teenage voices on the radio, but to *see* kids of thirteen and fourteen—they didn't look young. The whole thing had to be stepped down.'' Toward the end, the TV panels were given over almost entirely to lisping, stuttering tykes as young as four, doing stunts like creating Easter bonnets out of piles of ribbons and feathers. (Lou Cowan, who had moved to Manhattan, reportedly called his Chicago staff on that one: this was going too far.)

Aping ''Juvenile Jury,'' the Quiz Kids program became not much more than a string of cute sayings. Adlai Stevenson, two months after his 1952 Presidential defeat, asked the Kids whether they would like to hold the nation's highest office. Eight-year-old Harvey Dytch was dubious. ''The President has lots of worries. If an idea is wrong, they all blame it on the President.'' Other responses, ''My children would be the most popular children in the world. Maybe they'd even have a great big playroom.'' And, ''Mommy and Daddy and my brother would be very proud.''

''Quiz Kids'' had become almost a parody of itself. In 1954, it was gone, replaced by ''Lassie.''

Television was coming of age as a distinct medium. Networks expanded, antennas blanketed the nation, and a giddy array of new program choices from the New York entertainment capital displaced the simple old Midwestern shows. Cowan, by then a New York package producer, resurrected ''Quiz Kids'' there for nine months in 1956, with Clifton Fadiman, formerly of ''Information Please,'' as emcee. The new Kids, said the *Chicago Tribune*'s Larry Wolters, ''lacked the friendly warmth of the old Chicago group. They always seemed such good friends and not as competitive as the young New Yorkers. . . . I miss the touch of Joe Kelly, too . . . who didn't often know the answers himself. . . . That's a problem not confronting the omniscient Fadiman . . .'' A few months later, the show was off network.

The air of innocent fun and camaraderie had been a key to what made the Chicago show click. Those of us who traveled together shared exciting times. The competition came off sounding more like teamwork, with Margaret, perhaps, supplying the name of a character in a book that Pat couldn't quite remember, or Dick adding an explanation to Joel's solution. The staff, it was plain, had a whale of a good time putting the show together, and Joe Kelly made the whole thing a wonderful game.

The reversion to a highbrow quizmaster in the New York version— a concept rejected in 1940—apparently reflected Cowan's feeling that the Chicago show had become too watered down. But Fadiman committed the unpardonable sin: dullness. Because he clearly knew more than the Kids, they did not amaze him—nor the audience.

In the next three years, quiz games raced to a sensational fall. By that time, both Joe Kelly and John Lewellen were dead.*

The failure of the New York Quiz Kids program had been an aberration in the upward path of Lou Cowan, who at one point had thirteen shows going on the three networks. Some of his programs, like "Conversation," the first talk show, had intellectual appeal. But Cowan had a flair for the spectacular. Earlier in the season in which the transplanted Quiz Kids show wilted, he had grafted the old $64 question to a $64,000 stake. "The $64,000 Question" and its cousin, "The $64,000 Challenge," spawned a host of colossal copycats. Contestants sweated out their ordeal in isolation booths before fifty million viewers, while Cowan became president of CBS Television.

The bubble burst in 1959 with the revelation that Charles Van Doren had been primed to unseat Herbert Stempel, an unattractive but unbeatable champion on NBC's "Twenty-One." Van Doren confessed to a Congressional committee that his responses had been coached, down to the last perspiration-drenched second. The unmasking of Van Doren— an attractive young Columbia University English instructor with impeccable reputation and literary lineage, who had become a national folk hero while amassing $129,000—killed the big-money game shows for the next decade. The Congressional investigators turned up charges that contenders on CBS' $64,000 duo also had been fed questions and answers in response to pressure from the sponsor, Revlon. CBS cancelled all its quiz shows.

The result of the Congressional inquiry was the passage of stringent codes to enforce fairness and preclude prearrangement. The scandal and the landmark legislation wrought revolutionary changes in television. Networks wrested control from sponsors; advertising spots no longer were identified with a particular program. Shows were taped to avoid unexpected goofs. And executives experienced in live quiz and variety shows, like Louis Cowan, no longer were needed.

Although the chief allegations were against NBC's "Twenty-One," Cowan came under fire because of his previous connection with "The $64,000 Question." He had sold his interest three years earlier, only a

---

* Kelly had become emcee of "Totem Club," a fine educational children's program produced by Rachel Stevenson, but never again regained his Quiz Kids stature. In May, 1959, at the time of Kelly's fatal heart attack at sixty, Ralph Edwards was preparing a "This Is Your Life" tribute to him. Lewellen had produced "Down You Go," "Of Many Things," and other programs besides "Quiz Kids" for the Cowan organization and had written more than twenty children's books on science and aviation, some of them award-winners. In July, 1956 he died of leukemia at forty-six.

few weeks after the show's birth, when he joined CBS. But the Revlon shows were under his jurisdiction as network president. He protested ignorance of any rigging and even hired private eyes to check on the outside producers; the detectives reportedly found nothing.

CBS' own investigation, however, turned up evidence of tampering, and Cowan became the scapegoat. He was forced out and, smarting under the blow to his reputation, took refuge in the academic world, devoting his final years to the improvement of broadcasting and journalism.*

William S. Paley, chairman of CBS, explains in *As It Happened,* that neither he nor CBS President Frank Stanton had any doubt of Cowan's innocence, but adds: ''There was no getting around the charge that . . . as head of the network he should have known what had been going on for so many years.''

Said Fred Friendly, former head of CBS News: ''No one believed that he [Cowan] had played any part in the dishonesty. But his career and his elevation to the presidency of the CBS television network were so iden-tified with the quiz shows that it was impossible for him to disengage himself from the wreckage.''

Like Professor Frankenstein's, Cowan's creations had turned against him. Jay Sheridan, now a leading Chicago producer of industrial shows and films, sums up the feelings of the old Quiz Kids staff: ''Lou got caught in a media trap. I don't think he had a dishonest bone in his body.''

When the call came from the *Chicago Tribune,* I was a mother of two, and ''Quiz Kids'' seemed far behind me. The reporter wanted to know whether our show had been fixed. The spreading stench of the quiz

---

* Cowan was offered a vice-chairmanship of the CBS Board but resigned rather than be kicked upstairs, which he felt would be tantamount to a confession. He had been burned so badly that he even turned down an invitation from his friend Edward R. Murrow (another creative spirit who had outlived his usefulness to the network powers) to join the U.S. Information Agency, because he did not want the exposure. He became director of the Brandeis University Communications Center and then joined the faculty of the Columbia University Graduate School of Journalism, where he helped found the *Columbia Journalism Review* and then the Columbia-DuPont awards for broadcast excellence. He started a small, highbrow publishing house, Chilmark Press, was chairman of the board of *Partisan Review,* and founded an oral history library for the American Jewish Committee. He and his wife died in November, 1976, in a fire in their New York apartment, believed to have been caused by defective wiring in a television set. He was 66, she 63.

exposes had led the press to sniff for a rat in past Cowan productions. I murmured something negative and hung up.

"Quiz Kid 'Controls' Bared," the next day's headline screamed. The *Tribune* had gotten to Sara Kupperman, whose son Joel had blossomed into a music expert and had won $8,000 on "The $64,000 Challenge."

"I don't think the Quiz Kids shows were rigged," Mrs. Kupperman was quoted as saying. "But the producers knew pretty well what Joel knew and the questions were pitched sometimes so that he would have the first hand up. . . . The producers asked us for a list of books from time to time that Joel was reading, how far he had gone into them, what new interests he had developed. And it's possible that some of the questions were designed to take advantage of this knowledge."

Sid Friedlander, in the *New York Post,* pondered the distinction between showmanship and control. "Those radio Quiz Kids (their TV counterparts never had the same impact) captivated America with their quick wit. America can get over Charles Van Doren. But Joel Kupperman? Vanessa Brown? Joan Bishop?"

Rachel Stevenson, who had gone on to become director of children's programming for WTTW, Chicago's educational television station,[*] told the *Tribune* the Quiz Kids shows "were never in any way rehearsed nor were the children given any tips. . . . After the broadcast was over, we didn't see the children again until they reappeared for the next show a week later." Jeff Wade of the Wade agency insisted, "Our staff outdid itself in trying to stump the kids."

Nevertheless, Maxene Fabe, in *TV Game Shows,* asserts: "Even though the children were the mental prodigies of their generation, the Quiz Kids were coached before the show to make sure they did well. Such precautions would become a hallmark of all future Lou Cowan productions."

The implication that "Quiz Kids" was rigged is false, at least as far as the Chicago program was concerned. As Gerard Darrow said, "You can't fix kids. They'll tell." In New York, however, when Jack Lucal and two other Chicago graduates were recalled for a face-off with the new Quiz Kids in 1956, someone there told Jack a question beforehand and verified his answer. "I was scandalized," says Jack, now a Jesuit priest. "That never happened in Chicago. New Yorkers take the soul out of things."

---

[*] She received the McCall's Golden Mike Award for developing the first weekly television program for both deaf and hearing children. Among her many other educational productions was "The Humanities," done in cooperation with the University of Chicago.

Roby speculates that Cowan's New York underlings might have done some fixing without his knowledge. "He certainly didn't want *us* to rig them. He made a big point of that."

"Spontaneity was the life-blood of the show," says Lon Lunde. "It would not even have occurred to any of the behind-the-scenes people to tamper with it." Questions asked in the warmup never were used on the actual program. When little Frankie VanderPloeg was asked whether there was any advance preparation, he said, "Well, I come down and put on my cap and gown, and then I'm all prepared." To rehearse or coach the Kids would have destroyed that delightful quality. The fun was in the children's unself-conscious remarks and Joe Kelly's unplanned bloopers. As Kelly himself would say at the start of the program, "Anything can happen and probably will."

However, contrary to Jeff Wade's assertion that the staff was out to "stump" the Kids, the program was, in a sense, "arranged," as Dick Williams puts it (and Sara Kupperman implied). Because most of us had specialties, the mix of contestants and questions could influence the way things went. By juggling categories and playing up to known strengths, it was possible to put a seven-year-old on a competitive footing with fourteen-year-olds, or to set up a panel of eminent college professors for ignominious defeat by callow youths.

A ticklish problem was to play up the out-of-town Kids, at a disadvantage because they didn't know the ropes. Once, Rachel remembers, the effort backfired: she gave a team of Houston youngsters easier questions so the Quiz Kids would not beat them too badly, and the Houston kids won.

In directing questions up children's alleys, the producers tried to throw in something for each child, and to keep up with changing interests. "Sometimes we'd spot a child reading a book on a trip," Roby says. "That could open a whole new field."

Rachel, now a writer, producer and director for International Film Bureau, explains, "Our audience tuned in to see the Quiz Kids look good. Every time a question was missed, our ratings went way down." To forestall that danger, she would review the Kids' questionnaires for clues to what they might know about. "But the Kids never had any idea what we were going to ask. Part of the charm was in seeing the Quiz Kids figure out something. All of us were constantly on pins and needles."

With five bright panelists, there was a certain safety in numbers. And in case things weren't working, there were questions in reserve. Pat Conlon recalls such a time: "For some reason we couldn't do anything—

none of the five of us. Now—panic sets in at the table next to Joe Kelly. They were shuffling and having conferences. Joe started to sweat and said, 'Boy, we're giving away those radio-phonographs like hotcakes!' And so they threw questions in, easier ones.

"Put yourself in the position of the people running the show," Pat continues. "Days when we're blowing them all are a disaster, because then people won't tune back in, drink the Alka-Seltzer and all the rest of the stuff that's very important to their livelihoods. We'd come in there and blithely go on in our caps and gowns and answer questions. But jobs were on the line—careers."

And so, the need to show off the Kids' knowledge shaded at times into what Dick Williams calls semi-cheat. "If I was doing analytic geometry and was in Chapter 10," says Dick, "the math question on that week's show very likely came from Chapter 9. So my parents were obviously telling them exactly where I was, and I knew it. I was honestly doing a problem, and I had honestly not heard the problem before, but it was not exactly kosher either. It didn't occur to me as an ethical question then, and if it did to them, I think they rationalized it."

Once in a while, a parent might get a call: "Has Harve read Such-and-Such?" (Nothing specific enough to trigger a run to the library," Harve hastens to add) or "Does Naomi know anything about . . .?" ("And," Naomi smiles archly, "if Naomi didn't, Naomi certainly found out about it.") My mother, I remember, once was called to see whether I knew the clowns in Shakespeare. (I did.) These discreet inquiries or broad brush-up suggestions (which not all of us appear to have received) were an attempt to keep abreast of our specialties . . . a "testing of the waters" to make sure we could come through if certain kinds of questions were used. But, Roby insists, "we never planted a question out-and-out." Rather, as Jack Lucal puts it, "the effort was to find out what *we* knew."

Once Joan Bishop was approached backstage, in the heat of the staff's final question preparation on a personal appearance tour, and was asked if she knew what zucchini was. "Sure, it's a kind of squash," said Joan. On the show, there was a question about Puccini, Houdini, and zucchini. Another time, Joan was asked if she knew who Dmitri Mitropoulos was; she said he was conductor of the Minneapolis symphony. "But I wasn't fixed," says Joan. "I knew the answers."

Such isolated instances, arising from the nervousness of well-meaning, inexperienced producers staking everything on the unpredictable performance of children, were penny-ante stuff compared with what those with less delicate scruples would do on the big-money shows.

Without benefit of hindsight, those of us who were caught up in the situation went along and, as Dick says, rationalized it. It seemed not much different from being told what to study in school. Anyway, it didn't happen often. And everyone, audience included, wanted a good show.

But I always was somewhat uncomfortable about those occasional phoned feelers. Recently I asked Roby Hickok Kesler—now a widow and secretary of the board of trustees of her alma mater, Coe College—how she feels now about those long-ago calls. On the porch of her Cedar Rapids home, she sat back, hugging her knees. It obviously was the first time she had thought about it in that light. "In retrospect," she said simply, "it doesn't look very good, does it?"

If these mild disclosures shock or disturb, it is partly because the Quiz Kids image was rooted in the fond illusions of a naive age. The idea that an ever-changing panel of youngsters could answer anything and everything that might be thrown at them was about as realistic as the previous notion that child prodigies were freaks.

The program itself, by putting academic raiment on precocious tykes, fostered the impression that scholarship could be reduced to parroting facts, creativity to dashing off childish verse. The other scholastic trimmings—school bell, desks, slates, roll call, "report cards," the opening rendition of "School Days"—added to the aura of a classroom examination. But in fact, "Quiz Kids" was a *show*, and the running of it was show business. Entertainment value had to be the primary consideration.

"It was a game, that's all," says Pat Conlon, now an actor, "and all of us were players."

The message was a simple one. "Smart kids can be cute," as Harve Bennett puts it. The children and questions used, the contrast between the bumbling Chief Quizzer and his mighty-smart moppets, all were carefully measured ingredients of the program's appeal. "It was wonderfully orchestrated," says Naomi Cooks Mann, "with something for everybody. People think of it as an innocent bit of Americana. But it was American business."

The fact, for instance, that Naomi was discovered just as I approached puberty and gave up the trips was too convenient to be coincidental. So was the fact that I resembled Shirley Temple, and Naomi, Margaret O'Brien, each at a time when that particular child star was the cinema darling. And the fact that both of us were encouraged to wear pigtails until we were eleven.

The system of recalling three winners each week left the staff free (unless there was a tie) to balance the upcoming panel with old faces or give new ones a chance. (With the removal of competition in the televised version, the producers had a completely free hand in the casting.) The decision was influenced by the way a Kid "went over." As Claude Brenner says, "Judgments were made about our personal appeal and whether we were selling Alka-Seltzer or not." The sponsor may have had a direct say on occasion, as in the slating of Sally Ann Wilhelm—a Hoosier sweetheart from Miles Laboratories' home town of Elkhart, Indiana—who had (as she puts it) "a good German name and acceptable good looks" and eventually earned a regular spot on her own merits, ending up with the all-time female record. An Irish Kid like Margaret or Pat might be slotted for St. Patrick's Day, a musical one like Lonny or Joan as a foil for a guest pianist or singer, or a mathematical mind like Richard or Joel if the mail bag brought in a good math question.

The virtual absence of racial minorities reflected prevailing mores. It was a time when neither Satchel Paige nor Josh Gibson was in the major leagues, and nobody thought anything of it. To judge by the media, all "colored" people were servants like Jack Benny's Rochester or fools and scoundrels like Amos'n'Andy. (Cab Calloway did run an all-black quiz show for six months just before World War II, but it was cancelled.)

Lou Cowan, who helped produce wartime serials about problems of black soldiers and introduced black characters into soap operas, can hardly be accused of racism. Indeed, he and his wife Polly—a longtime civil rights activist who became a Mississippi freedom marcher in the 1960s and served on the board of the National Council of Negro Women— gave singer Mahalia Jackson her start at a time when black performers were persona non grata.

But in the climate of those times, few blacks even tried out to be Quiz Kids. ("If they did," says Rachel Stevenson, "we auditioned them like anyone else.") One black youth who grew up to be a Chicago lawyer was an avid Quiz Kids fan in his teenage years. He gave no more thought to the lack of black contestants than to "why my friends and I sat in a different section of the movie theater from the white kids. That was the way it was."

Anti-Semitism was rampant in the war years, a time of undisputed WASP hegemony. Yet a disproportionate number of Quiz Kid regulars were Jewish, including three of the four top wartime travelers, Harve, Joel and me. When we moved through crowds, there were loud remarks of "Oh, they're all Jews!" Richard Williams was (he laughs) our "house goy." When we went to see Henry Ford, a notorious anti-Semite, Kitty

Fischman said, "We'd better push you in first, Dick!"

"The owners of the department store that arranged our Seattle trip had a plush estate on an island," Dick recalls. "They invited the management of the show and my mother and me and nobody else, and we were conscious that it was because the others were Jewish."

Pat Conlon believes he was cultivated because "they wanted to get another Gentile." He explains, "Jewish kids happen to be brought up in a way that scholarship is important. Obviously, you want to reach the broadest possible audience, and if you have one Jewish kid after another, you may turn some people off."

Interestingly, Lou Cowan, a Jew, surrounded himself with a predominantly Christian staff and hired an Irish Catholic quizmaster. Once Cowan called Roby in. "How did it happen," he asked her, "that all five kids on the Easter show were Jewish?"

"I'll tell you how it happened," she replied. "They won."

Lou Cowan had two reasons for starting "Quiz Kids." He wanted to give bright children an opportunity and incentive to excel. And, of course, he wanted a successful show. Idealism and commercialism went hand in hand in the war bond and charity drives; the offering of scholarship keys to good students; the high school essay contest on "What America Means to Me"; and the annual Best Teacher contest. Such worthy activities catered to cherished cultural values and thus translated into higher ratings and profits in the good old American Way. So did the publicity about our idyllic home lives—walking our dogs, saying our prayers, helping our saintly-sounding mothers with the housework. "Quiz Kids" was brilliant PR.

But it was more than that. "What Dad believed," says Cowan's son Geoffrey (a Los Angeles communications lawyer who has revived "Quiz Kids" with Harve Bennett), "was that if you had a prize, you would study for it, and anybody could learn—that knowledge was not limited to the Ivy League." The same philosophy underlay "The $64,000 Question": the idea that a foot patrolman who was a Shakespeare expert or a black girl from Baltimore who was a crack speller could inspire others to learn. Cowan's wife Polly, brought up in a business milieu, was more cynical. She believed that prizes would only make people work for money, rather than for knowledge itself.

Lou Cowan was a trusting soul, and it was trust that brought him down. In the latter part of his life, he taught a media management course at Columbia University. Each year he would start off the class by drawing a big dollar sign on the blackboard. As Geoff explains in his book *See No Evil*: "Like it or not, profits are at the core of the industry."

It has been said of Lou Cowan that he was a man who should have been a college president rather than a network president. Looking back over his broadcasting career (Geoff says), "the one show Dad was most proud of was Quiz Kids." An old-fashioned show that celebrated knowledge. . . . A simple show from the heartland of America, that America took to its heart.

Celebrity at Seven

Boston. Hundreds of dark-eyed children who, as a news story told it, knew "only the narrow streets of little Italy," trailed us Quiz Kids one cold February day:

> At the Old North Church, throngs of quietly envious youngsters watched the privileged four allowed to climb to the steeple and ring the chimes, and followed them in whispers during their visit to Paul Revere's house. . . .
>
> Tattered autograph books and soiled sheets of paper were held out to the four far-traveled Kids, here to broadcast tomorrow night from Symphony Hall in a sell-out war bond promotion.
>
> One little girl of about 8, wearing a gingham dress and no overcoat, ran as near to the Kids as she could get.
>
> "I'll be listening Sunday," she called.
>
> They watched the famous four drive off in a cavalcade of motor cars.
>
> No one spoke for a moment, then the tot in gingham said suddenly, "I'm glad I'm not famous, just the same."

When I came across this story many years later, it struck me as ironic. How could that wistful child, close to my own age, have had any inkling that her ambivalence mirrored mine? Only on the road did I stay in fancy hotels and ride in chauffeured limousines with Important People as guides. When the applause died away, I was back in my lower-middle-class Chicago neighborhood, going to school and playing on the sidewalks like other children.

Mine was a far cry from the hothouse existence of the Shirley Temples. But it was not an ordinary life.

My parents were a pair of romantics.

My dad, Boris Duskin, was a latter-day Renaissance man, who tinkered with inventions, played varsity football at the University of Chicago, and taught himself to paint and sculpt; his lifelike busts of my little sister Bunny and me graced our mantel. He studied farming and nourished financially impossible dreams of becoming a psychiatrist, but settled for teaching high school chemistry despite the low pay and prestige, counseling troubled students in his free time. He was a memorable teacher— right up to his death in 1972, a host of graduates wrote to tell him so.

My mother, the former Rita Schayer, called herself a "bohemian." Short, dark and soulful, she had, in her youth, wallowed in Herman Hesse and Thomas Hardy while her friends dabbled in free love. She had relatives in vaudeville; an uncle, Andy Rice, wrote revues for stage and screen. Her grandfather was a scholar who raised sunflowers and communed with nature. Yearning to be a poet or a Shakespearian actress, she dropped out of the University of Illinois to enroll in Goodman Theater's drama school, but my father talked her into marriage instead, practically camping on her doorstep until she said yes. They wed on Robert and Elizabeth Barrett Browning's anniversary. ("Because they were originally drawn together by a mutual fondness for the poetry of the Brownings," explained a news item after I became a Quiz Kid. Someone sent them the clipping with a note: "Mutual fondness for POETRY????????????")

Mom worked as a secretary to put Dad through college but stayed home with Bunny and me throughout most of our childhood. Neglecting housework, she devoted herself to us. "What you put into a house," she would say, "must be done over and over; what you put into a child remains."

My parents made a virtue of the simple life. In my first seven years, we called four west side Chicago apartments "home" before taking root on the south side near Jackson Park. Our furnishings were secondhand bargain treasures (a tradition I've enjoyed carrying on). There was perpetual clutter: stacks of yellowed piano music; sheafs of manuscript for the chemistry workbook Dad wrote; Mom's longhand scribblings, at which she labored lovingly into the wee hours; and everywhere books, books, books.

It was a home filled with laughter and a sense of what life should be. Creativity was our bread and butter. Hardly anyone ever ate at our dining room table. When not covered with papers, it might be spread with drying clay lumps recognizable only to their small creators, or, at Christmas, with masses of crepe paper, feathers and scraps to be assembled into gifts and decorations. (Our ecumenically-minded mother let us have a tree until I was eleven, with the grudging assent of our father, who as a young child had witnessed frightening pogroms in his Polish shtetl.) Birthdays and other special occasions called for original rhymes. We cut up old greeting cards and used the pictures to make our own. The four of us took long walks, singing at the top of our lungs and concocting continued stories.

Our clothes were castoffs from well-to-do relations. Items hopelessly out of style became costumes for the impromptu fantasies my sister and I acted out. Once we pretended to be fairies dressing up as children.

Bunny and I played Red Rover and jumprope with the neighborhood gang but stayed outside when the others ran in to listen to "Terry and the Pirates." "Let's Pretend" was our speed. Our parents disapproved of adventure comics; we had classic comics instead.

Mom shared with us her bountiful love of literature. At two, I could repeat Eugene Field's long poem, "Little Boy Blue." Later my mother read aloud a chapter a day from the Bible at lunchtime. I liked the Book of Ruth; I had been named for her.

Someone had given us a little table with the alphabet on it, and my mother fed me there when I was small. When we went out, I would ask what signs like D-R-U-G-S and S-T-O-P said. Mom would drop me off at the library to look at picture books while she shopped. One day, before I was four, she was surprised to find a crowd surrounding me: I was reading aloud. (Not *too* surprised, though—she had read early herself.)

By five, I had gobbled up Aesop's *Fables* and was well into Lamb's *Tales from Shakespeare.* Mythological gods and goddesses were my familiar companions. I could hardly wait until I would be old enough to take a bus to the library alone.

My early life and education centered on my home; school was incidental. I leapfrogged through first and second grades in a matter of weeks. The principal at Pope School wanted to advance me even more, but my mother, who had skipped a year and a half herself, was concerned that I "remain a child." My teachers let me do extra work or bring books to read while my classmates plodded through primers.

"My attitude was that the child should lead," says my mother. "I never deliberately taught anything. I believed in an enriching environment. I didn't buy mechanical or wind-up toys. I always had construction paper, pencils, crayons and coloring books around."

The watchwords of my mother's faith were "wholesome," "well-rounded," and "creative." When she saw me turning into a bookworm, she immediately ordered *Children's Activities,* a magazine full of things to make and do, which kept Bunny and me busy and happy for hours. Roby Hickok wrote in *The Quiz Kids,* "Rita is like an intellectual seeing-eye dog—gently guiding and directing her daughters down the avenues she thinks they'll enjoy." At Mom's suggestion, I organized neighborhood clubs to put out newspapers, present magic shows, and perform the melodramas I wrote and directed. (Usually all the characters got killed off in the first act.)

While my imaginative inclinations derived from my mother, Dad was the source of my logical mind, perfectionism and passion for truth. From Mom, I learned to dare; from Dad, to care about getting things right. As a teacher, he came home earlier than most fathers and had more time to spend with me. He asked to see everything I wrote and made me correct each error. I dreaded showing him my work but learned to put excellence above pride of authorship.

Dad touted scientific thinking. He investigated notions like spiritualism and holistic healing at a time when most people dismissed such stuff as poppycock. A patient problem-solver, he made me one. "Science seems like magic," I wrote in my diary, "but if you study it, you can explain it."

My self-taught parents convinced me that I could teach myself almost anything. At seven, I learned to type, after a fashion, from a manual Dad brought home. When the Quiz Kids visited Henry Ford, I busied myself copying his autograph and turned out a reasonable facsimile. ("Hope you don't grow up to be a forger," Ford teased.) When Bunny, who showed vocal talent, began studying music, I picked up her piano book, breezed through it in a week, and started taking lessons too.

Our walls vibrated with song. Dad thundered Caruso arias in the bathtub and stroked a musical saw. Mom sat at the piano singing with Bunny and me by the hour and traipsed halfway across the city with us on buses and trains for our lessons. When we made up melodies, she bought us composition books. When we spouted poetry, she wrote it down.

Our accomplishments, no matter how minor, were lavishly applauded and shown off to relatives—reluctant command performances on our part.

"Gifts," Mom told us, "are meant to be shared."

Like my mother, whose poetry collection eventually was published, I was constantly getting ideas for books: a sequel to the Oz series; my autobiography, "Figs and Thistles"; a tale called "The Cobbler's Son and the High-Born Lass on a Barren Planet." At nine I wrote an essay on "Materialism and Idealism":

> Society is full of materialism. There isn't enough idealism in the world. . . .
>
> The materialistic person is one who *overdoes necessity* and thinks only of ways to promote his success, help him earn money, and similar things, which all add up to the *perpetual desire to be a Big Shot.*

During the war, my prolific hand churned out patriotic verse, some of which got published, thanks to my Quiz Kids connection. I would stop and salute every time I passed a flag, and was thrilled when my poem "Wouldn't It Be Wonderful?" ("If only all the world were friends . . .") drew $3,500—perhaps the biggest price in the history of poetry— at a war bond auction that included possessions of such world-famous figures as Madame Chiang Kai-shek.

There were disappointments, too. When *Seventeen* asked me to write an article, the editors returned it, claiming my mother had written it. She hadn't.

When, at twelve, I wrote and illustrated a real book, an adventure in which the chemical elements come to life, it was a family affair. Mom, the promoter, landed the contract with Dodd, Mead and Company after a New York Book Week luncheon at which I represented the school-children of America. Bunny was the inspiration—the story was to be a painless way to teach her chemistry. Dad, my collaborator, furnished the facts. On nightly walks, my family helped me thrash out plot and characterization. In the mornings, I wrote my daily three pages. In the afternoons, we revised them, assembly line style, on the dining room table.

The ecstasy of receiving my own published book in the mail confirmed my desire to write. Earlier, I had collected my poems under the title "The World and Myself." Now I penned in my diary: "The world is one unit and I am another, and the bridge is . . . *Chemi the Magician.* . . In this hour I have the world in a little red book."

"I always expected fame to come to our family," says my mother, who claims to have ESP. "I just felt we would be discovered."

To help things along, when I was six, she wrote to "Quiz Kids" unbeknownst to my father, who might have nipped the idea in the bud. When the questionnaire came, she persuaded him that I would enjoy the "game" and deserved the recognition. "Praise Is a Hunger," Mom titled one of her published articles, and she was hungry—her family had mocked her as a poetic dreamer.

Dad's craving was for a normal family life. His father, a wealthy department store owner in Lunienz, Poland, had died before Dad's birth, leaving a large family from a previous marriage. Dad's mother, resented as an interloper by her deceased predecessor's kin, took her older children to America but was forced to leave her infant son with an uncaring step-grandmother. He grew up believing his mother was dead until, at nine, after repeated efforts on her part, he finally was sent to join her . . . smuggled out of Czarist territory, seasick during the two-week voyage in steerage, then abandoned at Ellis Island by his paid guide and left to wait ten days, unable to speak a word of English, until a stepbrother came to claim him. He never quite laid those ghosts to rest.

So, although the Quiz Kids producers wanted to put me on immediately, Dad insisted that our family's planned summer vacation in the Indiana Dunes come first. He also stipulated that if I showed any signs of becoming spoiled, I would be taken off the program. Before my first broadcast, he crouched for an eye-to-eye talk. "They're going to make a big fuss over you," he warned me. "But don't forget—there are a lot of important people in the world. Don't think you're the only one."

As foreseen, I was an instant hit. At seven, outnumbered four to one by older boys, I "defended the academic reputation of womanhood," as radio columnist Don Foster put it. When I identified the final opera in Wagner's Ring cycle as *The Dusk of the Gods,* twelve-year-old Richard Banister tried to correct me: "It's Gott-dam . . . Gott-damm . . . " As the producers shuddered in consternation, I shot back, "He means the German name, *Gotterdammerung,* but in English it's what I said."

I knew Shakespeare, opera, and the Bible "better than most kids know the multiplication tables," said *Senior Scholastic.* In a quizdown with five University of Chicago professors who could name only four of Jacob's twelve sons, I supplied the other eight. I could trace Biblical genealogies and, to the amazement of Scriptural scholars, discovered an obscure discrepancy in two lists of the sons of Saul.

Such "phenomenal" feats were typical among the Quiz Kids' inner circle. "Children naturally have retentive minds," Gerard Darrow's Aunt Bessie once explained. "They have nothing to worry them as grownups have." Immersed in books, I could remember just about everything I read—something I wish I still could do. To a degree, my memory was photographic; I could picture what I had seen on the printed page.

Often I've been asked whether I was nervous before the show. There was a pang of anxiety just as we put on our caps and gowns and marched out to our places in front of the mikes. But once the red "On the air" light flashed, the adrenalin began flowing.

My mother soon realized that I needed a more organized curriculum. She bought me basic works in my fields and started me on *Time* magazine. When we went on tour, she had me read up on the destination city; usually that was good for at least one question. Studying was no chore. It was not unusual for me to tear through a volume of *World Book* for curiosity's sake, or to reread *The Secret Garden* for the fourth time.

When I was almost nine, I woke up early one Sunday morning and began browsing through Dad's chemistry books. I knocked on my parents' bedroom door, brimming with questions. Dad turned to Mom and said, "*This is* real *nachus.*"

From then on, I perpetually nagged him to make up problems for me to solve. He began bringing home experiments for us to try in the kitchen sink. Mom was afraid we would blow up the place.

The "Quiz Kids" staff welcomed my new enthusiasm. Now they could play up the anomaly of a girlish voice answering questions about uranium isotopes, alpha particles, and covalent bonding. One press release ran: "She has a mind like one of Daniel Boone's traps . . . . a strange combination of fantasy and cold logic expressed in her two ardent loves . . . literature and chemistry. She grasps chemical formulas the same way she does an operatic plot."

My publicity dwelt on the distaff side of my personality. With fat blonde curls and short-waisted pinafores, I was "the little darling of the Quiz Kids," "a charmer with an infectious giggle," "a casting director's dream of Alice in Wonderland," "a quaint little fairy." My favorite dolls and stuffed animals accompanied me to broadcasts and trips. Girls in other cities flocked to cheer me.

I was constantly trying to disprove the notion that mine was the weaker sex. When we visited Father Flanagan's Boys Town, I wished aloud that there was a Girls Town. I announced my disappointment that so few of the Quiz Kids contest-winners were females.

Undoubtedly I was not the most brilliant girl who ever tried out for the program, though I was bright enough. What I had were tenacity and a show-stealing candor.

Joe Kelly said, "Isn't it just like a woman?" every time Ruthie
Duskin summed up for the Quiz Kids. Whatever the question,
whatever the answer, Ruthie was right there at the end. . . . Her
technique in covering up holes and fumblings won enthusiastic
applause from an amused audience. . . .

Ruthie's feminine charm and vivacity seemed to prove that a
woman can get to high places even though the fabric of her information is pretty diaphanous.
—*Boston Post,* February 21, 1944

Her uninhibited answers and even more uninhibited questions in a
voice of breathless urgency livened the air wherever she was.
—*New York World-Telegram and Sun*, April 14, 1956

In the British Columbia government house, when our guide pointed
out the King's suite at one end and the Queen's at the other, I asked
loudly, "Why don't the King and Queen sleep together?"

At the formal luncheon, the hostess caught me staring into space. "A
penny for your thoughts," she smiled.

"Oh," I replied, "I'm just playing a thinking game that I play when
I'm bored."

When Roby Hickok took me at age eight to see Maurice Evans in
Macbeth (my first taste of live Shakespeare), we found the actor backstage, applying his makeup. He put his arm around me with a playful
tickle and begged, "Now, don't yell out if I make a mistake."

As Roby tells it in her book, I did everything but. In excited stage
whispers, I kept her and our immediate neighbors informed of what was
coming next. When Evans entered with bloody hands, I stood up and
cried, "He's killed Duncan!" I recited Lady Macbeth's sleepwalking
speech right along with Judith Anderson.

Afterward, I asked Evans why there had been only two murderers when
the bard called for three. And why hadn't they brought Macbeth's head
in on a platter?

"I'm going on tour and may need it," he deadpanned.

The great Shakespearian actor set an example of humility. He signed
himself in my autograph book, "A poor player that struts and frets his
hour upon the stage and then is heard no more."

My "sensible parents" (as Roby called them) were careful to keep me
from getting a "swelled head." Mom shut herself in a closet, out of my
earshot, to take the avalanche of congratulatory calls. Telegrams, letters

and clippings piled up in packing cases, out of sight.

For a while I didn't even realize I was on the radio. Being so young, I had been given several auditions; the broadcast seemed like just another. When a girl on my block said she had heard me, I told my mother, "I didn't see her there."

Four months later, I was in New York making movie shorts. We lunched with Cecil B. DeMille and met Eddie Cantor, who called me "remarkable." Mom wrote to Dad, "It all reminds me of that childhood story about the pot of gold at the end of the rainbow."

Dad fired back: "You certainly are leading the rounds of celebrities. Hope you take it in stride and especially counteract *any adverse* effects of praise." To me he wrote, "Remember, don't let anything make you proud and haughty, like Cinderella's stepsisters."

"Rest assured," Mom replied, "Ruthie is not being spoiled. I do appreciate the fact that I am getting in on experiences . . . which few persons are privileged to do . . . but the pomp and ballyhoo don't impress me. It is grand to have a vacation at someone else's expense and to have a sweet child whom everyone admires . . . whether people know she is a Quiz Kid or not."

Four years later, arriving at the New York Book Week luncheon, I hung back as we approached the room set aside for honored guests. "The sign on that door says 'Celebrity Room,' " I told my mother.

"*You're* a celebrity," she informed me, amused that I didn't know it.

The thrill of that event was getting to meet (and later correspond with) one of my favorite authors, Dorothy Canfield Fisher. I was much less impressed with the Eddie Cantors; in fact, I barely knew who they were, since I seldom listened to the radio and my family rarely could afford a movie.

Inevitably, the question of putting me in pictures arose. Shortly after my Quiz Kids debut, Judy Garland (my favorite actress) called me to her Blackstone Hotel suite. She wanted me to play Amy to her Jo in *Little Women,* but nothing came of it.

Judy hugged me and asked me to write a poem for her. "She's like a real person, not a movie star," I told my mother as we left.

In Hollywood, Vanessa Brown's mother put mine in touch with David O. Selznick's office. Selznick's secretary suggested we stick around—something might turn up. But Mom by then was repelled by the dreary, unnatural lives of film children, and anyway, Dad would never have stood for it. She wrote to him: "Hollywood is the bubble and bauble that you think it." When we got home, there was a letter from an agent interested in promoting me to remake Shirley Temple's films. He asked my parents to send photos. They never did.

Despite her vicarious pleasure in my plaudits, Mom tried to keep things in proportion, reminding me how much enjoyment I was giving some invalid or doting spinster. She quoted from Matthew: "What is a man profited if he shall gain the world and lose his own soul?" And she held up as an object lesson Orson Welles' Citizen Kane, who built a formidable communications empire but never got over his childhood lack of a loving home.

A real concern was how our extended absences would affect my sister. A playful elf, Bunny craved affection.

When we began traveling with "Quiz Kids," Bunny, then five, lodged with relatives or friends; Dad would see her after work. Bunny remembers being "very homesick." "The people I was staying with wanted me to eat peanut butter. I had never tasted it, and I refused. I stalked off and sat on the swing feeling sorry for myself." Three days before our return, when Dad came to visit, Bunny started to cry, "I want Mom right now."

Later Mom got permission to bring her along to Salt Lake City. John Lewellen held her on his lap on the train and put her on the air to sing a song. Thereafter she made occasional appearances, especially on anniversary specials, when the tiniest quiz babies were pitted against graduates.

Mom and Dad saw to it that Bunny got other strokes for her singing ability. We joined an All Children's Grand Opera Company, where *she* starred while I played supporting roles.

Trying to equalize Quiz Kids rewards, our parents bought Bunny duplicate gifts, when they could, and cashed some of my bonds (with court permission) to outfit us both and send us to camp. School authorities were warned to treat us alike. Bunny won plenty of honors herself, including high school salutatorian, and was selected as one of the top seniors in Chicago. But all along, she faced questions like "Are you as smart as your sister?"

Many people have asked me how Bunny reacted to the Quiz Kids business. Yet she and I never discussed it until July, 1981, when I visited her and her family in their Phoenix home.

"When you're very young, everything seems to be natural," said Bunny, wife of attorney Sandor Shuch and mother of two teenagers. "It didn't occur to me that other people might not have someone in their family on the radio." That she was on the show less than I didn't bother

her much. The only time she was really sorry was when she went to college and wished she had "that nice nest egg." It seemed (she told me) that "Quiz Kids was your thing and opera was mine, and we each participated in the other a little. I didn't feel competitive with you. You were my older sister—I looked up to you. I was jealous of Bonnie Roberts [a girl in my opera group]; she was my age and we competed for the same roles."

Her "Quiz Kids" appearances sharpened her competitiveness and gave her the feeling of being "in on things," without putting her under pressure. "I didn't have to study, I wasn't put on the spot. It was like being the baby of the family—I could just be cute and cuddly and everybody would accept me. I didn't have to perform that well, and when I did, everyone was pleasantly surprised. Once I answered a question about snakes. I had just studied about it in school. I felt good because it was a question they never expected me to answer.

"*You* had to overcome expectations that you would be snotty. I didn't have that, because I wasn't the famous one."

My parents told me I was lucky to be a Quiz Kid, and in many ways I was. Certainly it was far more stimulating than grammar school. I liked competing with such high-powered rivals as Harve Bennett Fischman and Richard Williams and having adventures with them on trips. I loved playing Monopoly on the train and being lulled to sleep in the rolling cocoon of an upper berth. I appreciated the chance to touch my country's history and to see its beauty. I enjoyed the sense of power when, at ten, I substituted for Joe Kelly, and later, in my two-year Quizdown stint. Above all, "Quiz Kids" proved to me what I could achieve.

But of course, there was a price. I got bored posing for pictures. I hated signing autographs, preferring to collect them (even from other Quiz Kids). I resented being pointed out at school ("She plays like other children!") and being called out of class to read for visitors and older students. (In fact, I got my mother to tell the principal to put a stop to it.) At recess, schoolmates would back me to the fence, pestering me with questions and begging for help with their work.

When I wrote home from camp that I was getting teased because the director had introduced me as a Quiz Kid, Mom gave me moral support by mail:

> . . . To be a person of distinction is certainly nothing of which
> to be ashamed, but rather a cause for honest yet modest pride,
> gratitude for being so favored. . . . Use your position with dignity,
> and be an example of a person whose head hasn't been turned by

fame. But don't make the mistake of bending over backwards with false modesty like Uriah Heep and his 'umility.

I wasn't ashamed of being a Quiz Kid, but talking about it (even to people who were genuinely interested) seemed like bragging. Once a kindly woman struck up a conversation with me on a train. "You sound like Ruthie Duskin," she said. I never let on that I was.

I wanted to be accepted for myself, not as a quiz whiz. I discounted my abilities; they seemed quite natural to me. The more I knew, the more I realized I did not know. Yet others seemed to assume I knew it all.

"Doing your own thing" was not yet in vogue; the last thing anyone wanted was to stand out from the crowd. When, at ten, I won a scholarship to the University of Chicago Laboratory School, my new seventh grade classmates greeted me with autograph books. If I signed, I was branded "stuck-up"; if not, "standoffish." If I answered questions in class, I was a "showoff." One of the popular girls took me aside and advised, "Don't raise your hand so much. Boys don't like it."

Although I longed for people to forget I was a Quiz Kid, I was unwilling to stifle the qualities that made me one. (Even in college, my irrepressible hand shot up. Says my husband, whom I met there: "You were the only girl who would speak up in class.")

Wanting desperately to fit in, I stopped going on Quiz Kids tours. Now that I was in a private school with my intellectual peers, missing classes and after-school play rehearsals was no trivial loss; and Quiz Kids relationships, as I approached puberty, could not replace normal social ones.

My parents encouraged my decision, even though it meant an end to my preeminence as "the Quiz Kid girl." All along, Dad had harbored resentment of our "gallivanting," though he and Bunny had been good sports. Mingled with the glowing reports in my mother's letters had been "nostalgia for our home and the quiet unpretentiousness of our lives." In the six months before we cut out the traveling, Mom and I were away on our birthdays and my parents' anniversary. On the latter occasion, Dad wrote to her: "You'd better make this your last trip. Save some traveling for both of us in our old age."

At the Lab School, social life was tightly clannish. While I made a few close friends, I was painfully conscious of being two years younger and a foot shorter than everyone, and a Quiz Kid to boot. Being named Miss Pigtails of 1944 by *Polly Pigtails* magazine didn't help. Team games were my downfall; I was always the last chosen. Not until I was nearly forty and took up tennis did I realize that my "lack of coordination" actually had been simply a lack of physical maturity.

In retrospect, I may have blown my social problem out of proportion as well. What I thought my peers thought of me may have been largely a figment of my own anxiety. A woman with whom I occasionally play tennis these days, who was part of the athletic "in" group at the Lab School, recently told me, "It was exciting to know someone who was on the radio."

After tenth grade, the final year at the Lab School, I could have gone on to the University of Chicago under the accelerated Hutchins plan, as a number of youngsters, including some Quiz Kids, did. But I already was two years ahead, and college at fourteen seemed absurd. Instead, I finished up at South Shore, a public high school.

Intellectually, the place was pretty barren, but socially it was blossom time for me. Upon my arrival, the school paper ran a story: "Discovery! Quiz Kids Are Human, Too, Just Like the Rest of Us." I shot up to five-foot-six, joined a sorority (as I did again in college), and began dating regularly. I abandoned my bookworm tendencies; to this day, I am more a doer than a reader. I was feature editor of the school paper and had the lead in the senior play. (Unfortunately, I giggled all the way through— as in my Quiz Kids duet with Bing Crosby.)

Still sensitive about the egghead image, I chose Northwestern's wholesome atmosphere over the unrelentingly cerebral University of Chicago— a decision I have half-regretted at times. I came to college with the watch and typewriter I had been given at my Quiz Kids graduation. My quiz days were over, except for brief appearances on "College Quiz Bowl" and Cowan's "Superghost" and "It's About Time."

Arriving on campus, I met the usual razzing with unaccustomed equanimity, seeing with sudden clarity that anyone whose friendship I valued would accept me for myself. When I was elected scholarship chairman of my dorm corridor the first week of school, a girl across the hall complained loudly, "I don't want a Quiz Kid telling me how to improve my grades!" My roommate burst into her room and said, "I don't know what you think a Quiz Kid is, but I didn't even know Ruthie was one!"

Quoth the *Daily Northwestern*: "Miss Duskin violently disputes the rumors that a Quiz Kid is an untouchable being. She plans to lead an active, normal life here." Two years later I was editorial assistant on the *Daily* and an editor of a student magazine.

"Would you rather be told that you're smart or beautiful?" asked Rick DuBrow, a fellow-toiler on the *Daily*.

"Beautiful," I replied instantly. "I know I'm smart."

In high school, I had tied for valedictorian. At Northwestern I won an award for highest freshman grades, maintained a nearly straight-A record, made Phi Beta Kappa, and graduated with highest distinction, having gone through on partial scholarship, with an honorary full scholarship my senior year.

My graduation was a triple celebration. It was my first wedding anniversary and the day after my twentieth birthday.

Pat Conlon, a younger Quiz Kid colleague, tells me that a ripple of surprise went through the ranks when the news came back that I had married at barely nineteen.

The path I took, from college on, was (for my generation) characteristically female, considering how I had been set apart. In a way, my early marriage was both a fitting conclusion to an accelerated childhood and a welcome escape into normality. Femininity, of course, had been the key to my Quiz Kid appeal. I epitomized the bright young woman who had been given mixed signals: lavishly praised for distinguishing myself but bred to comply, independent-minded yet needful of approval, outspoken though loath to offend. I thought of myself as special and expected great things of my future; yet rather than laying plans, I drifted through life assuming (as my childhood experience had led me to do) that some sure hand would pluck me up and find me a place in the sun. My aspirations were unfocused and not really my own. It was inconceivable to me that I would end up "just a housewife," yet in my mother I saw the possibility of falling back on that option—for a while.

Nor did my parents press me; whatever I did was wonderful to them. When it came right down to it, my "bohemian" mom was a Jewish mother, and my making a good marriage was "a consummation devoutly to be wished."

As a child, I had changed ambitions yearly: poet, actress, heroine, teacher, chemist, writer. But my one enduring goal had been to be a wife and mother and live happily ever after. From the age of six, I was boy-crazy in an innocent way. When Chico Marx got affectionate with me, I blushed, "You're the only man I've ever kissed—except my father, my uncles, and boys." At nine, I had a highly publicized "engagement" to Quiz Kid Harve Bennett Fischman, a suave four years my senior. At the Lab School, I ran through a series of unrequited crushes. At fifteen, I was talking marriage with my high school steady, a fervent physics student who reminded me of my father. At seventeen, I was engaged.

In a Quiz Kids movie short, I had been asked which Shakespearian character I would like to wed. "Hamlet," I said—"but he's not a man of action, and I'd like to marry a man of action." Gilbert Feldman fit the prescription, his idealism deeper than mine, his activism undeterred by prevailing opinion. He alone led his delegation in a walkout from Northwestern's 1952 mock political convention in protest against the selection of Red-baiting Senator Joseph McCarthy as keynote speaker. (The incident made the papers, and McCarthy came looking for Gil "to set him straight," but he had gone home for the weekend.)

I first met Gil in the Northwestern library, early in my freshman year. Far from being threatened by my brains, he sought me out. He had listened to the show but "wasn't especially awed": he knew many of the answers. Highly competitive, he aimed to top my English grade. He scored second in a class of four hundred; I beat him (he remembers) by two points.

Gil's roots are different from mine, his middle-class Jewish family solid and worldly-wise. His father was vice-president of a furniture company. His mother, carrying on the tradition of her Old World parents who had put two sons through medical school with the earnings eked out of a dry goods store, devoted herself to raising her sons the doctor and lawyer.

Gil and I complemented each other. Compared with other girls he had known, I was exceptionally serious-minded but amazingly unsophisticated. He, coming from a business-oriented family, knew more about practical affairs; I was absorbed in matters of the mind. We talked philosophy, literature and politics and vowed that our marriage would be one of equals, a rarity then. I encouraged his inclination to be a union attorney and, in the early years, helped him with his briefs.

My own career choice was more difficult.

I have always agonized over decisions, searching for the perfect answer. Once, on Quiz Kids, Joe Kelly asked me to tell my favorite riddle. I demurred. "You know thousands," my mother remonstrated afterward.

"I was trying to decide which is my favorite," I explained. When Gil and I picked out my engagement ring, I sat in the jeweler's for an eternity, unable to make up my mind.

My career thoughts in my first three years of college had been similarly inconclusive. Influenced by my mother, I had enrolled initially in Northwestern's renowned journalism school. But with so many enticing liberal arts courses to choose from, I hated to fill my schedule with vocational requirements.

Meanwhile, I was growing away from Quiz Kid values. I remember how crestfallen I was when I got my first B in a literature course (one in which, incidentally, Gil evened the score with an A). I went to the professor, Bergen Evans, to ask what was wrong with my essay. "Nothing is wrong with it," he replied. "It merely lacks the spark of originality I look for in an A paper." Evans opened my eyes to a level of thinking beyond merely knowing the answers. A sociology professor, whom I interviewed for a journalism assignment, lectured me on the difference between scholarly research and the sort of surface investigation I was doing. Again, the emphasis on depth.

What confirmed my disenchantment with journalism at that point was the month I spent in New York as a *Mademoiselle* College Board editor, the summer after my freshman year. Poet Sylvia Plath, who was on the same board the summer before, evoked in *The Bell Jar* the emptiness of that scene.

My childhood course had been subtly guided by parental example: now I switched to my future husband's major, political science. But by the time we married two years later, with Gil in law school and my graduation looming, I still had no career plans. Bergen Evans had told me how fortunate he felt to be paid for doing what he would gladly pay to do. To love one's work, to affect others, to do something worthwhile seemed vital to me. I was not ready to write—I had nothing, yet, to say. I vaguely considered graduate school, but no single field consumed me. Though I had won honors in political science, it remained more Gil's love than mine.

Since I enjoyed working with children I decided to be a teacher like my father. With one year to go, I squeezed in enough education courses for a certificate and landed a seventh grade social studies and English position. "Why do you want to do that?" one of my professors lamented— "You could teach college." But financial needs aside, I was impatient to get out into the world.

Within six months, I was on maternity leave. An "accident."

In college, I was deeply affected by David Riesman's *The Lonely Crowd* and by the existentialist philosophers. I wanted to be autonomous, to act rather than react. I believed that each moment was an opportunity to create oneself anew. Yet often I slid into imitative or unplanned choices: my major, my career, and finally, parenthood.

My disappointment at having to give up the work I had so tardily settled upon was real. I was enjoying my students and the creative challenge of teaching. And I was not one to leave things unfinished. Still, surrender did not come terribly hard. As a child, I had loved playing with dolls. As a camp counselor, caring for other people's children, I had ached to have my own. I had no doubt that I could pick up my career later.

In my waiting months, I thought about my mother, hoping I could match her example. I felt, as had she, the awesome responsibility of a life in my hands. As with her, my children would come first. So, like most mothers of my generation, I never considered going back to work full-time while my youngsters were small. But I did keep a hand in, through tutoring, Sunday School teaching, and leading Junior Great Books discussions in my Highland Park, Illinois community.

Intent on building his law practice, Gil left most of the child-raising to me. During the nesting years, our "union of equals" assumed more conventional proportions. I read *War and Peace* and *The American Scholar* while nursing my babies and produced one magazine article when my firstborn, Steve, was a year old. But I felt so guilty about putting him in his playpen, crying, while I pounded out copy for a deadline that I wrote nothing else professionally for seventeen years. I would read the Northwestern alumni news with the sinking feeling that my contemporaries were outdistancing me.

The first time I lost on Quiz Kids, I sobbed, "Mommy, I failed."

"No," she assured me, "you never fail when you do your best."

As a top Quiz Kid, though, I internalized the message that my best was *the* best. I felt my early success as something to be validated by future achievements. My sense of singularity had a flip side: the conviction that everything I touched would be golden. And it was . . . so long as I remained in academia.

Now, like my mother before me, I concentrated on being the best mother, channeling my ambitions through my children. I was an achiever; they would excel. I was competitive; they would be winners. Gil's attitude reinforced mine. Ours was a double standard, more demanding for us and our young than for outsiders.

But parenting is not like being a Quiz Kid or earning a Phi Beta Kappa key. As a young, inexperienced mother dealing with a sensitive, highly individualistic son, I was filled for the first time with fear of failure. The conventional wisdom stressed adjustment and conformity. Trained to

please and ambivalent about my own childhood differentness, I felt
uncomfortable when Steve's behavior departed from the norm. I
remember vividly, for example, my mortification when I visited his
nursery school and saw him sitting in the story circle, his back firmly
planted toward the teacher: a clear statement that listening to her was not
what *he* wanted to do. To let him live his own life and become his own
person was a lesson it took me years to learn.

My daughters were born with visual defects, more serious in the case of
Laurie, the elder. When told that she might need special schooling and
large-print books, I was stunned. Her imperfection struck me as a personal blow, the harder to bear because nothing could be done. As things
developed, her vision certainly did not hold her back. She graduated cum
laude from Smith College and now is at the University of Chicago Law
School. But for me, being forced in her infancy to accept the fact that
there are some things I cannot change was a humbling lesson.

All three children, now seventeen to twenty-seven, are bright and
talented. They turned out to be fine, accomplished young people. But in
the early years, my husband and I put far too much emphasis on our expectations for our musically gifted son—a mistake of which I, having been
put onstage as a child, should have been more wary. Excited by Steve's
ability, we pressed him into competitions he did not enjoy and made too
much of his performance. Now he plays the piano only when it suits his
purpose. "It's okay," he says, "if it doesn't become your whole
identity."

My sister, too, turned away from her music for a while in young
adulthood. "I needed those years of not singing," she says, "to discover
other ways of relating to people. I was popular because I could sing; I
wanted people to like me for myself. Applause is not a substitute for
love."

Like our mother and me, Bunny has devoted most of her efforts to her
children—"although I haven't sacrificed everything for them," she says.
"My kids didn't get all the lessons and camps and exposure to poetry and
theater that we got. Mom would rather have done without necessities
than for us not to have our lessons."

I, on the other hand, felt driven to duplicate my childhood for my
children. I steeped them in a brew of music and literature foreign to many
of their video-saturated contemporaries. Having, at a tender age, seen
the pop idols, warts and all, I had a jaundiced view of mass values that
echoed my parents'. Television and comics, I proclaimed, were not con-

structive. Advertised action toys that left nothing to the imagination were junk.

Yet no matter how much I sat with the children at the piano, how many lessons I chauffeured them to, how many original shows they put on, how many museums we visited, how many clever theme parties we gave, in my eyes my efforts fell short. Even now, I get irrational guilt-pangs about things my offspring do not know.

Still, time and experience did make a difference. By the time Heidi was born, seven years after her sister and ten years after her brother, I was a more relaxed, self-confident mother, Gil (now well-established in his profession) a more involved father. And there were two surrogate parents, Steve and Laurie, for balance. The joy of raising that baby knit our family together as never before. "Every child should be a third child," I said.

My renewed sense of self-assurance and self-esteem derived in part from the twelve years I spent (both before and after Heidi's birth) leading Junior Great Books discussions and coordinating the program in my suburban community. The emphasis in Great Books is on thinking for oneself; and my preparation sessions with co-leaders who became intimate friends yielded delicious moments of self-discovery.

The counseling I obtained when my son was small had helped me develop my own style of nurturing; and my parents' move to Florida may have freed me, unconsciously, to stop seeking some sort of quasi-parental approval through my children. Resolved to stop "smothering" them and to encourage independence, I allowed them as much as possible to make their own decisions and learn from the results—especially concerning things that really were their business. "We had fewer rules than most of our friends," says Laurie. "We had no curfew, but there was an expectation that our time would be well-spent."

While Laurie sees her upbringing as positive, her brother reacted against its serious intensity. "One of the themes that runs through our family," says Steve, "is that it's not okay to be average. It's almost required that we stand out. We all get a lot of satisfaction and admiration from the work we do. We find situations where we're looked up to and can make a contribution. But we don't get as much satisfaction from the ordinary parts of life.

"A lot of great things come from people who don't feel okay unless they're doing great things. But it's like an addiction—you suffer if it doesn't work."

My story has a familiar denouement: the midlife career. While I always had intended to resume employment when my children grew up, the feminist movement and the example of successful younger women sharpened my determination to become a financially contributing member of our household and to take charge, at last, of my life.

My sense of purpose was strengthened by my discovery, in my thirties, of a new brand of religion, Humanistic Judaism, which stresses personal power, independence, and responsibility. For ten years I taught in my Humanistic temple, helped develop its curriculum, and wrote for its periodicals. This work led, through a personal contact, to the resumption of the writing career I had put aside nearly two decades before.

Up to that point, most of my activities (Junior Great Books, religious school, PTA presidency) had flowed from the maternal instinct—the desire to enrich my children's education. The year before I turned forty, after my father's death and my son's departure for college, I took a part-time job as a staff writer for Lerner Newspapers, a weekly chain. For nearly eight years, I covered community news and wrote award-winning features and columns, freelancing on the side. Writing at home, I was able to remain available to my children. The more self-directed I became, the more self-reliant they grew. I won a tennis trophy, burying my old sports bugaboo. I felt ten years younger.

Once, in my immaturity, I had dreamed of going back to writing when I had some burning message to impart. Now I began to see the satisfaction in informing my neighbors about admittedly mundane things that affected their everyday lives. My long experience with questions and answers translated into canny interviewing and a compulsion to get to the bottom of things, and my old irresolution became a plus: the ability to see both sides. Going after scoops rekindled my competitiveness, but I strove for accuracy, remembering my childhood distress at being misquoted.

Each Thursday, I confess, when I opened the door and saw the newspaper lying on the stoop with "by Ruth Feldman" on the front page, I felt a thrill. Getting public recognition again, I realized I had missed it. The performance instinct still is strong; while I measure my achievements by an internal yardstick, I do find applause sweet.

A family connection opened a new avenue: writing educational filmstrips and videotapes, which, in turn, led me into shooting slides. I bought my first SLR camera and discovered an unsuspected knack. Assignments have taken me to the Carib Indian reserve in the wilds of Dominica and to the hogan of a Navajo medicine man. My professional activities have been in fields for which I lack the customary credentials.

Reporting and photography skills were relatively easy to pick up; but my liberal education and varied life experience have proven invaluable again and again in tackling assignments.

My other big asset, for which I thank my parental and Quiz Kid training, is the nerve to try. Deep down, I still believe that I can do just about anything I set my mind to, whether wallpapering and furniture refinishing, writing a marionette show, or interviewing Andy Warhol and John Anderson.

Of course a gap of decades is not easily vaulted. Having been accustomed, as a child, to unsought acclaim and praised for modesty, I had to learn to set strategies and sell myself. Expecting to be catapulted ''up there'' again, I became irrationally depressed when it didn't happen. Only after achieving some adult success did I put ''Quiz Kid'' on my resume and insert Duskin in my byline.

My sister, too, has the feeling that she should have accomplished more. ''I don't know if it was Quiz Kids so much as Mom and Dad and their expectations, and winning school awards and singing in operas. Then you get out into the big world and you're just a small cog in comparison with others. I feel I had a lot of promise I didn't fulfill.'' On second thought, Bunny reflects, Quiz Kids may have been more of an influence than she realized. ''I do feel that I should have achieved greater heights—and why didn't I? That I was one of the select few, and I should have become famous or created some brilliant new idea. Rubbing shoulders with stars like Jack Benny, being on the radio, makes you feel you should have done more.''

What Bunny has done, besides mothering, was to co-found two Jewish day schools her daughter attended and to serve as assistant director during a ten-year struggle to keep the schools afloat. Now, with her daughter in high school, Bunny has returned to school herself for a master's degree in her original field of social work.

For me, surviving emergency surgery three years ago at forty-five awakened a new sense of urgency and ''born-again'' opportunity. For a long time, I had thought of leaving my newspaper job; and in 1981, I did. The paper was no *New York Times,* and I had learned and grown there as much as I was going to. With my last child in high school, I was ready to move beyond my home and community. Drawing upon my teaching, writing and audiovisual experience, I helped put together a training course for Motorola and supervised a pilot test in Phoenix, earning as much in three months as I would have made in a whole year at my newspaper job. It was my first direct experience with the corporate world, and making good there was a real ego-boost. In addition, I have intensified my photomarketing, with increasing success; continued writing filmstrips; and done some magazine pieces, including a detailed analysis of Senator Charles Percy's Mideast positions (the lead article in the premiere issue of *Jewish Chicago*).

Giving up my safe newspaper spot to seek work with more challenge and potential was a step toward owning my life. Writing this book— integrating the separate strands of my past—is another.

The *This Week* piece I wrote upon my Quiz Kids graduation concluded: ". . . let us be careful that in our eagerness to grow up we put away only the narrow *childish* attitudes and . . . retain the wonderful, *child-like* qualities . . . curiosity, energy and love of life that made our childhood so rich."

If I had it to do over, would I be a Quiz Kid? Probably. I am what I am, and the past is history—my history.

Little Ruth has learned to stand.
With her own tiny hands
she grasps the pillars of her crib
and by the tremendous force of her desire
pulls herself up.

Tossing her head proudly, she draws herself erect
as though inhaling the rarified atmosphere of high places,
and laughs the uncontrolled
and uncontained laughter of a child—
A laugh of triumph
of one who has achieved something long desired.

When night comes, she will not sleep.
As many times I lay her down,
so many times she rises
and stands there in the dark
calling to us to come and see.

Realizing at last that there will be
no more response to her calls,
she bursts into heart-touching sobs
as though the audience has considered
applause between the acts sufficient
and has requested no curtain calls.

Soon her cry becomes a whimper.
And as one who has given a splendid performance
at last gives way to sleep,
hugging happiness until fatigue overwhelms her,
so our little one nods her head,
unconquerable and unquenched.

—Rita Duskin, 1935 (adapted from *The Frugal Chariot,*
   Windfall Press, 1970)

Ruth Duskin at age seven, sitting on her Quiz Kids fan mail.

Jack Benny, the Quiz Kids' host, arrives with them in Hollywood in 1941.
Front, left to right: Gerard Darrow, Richard Williams, Claude Brenner.
Back: Joan Bishop and Cynthia Cline.

Jack Lucal, Gerard Darrow, and Richard Williams give the wartime ''V for Victory'' sign.

Gerard Darrow hugs Donald Duck, a present from Walt Disney. With him, left to right: movie actress Gloria Jean, Disney, Joan Bishop, Richard Williams, Cynthia Cline, and Claude Brenner.

Gerard Darrow enlightens Ruth Duskin about his favorite subject, birds.

Joel Kupperman and Ruth Duskin with Fred Allen and his wife Portland.

Joel and Ruth with the Lone Ranger and Silver.

Ruth Duskin backstage with Shakespearian actor Maurice Evans before his performance in *Macbeth*.

The Quiz Kids roll into Portland, Oregon. In the car, from left: Richard Williams, Ruth Duskin, Joel Kupperman, and Harve Bennett Fischman.

Ruth beats future Nobel prizewinner James D. Watson—as well as Jack Lucal, Margaret Merrick, and Claude Brenner—to the answer on a Bible question.

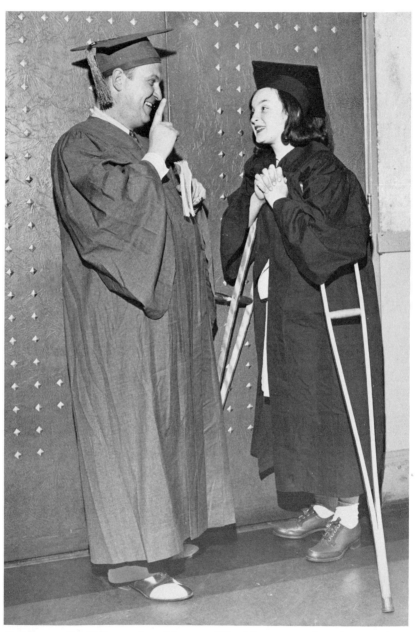

Quizmaster Joe Kelly cautions Margaret Merrick not to peek at the questions on his cards.

The Quiz Kids with Chico Marx. From left: Gerard Darrow, Claude Brenner, Richard Williams, Margaret Merrick, Joel Kupperman, David Prochaska, Ruth Duskin, and Harve Bennett Fischman.

Guest Quizmaster Bob Hope struggles with an arithmetic problem while Joel Kupperman, math whiz, looks on.

The Quiz Kids stump guest Quizmaster Eddie Cantor. From left: Joel, Gerard, Harve, Richard, and Ruth.

Guest Quizmaster Bing Crosby hits a high note with Gerard and Ruth.

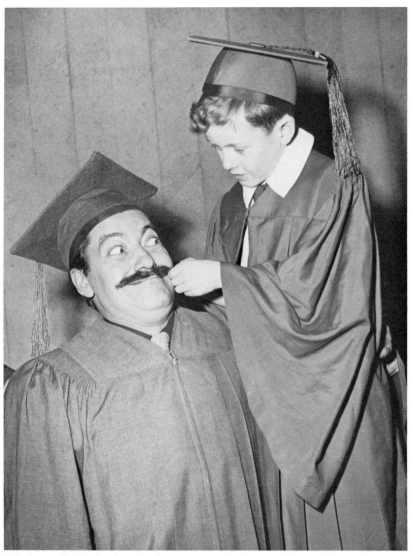

Is it for real? Pat Conlon checks out guest Quizmaster Jerry Colonna's mustache.

Ruth lends her jumprope to another guest Quizmaster, University of Chicago professor Leon P. Smith (father of Quiz Kid Elinor Smith).

Vanessa Brown (Smylla Brind) appears in the Quiz Kids' "schoolroom" at Studio E in the Merchandise Mart, along with Harve, Bunny Duskin (Ruth's sister), Richard, and Claude.

Vice President Henry Wallace meets in his Washington office with Harve, Margaret, and Richard in 1943.

The Quiz Kids return to Hollywood in 1943. Here they lunch on the set with Peggy Ryan and Donald O'Connor. Passing their autograph books are, from left to right: Ruth, Gerard, Harve, Joel, and Richard.

At the Hollywood Canteen, Harve makes good on a bet with a kiss from actress Jinx Falkenburg.

Part Two:
Here They Are—the Quiz Kids!

Gerard Darrow: Fallen Robin

At seven, he was the youngest of the original Quiz Kids, darling of millions.

At nine, he made the cover of *Life*.

At forty-seven, Gerard Darrow died . . . a man in broken health who had spent a good portion of his final years on welfare.

A routine death notice appeared in the *Chicago Tribune* February 3, 1980. The small item was easy to miss. No mention of his having been a Quiz Kid. No accompanying story. The press did not pick it up; apparently no one recognized the name.

His Quiz Kids associates had lost track of him. Hardly any knew of his passing.

Never married, he had been living with a ninety-one-year-old aunt. A handful of mourners attended his wake. One young man broke down and cried: Gerard's neighbor of ten months and only friend, Gino Stockero.

"He wanted to die," says Gino. "He felt his life was over, there was nothing left. He aged way before his time."

Eight years earlier, Gerard (in an interview published under the alias "Bruce Fletcher" in Studs Terkel's *Working*) had said "I don't know what's going to happen to me. It would be much more convenient if I had cancer and passed away and [people would] say, 'Oh, how tragic,' and I could have the peace of the grave."

In 1940, he was Baby Gerard, "the sparkplug of the Quiz Kids." Before he could tie his own shoelaces, he regaled listeners week after week with colorful descriptions of bird habits and habitats.

He spoke of his feathered friends as if they were intimate human pals. Asked which bird is most henpecked, he replied, "The male phalarope. Nature has given the female brighter plumage, and she does the courting. She thinks it's leap year all the time. She makes the male sit on the eggs and care for the young, while she goes off. She probably goes to play cards with the other birds."

This "pint-sized William Beebe" outdid the noted naturalist in a spell-down on varieties of ducks. He knew "the whole animal kingdom from Aardvard to Zebu," said *Cue* magazine. He could explain "the exact difference between a frog and a toad, a crocodile and an alligator, down to length of snout or sliminess of skin." He knew that camels' cuts don't heal and that Pacific Coast Indians used the oily candlefish for torches. ("It makes a good light but smells awful.")

His memory left his elders gasping. Identifying Vallisneria, Cabomba, and Sagittaria as aquatic plants was a snap. Before he ever studied geography in school, he could name hundreds of cities, rivers, and mountains. He recited Greek myths in toto. He had a triple-track mind: he could read a book while listening to the radio, tune in on a nearby conversation, and repeat all three verbatim.

Publishers sent him science books for comment. When John Kieran of "Information Please" put out a book of *Nature Notes,* Gerard ("the John Kieran of the Quiz Kids") reviewed it for *Time.* He offered faint praise: "Children of six could enjoy this book. It's pretty elementary. The only thing I found out that I didn't know was how to make feeding stations for hummingbirds."

When Gerard was told he was to meet Kieran at the National Audubon Society's annual meeting, he burst into tears. But Kieran had not been offended. The two nature-lovers had a nice talk about water ouzels and redpolls before Gerard got up to answer questions for the five hundred society members . . . all the while holding his pet salamander in his pocket and taking it out from time to time to make sure it was all right.

The nine-year-old must have felt right at home. The year before, he had been voted a member of the society, as well as a life member of the Chicago Academy of Science. His ambition was to be an ornithology professor; at times he sounded like one.

Gerard was "clearly a prodigy," *Life* proclaimed, "and, as such, subject to intense and frequent study by an army of scientists. Seeking in vain for some clue either in heredity or association for Gerard's tremendous interest in ornithology, they have come to the meager conclusion that Gerard must like birds.''

Once another boy asked Gerard how to become a Quiz Kid. ''Well,'' said Gerard, ''you go to the library and ask for a lot of books, and you take them home and read them all and go back for more.'' In Gerard's case, there was a little more to it.

Gerard Brendan Darrow came from enterprising stock. On his mother's side, there was a line of Michael McDermotts: a surveyor who mapped the Canadian wilderness for the British crown and laid out much of Milwaukee; a contractor for the Chicago drainage canal, elevated train system, and Field Museum of Natural History; and an Olympic swimmer. The boy's father, Joseph Darrow, had put himself through night engineering school, then gone to work buying up rights-of-way for Samuel Insull's power lines. But by the time Gerard was born in Gary, Indiana, his father, like many in 1932, was temporarily unemployed, his fortunes having crashed with Insull's utility empire.

Gerard, who bore the name of the patron saint of mothers, never knew his own; Irene McDermott Darrow died of encephalitis four months after giving birth. Joseph Darrow moved his newborn son and his three older children, ages ten to thirteen, into his parents' six-room apartment on Chicago's south side, where his sisters Bess and Clara lived. Baby Gerard slept in the dining room, while the other eight doubled and tripled up in the bedrooms.

Bess, warm and plump, took the babe under her wing. ''He's like a skinny little robin that has fallen from its nest,'' she would sigh.

By six months, the infant was speaking a few words. By two, he could recall anything read to him. To keep him occupied, his grandmother or Aunt Bessie would cuddle him in a rocker and read whatever came to hand.

One day his grandmother happened to pick up his eldest brother's Boy Scout bird manual. Little Gerard was entranced with the brightly colored pictures. Over and over, the two women would read him the names and descriptions, and he would parrot them back. Soon Bessie was bringing home books on birds, butterflies, bees, flowers, shells, rocks, and fish. She would read to him at mealtime to get him to finish his oatmeal, and he would sit on the floor poring over the pages for hours.

By the time he was four, he could identify hundreds of birds, and Aunt Bessie would call in the neighbors to applaud. The *Chicago Daily News* got wind of the "prodigy" and wrote him up. When Lou Cowan consulted the paper's files for potential Quiz Kid material, Gerard was an obvious choice.

The only original Quiz Kid under thirteen, he was singlehandedly responsible for the show's smashing success. His knowledge amazed listeners; his high-pitched, deliberate speech and unconscious wit won their hearts. As *Life* observed, the long drawn-out "Well-l-l-l . . . " with which he launched each answer became as familiar as FDR's "My friends . . . " Asked how many antlers Santa's last reindeer could count on the heads of those in front, the other Kids blanked. Gerard piped up: "None, be-cause a rein-deer can't count."

He did not yield the mike easily. Once Joe Kelly asked him to sing a bit of "The Three Little Fishes." Gerard sailed through three verses, ignoring Kelly's remonstrances. Afterward he explained, "I am sure the peo-ple would want to know that the lit-tle fish-es got safe-ly back to their moth-er."

His genial father took him out for a chocolate soda after each broadcast—a treat the boy treasured more than his mounting stack of $100 bonds. Gerard confessed that he was afraid he might cry if he lost. "You're too big to cry," his father replied.

Bumped after nine straight appearances, Gerard did not cry. But his fans did. "I am absolutely heartbroken," one letter ran. Another outraged writer threatened to "buy no more Alka-Seltzer until Gerard comes back." He soon did, and the custom of recalling popular Kids was established.

"Gerard's weekly stint is an almost indispensable moment of sparkling relief in the vast cacophony of dullness and mediocrity broadcast over U.S. networks," wrote Sidney James, *Life*'s Chicago bureau chief, in a five-page cover story. Because of the lad's phenomenal memory, he was "an object of nationwide curiosity. . . . His habits, his clothes, his menu, his size, his weight, indeed, every separate, unrelated fact about Gerard is eagerly seized upon, mulled over and discussed by his admirers and detractors. . . . Gerard's conversation, which reads alternately like the *Encyclopedia Britannica* or the 'Bright Sayings' column, is carefully taken down and chronicled in a one-man *Congressional Record*."

This "mastermind in short pants" was described as a "regular boy" who loved to swim, roller skate, roll in the snow, and splash through mud puddles. Aunt Bessie was forever wiping him clean. He showed up for the filming of a Paramount movie short with a bruised chin; he had fallen off his new Christmas bicycle despite Bessie's warnings. *Quiz Kids Magazine* reported that he owned more than four hundred volumes on nature and other subjects, but his prize possession was his comic book collection. His pet peeves were shoes in summer and heavy underwear in winter. His favorite personage was the Good Humor man. Once he punched an older boy who called Quiz Kids sissies.

Yet Gerard's preoccupation with flora and fauna set him apart from ordinary children. His pen pals were eminent scientists. He played with pets, not toys. He woke his sister by putting his salamander in her hair and drove Aunt Bessie wild by collecting live insects; once she found fifteen caterpillars crawling around the kitchen. A retinue of turtles followed him around the house. His menagerie included a cocker spaniel named Rusty, twin lovebirds, Bill and Coo, and a two-foot alligator named Snappy (a gift from the Cleveland zoo) that bit everyone in the family but Gerard. He told reporters he wanted a baby vulture.

It was an unusual environment—living in close quarters with so many older people—for a little boy who yearned to be an explorer like Frank Buck and bring back live specimens from Africa. Instead, Gerard had to content himself with forays into the woods near his family's summer cottage. The tiny converted back porch breakfast nook, where he bunked with his brother Mike, overflowed with the younger boy's expanding collections of bird's nests, fossils, shells, pressed flowers, feathers, mounted butterflies, moths, and beetles.

His two older brothers paid him scant heed. Once, when they were going pheasant-hunting, the passionate bird-lover stuffed their gun barrels with paper. Reprimanded for endangering his brothers' lives, he muttered, "Anybody who would kill a pheasant ought to be killed."

When Gerard went on Quiz Kid trips, his family was under strict instructions to wire him if anything should happen to his pets. On at least one occasion, he vainly pleaded to take his alligator along.

He did get to take his favorite snapping turtle to Washington to visit Mamie Eisenhower. At the White House, when colleague Cynthia Cline presented Eleanor Roosevelt with a Quiz Kid key, Gerard unpinned his own key and gallantly handed it to the First Lady to give her husband "in token of the fine work he has done." Added the eight-year-old diplomat: "I'm for him and I've always been for him." Later Gerard explained his gesture: "Mrs. Roosevelt had a key, and I didn't want the President to be jealous."

Normally, tact was not Gerard's strong suit. In New York Mayor Fiorello LaGuardia's office, the smallest Kid touted Chicago's superior cultural attractions. "The Little Flower," unperturbed, winked and told him, "Even if you stay little, you might grow up to be mayor of a big city."

Wherever the Quiz Kids went, Gerard was the center of attention, and he knew it. At Hollywood's alligator farm, he mounted the beast Dorothy Lamour had ridden in her latest film escapade and asked the startled attendant, "How large is an alligator's brain?" He chided Paramount for having used nonindigenous camels in *The Road to Morocco*—"They should have been dromedaries."

Screen idols sought his autograph while he collected strands of hair from Claudette Colbert, Gloria Swanson, and the rest. He had a screen test with Roddy McDowell, patiently enlightened Jack Benny about the difference between echidna (an Australian mammal) and nilgau (a type of deer), and posed for photographs reading a thick book of Spinoza while Benny read the funnies. Gerard was said to be the only person who ever changed a line in a Benny script and got away with it.

In fact, Gerard got away with murder.

> . . . Gerard was posing with Bob Hope and Paulette Goddard. A big moth settled on one of the lights set up for the picture. Gerard waited, expressionless. When the moth ventured close enough, Gerard grabbed him with a boarding house reach, dashed across the room, locked the insect in embarrassed Aunt Bessie's purse, dashed back to pose again. Everybody roared with laughter except Gerard.
> —Gene Farmer, *Cedar Rapids Gazette,* April 26, 1942

Bessie and the Quiz Kids staff had to be constantly on guard for fear the uninhibited child would say or do the wrong thing. When the Kids visited W.C. Fields at his hacienda, Gerard lectured Fields, a notorious lush, on the evils of alcohol. Gerard said he had made a study of the subject and offered to tell Fields about it, but was hurriedly whisked away.

Gerard may not have endeared himself to Fields; but with his cherubic face, rosy cheeks, wide eyes, slicked-down hair, and immaculate suits, he captivated grandmotherly types. On the Quiz Kids' second Hollywood trip, a contingent of elderly ladies met Gerard at the train. They were so taken with him that Aunt Bessie, who accompanied Gerard on his Quiz Kids jaunts, invited them all to tea.

"Aunt Bessie really swung," Gerard told *Texas Magazine* years later. "She got along well with people like Fred Allen and Jack Benny. This was a great asset to me." Kind, garrulous Aunt Bessie gloried in her nephew's spotlight. After all, in great measure she had made him what he was.

Throughout Gerard's childhood, Bess was his closest companion and confidante. She pampered him, clucking indulgently at his mischief. He knew how to get around her by quoting Scripture when he misbehaved. She fussed about his diet but let him eat box after box of popcorn "with real butter on it."

Instead of writing in a diary, he dictated to Aunt Bessie. This entry was printed in *Coronet* magazine:

> I was scared yesterday when I got the second notice for my dog license. Aunt Bessie had no pity. She said I had squandered the money that I should have saved for Rusty's license, and if he had to go to the dog pound it would be my own fault. I was terribly worried trying to think how to make some money. Finally, I got an idea. Whenever I pull out a tooth, I put it under my pillow and the fairies take it and leave a piece of silver. So I managed to work out four loose teeth. Aunt Bessie looked kind of funny, but when I woke up there were four half-dollars under my pillow—enough to save Rusty.

Bessie continued to read to Gerard long after she had taught him to read. She looked up answers to his perpetual questions and, when he became a Quiz Kid, sat by him each week to help him study—sessions he appeared to enjoy. On tour, she saw that he completed his school assignments, a task he approached less willingly.

His scholastic performance was surprisingly spotty. He did poorly in first and second grades but was skipped the next year, after he became a Quiz Kid. He could read eighth grade material but fell down in spelling, penmanship, and arithmetic ("There's no romance in it.") Once he explained to his father: "When I put down the number 11 on my paper, it looks like a stork's legs, so I begin to think about storks. Number 8 looks like an owl . . . and by that time, I forget to do the problem."

He was in some ways far ahead of his peers, in others, childishly naive. His formidable knowledge had startling gaps. In July, 1941, as the United States weighed entry into the war, someone jokingly asked Gerard if there was a bird large enough to carry off Hitler. "Who's he?" responded the eight-year-old prodigy. When classmates twitted him about his belief in Santa Claus, he told Aunt Bessie, "I don't care if those kids think there's no Santa Claus. A lot of them don't believe in the Darwinian theory, either.''

Although gushing journalists portrayed Gerard as ''lovable'' and ''unspoiled,'' his schoolmates saw him as smug and pedantic. The principal at Bradwell School was constantly finding reasons to put his star pupil on the stage. Once, when a movie on thrushes was being shown, something went wrong with the sound track. Gerard, who had seen the film that morning, completed the narration from memory. Another time, giving a slide lecture, he stamped his foot when the other children failed to identify a specimen on the screen. ''This bird is found in all your back yards,'' he railed. ''What do you kids *do* with your spare time?'' He ran a mini-Quiz Kids contest; one of the low scorers laid for him and beat him up.

Schoolfellows ridiculed and avoided him. Ex-Quiz Kid Harve Bennett, who attended the same school, remembers: ''Here's a child with wide, strange eyes and a strange way of talking, who's describing the tropical birds of West Pago-Pago, and you say, *What world does this child come from?* One had only to listen to Gerard on the radio with any degree of intelligence to know that he was not in the mainstream of American life. In person, he had Bette Davis mannerisms that looked like someone portraying neuroticism. I, even as a ten-year-old, knew intuitively that Gerard was headed for a lot of trouble.''

At first, Gerard enjoyed socializing with the other Quiz Kids. He loved clambering through the upper berths of Pullman cars at night and playing Monopoly by day. He was tight-fisted with his play money; we called him ''little Scrooge.''

He was nine when I arrived as the new Quiz Kid baby. Then six-year-old Joel Kupperman, the lisping ''math genius,'' came on and totally eclipsed Gerard. Bessie Darrow set her lips and fought to keep her nephew in the forefront.

He, more than any of the others, ''played to an audience,'' says Roby Hickok Kesler. ''It wasn't a healthy thing for him.'' He would pause to take off his owl-like glasses before posing for pictures and would smirk knowingly when he gave an answer. ''*I'm* Gerard *Dar*-row,'' he introduced himself imperiously. He delighted in annoying adults by pretending to ignore what they said, then repeating it word for word when called to account. Once when Joe Kelly asked for the name of a rare bird, Gerard gave Kelly's name in Latin.

The second California trip was Gerard's last hurrah. A few months before, Joel had made a movie with Donald O'Connor—a fact that rankled with Bessie Darrow. She confided to my mother that MGM, at the height of Gerard's early fame, had offered him a contract, but it would have meant quitting "Quiz Kids" and Lou Cowan refused to release him. According to Bessie, Cowan said he had spent $36,000 on Gerard's buildup and wasn't about to see his investment evaporate. Now, Bessie said, Cowan was willing to make amends by trying to set up some studio contacts for Gerard. But young Darrow at eleven was not photogenic.

One memory of that trip remained with Gerard for years. At a Hollywood Bowl war bond benefit, he had sat next to twelve-year-old Elizabeth Taylor. Miss Taylor, as he called her, told him she disliked being in movies, but her mother forced her. Almost a quarter-century later, Gerard commented to *Texas Magazine* on her turbulent life: "She can't help it. She's like a wave in the ocean that's forced to drift along with the tide."

With ninety Quiz Kids appearances, Gerard was the sole survivor of the original panel. Now, despite a letter-writing campaign apparently orchestrated by Aunt Bessie, he made a premature exit. Harve, Joel, Dick Williams, and I continued the war bond circuit, with Gerard's place filled by local contest winners.

The backstage gossip was that Gerard had been quietly dropped. Says Harve, now a successful television producer: "As he neared puberty, the excesses of personality were becoming difficult to support in a commercial medium. That which had passed as eccentric was becoming aberrant. There was a latent homosexuality that was beginning to assert itself on microphone.

"He was the kind of kid that other kids in my school referred to as a 'fruit.' He had a 'limp wrist.' Nowadays perhaps there's more tolerance of that. God knows, in our time, there wasn't. I suppose if I had been the producer of that show at that time, I would have said, 'Let's ease him out.' "

Dick Williams conjectures that the clincher was a San Francisco press conference at which Gerard sat in a corner wolfing popcorn and refused to do the "trained seal act." Gerard also managed to get lost in the crowd at Oakland just as we Kids were to launch a ship, and then had a tantrum at having missed it.

"Gerard bombed on that trip, and they didn't have him back," says Dick. "Of course it was a management decision—it always was." According to Roby, "He just faded away. As he got older, his specialty was too limited."

Gerard himself "wondered what happened," as he told Studs Terkel three decades later. He surmised that his "obnoxious" ways had become "intolerable," and "it was considered wise that I retire early." From then on, he was "just plain" Gerard Darrow.

One person who wanted Gerard off the show was his father, who (according to Gerard's brother Joe, a retired businessman) felt the program was interfering with the boy's schooling: "He had too many irons in the fire."

The father, who had remarried, decided to take a stronger hand in his young son's upbringing. He brought a reluctant Gerard to live with him and his new wife, to whom Gerard took a passionate dislike. Bess had built him up, babied him. His stepmother did not. Although pleasant enough in public (Gerard later told Gino Stockero, the friend of his final months), she needled him in private and turned his father against him. His two stepbrothers were popular, underlining Gerard's isolation; their friends called him "weird." He often ran "home" to his grandmother and aunts a block away.

To complete the radical changes in his life, his father pulled him out of Bradwell in mid-semester and enrolled him in the University of Chicago Laboratory School. Gerard was put back a year, so when I entered seventh grade there the following fall, I found him in my class. In this small private school where social life was clearly divided between the "ins" and "outs," Gerard was definitely out. He developed a reputation for annoying girls and became the butt of locker room jokes. He was president of a rock-polishing club that dwindled to one other member. Dick Williams, then at the University of Chicago, remembers seeing graffiti scrawled on the nearby Illinois Central platform: "Gerard is a pig."

Nevertheless, Gerard liked the Lab School. The counselors "knew how to handle him," says Rachel Stevenson, with whom Bessie Darrow kept in touch. "They let him sit in a tree or whatever." Eventually he made some friends and even became a student council representative.

Gerard's father told the counselors that his son had been overly sheltered; his aunts had not allowed him to play ball like other boys. Following his father's wish, Gerard went out for intramural sports. Although thin and poorly coordinated, he persevered and won baseball and swimming awards.

Whereas his I.Q. in public school had tested only slightly above average ("I.Q. tests are the bunk," Bessie had scoffed), an individual Stanford-Binet at the Lab School registered 144. On achievement tests, he ranked in the top quartile nationally. He pulled high grades in French and music but C's and D's in English and math. His uneven showing was a constant source of mortification. When he didn't know the answers, teachers rubbed it in.

A crotchety old schoolmaster who banged out opera tunes on a scarred upright piano awakened a love of music that became the focus of Gerard's adult life. As a child, he had scorned "hotsy-totsy stuff"; his taste had run to compositions like *The Carnival of Animals* that fit his zoological bias. Now he learned to identify symphonic themes by catch phrases sung to the melodies. Here was fresh fodder for his voracious memory.

By the time he got to Millikin College, he knew vast quantities of music and had begun amassing a record collection befitting a connoisseur. He studied voice, piano, theory and harmony, but being tone deaf, decided to become a musicologist—an authority on music as he had been on birds.

Before he was able to get hold of his Quiz Kids money at twenty-one, he apparently was on his own. He later told ex-Quiz Kids Dick Williams and Joan Bishop a scarcely believable story about having to pilfer baskets of wilted lettuce to eat at Millikin.

One day, Gerard got on a train for New York and began working his way through Columbia University night school as first a factory hand, then a servant in an exclusive men's club, and finally a cafeteria busboy. He would scream at lazy co-workers and would sing loudly offkey while pouring coffee, until customers begged him to shut up.

His family assumed he had gone to Columbia because a friend from Millikin had. But according to Gino Stockero, Gerard went east to escape the family. "He had had so much attention, being so young and a Quiz Kid, and then after that, they put so much on him to be an achiever that he had to get away. His brothers were doing well during those years when he was finding himself in New York, and he was not."

Joan Bishop, who was pursuing a musical career, invited Gerard to the Manhattan apartment she shared with her mother. "He was living in some dump on Third Avenue," Joan remembers. "He wasn't even eating. We gave him a couple of pork chops and cupcakes. He did have his fish tank—he told us about his fish. He looked terrible. His hair was unkempt, real long. His socks were hanging down and his shoes were unshined. And he was badmouthing the [Quiz Kids] show, saying it had ruined him. He didn't think it was good for kids." Joan was impressed, though, with Gerard's musical knowledge: "He was telling me about operas I wouldn't think anyone would know."

Four years later, Gerard met Joan and Dick Williams at the hotel where she was singing. "He was kind of creepy," says Dick. "He seemed pathetic. There was something furtive about him. You just felt he was psychologically damaged.''

Gerard took classes at Columbia on and off, maintaining a B-plus average. ''He kept changing courses,'' says his brother Joe. ''I thought he'd be one of these guys that keep going to school all their lives.'' But the Quiz Kids money ran out. ''I'd like to get on that $64,000 Question,'' Gerard told a reporter who tracked him down.

Through Columbia, he found a job as a proofreader for a Wall Street law firm. He enjoyed the meticulous work far more than slinging hash. As he later told Studs Terkel, ''the law firm brought me back to the fact that I was not just somebody's scullery maid. The people either liked me very much or hated me with a purple passion. But I was respected. I've been respected on every job I ever had.'' When he left, half the staff of lawyers gave him a farewell luncheon. ''I was asked to make a speech,'' he told Terkel, ''and I was much applauded.''

At twenty-seven, he got his break: he was asked to lecture for the New York Society for Recorded Music. Next came a chance to substitute on a radio show. With his deep voice and familiarity with musical minutiae, he soon had his own program, ''The Language of Music.'' He spun classical discs and interviewed guests like Pierre Monteux and Walter Slezak.

A year later, he answered an ad for a musical expert, fluent in languages, to help run a west coast station. He knew French, German, Italian, and a smattering of other tongues. He packed up his 10,000 records, three cats, two guinea pigs, cockatoo and Mynah bird, and moved to Bellingham, Washington. But the station signed off after eighteen months, and he roamed down the coast, selling encyclopedias. He landed in San Francisco, where he became producer-commentator of a four-hour Sunday program of rarely-heard long works. He had found his mission: to make good music accessible to anyone who would appreciate it.

A year later, he turned up in Houston, hosting KLEF's classical programming. Music-lovers enjoyed his immense store of witty anecdotes and encyclopedic information.

The station profiled him in its program guide.

Once the child idol of millions, Gerard is now just another grown-up trying to keep a few jumps ahead of the bill collectors. He is a mature, balding gentleman; a man of considerable personal charm with a gentle wit, a very generous nature, and most considerate of those around him. ''Everybody expected all kinds of things of me,'' he says retrospectively, ''but I was no longer the bright little boy. I had to learn to become a bright adult. I'm still working on that.''

. . . Gerard made the [Quiz Kids] show sparkle . . . and we think he still does! He disclaims that he was ever a child genius. ''I just had a great memory . . . which isn't as good as it used to be.'' We know better. Whenever there is a musical question . . . we just ask Gerard. Nine times out of ten, he has the answer on the tip of his tongue.

Those nine years as a classical disc jockey were, as Gerard later told Studs Terkel, ''the happiest times of my life.'' One job, he said, ''consumed me day and night for a year and a half.'' He hobnobbed with the likes of Sir Thomas Beecham and Lotte Lehmann, threw extravagant catered parties, partook in deep discussions. He was in his element. Then, once more, success soured.

He had a falling-out with KLEF's management and could not find another job in the field. At thirty-six, his career was over. He later told people that nobody wanted to hire someone his age, that he had run into bad breaks.

His aunts persuaded Gerard, who had been ill in Houston, to come back to Chicago (a decision he later regretted). ''No matter how old he was,'' says Gino, ''they always treated him like a boy.'' Gerard, for his part, felt responsible for the two aging women. It was his first home-coming in the decade and a half since he had boarded that New York train. He had not even come in for his father's funeral.

Unable to reestablish himself as a radio announcer, Gerard took a job tending roses for a florist in the western suburbs, near where Bess and Clara lived. Three years later, he called WFMT, Chicago's fine arts station, hoping for an opening. That was when Studs Terkel, who hosts a show on that station, interviewed him as ''Bruce Fletcher.''

''As soon as you saw him, you knew there was something wrong,'' Terkel says. ''He was an outsider. He looked down on others. The classic lost figure.''

Short and stout, Gerard spoke in a distinct, formal manner reminiscent of his early diction. His hair had begun graying at twenty-one; by thirty-five, he had lost most of it. He felt his body had undergone a sort of male menopause. ''The years went by quickly when I was very young . . . when I should have been having fun,'' he told Terkel. ''I became a concerned old man at a very early age.''

Now he was ''in retirement,'' living in a cheap room and savoring the "peace and quiet and privacy" of the greenhouse. "Everyone says, 'Bruce [Gerard] is hard to get along with.' Bruce [Gerard] is not difficult to get along with if I had intelligent people to work with, where people are not after me or picking on me . . . " But he missed the music business: "I blossomed forth like the roses in the greenhouse. I was in my own kind of work."

The published sketch in *Working* glossed over his good years as a music announcer, dwelling on the menial jobs and his condemnation of "Quiz Kids." In better days, he had called that experience "broadening and demanding," mentioned the fun of travel and meeting celebrities. This time he poured out his bitterness: "I can't forgive those who exploited me. . . . Had I grown up as others did, I would have come out a much better person. . . . I wish it had never happened."

Shortly before Lou Cowan's death, ex-Quiz Kid Patrick Conlon dropped by his office, seeking permission to revive "Quiz Kids." Cowan was troubled. He had read *Working*.

"Do you think anybody was really hurt by the show?" he asked.

"My answer," Pat recalls, "was that for people who were in trouble already, it was not going to help. Gerard Darrow was going to have problems no matter what."

"He was already so affected," says Dick Williams. "It was unfortunate to rave over his mannerisms and then, when what had been cute was no longer cute, suddenly the poor kid was shunned."

Says Harve Bennett: "Gerard was a lonely kid raised of a maiden aunt. Aunt Bessie gave him protection when he needed it, but she also gave him overdominance. I had hoped he might have become, perhaps, the curator of a museum. A lot of people who as children are very odd turn it to their advantage when they grow older. That Gerard had turned it destructively against himself was sad, and that he blamed Quiz Kids was doubly sad."

Gerard stayed at the House of Roses for five years, until he no longer could bear the 116-degree summer heat in the greenhouse. He solicited prospects for an Arkansas land deal that was declared illegal, then made a final stab at seeking broadcasting work in San Francisco. Back in the Chicago area, he drove a van and sold plants by phone, making at most $140 a week. For several years he was on welfare, living in a rooming house with two cats and a canary and helping to care for Bessie, now in her eighties and wheelchair-bound.

When Bess was killed in an automobile collision, Gerard got rid of his pets and moved in with Clara, who had been injured in the accident. He cooked her gourmet meals with groceries purchased with food stamps and newspaper coupons.

"He felt he had lived his life," says Gino Stockero, a resident of the Wheaton apartment complex to which the pair moved in spring of 1979. "The only thing that meant anything to him anymore was staying with his aunt. She was his only real family."

Gerard's relations with his brother Joe, his only natural sibling still in the area, were pleasant but distant. As for the stepmother and her one living son, Gerard refused to let them in the house. "He was completely unreasonable," says Gino. "He would throw tantrums when anyone mentioned her name."

Gerard's family, says Gino, "frowned on his not working all these years. They would say, 'So-and-so is doing this and that, and you're not making much of yourself.' Gerard was very emotional. You could hurt his feelings very easily."

The elderly aunt admonished her nephew for wearing striped coveralls to church. "The Lord doesn't care how I look, as long as I go," Gerard would insist.

"He felt he was different," says Gino. "He felt he had become fat and ugly. He had no social life, no real friends. He just stayed on his own."

The two men became acquainted when Gino, who was doing part-time maintenance work to finance his psychology studies, came over to help Gerard and his aunt get settled. A thirty-three-year-old Vietnam veteran, Gino had traveled widely and seen all kinds of people. He says, "I don't like people that come out of the same mold. I like people who are different, as long as they're genuine."

To Gino, Gerard was "the most intelligent man I ever knew. Such a source of knowledge for me. He was forever correcting my vocabulary. He had an amazing way with words." He could be (Gino says) egotistical and argumentative but also enthusiastic, entertaining, and original. He would mimic people, caricaturing them as monkeys or birds. Gino's friends and professors who met Gerard "remembered him and were impressed by him."

They were an unlikely pair. Gino, trim, athletic and "one hundred percent Italian," with shiny black hair, wore sneakers and tee shirts, and worked out with weights. Gerard, bald, bloated, and Irish, wore thick glasses, baggy old pants, and threadbare coats, and spent most of his time reading. No one would have guessed there was only fifteen years' difference in their ages. They did have one thing in common: Gino, too, had lost his mother in infancy. "He loved me as a person and looked out for my welfare," says Gino. "If I needed something, he was there. He considered me the brother he never had."

Soft-spoken, sincere Gino was an appreciative audience for Gerard's tales of his high life as an announcer and of his demeaning years working in fast-food establishments and the like. Gerard advised Gino about his love life. And he confided in Gino about his own.

"Gerard was a confirmed homosexual," says Gino. "He felt great toward someone that would accept him for what he was, not some kind of oddity. He started opening up and talking about things that he had kept in himself for so long. He told me that he'd never made love to a woman in his life. He grew up in a time when homosexuality was very frowned upon. He was emotionally unstable, with all that guilt."

Gerard made some tentative overtures to Gino. "I told him I don't have any inclinations to it, and it didn't seem to put any crimp in our relationship. Sometimes when he would leave, he'd grab me and kiss me on the cheek, real emotional-like. I wouldn't get all tense about it. To him that was like kissing a beautiful girl good-bye."

Gerard told Gino about an older man with whom he had had an affair— a colonel who had a mountain resort, whom he "really missed"—and asked Gino to make inquiries about where he could meet gays in Chicago, but nothing came of it.

With women, Gerard enjoyed "putting 'em on," feigning interest to make them uncomfortable. Once, in the course of a long afternoon of fast-paced repartee with John Monaghan, a fellow-Irishman he met through Gino, Gerard spun a tale of having been a ladies' man. At Columbia, according to Monaghan, Gerard claimed he had had the pick of the litter. "He said he got a case of the clap and couldn't father a child. By the time he figured out what was going on, it was too late—the doctors couldn't do anything. He didn't like women because of it. He had an IOU to settle. 'When they get too uppity,' he said, 'I can browbeat 'em. Because I am the whiz kid.' "

At the time of this conversation with Monaghan, Gerard had just heard of the death of a singer with whom he had been close, and he wept hysterically. Mingled with his sorrow was anticipation of his own end and mourning for the child he never would have. "When I die," he sobbed to Monaghan, "there will be no more Gerard. It will be the end of the whiz kid."

"He'd burned himself out," says Monaghan. "He never grew up the way the rest of us did. He said, 'God! Information kept getting put on me.' He couldn't relax: 'You're a genius, you're a child prodigy, you're supposed to be the best. What do you *mean* you don't wanna do it?' He said, 'You don't know what it's like being marked as the brain of brains and not always coming out a winner. It's a stigma you can never shake. If you're Mickey Mantle, at forty-five or fifty you're going to stop hitting home runs. But the brain isn't supposed to give out.' "

It must have been an extraordinary outpouring for Gerard, who seldom spoke about Quiz Kids and was touchy when teased about it. "His attitude was, it was past and that was it," says Joe Darrow.

Yet once, when Chuck Schaden played a Quiz Kids tape on his old-time radio show, Gerard called in to say he had been one. "Being a Quiz Kid and being at the classical music stations were the two most fantastic experiences of his life," says Gino. "He got to be what he wanted to be, express his intelligence, and that made him happy. It built up his ego, though, to the point that he might not have been able to live up to it. Being so young and treated the way he was, and going to the places and doing the things he did, and thinking so highly of himself compared to another kid his age, and then—from one extreme to the other, working in a restaurant for seventy dollars a week. Life was a letdown."

Since he had come back to Chicago, Gerard's allergies had been acting up. So when he noticed his face and body swelling, and his eyes becoming sensitive to the sun, he got his prescription renewed by phone. He was taking his aunt's codeine pills, too. And, says Gino, he was an alcoholic. "It started when he was living high on the hog. In later years, if he could get his hands on it, he would drink two bottles of champagne at one sitting."

The mixture of drugs and alcohol must have worsened his condition. But despite depression and ill health, he never completely gave up his dream of returning to the music business. Gino got him an interview for station manager at a nearby community college, but someone else got the job.

In the fall, a few months before his death, Gerard finally found work proofreading engineering documents for $200 a week. ("Excellent candidate—don't be fooled by appearance," the personnel interviewer noted.) No matter how sick he felt, he got up and went to work every day. "He was very proud of himself," says Gino. "After so many years of not working, and then coming back, being able to pay the bills and buy the food he wanted and go do the things he wanted to do—that made him feel good, because then his family had nothing to criticize him about.''

At Christmas, he bought his aunt some jade jewelry. ''Oh, Gerard,'' she said, ''you shouldn't have. At ninety-one years old, I'm not going to wear this stuff.''

''She didn't realize how much it meant to him to show his love and appreciation,'' says Gino. ''He just broke down and cried and cried.''

Gerard saved to go to concerts, plays, and old movies. He missed his record collection, which he had donated to Rice University when he left Houston, reserving only a few albums with personal associations. He had just a cheap record player. As his condition worsened, he spent more and more evenings in his bedroom, reading or watching educational television programs about spiders and snakes. His interest in nature remained strong, and so did his memory and curiosity. He would irritate Clara by reminding her exactly when and where she had acquired a certain item. He was fascinated with Africa and talked eagerly with a Ghanaian youth leader Gino brought over.

As time went on, Gerard became so listless that he could hardly drag himself to work. He was hospitalized with a diagnosis of a congestive heart condition. ''They found a blood clot on the lung and operated,'' says Joe Darrow. ''He went into a coma and never regained consciousness. For about three days, machines were keeping him alive. The doctor said he wouldn't come out of it. Finally they pulled the plug.''

Gerard died alone, of kidney failure. ''It was a shock,'' says Gino. ''It really hurt.'' The card distributed to the few mourners at the funeral bore a prayer of St. Francis of Assissi. On the reverse side was a picture of the barefoot saint communing with his beloved birds.

A year and a half after Gerard's death, there was as yet no marker on his grave. According to Joe Darrow, the subject was ''in abeyance.''

Gino fell heir to Gerard's books and records. ''As soon as I can afford a stereo, I'm going to get into this music,'' he says. ''This has sentimental value. I knew a great person and a real friend.''

Gerard Darrow was a boy with an unusual hobby and a spectacular memory, who was laden with an inflated image and spoiled by attention and overindulgence. Yet for a time, he overcame his personal difficulties and found satisfying work in a field he loved, before the womb of his family enveloped him again.

On a Quiz Kids Mother's Day show, the children were asked to make up poems. Gerard, age eight, composed an elegy:

Although my mother's dead,
And my aunt's taking her place,
I want to see my mother
When I go up to heaven
In her white cap and lace.

Joan Bishop: Velvet Voice

She identifies totally with the Quiz Kid experience.
It's been a really important part of her life.
    —Geoffrey Cowan

Some of us have downplayed our Quiz Kid identity. Joan Bishop plays it up. After years of performing in posh Manhattan lounges, she still snags an occasional interview as a former quiz queen. "Original Quiz Kid" gets top billing on her resume.

"Chicago's Versatile Child Prodigy," as the *Herald-American* once called her, Joan at four sang Brahms' Lullaby on the radio in German and English. At five, she gave a piano recital, sliding along the bench to reach the ends of the keyboard and finishing with a toe dance. At six and seven, she played at the Chicago World's Fair.

A natural mimic, "Joannie" picked up her passion for music from her mother, Irene Eccardt Bishop, who had played piano at nickelodeon theaters for twenty years before her marriage. At ten, the child gave her own concert in the Auditorium Theater and at eleven was chosen by Frederick Stock as soloist for a Chicago Symphony youth concert. At the audition, she played for Stock a Bach prelude and the first movement of Mozart's D Minor Concerto. While she was playing, he walked to the edge of the stage and called out to her mother, sitting in the empty hall, "Iss dot da only vun ya got?"

At thirteen, bubbly blonde Joan was one of those chosen for the first Quiz Kids panel. "I went to my piano lesson," she remembers, "and my teacher said, 'There's a man here from a radio program who wants to interview you.' '' The man was Louis G. Cowan, who had gotten wind of her from a two-year-old newspaper clipping about her Chicago Symphony performance.

Joan, as Cowan found, was "the girl with the miraculous ear." She could pick apart a five-note chord, could tell whether a knife striking a glass of water emitted an F or F-sharp, and could sing any note on demand. "You laugh in the key of A," she once told Roby Hickok.

Poised yet unassuming, Joan answered questions with crisp dignity; she did not guess. When Jack Lucal identified a fragment of Rachmaninoff's Prelude in C-Sharp Minor, she noticed that the piece had been transposed a half-step down. She could "spot a misplaced quotation in poetry or literature" as well, the *New York Journal and American* observed, and she didn't mind correcting her elders, as columnist E. V. Durling discovered:

> Do I have to keep on my toes? Now the quiz kids have become readers of mine and are checking on me. "So you don't know who the first strip teaser was" writes Quiz Kid Joan Bishop. "Tsk! Tsk! Mr. Durling, how about Salome?"
> —*Chicago Herald-American*, July 26, 1942

Joan's excitement crescendoed when she was picked for the early Quiz Kids tours. In New York, police sirens led the way to the office of Mayor Fiorello LaGuardia ("a funny little man, very courteous"). At the White House, Eleanor Roosevelt was a "charming, gregarious" hostess, "a little bit giggly."

The trips were thrilling to a girl whose parents had lost everything in the Crash when she was three—"old enough to know we couldn't buy things." Her father, John Bishop (originally Biskup), had been brought over from Czechoslovakia by parents looking for streets paved with gold; while Joan was growing up on Chicago's north and west sides, he was a sometime bookie with gangland connections and worked for the city sanitation department. ("He certainly never shot anybody or packed a gat," Joan hastens to add. "I remember Bugs Moran—we went to his apartment. Sweet as he could be.")

One night superstitious Joan wished on a star that she could go to Hollywood. The next day, the Quiz Kids office called to say she was going. It was a magical three weeks for the starry-eyed adolescent, who stepped off the train like Cinderella alighting from her pumpkin coach. She sat in on Deanna Durbin's voice lesson the day before the ingenue's wedding . . . lunched at Walt Disney studio (Snow White salad, Duckie fruit plate, and Grumpy Delight) . . . watched the fabulous floor show at child star Jane Withers' fifteenth birthday party . . . met personalities like Bob Hope and Groucho Marx, who wrote in her autograph book, "There's no face like Joan." The Kids got gold watches from their host, Jack Benny; Joan never wears hers for fear of losing it.

The first Quiz Kids movie short opened at the klieg-lighted Chicago Theater with all the trappings of a Hollywood premiere. Notables like Mayor Edward J. Kelly were there, and stars like Rudy Vallee, Dorothy Lamour, and John Barrymore sent telegrams. Joan "scored the hit of the evening" when she stopped a slide trombonist at the exact tone she had been told to catch, reported C.J. Bulliet in the *Chicago Daily News.*

Two weeks later, when Joan went back to see herself in the film again, bandleader Phil Harris spotlighted her in the third row. Wrote Wauhillau La Hay of the *Chicago Sun*: "A friend of mine on the Benny show told me that every boy in the Phil Harris band was amazed at Joan's perfect pitch."

"When I'm married and have a child," Joan at twenty-three told columnist Earl Wilson, "I'm not going to send him—or her—to school. Schools are like names. Sometimes a child finds himself saddled with one he doesn't like and it hurts him." Joan did not go to school. "I don't know how we got away with it," she laughs.

"She learned everything by herself," her mother explained to Muriel Fischer of the *New York World-Telegram*. "Why, I never even held Joan's hand to teach her how to walk. One day she simply walked out of her bedroom. And that was that." Irene Bishop found her only child "a bit overwhelming at times." At three, Joan began reading by following the funnies read on the radio. Soon she was consuming two newspapers daily and taking the encyclopedia to bed. (Her I.Q. was published as 157, though she thinks it was only 117.)

When it came time for schooling, her parents gave her a globe, atlas, dictionary, and blackboard and let her go her own way. She learned history and geography from her stamp collection. ("I knew countries most people hadn't heard of—to me they were old friends.") Her first arithmetic lesson was her mother's cutting up a potato to illustrate the relationships between half, quarter, eighth, and sixteenth notes. (Her math is admittedly weak: "What do I need long division and trigonometry for?")

She did not miss going to school with other children. ("They sort of envied me.'') Rather, she believes she "missed out on a lot of unplea-santness. I probably would have been bored stiff. I might have been pushed ahead, and it probably would have affected me.'' She played with neighbor children in the afternoon. "I used to correct their homework. The spelling of some of those kids would knock your eye out.''

Mrs. Bishop felt her daughter could better utilize the five hours a day she would have wasted in school by practicing the piano instead. Which the little girl gladly did, setting her own schedule and putting a "Do Not Disturb'' sign on her door.

At her first recital, as the chubby five-year-old cooed Brahms' Lullaby to her own accompaniment, someone coached, "Louder!''

"You can't holler a lullaby and put a baby to sleep,'' the moppet shot back.

Music was her major preoccupation—"maybe seventy to eighty percent of my interest as a child.'' She studied piano on scholarship with Moisse Boguslawski, who gave concerts for culture vultures, and then went on to artist-teacher Franklin Stead at the now-defunct Cosmopolitan School. She could "reach octaves with the thumb and third finger,'' the *Michigan Daily* marveled when the Quiz Kids came to the Ann Arbor campus to challenge (and beat) a team of professors. "She has a natural free arm movement which takes others years to acquire and slim, strong hands indicative of a great musical future.''

But piano was not Joan's real love.

"I always wanted to sing. It was just in me.''

Joan Bishop Barber and I are getting reacquainted over eggs Sardou at the Greenery, a froth of a luncheon spot on New York's upper east side, near Joan's apartment. In her lapel is an animal rights button; she orders vegetarian.

Forty years ago, Joan Bishop was voted "prettiest Quiz Kid.'' At fifty-four, the round face has become a bit puffy, the blonde hair bleached, but the bright eyes and chummy warmth are undiminished. Rosy makeup, regal bearing, and rainbow-framed glasses bespeak a woman still image-conscious. She smokes Carleton 100's. Her earrings are musical staves.

She speaks in the well-modulated tones that won her the New York title in NBC's Search for America's Most Beautiful Speaking Voice. "When I was about four, we had one of those old wind-up victrolas in the basement, and I'd take Mother's operatic records down there. She had marvelous 78s, only one side. I had a little rocker, and I'd sit and rock and listen and cry. They were so beautiful. I said, 'Oh, I want to do that.' ''

At five, she saw her first opera, *Aida*. Dazzled, she made up her mind to be an opera singer, but concentrated on piano while waiting for her vocal equipment to mature.

"Quiz Kids" brought her rich mezzo-soprano voice to public notice. In Atlantic City, the Kids shared billing with Metropolitan diva Gladys Swarthout, one of Joan's idols. Joan answered a question by singing a snatch of her old standby, Brahms' Lullaby. Afterwards, a fan came up to compliment her. "Boy, did that make my evening!" she beams. "Here Swarthout had sung, and this man tells me *I* had a beautiful voice!"

Said a Christmas publicity release: "The best gift of all for Joan would be voice lessons which her family cannot afford, and tickets to next year's opera . . . It was a bitter pill this season not to be able to attend even one."

As the top female Quiz Kid of 1941, Joan earned $1,400. At fourteen, she began vocal lessons at the school where she took piano. By fifteen, she knew fifty arias in French, German, and Italian. "Mother wants me to be a pianist, but singing is what I like, so that's what I'm going to keep on with," she told *St. Paul Pioneer Press*.

Her linguistic training was obtained at a translation bureau where she enrolled after joining Quiz Kids. "On the first program, none of the Kids could say what school they went to, because I couldn't say, 'Duh, I don't go to school at all.' So John Lewellen told my mother she was going to have to send me to some kind of school. We found a place that was basically a language school. So then I could say, 'I'm Joan Bishop, I'm thirteen years old, and I go to the Chicago School for Adults.' That's the only school I ever went to."

She relished the companionship of her Quiz Kids "classmates" and reveled in the spelling bees and mental games they played while traveling. But the trips stopped for Joan, to her chagrin, with the advent of younger Kids like me. At sixteen, she graduated after thirty-one appearances, returning occasionally to pinch-hit for Joe Kelly. On one such occasion, she played Chopin's Revolutionary Etude, and Lonny Lunde, the new musical prodigy, identified it.

The Quiz Kids graduation, the only one she ever had, is a special memory. It was Christmas, 1942. "Joe Kelly said there was something under the tree for me. I opened it, and there was a tiny cedar chest. The card said, 'The full-sized edition will be delivered to your home this week.' '' It was exactly what she wanted—a place for the keepsakes she had been storing in boxes.

Today that cedar chest sits on the bare wooden floor of her third-story walkup apartment, two blocks from the East River. The single barn of a room is crammed with old sheet music, books, records, pictures, clippings, and faded memorabilia. "Controlled chaos," Joan laughs.

One of the items in her scrapbook is from a *Chicago Tribune* Inquiring Reporter:

> Although I have all the time in the world to do a task . . . I can't seem to slow myself down to a normal pace. I dress in a hurry, eat in a hurry, and do everything in a hurry. When I'm in one of my rushing streaks mother sometimes asks me if I'm trying to catch a train.
>
> —Joan Bishop, graduate Quiz Kid (age 17)

Professionally, too, Joan was dashing for a train. The thrill she wanted, as she told the *New York Times,* was "to sing a big role in opera with a large audience." When she was only fifteen, she sneaked into Chicago Opera Company auditions advertised for singers sixteen and up; reporters who recognized her as a Quiz Kid gave her away. At seventeen, she sang in operetta choruses and did a solo from *Carmen* with Olsen and Johnson's variety show "Sons O'Fun." At eighteen, she made her operatic debut as Siebel in a workshop production of *Faust.* That year she was accepted for the Chicago Opera chorus and learned sixteen shows in thirteen weeks. Her only role was a three-liner as the page in *Rigoletto,* but, says Joan, "it was wonderful to be there." It was the company's second-to-last season.

At nineteen, she hit the Big Apple. "Having been here two or three times with the Quiz Kids, I was nuts about it. I couldn't wait to be old enough to fly the coop." When a Los Angeles troupe bound for an eastern tour with *Desert Song* came through the Windy City, she hopped aboard.

After the show closed, Joan found a piano job in a Greenwich Village restaurant, The Music Box. She wrote to *Ex-Quiz Kid Resume*, a yearly newsletter of graduates' doings:

> All of musical New York dined there—Giuseppe de Luca, Wilbur Evans, Carol Bruce, Percy Faith, Raymond Paige—and of course I met and sang for all of them. Julius Huehn of the Met remembered me from the QK show. I did several roles with the San Carlo Opera Company* at Center Theatre, Radio City. Jack Benny came to town

* Her biggest role was as Kate Pinkerton in *Madame Butterfly.*

and I went to both his broadcasts. . . . I expect to be doing weekend performances in the Catskills. We call it "The Borscht Circuit."

As a Quiz Kid, Joan had been asked in what period of history she would like to have been alive. She said, "When Tschaikowsky conducted the initial concert at Carnegie Hall." At twenty, she got to sing there, as she reported to the *Ex-Q.K. Resume*:

JOAN BISHOP OFFERS
MUSICAL CHEF-d'OEUVRE

Recipe for a busy life—or let this happen to you—it's fun!

1 Carnegie Hall concert

2 Madison Square Garden appearances

Toss in one each at Grossinger's, Grand Ballroom of the Astor, and the Wedgewood Room. . . .

Sprinkle freely with 95 pieces of lettuce won at Monmouth Park track

Now simmer at Atlantic Highlands, New Jersey

Set to cool each evening on bandstand at Log Cabin Inn

Recipe for fall seasoning:

20 weeks on concert tour of midwest. . . .

The Carnegie Hall concert turns out to have been a joint recital with three other comers. The Madison Square Garden appearances? She sang the national anthem.

The twenty-week concert tour was a 16,000-mile circuit in a Willys jeep. In some 250 schools and lodge halls, she played Chopin's Revolutionary Etude on pianos with low stools, Coke bottle stains, and popcorn stuck between the keys, and sang a conglomeration of opera, boogie, folk songs, and light classics. At intermission she would give a little speech about Quiz Kids and show her Jack Benny watch. ("See, he isn't so cheap after all. Of course, it would be even nicer if it would run . . . ") She remembers fondly the young audiences that stayed past the last school bell, begging for more.

Meanwhile, true to her "staunch Q.K. upbringing," she took first place in a radio music quiz, beating out Fred Allen's bandleader, Al Goodman, and made several appearances on a video quiz with Faye Emerson and Al Capp. She performed at a private party for the Duke and Duchess of Windsor and gave radio concerts with composer Vernon Duke ("April in Paris"), who autographed his picture to her, "From the ArchDuke to the ArchBishop."

Six years after Joan's operatic debut, Bill Irvin of the *Chicago Sun-*

Times reported that the twenty-four-year-old was "well up the ladder on her climb to musical success."

When Joan first came to New York, Roby Hickok had written: "She is giving herself six years and then she hopes to invite all ex-Quiz Kids and staff to the Met. I'm taking odds that we'll be there—center section."

Roby lost her bet.

Joan never even tried out for the Met. ("Chicken, I guess.") She did use the remnants of her Quiz Kids money to finance summer study in Italy with Walter Tassoni, who later conducted the Seattle and San Diego opera companies. But Tassoni discouraged her.

"It was kind of a foolish time to go [to Italy]," Joan says. "La Scala wasn't open. I never even got inside."

An operatic tour of Central and South America was cancelled. She sang in the choruses of two Broadway musicals, *Magdalena* and *The Gay Life,* won $500 on a Kate Smith talent show, got a watch for singing "Can't Help Lovin' That Man of Mine" on the Johnny Olsen show, joined the NBC-TV Opera chorus, but never had an important professional role.

"I did have something of a standout thing in *Dialogues of the Carmelites* by Poulenc. I was a nun who got guillotined in the French Revolution."

When asked about the frustration of her early hopes, Joan responds philosophically. "You have all these glowing ambitions when you're fifteen. . . . I would like to have made it as a big-time opera singer, but I wasn't going to slit my throat if it didn't happen. There's such a narrow field, and it's getting worse all the time. Actually, I got so involved in the other parts of my career . . . the pop stuff. . . . And I really had to make a living. Opera doesn't pay well unless you have great talent.

"Perhaps I was honeycombed—a jack of all trades. I loved both the playing and the singing. And I'm glad I could do both. It kept me in nylons for a long time."

She settled into a continuous series of lounge engagements, supporting herself and her widowed mother, who had come to live with her. Every time she opened a new place, her picture would appear with the legend, "Joan Bishop, former Quiz Kid." ("It was a press agent's gimmick— I don't think it ever got me a job.")

"I'd say in all modesty that I was one of the better ones. I had a vast repertoire, I could play virtually any request. I had fifteen years of real beauty, making a good living. The highest paying job was at the Waldorf, which in those days was $250 a week (that would be like $500 now) plus tips.''

She remembers one evening at the Sherry Netherland, where she was getting $160 a week for shorter hours. ''There was a nice man at a table by himself with a telephone, and I found out he was a wealthy oil man from Texas. He asked for *My Fair Lady*, and he sent the busboy over with a bill. Then he wanted *West Side Story*, then *South Pacific*, and each time a bill came over. Finally I'd been playing for an hour and a half and he said, 'I'm going broke here, you'd better take a break.' I gathered up my bills and went into the ladies' room. First I found three ones, then a ten, then a fifty, then a hundred. I had $163, which was three dollars more than my weekly salary. Biggest tip I ever got in one fell swoop.''

If the piano jobs paid the rent, the NBC Opera provided glory-by-association. She mingled in the commissary with Nicola Moscona, Giorgio Tozzi, Zinka Milanov (''the only one who was uppity'').

Going through her photo albums, she pauses at a glossy of an NBC musical based on the life of Handel. ''That's me next to Maureen O'Sullivan. First they had some gown on me that they didn't like. So they went and got this beautiful maroon velvet with a mink collar, but it was about a size 8. It had to stay open in the back, with a couple of big safety pins—and here's the orchestra behind me. So I turned around to the guys and said, ''I dreamt I sang the *Messiah* in my Maidenform bra'!''

Her one big deprivation was that working nights kept her from going to the opera. But she did have a date with Metropolitan baritone Lawrence Tibbett. ''He was a dear. He did Rigoletto when I had that little bitty role, and then it turned out he lived down the block from us on 56th Street. Mother came back from the supermarket one day and said, 'Guess who offered me his grocery cart? Lawrence Tibbett.'

''One day I was practicing—the piano was in the window—and he walked by. I immediately went into *Traviata*—la-rium, bup-buh-bum, bup-buh-buh—and he turned around and talked to me through the window.'' Later he came over to the Madison Hotel, where she was working, and another time took her to dinner at the Stork Club.

In 1957, Joan, playing a Fifth Avenue cocktail lounge, told the *New York Post*: ''I don't think I expected this much. . . . I ask very little in life. I try everything, but I wouldn't say I knock myself out.''

In 1976, a few months before Lou Cowan's death, Joan wrote to him that she had an ''ideal job'' at the Biltmore. Now she is unemployed.

"They're hiring men, mostly, and I got sick of calling agents. The business isn't the same—this perpetual rock and roll stuff. They expect you to have your own keyboard and amplification system and drag those things to jobs, and I simply don't want to be part of that. I want to walk into an elegant hotel on Fifth Avenue at six o'clock and finish at twelve."

Her piano goes untouched. This woman whose whole life was music . . . who once could play Chopin's E Minor Concerto, the Grieg, the Liszt E-Flat . . . now plays nothing at all. "I just don't feel the urge. I got tired of it. I've been at it so long."

She has let her voice go; she disdains singers who "don't know when to quit." She does not sing even for her second husband, John Barber. "I never sang for my father, either."

Like her mother, she wed late. Her first real date was with Jack Lucal, to his senior prom. '("That's what made him become a priest, I think!") Her first marriage was at thirty-eight, to Walter Boone Williams, a divorced man thirteen years her senior. She is childless: "We were both too old to start a family."

She is not sorry about having waited so long to marry, though she sometimes wonders what her child, if she had had one, would have been like.

"When I was eighteen, I thought, 'I've got to have children by the time I'm twenty. I guess I got rolling on my career and realized that it was more fun. I fell in love a couple of times, but not enough to make me want to give up my career." Her nocturnal working hours, she feels, would have conflicted with domesticity. "People used to say, 'How come you're not married?' And I'd say a husband would be an intrusion in my happy life."

In 1965, Boone, a minor Shell executive in New York on business, dropped in at the Roger Smith Hotel, where Joan was playing. "He was the only guy in the place," she remembers. "It was raining cats and dogs. He waddles in, goes to the bar. I was playing 'Stormy Weather.' He brought his drink over to the piano and said, 'Topical music, I see.' Turned out he loved opera, Romberg. He had a fine tenor voice." Joan moved with Boone to his suburban New Orleans home. "I'd been working so many years, I felt if I retired a little early, I had put in my time and paid my dues. I didn't miss it. I could always sit down and play something."

The time in New Orleans was hard. Her mother, who had followed the couple down there, died. Boone was hospitalized eleven times in the six years before his death.

Meanwhile, Joan did volunteer work at a community center, teaching black youngsters needlework, and was the only white member of a literary club. "I was on my soapbox a little bit in my own private way. I had blacks coming to visit me. I was the talk of the neighborhood. When I was selling the house, a woman down the block said, 'I hope you don't sell it to niggers.' I'd have liked to do just that, to fix the neighbors."

Joan met John Barber when she contacted the AFTRA office looking for job leads to get back in circulation. "I said, 'Gee, this is a cute guy! He's six years *younger* than I am.' "

Now, with Joan no longer employed, John—an actor whose plum was emceeing a fight scene in *Mandingo* with James Mason—supports the two of them with a nine-to-five office job, picking up roles when he can. (Once he played Santa at Macy's.) At the moment, he is Dr. Gibbs in a two-week run of *Our Town* at a midtown church.

Short, dark, and Irish, John has a mustache and sideburns and speaks with a hint of the Alabama hills. "He looks a little like Omar Sharif," says his obviously prejudiced wife. A radio historian by hobby, he combs secondhand book counters for a copy of the *Quiz Kids Dictionary* that (Joan laments) she lent out and never got back.

Did Joan's having been a Quiz Kid turn him on? "No," he smiles, "Joan Bishop as a woman turned me on." But Joan confides, "He talks about it like crazy." With John's prodding, in 1975—the thirty-fifth anniversary of the first Quiz Kids broadcast—she wangled interviews for herself and Jack Lucal on the "Today" show, "A.M. New York," and "Straight Talk."

In the kitchen, Joan unloads a six-pack of beer for John and my husband Gil, and food for the two cats. A frugal shopper, she clips coupons. She and John have a nest egg put away for their declining years. "As long as we have a roof over our heads that doesn't leak, and we can buy a tape and maybe occasionally go to the theater, that's enough. There are a heckuva lot of people who have much less than we have."

She considers this the happiest period in her generally happy life. "John is wonderful and healthy, and I'm being a housewife in the only city I really love." Though "all for" women's liberation, she is "quite content" cooking for John and helping him with his lines when he lands a part. "I can live it vicariously, as my mother did when I went into the business."

She does not think of herself as retired—"We don't really retire, ever, until we die. People say, 'What do you do all day?' I don't know, the time just goes, between keeping house and shopping and reading the paper. I'm always doing something. I sure don't watch soap operas.

"Some of these game shows are awful, like Let's Make a Deal. If you know your own name, they give you $10,000." She does enjoy matching wits with the contestants on "Wheel of Fortune." Years ago she tried out for "Password" but married and moved to New Orleans before she could go on. Later she made a trip back to New York for the "Who, What, or Where Game" and won $1,140 plus a barbecue grill and toaster. She subscribes to a contest magazine and has won a "dandy set of pots and pans," a camera, and a picnic cooler. "One of these days it will be a trip to France. I'm always an optimist."

She has studied braille and done recording for the blind, as well as animal protection work. "I was always a student. I think Quiz Kids intensified that. You'd think, 'Gotta remember that, it might be a question.' I still read everything but the used car ads and try to remember."

She solves the *New York Daily News* Double-Crostic religiously and even has crossword toilet paper. When she heard that ex-Quiz Kid Pat Conlon had won a bundle on the "Who, What or Where Game," she looked him up and invited him and Jack Lucal over for an evening of reminiscing. They "literally attacked" a six-foot crossword puzzle hanging near the door.

"An airplane takes off from New York City and makes a flight to Chicago in an hour and twenty minutes. Later that day it makes the return flight, but it takes only eighty minutes. How come?"*

Joan is testing us, at dinner, on her favorite puzzler, one she put to her fellow-Quiz Kids and an opposing team of 4-H clubbers forty years ago. "We were all quizzing each other before the program, and I posed that question. When we did the show, the same question happened to come up. All five 4-H kids raised their hands, but the other four Quiz Kids did not, even though I'd given them the answer. They felt it was Joan's question. Their loyalty really touched me."

"Quiz Kids," to Joan, was far more than a show. With no siblings or schoolmates, her social as well as intellectual life in the crucial adolescent years revolved, to a great extent, around the program. In a very real sense, "Quiz Kids" was her school, the contacts she made there her old school tie. "A great keeper-in-toucher," she corresponds with at least a dozen former colleagues and tried to arrange a fortieth anniversary reunion.

---

* The flight times are the same.

She is a fount of anecdotes. Like the one about the stockyards rodeo, when a donkey pulling the Quiz Kids in a little painted cart balked and a passel of cowboys and clowns lifted the cart (donkey and all), with Joan still in it, onto the stage. "The audience was in hysterics, and Ben Bernie, the emcee, says to me, 'Well, you'll really have something to tell your grandchildren, won't you, Joan?' The cart, by the way, was borrowed from a wealthy little boy named Mickey Jelke. When the race track scandal broke, I said, 'To think I had a ride in his Sicilian cart!' "

At heart, Joan Bishop is still the star-struck girl who ran around Hollywood, autograph book in hand. Her reminiscences of her professional years are laced with names like Jerry Lewis and Hugh Downs. She was "great friends" with Arthur Godfrey's mother: "We used to play gin rummy at her apartment."

On the tapestry-draped piano are an autographed photo of singer Dennis Day and two pictures of Jack Benny: one taken when he met the Quiz Kids' Hollywood train, the other with Joan in 1974, shortly before the comedian's fatal illness.

She had come to see him do a benefit. ("He seemed fine, he was jovial.") As she approached him in the receiving line, she held out the old 1941 picture. He was puzzled; then recognition dawned, and he called over his manager, Irving Fine: "Irving! Irving! He's got to see this picture. My God, I look younger now than I did then." (In his later years, he had darkened his silver hair.)

"We talked about Quiz Kids a little," Joan remembers, "and he autographed the back of the picture: 'To Joan . . . Yes, I remember . . . Jack Benny.' Three months later, he was gone."

Dennis, whom she had met on the Benny show, she last saw in summer of 1980, when he was doing the Westbury Music Fair. "He's a prince. Hair's a little thin, the voice isn't what it used to be, but—it was as if I'd seen him the previous week."

She pops more riddles and challenges us to a Scrabble game, but time runs out with music talk and memories.

A few weeks after our visit, a letter comes from Joan, enclosing a review of John's performance in *Our Town* ("meticulous portrait from a bygone era").

. . . Sold the piano yesterday to a friend—I know it'll have a good home. . . . Yes, it's finis—someday I might take it up again but as of now I have no desire.

Are you and Gil familiar with the great tenor Josef Schmidt's records? Should've played one for you. . . .

. . . And now for a bit of trivia—if H_2O is water, what is H_2O_4?* How do you pronounce GHOTI?** (This one's attributed to G.B. Shaw) . . .

As ever,

Joan

Joan Bishop is the quintessential Quiz Kid. But one puzzle she never solved: she never figured out the right moves to get where she said she wanted to go. Her fantasy of opera stardom proved to be a pipe dream fed by Quiz Kids hype.

"She worked very hard but never got the breaks," says Bunny Kreisman, a musician friend who has known Joan since her teens. "She was an exquisite pianist, had a glorious voice. She was never out of a job, but it wasn't what she really wanted."

"It's everybody's story," says Sheilah Brenner, one of Joan's closest Quiz Kid friends. "Not everybody reaches the heights or accomplishes what they set out to do."

Bubbles Silverman was another curly-headed blonde child radio star, born three years after Joan Bishop, who listened to her mother's records and dreamed of becoming an opera star. Bubbles—as the coloratura, Beverly Sills—made her dream come true.

There are important differences between the two stories. Sills was a voice prodigy, while Joan's early recognition was primarily for piano; possibly she might have had a better chance for success as a concert pianist. Sills' childhood radio career was as a singer (on Major Bowes' Amateur Hour), Joan's chiefly as a quiz show performer. Sills quit radio at twelve, just about the age Joan started. Sills, throughout her youth, studied with a top teacher and later had mentors who guided her progress. Joan's first voice teacher of major repute was the one she had in Italy for a few months at twenty-two. She had no mentor or manager; a babe in the big city, she did everything on her own.

Most important, Sills had the singleminded determination to make it in opera. In her late teens, she cut out Broadway diversions to concentrate on serious training. Like Joan, she sang for a while in club lounges, helping to support her widowed mother. But she left that work and, starting with lesser opera companies, eventually tried out seven times for

---

* Water is for drinking, bathing, etc.

** Fish. (GH as in enough, O as in women, TI as in motion.)

the New York City Opera before being accepted there.

Joan perhaps was less than adept at managing her career, too timid, too easily discouraged. There was a scattershot quality about her, a predilection for show biz that distracted her from pursuing her stated goal.

Joan's case suggests that the qualities rewarded on the Quiz Kids show were not necessarily those likely to win comparable rewards on the outside. No doubt she hoped her Quiz Kids contacts would open doors, but those doors were not the ones that lead to a serious artistic career.

Today, Joan seems genuinely happy. A here-and-now person, an accepter, not an analyzer, she has been realistic enough to appreciate what considerable success she has had in music and now in marriage. "I don't think I'd have done anything differently," she says. "And there's no use thinking about it now. There's not a darn thing I can do about it."

The cessation of her career accentuates her fondness for her long-ago Quiz Kid past. "I didn't want it to end," she says. "I remember saying to someone right after I graduated, "If I were to die tomorrow, I'd have had a wonderful life."

Claude Brenner: Immigrant Charmer

*Americans say of their country, "America is the golden land
of opportunity" . . . . That this should ever be proven to me . . .
a short fifteen months after landing in New York, was so remote a
possibility that it never even materialized as a thought. . . .*
—Claude W. Brenner, *The Outspan*, Nov. 5, 1948

"We're not masters of our destiny," says Claude Walter Brenner.
"Life is full of accident. It's being in the right place at the right time."
That Claude was in Chicago when "Quiz Kids" began was due to a
fortuitous series of events.

A "pure-bred Litvak," he was born in Pretoria, South Africa, of
Jewish parents whose families had fled Eastern European pogroms. His
father, S. David Brenner, who had a general store and hotel in the coal
mining area of Natal, died in Claude's infancy. Claude has "astonishingly
clear" memories, from the age of two or three, of gazing at the
smoldering ruins of the family hotel while cradled in his uncle's arms,
then of going to live with relatives in a little house by the railway line,
where he watched the trains go by and dreamed of being an engine driver.

On his eleventh birthday, Claude, with his mother and older sister
Sheilah, set sail from Johannesburg and reached the United States two
weeks before the outbreak of World War II. The timing of that voyage
changed the course of their lives.

It was, Claude figures, his tenth transatlantic crossing, counting the
separate legs of the Capetown-Southampton-New York triangle. His
mother Frances Brenner—a strikingly handsome woman, gentle but
strong-willed—had used Irish sweepstakes winnings to take her children
to visit relatives in England and America when Claude was about four,

and later had studied at the National College of Chiropractic in Chicago. This time she planned a short stay, intending to complete her course. She had postponed the trip twice. The date set, she planned to leave the children behind in boarding schools, then changed her mind and decided to take them along and board them in the Chicago area.

But with the onset of war, the British pounds she had brought were drastically devalued, and the family was stuck for the duration. The three lived in genteel poverty in a single room. Sheilah and Claude had summer jobs as hotel clerks, and their mother worked as a secretary.

At twelve, Claude, who had whipped through Johannesburg's best boys' school, was a freshman at Senn High School alongside his fourteen-year-old sister; he had skipped thanks to an I.Q. test that measured 149. When "Quiz Kids" started, he began collecting clippings. ("I can still remember my reaction to the first program: *Oh my God, these are smart kids*.") A cousin who did radio commercials ("Mommy, I want a Salerno butter cookie . . . ") and knew Joe Bailey of the Cowan office gave him Claude's name.

"I just got swept along," says Claude. "Why wouldn't one? The public exposure was appealing, certainly ego was involved, and given our economic circumstances, the $100 war bond was a great selling point. Here was the mechanism to put me through college. But I don't think I consciously made that crass materialistic decision. It was all rather naive, and we were rather passive about it."

On Christmas, 1940, Claude Brenner became a Quiz Kid, and on New Year's, Sheilah, nervous and uncomfortable, made her one-and-only appearance. That evening, Claude tied for first.

With his big, dark eyes, eager smile and perfect manners, he was "the most ingratiating kid of the lot," wrote Weldon Melick in *Coronet*. "A polished little gentleman," pronounced the *Chicago Sun*'s Wauhillau La Hay. "Claude is going to go far. He could sell me some insurance right now." When he went off the panel, he was recalled by popular demand and was given an ovation on his return, something that had happened to only one other Quiz Kid, Gerard Darrow.

Claude's knowledge was as broad as his British accent; he lent an international flavor to the show. As *Quiz Kids Dictionary* observed: "When Claude . . . talks about London, Madeira, and Trinidad, he talks from personal experience, and when he answers questions on geography, he usually has seen the places he mentions so glibly."

He knew, according to press reports, four languages. ("Probably English, Afrikaans, and some Hebrew and Latin," says Claude. "In those days, everything we knew or did had somehow to be magnified into larger-than-life proportions. Embarrassing.'')

> Claude Brenner, the Quiz Kid who has lived most of his twelve years in South Africa, knows his America nevertheless. That was Claude who identified the sounds of a whirling malted milk mixer and the ''fizz'' of soda water.
> —*Chicago Times,* February 14, 1941

He had horse sense, as one of his teachers remarked. On the show, he solved the following head-scratcher:

> A man went into a butcher shop and ordered a pound of meat costing 30 cents. While the butcher had his back turned, the man took a half-dollar the butcher had carelessly left on the counter.
> He paid for the meat with the butcher's own-half dollar and walked out with the meat and twenty cents in change. On the way home he repented and went back to pay the butcher. How much did he owe?*

His childhood ambitions had run the gamut from ''great renowned artist'' to concert pianist to ''world-famous inventor.'' (''Notice this need for fame at an early age.'') By ten, he was captivated by ''aeroplanes.'' He learned to recognize them from the *Spotter's Guide,* built models, wrote aviation articles for *Quiz Kids Magazine*, and decided to be an aeronautical engineer. He spent most of his ten-cent allowance on miniature planes and tin soldiers—British, of course.

His teachers at Senn reported in the *Journal of Education* that Claude was popular, hard-working, and unusually modest. (His South African schoolyard ethic forbade self-praise.) The Quiz Kids competition, the teachers said, had spurred his intellectual curiosity and given him poise, inspiration, and a ''keen desire'' to pursue his education.

In his junior year, Claude was offered a full scholarship to Lake Forest Academy, a prestigious North Shore boarding school—a ''wild coincidence'' that flowed directly from his being a Quiz Kid and set him on the road to success. Someone in the admissions office, in cleaning out the files, came across a letter of inquiry that Claude's mother had written three years earlier, before coming to the States. ''That's a familiar name,'' said the director of admissions. He called a Lake Forest alumnus who was on the Quiz Kids staff and said, ''We must have him at the academy!'' And so, every week on the radio, Claude would say, ''I am Claude Brenner and I am fourteen years old and I am a junior at Lake

---

* Fifty cents.

Forest Academy.'' The assistant director of admissions told him the following year, ''We have fifty new boys, and thirty-five are due to you.''

Claude graduated from the academy as valedictorian in June, 1944, and from ''Quiz Kids'' in July. His parting gift was a suitcase (now in his attic); he packed and left immediately for M.I.T., where, thanks to his rigorous Lake Forest training, he had won a partial scholarship. He was not quite sixteen.

He had appeared on the Quiz Kids program seventy-one times, including a couple of occasions when he substituted for Joe Kelly (''That was marvelous—I knew all the answers!''), and had traveled to New York and Hollywood. It had been ''three and a half years of delightful experiences which I shall never forget,'' as he wrote in *The Outspan,* a South African national magazine, when he returned there briefly at twenty.

By then he already had earned his bachelor's and master's degrees from M.I.T., on an accelerated wartime schedule, and had made Phi Beta Pi, the engineering honorary. ''It's everybody's bet,'' Roby Hickok wrote, ''that Claude will be a topnotch engineer who will contribute a great deal to the science of aeronautics.''

Claude's magazine piece concluded:

> Had I never been a Quiz Kid, the whole course of my nine
> years in America, and probably of my future, would have been
> totally different. I have seen the results of American free enterprise
> and commercialism . . . and have come away convinced that
> America is the golden land of opportunity.

''Quiz Kids marked me for life.''

Hardly have I gotten my coat off when Claude Brenner greets me with that melodramatic statement, one on which he will elaborate at length during my stay in his Lexington, Massachusetts home.

The accent is cultured as ever. The hair is thinning, but the complexion is still ruddy, the brown eyes animated behind horn-rimmed glasses. Sudden gestures punctuate his masterful diction, which occasionally lapses into ''swell,'' ''golly gee,'' and ''oh, fiddle faddle!''

Claude is delighted to see me, though it took him six weeks to answer my letter.

> Please accept my apologies for apparent churlishness, but my
> delay in replying reflects my ambivalence on the whole business of
> Quiz Kids. . . . While there is no question that there is gratification

—smell of the greasepaint, roar of the crowd—in having one's name in print . . . I think that I, in the end, feel that history must be served. . . .

The truth of the matter is that I would feel a lot more comfortable telling the world about myself . . . were this year not such a difficult one for me. My marriage broke up, and my professional career took an unexpected redirection (what a euphemism!). Still, there've been a number of pluses overall, and one presses on to recover. I suppose, also, at age 52 I must come to accept that having been a Quiz Kid (maybe it's the "kid" part that one has to deal with) is an inescapable fact. But I'm never sure when we stop trying to meet other people's expectations because of that fact.

"Our family is a shambles," he tells me sadly, soon after I arrive. "These last fifteen months have been exceedingly bleak for me." Yet even though his unwanted divorce has just come through and he has undergone a stressful separation from his latest job, Claude Brenner is in remarkably good humor. His tendency to self-pity is tempered by realism and whimsy; one can imagine a stern Victorian schoolmaster in his head, pulling him up short when he begins to get carried away.

I have heard him called mercurial, but as a host, he is the old, impeccably charming Claude, warm and winsome. A man who sets his breakfast table with cloth napkins. In his kitchen hangs an Afrikaner motto: *Alles sal regt kom* ("Everything shall come out right").

Claude is an "unreconstructed romantic," a believer in happy endings. He and his ex-wife were the nearest thing to childhood sweethearts; he met her, a descendant of generations of English, when he was working in the mother country for a year. He was twenty, she sixteen. But she married someone else. She and Claude reunited twenty years later—his first marriage. He never adopted her two children, though he loved them as his own. The union, he says, "was just a fulfillment for me, absolutely total. We were perceived to be, if such a thing were possible, the ideal marriage." He cherished his dinners with his wife, a nightly ceremony of candles and wine. But after ten years, "things went sour."

Now he lives alone in his gracious colonial home with two cats, whom he treats like children. "My total life impression is of sharing a room with my mother and sister, so this house was just a pinnacle for me," he explains. The mantel, walls, shelves and tabletops hold keys to Claude Brenner.

A small menorah. "I am a 'revolving door Jew'—in at Rosh Hashanah, out at Yom Kippur. I never belonged to a temple, I don't observe the dietary laws, but I am very Jewish . . . I understand the specialness of being a Jew that only Jews understand, and I want to preserve it. I feel guilty that I escaped the concentration camps, that I didn't suffer. When it really comes down to it, I think I do believe in God—I wouldn't say a God watching over me, but in total control of everything. Of course, my intellect gets in the way and says that's ridiculous.''

A British monarch mug collection. ''In 1957, I finally decided to forswear queen and country and become a U.S. citizen. But I still have the strongest possible emotional tie to England. I can't conceive of going to Europe on business without stopping off there.''

A picture of Claude as chief commencement marshal at M.I.T., where he is a trustee and past president of the alumni association. ''M.I.T. is the place where I matured, where I made my lifelong friendships, where I was able to prove myself for myself rather than for what others expected me to be.''

A perpetual motion toy . . . back issues of National Geographic . . . golf trophies . . . a squash racquet. A clump of Quiz Kids books in one corner of the crowded bookshelves. His childhood favorite was Swiss Family Robinson, which appealed to him ''because of the way they built such an interesting life out of the wilderness, took advantage of the natural resources, and how cozy it all was''—a reaction that foreshadowed his current professional concerns as president of a Boston-based energy consulting firm.

The living room, this March evening, is chilly; the thermostat is set low. Claude sits, in mohair sweater and ascot scarf, like the lord of a drafty English manor, plying me with cheese and hazelnuts. Positively evangelistic on the subject of conservation (''We have no right in this country to waste the energy we do, living in a world that doesn't have enough''), he has formed his own company, Commonwealth Energy Group, to help industries plan for efficient energy management and develop alternate sources.

The entrepreneurial role is new to Claude, who has climbed the ladder in companies involved in aerospace and other innovative technologies. (His salary in his last vice-presidential job was $60,000.) He moved into the executive end because ''that's where the power is, where the responsibility is, where the recognition is, where the bucks are. I must lead. I really must, I'm driven to lead, and people respond to my leadership.''

Not an inventor but an implementor, he can ''understand what the designers are doing and guide it so all the pieces fit together.'' He has run the gamut from atomic test instruments (''Thirty years ago it was the right thing to do'') to solar power. He has headed projects as diverse as strobe beacons for Gemini, Apollo, and Skylab orbital rendezvous; a color television sensing element for the Viking Mars landing; cathode ray tubes for the Los Alamos and Livermore laboratories; optically-tracked missiles; computerized laser printing; and automated color-sorting of cigars. He is author of more than thirty papers, articles, and book chapters.

Claude Brenner is not one to work for a General Electric or Honeywell. (''That would be routine and boring.'') Rather, he has looked for a small company ''with an interesting personality, doing interesting things in a new and different area.'' Companies like DeHavilland, the British firm that developed the first civilian jet (''It made its maiden flight on the 27th of July, 1949, and I was there to see it''); Allied Research Associates; EG&G, Inc.; Laser Graphic Systems Corporation; and most recently, Northern Energy Corporation, which operates a federally funded regional solar center, of which Claude was deputy director.

His new firm's slogan: ''The basic danger of the world energy situation is that it could become critical before it seems serious.''* Ultimately, Claude envisions a safe, secure energy system based on a combination of exotic technologies, free of dependence on oil and coal. ''Overall,'' he says, ''energy is a political problem. The technology is there. The people who say we ought to ban nuclear or concentrate on one thing or another are out of their minds. We need all the energy we can get from all the sources we can get. Otherwise we're doomed. I talk and talk and talk and talk and talk to presidents of companies and chairmen of the board, and I realize I've won them over when they say, 'You scared me.' I say, 'Right. I intended to scare you.' ''

''I am so conditioned,'' Claude smiles, ''that I will answer any question. Because that's what success was: they asked a question and you answered it.''

The question Claude finds hardest to answer definitely is how ''Quiz Kids'' affected him. ''I am of two minds about it. It was an incredible experience. Certainly there was the travel, the attention, the hoopla of getting to meet famous and important people. (Like Clark Gable, whose autograph might be worth a fortune if I, in my compulsiveness, hadn't decided that, written in pencil, it might fade away, so I went over it in ink!) There was excitement and pleasure and joy. It put me through

---

* *Energy: Global Prospects: 1985-2000* (report of a world workshop on alternative energy strategies, 1977).

college and enabled my mother, then, to put my sister through. It changed my life in fantastically remarkable ways.

"But there is no free lunch. There is an emotional payment that I may be continuing to make in deep and subtle ways. I think, on the whole, it was an exceedingly damaging experience. I believe it shaped me in terms of my responses to life's pressures. To the question, on balance would I have done it again—knowing what I know now, would I allow my child to do it—" he shrugs and flings out his arms—"it remains an open question. I honestly don't know."

Claude and ex-Quiz Kid Vanessa Brown faced such questions in 1964, when they were guests on David Susskind's talk show along with four other onetime "prodigies": pianist Lorin Hollander, author Gore Vidal, harpsichordist Ruth Slenczynski, and dancer Alicia Markova. Claude, then thirty-five, felt out of place. He never had considered himself a prodigy, just a brighter-than-average kid with an engaging personality and a "terribly retentive memory."

In the dressing room, Vanessa greeted Claude like a long-lost friend. "She was all sort of gooey about it," he remembers. "I was surprised she knew who I was—she'd only been on the program a few times."

Vanessa asked Claude what he was going to say.

"I'm going to say how awful it was."

"Oh, you can't say that! It was wonderful!"

The actress figured that Susskind wanted the "prodigies" to commiserate about their unhappy childhoods, and she enlisted Claude and Hollander to foil him. (Vanessa recalls: "We managed it very well, with winking signals. Any time the thing dropped a little, somebody would come up with a *happy* story about their past. Susskind would not speak to me at the end.")

But Claude was not going to go along . . . not until Susskind asked him the opening question. "He insulted me. He turned to me with his glazed eyes and said, 'Ah, Mr. Brenner, you were a Quiz Kid. What were you doing when normal children were playing with their trains?' And I said, '*I* was playing with my trains, Mr. Susskind. *I* was a normal child.'

"I wasn't going to give *this* guy any grist for any mill that said we were different. Which, of course," he adds, "we were. We inevitably had to be. I don't think you can expose malleable young people to that kind of attention and pressure and expect them to come out of it whole."

After the Susskind taping, Claude took Vanessa to Sardi's, so he could brag to the guys at the office that he'd had a drink with Vanessa Brown.

The true story of the electric train: Claude's mother (who died the year of the Susskind interview) had promised him one (which he desperately wanted) if he stayed on the program ten times in a row. He stayed on only nine times, but she said he could have it anyway. "I said, 'No, I don't want it.' I've had a raging battle with my psychiatrist over whether that was her pressure to make me win. My sense is that Mother couldn't afford an electric train and that was her way of delaying."

We are lunching at his office, a converted condominium apartment in Winchester. He has opened a can of soup and fastidiously poured it back. ("You don't want lumpy tomato soup.")

"Winning was big for me," he reflects. "Once you entered a competition, you entered to win. I wanted one thing out of that program: to survive. Not to be like the mass of kids that didn't. I was constantly on my mettle throughout my life. Always the sense of *Am I going to make it tonight?* Even today"—his finger jabs the air—"I still haven't escaped the business of being a Quiz Kid, and I'm *fifty-two years old, for God's sake,* and a successful professional man."

The need to come out on top is something that, as a child, he "perceived to be expected of me—by myself, and very subtly, by my mother. Mother was not a pushy person; she abhorred grossness of behavior. But she was very controlling in her way, a strong figure in the background. She idolized me." She was not, he hastens to make clear, a stage mother: "She stayed out of it. Occasionally she would press me a little, to fulfill the Quiz Kid obligation, as it were; but there was no coaching. Only one time, in the interview, I think she mouthed an answer to me. But generally, she worked not to let it go to my head, by playing the whole business low-key."

Nevertheless, "we lived from Wednesday to Wednesday. It was there under the surface, inescapable, as elemental a part of our lives as having to go to school in the fall and finishing in June."

"One of the great sadnesses of my life," says Claude, "is that I secretly wanted to show my scrapbooks to my children but never did. I felt the kids had enough trouble competing with a strong, controlling father without having to live up to his accomplishments."

His scrapbooks fill four tattered volumes. The title: "Sheilah and Claude Brenner." ("She was the oldest—she got top billing.") One of the early clippings is a January 1, 1941 wire service report:

> A 14-year-old girl will attempt to follow in her 12-year-old brother's footsteps when Sheilah Brenner of Chicago makes her debut on the Quiz Kids tonight.

Claude believes his Quiz Kids success may have been a source of unspoken resentment on his sister's part. "Once she opened up and revealed how deeply she felt about it." It happened in 1963, when Lou Cowan was seeking updates on his former brood. Sheilah, still in the Chicago area, got a call, not Claude. "She said to me, 'That's surprising. Why did they contact me and not you?' And I said, 'Why is that surprising?' And she said, 'Well, after all, *you* were the *star*.' "

"I have always," says Sheilah Brenner Lang, "basked in my brother's reflected glory. People who knew us in high school would say, 'Hi, Sheilah, how's Claude?' This has been the story of my life. It became kind of a joke. It never bothered me.

"The only thing is, I think it's time to put it away. Quiz Kids is very juvenile. It's peculiar when you're fifty-five years old to go out and someone introduces you, 'Do you know her brother was a Quiz Kid?' It was a long time ago. I'm astounded it's still recalled."

A heavyset woman, sitting in her Skokie, Illinois, living room with its grasscloth walls and plastic-sheathed beige upholstery, she exudes strength, dignity, certainty. Though Claude suspects "it must have been tough on her to be a tagalong," she insists his Quiz Kids broadcasts and trips were "a marvelous, happy experience. Everything to me was an excitement." When she would ride home on the elevated train after the program, she would think, *Do these people know he was on the radio tonight?*

"For me," she says, "Claude was always on a pedestal. He was the one who had to accomplish, and I"—she smiles—"was the little nebbish that stood behind."

She dismisses her ill-fated Quiz Kids appearance as "a one-shot brother-sister gimmick." She is still pinching herself about her good fortune in getting to go to Northwestern on money that, without Quiz Kids, would have been set aside for Claude, the man of the family.

Now she has taken over as president of her late husband's dental manufacturing firm.

"I feel quite secure," she says. "My mother made it that way. I never felt deprived of anything. Ever.''

In contrast to his sister, Claude is—beneath the playful wit and gentle sophistication—a brooding, demanding perfectionist.

"He hasn't had an easy life," says Sheilah. "We never had a home, per se, and he went off to boarding school, and then he was out on his own at M.I.T. at fifteen. He never came back after that. All these were wonderful, exciting things, but hellishly frightening. I can just see my mother and myself standing at the station, and this little boy walking down, weeping to pieces. And he came to M.I.T. as a Quiz Kid and had to live up to that—or live it down.''

My visit gives Claude the opportunity to pour out the dark side of his feelings about the Quiz Kid experience to ''someone who really understands.''

"I always felt I was something of a freak," he confesses, "that the public was gawking at these young people who had that quirk in our minds which allowed us to remember facts." Though *Coronet* magazine once called him "the typical Quiz Kid . . . highly endowed in every single attribute," Claude says he has no illusions about why he was selected. "The spice I added was my accent, pure and simple. I got so sick and tired of being described as the boy with the 'smooth British accent.' Is there a rough British accent? I used to think I was the dumb one, and my accent was my only asset.''

In the early days of the program, he recalls, "some noted educator would stand up and say what wonderful, normal children we were, and how this was of value to the entire nation. That kind of crap. How could he tell? He'd never met us. He saw a bunch of trained seals. We had to smile and be pleasant and not show our disappointment when we lost. We weren't allowed to act like normal children—we weren't allowed to have any hurts.

"We were, in fact, show business personalities, and we were shockingly underpaid. Yet if they had placed a larger monetary value on it, it would have taken away the flavor of delicious naivete.

"Don't misunderstand me," he adds. "There was no force driving me to participate. I could always have said no. Not that I would have; I enjoyed it. Sure we were exploited. Miles Laboratories profited enormously from that. I was exploited by Lake Forest Academy. But I got myself a scholarship to a damn good school, and I'm grateful for it.''

Despite the good times on trips, he felt no real bond with the other

Kids. "These weren't my friends, they were people I competed with. We put on our caps and gowns and said the usual dumb things that kids say to each other. But there was always the sense of faint strain: *When you win, I lose. I knew the answers, why do you get called on?* This was more than normal school competition—this was competition in the public eye, competition for fame and fortune."

Unlike some of us, he never went on any other quiz show. "What would be the point? I've been in some respects denigrating my experience, yet Quiz Kids was *the* quality show."

When he was asked to be on "the $64,000 thing," the prospect evoked anxiety. "There would have been the same kind of punishment I used to get: 'You mean you didn't get 100 on the test? You mean you didn't make it past the $8,000 plateau? Come on, Quizzie, don't you know the answer?' I really took a beating about being a Quiz Kid."

Some of the comments scrawled in his Lake Forest yearbook tell the story: "To my pal with the I.Q." . . . "To 'Quizzy' Claude the 'brain' . . . "To Brains from lack of brains" . . . "To my little quiz friend . . . All the luck in the world to a damned genius" . . . "To the 'Great Brain.' Thanks for the help in English."

Claude's arrival at Lake Forest had been much-heralded, and petty jealousies were greatly magnified among this coterie of 135 boys who lived, ate, studied, and played together. Claude alone was allowed to miss chapel and study hall so that he could do the show on Sundays. He was called stuck-up if he inadvertently failed to return a greeting.

Although he loved Lake Forest and threw himself into every activity (worked on the newspaper, acted in plays, took yearbook photos, led the debating society), he "felt a veil" between himself and other kids. Being youngest in the class and slow to mature contributed. "I wanted desperately to be accepted. I had lots of friends, but I was classed with the brainy crowd, not the sports heroes. I don't think I would rather have been friendly with the 'in' group, but I wanted to be able to make the choice myself."

An "indifferent" athlete, he helped organize a soccer team and went out for his varsity letter to show that he was "a normal kid." When he proudly marched up to receive the letter, there were mutterings from the school jocks. "I wondered if I had really earned the letter or if I had gotten it because I was the Quiz Kid."

He might, he acknowledges, have "suffered the same rejection" in any case. "Certainly kids tease, kids are cruel. But it wasn't merely one teenager teasing another. Our teasing was a result of our being national figures. We were household names. In a sense—God, this sounds grandiose!—we were national property.''

One evening his mother took him to the Chez Paree with some out-of-town friends. ''They whispered to the emcee they had a Quiz Kid at the table. So the fanfare and spotlights were thrust upon me. I hated it.''

After his Quiz Kids graduation, ''I wanted to get it behind me. I used to keep it as quiet as I could. I would not permit my mother to tell anybody who I was.'' (Yet four years later, he had ''no qualms'' about writing an article about it for a South African magazine, and once he returned to emcee the show when he was in Chicago—''So I was ready to trade on it, on my own terms.'')

The M.I.T. humor magazine welcomed him with ''a scathing paragraph.'' When he went to pick up his midterm grades, a classmate jibed, ''Come on, open the envelope—I want to write my parents that I beat the Quiz Kid.'' The attention faded quickly however. ''M.I.T. was a chastening experience. When you came having graduated first in your class, you discovered that everybody had graduated first in his class. There were a lot of people who'd never heard of, and didn't care about, Quiz Kids.'' Although Claude did well academically, he was not tops; he was too busy editing the student newspaper, playing the lead in shows, and singing in the glee club. ''In the end, I was elected permanent class president and was a leader of all the clubs I was in. That was my fulfillment—*I can do it on my own.*

''Except at graduation. Just as I was being handed my diploma, some people leapt up right in front of my family and said, 'Oh, that's the Quiz Kid!' ''

The tag continued to plague him. His graduate school roommates, suave naval veterans, ''would exploit my Quiz Kidness to the limit. We used to go out to dine, and they'd say in a loud voice, 'I wonder if these lucky people know they have a Quiz Kid in their midst.' '' If the waitress was particularly attractive, his roommates would nudge him to show his Jack Benny watch. ''They'd get the date with the waitress; I wouldn't.''

When he would go to a party, he recalls, ''conversation would cease, there would be whispering, and in would walk Claude Brenner, the Quiz Kid. I wanted to make it with a girl because I was charming and good-looking and debonair and dashing and persuasive and seductive, not because I was a Quiz Kid. I want to be a success because I'm competent in my profession, not because I was a Quiz Kid.

''I used to think I'd reach a point in my life when nobody would remember that anymore. . . . 'Did you know Mr. Brenner was a Quiz

Kid?' If I had a dollar for every time somebody said that, I'd be rich. Somehow it tracks me into companies even where I'm not known.''

When the *Boston Globe* expressed interest in profiling him (''Quiz Kid Continues To Make Good''), he had ''a great clench in the stomach.'' Yet, he admits, ''my intellect tells me that the fact that I was once such a person is no different from having been one of McNamara's 'whiz kids.' If one of my colleagues had an article written about him and had some unique thing like that in his background, I would say, 'Isn't that interesting!' Why do I feel there is some kind of stigma and a little bit of a putdown: *Look, the oddball made it?*''

Driving through historic, wooded Lexington, Claude points out the landmarks with evident pride. He settled in the Boston area, he explains, after discovering that there was no aeronautical work in his native South Africa and concluding that advancement in England would be slow for a Jew from the non-managerial class.

The cold war was raging, and the aircraft industry was not hiring aliens, so he took a job offered by his former thesis advisor, at M.I.T.'s research laboratory. There were no openings in his field of aerodynamics, so he was stuck in aeroelastic structures, a new field in which he had taken ''the obligatory junior course.'' He wound up an expert and, with a classmate, started a company that fabricated wind tunnels, then branched into other phases of engineering.

At twenty-nine, he was a scientific advisor for B-52 tests on Eniwetok atoll. At thirty-three, he headed a seven-man task force that set up all the instruments for the navy's first live test of nuclear anti-submarine rockets. ''We, in effect, pushed the button that detonated every weapon. I did the countdown, and it was our signals that launched things, turned timers on, opened camera shutters across the Pacific.'' Despite a few hairy moments when the clock developed a bug just before zero hour, ''we did it! The commodore came up to congratulate me, and I said, 'I've got a confession to make. I've never done this before.' ''

Life is an adventure to Claude. He advises students, ''What you prepare yourself to do is irrelevant in the end. Your career can take you anywhere. Educate yourself as a whole human being.'' Academic qualifications, he believes, are less determinate than ''the chemistry inside you.''

Claude's chemistry is passionately eclectic. ''Variety and change are to me critically important. I have catholic tastes in virtually everything.''

He has flown more than a million miles, has been in every state but seven, keeps a record of each plane in which he flies, and takes umbrage when he finds himself in the same vehicle twice: "The objective is to fly in every aeroplane of the fleet."

He loves his work and labors diligently, but "work is not paramount. Life is living, and one has to savor all of it." He has even done needle-point ("the mathematical precision fascinated me") and constructed light verse ("a way of counting sheep").

HOW OLD WAS ST. GEORGE?

The day that I turned forty, I was confident and glad
Champagne and dinner at the Ritz—I celebrated well
The best years life would offer, better yet than those I'd had
Still promised opportunities at which I'd yet XL

It's now a decade later, and my fiftieth draws near
The lines and thinning hair foretell the tolling of the knell
Must I at last confess that middle age is really here?
With all the dragons yet to slay, confession hurts like L
     —Claude Brenner, 1978

"I'm in the last quarter of my career," says Claude. "There's not much time left. In recent years I have been (to use a cliche) upwardly mobile to some level that I'm unable to define. There is this need to succeed . . . recognition is important . . . "

Yet until a conflict with his boss at the solar center forced his hand, Claude—with his working class origins—was hesitant to go out on his own. "He said he didn't want the responsibility," says Sheilah, "yet when he works for somebody, he gives 350 percent of himself, works and worries himself to pieces as if it were his own."

Claude explains, "The feeling that I have to answer to a higher authority goes back to the issue that there's always somebody up there testing you. In my Quiz Kid and university and life experience, I've always been a strong Number Two. I was never the Richard Williams, if you will. Executive vice-president, vice-president of operations, I perceived that to be my lot in life. I was comfortable in an environment where there was structure and my role was well-defined, and I knew how to function."

Now that he has made the move, his objective is "to have a small, quality class company, and if people have a problem with energy, they'll immediately say, 'Commonwealth Energy Group—those are the people to go to.' I would like to have it wax and flourish, not so much because I want to make a million dollars, but because to be the president of a company that has made that kind of money is a mark of success.''

But he adds, ''I think it would never be quite enough. One never gets enough.''

Despite all his accomplishments, Claude Brenner is tugged by an undercurrent of self-doubt: ''the tempering fire in the failure of one's soul.''

The sense of ''who-am-I-to-achieve'' goes back to childhood. (*Am I on the show because of my accent? Did I really deserve my soccer letter?*) In a way, he feels, the Quiz Kid experience set him up for a fall: it made him squirm to find out how much he did not know.

''I am finally at the stage where I'm making a conscious effort to say, *I'm as good as the next man.* There is no reason why, if I have a question to ask at a conference, I shouldn't fling my hand up, because normally I will ask a better question than most people do.''

He has been appointed chairman of the visiting committee to M.I.T.'s humanities department, a task that pleases him mightily because of his belief in educating technologists to be ''citizens of the world.'' Yet, he muses, ''here I am, sitting with the dean of humanities, the provost, head of the department, president of the school. . . .'' (Stage whisper) *''They're going to find me out!''*

''When I describe myself and my life situation,'' says Claude, ''it's terribly important that everybody know everything—both sides. If you got me talking about my marriage, and the reasons for its breakup, I would feel compelled that you knew how she felt.''

He acknowledges his responsibility for the strains on the relationship: his ''short fuse, low tolerance level, and excessive compulsiveness'' . . . his difficulty in trying to be a father to his wife's children without having had a father of his own . . . his ''dumping'' on the family, at a time when the ties were particularly fragile, his frustration about the other ''divorce'' from the man he worked for and had considered a close friend and father figure. Although Claude has taken sensitivity training and prides himself on openness in business, he was unaware of the depth of his wife's unhappiness until too late; she had taken up with a bereaved neighbor. ''I've spent two years in therapy, understanding that it wasn't all my fault,'' he tells me. ''As one of my friends said, 'You and your Jewish guilt.' ''

''I can say, 'If only I'd done that differently. . . . ' But there's an inexorability about what happened. The forces that impinge upon us come from so many directions—you can't blame any single event.''

"So,'' says Claude, "the question comes back to the extent to which we were influenced, controlled, governed and shaped by the Quiz Kids experience. I would say strongly, but not exclusively. Perhaps I was laying all my emotional difficulties on that experience, and that is unfair. There were other factors going on in our lives. Our families—but our families themselves were inevitably shaped by our Quiz Kid experience. There's an interweaving of cause and effect that becomes a seamless web. You can't run a controlled experiment. We will never know whether we were Quiz Kids because of the kind of people we were or whether we're the kind of people we are because we were Quiz Kids.''

I have told Claude my own feelings toward our shared past, and I have seen his moist eyes and kindred smile. The thought that he was not alone in feeling shy, inadequate, and different is a revelation to him. He likens it to falling in love and to the pain of his marital collapse: "I thought nobody in the world had ever felt this way before.''

We are dining at a Greek restaurant. The wine is warm and so is the mood. Claude tells me the worst word he knows in Greek and talks of places he has not yet been. Peering over the top of the menu, he rolls his eyes conspiratorially, curls his lips, and mugs: "Hush! There are Quiz Kids at our table.''

He recalls the time when, as a young man seeking worldly wisdom, he visited George Kamen, who had handled merchandise promotions for the Cowan organization, in his Fifth Avenue New York apartment. ("He did the most sophisticated thing you could do—he put a drop of pernod in a glass, rinsed the glass of pernod, and made a martini.'') Claude has never forgotten something Kamen told him: "You *are* different. Remain as different as you are, otherwise you'll simply be one of the crowd. If people remember you for your difference, you'll succeed.''

Claude leans forward, intent. "The thing is, I have an unfortunately strong need in this never-ending search for truth to see things as right or wrong, black or white, good or bad, even though I know that the shades of gray are infinite. That we were Quiz Kids is a fact of life. We benefited from it materially, intellectually . . . and I think the jury will forever remain out on whether we were punished emotionally.

"As I reflect on what I've been saying, I have a sense that I have overstressed the negative feelings, perhaps because there was a cathartic process being served. And that really, in balance it was a wonderful, positive, interesting, useful, unique, not-to-be-rejected experience. Having been a Quiz Kid is nothing to be ashamed of . . . nothing to hide, but something to be proud of.

"And we've now come full circle to the question: If you had it to do over, would you? And I think the answer would be: *Yes . . . even so.*"

Jack Lucal: Called to the Cloth

Jack was very, very serious-minded. You'd have to be to become a priest.
    —Ex-Quiz Kid Richard Williams

Jack has a dry sense of humor. He's very outgoing. He's not holier than thou—he'll take a glass of wine. He calls at eleven to have lunch at twelve.
    —Ex-Quiz Kid Joan Bishop

At the Quiz Kids' first anniversary party, the Kids dressed as what they hoped to be when they grew up. Fourteen-year-old Jack Lucal came as ambassador to China, though he had talked not long before of becoming a priest. Since his first visit to Chinatown, at nine or ten, he had been a Sinophile. At fifteen, he began learning Chinese. The title of his high school commencement speech was "East Meets West."

"And that interest," he says, "led me to the Jesuits. I thought I might be sent to China, like the great missionaries of the seventeenth century."

China is one place the Rev. John Alanson Lucal, S.J. (Society of Jesus), has not been yet, though he has seen much of Africa, Europe, and the Middle East and has studied eleven languages, from Greek and Latin to Amharic and Swahili.

The slender white band tucked under the pointed collar of his black knit shirt is the only tipoff that the fifty-four-year-old man in the neutral-colored suit, facing me across the lunch table, is a cleric. Our reunion is in Chicago, where he has stopped off en route from officiating at his niece's wedding. The postscript on his letter said, "I hope you will call me Jack . . . in the QK tradition."

Jack Lucal has weathered well. His faintly lined face is spirited, his words measured but forceful. His longish brown hair has receded some, and there are white streaks in his mustache and Vandyke beard. Clear blue-grey eyes, benign yet piercing, smile good-humoredly through thick lenses. His ready laugh is self-effacing.

In his assignments as a Jesuit, he has reconciled his two childhood passions, politics and religion. His current post is with the International Labor Organization in Geneva. Unity is his leitmotif; his vision, universal. His vocational ideal: "to work as a priest in the creation of greater world community."

As he recalls his early spiritual stirrings, a trace of the youthful Jack flits across his features. "I was fairly religious as a boy, although I didn't go to a Catholic school. We lived in a very Protestant suburb, Oak Park. Being a Catholic, you stuck out. It put me on the defensive. When I walked to and from school, I'd frequently stop in the church."

Three of his grandparents were Protestant, only one Catholic: his mother's mother, a devout Irish-Alsatian whose lineage included a priest. Jack's mother, Helen Strong Lucal, transmitted that heritage to her son. His father, Alanson Lucal, a tire dealer who had grown up on an Ohio farm and majored in physical education, "wasn't really anything that we could find out. He went [to church] with us on Christmas and Easter." Twelve years before his death, quiet Al Lucal finally converted to Catholicism while recovering from a heart attack, shortly after Jack entered the novitiate. Jack recalls: "He said to me, 'You know, this is the first time I've ever had an opportunity to think about religion. I've been too busy making a living.' I gave him some of the traditional arguments, and he said, 'Oh, that's all very interesting, but the real reason, if I became a Catholic, would be because of your mother's example all these years.' "

Helen Lucal, convent-educated, sent her son and daughter to the excellent Oak Park public schools because they had two rooms to a grade, while the parochial schools had two grades to a room. Jack learned his catechism in Sunday school.

"We had a book of Bible stories. I can remember vividly the one about the Jewish high priest, the plate, the Holy of Holies. I was fascinated." In eighth grade, he did a vocational workbook, cutting and pasting pictures of the vestments worn by Catholic priests. "At twelve or thirteen, you're impressed by externals: dressing up and being up there where everybody's looking at you, being an *important person*. As I grew older, the inner meaning became more significant."

Thoughts of a priestly calling receded, for the time being, after Jack became an "important person" on "Quiz Kids." The program went on the air the summer before he started high school, and he joined the board early in September. He was thirteen. "Everyone was talking about it in Chicago. It was my parents' idea for me to apply. We were listening, and I was answering some of the questions."

His grade school principal wrote on his recommendation: "Jack is a very capable pupil of the near-genius type." He was strong on history, geography, and politics and "pretty good on Bible stories." He "might answer a music question or something on Shakespeare." He tossed off stumpers like "What element now found on earth was first discovered on what heavenly body by the use of what scientific instrument?"

Inside of four months, he held the record for consecutive wins: fifteen straight, with eight first-places. "The DiMaggio of the Quiz Kids," one newspaper dubbed him. "The ace Quiz Kid," saluted another. Only advanced age kept him from being one of the all-time champs. When he retired at sixteen, he had appeared sixty-eight times in twenty-seven months, more than anyone but Richard Williams.

Things came easily to Jack. It was no effort for him to recall what he had learned. He read three newspapers a day, along with the World Book, Mark Twain, Rudyard Kipling, Robert Louis Stevenson. His room was papered with maps, and he kept neatly catalogued collections of stamps, coins, medals, travel folders, and historic headlines. He learned Morse code and rigged up a telegraph system between his room and his younger sister Janet's.

Helen Lucal, dynamic and self-assured, was the mainspring behind her son's development. From the time he was two, they had talked each night about the day's happenings and, later, about historical personalities. An Oberlin University graduate, Mrs. Lucal had taught high school music; she started giving Jack piano lessons at four—but only on his own initiative. "If you are not interested," she would tell him, "we mustn't waste your time or mine." Reason, not punishment, was her method of discipline.

Jack's parents stimulated his interest in world affairs with dinner-table discussions of clippings his mother cut out. The whole family would end up sprawled on the floor, checking disputed points in the encyclopedia. When Jack expressed an opinion, his parents played devil's advocate, making him back up his views. After he became a Quiz Kid, his mother acted as "research secretary," briefing him on current events. (Janet declined to try out for the show; she was proud of her brother but preferred not to be in his shadow.)

Jack had an embarrassing habit of airing the family linen coast-to-coast. He revealed, for example, that it was his mother who had proposed to his dad. Emceeing a contest between Quiz Kids and their parents, Master Jack twitted his mom, "I know how old you are, but I shan't tell."

But his most-quoted comments were of the God-and-country variety that warmed the cockles of America's heart. When the Kids were asked what historical event had most profoundly affected mankind, Jack's electrifying choice was "That the Son of God became Man and lived on this earth." Which three books would he save if all the rest had to be destroyed? The Bible, the Constitution, and "a history book, so that people could be guided by what had been done."

He was fervent about foreign policy, pious about patriotism and public service. At his grammar school graduation, he delivered a prize oration on "What the Flag Stands For." He rounded up thirty-six pounds of old records, newspapers and magazines for the Red Cross and made his friends buy ten-cent defense stamps as tickets to play on his ping-pong table.

When 1940 Republican Presidential nominee Wendell Willkie asked the Quiz Kids what they expected from their system of government, others mentioned freedom of speech and fine schooling. Jack Lucal preached, "Children have the benefits [of liberty] but they also have the responsibilities, and they must guard these responsibilities or our democracy will be lost." When Willkie failed to oust Franklin Roosevelt from the White House, Jack compared the candidates to Quiz Kids, who won or lost "with a smile," and exhorted "every citizen to support with true loyalty the choice of the majority of our people."

Handsome, clean-cut and studious, he was the sort of young man who looked at home in a suit, tie and glasses. But he had his boyish side. He disliked haircuts and emptying the garbage. He liked fishing, loud socks, Carmen Miranda and Groucho Marx. When the Quiz Kids went to Hollywood, Jack drove staff members crazy imitating Groucho's tilted gait. When the Kids, as a prank, locked their mothers in their hotel rooms, Jack was the one who turned the key on Bessie Darrow.

Aside from being the last chosen for ball teams, Jack was a popular, all-round kid, his basement a constant gathering-place. He was president of his grammar school class, captain of patrol, editor of the yearbook. His classmates and teachers voted him the American Legion award for scholarship, leadership, service, honor, and courage. Summers, he helped in his father's tire shop, laid streetcar rails, washed windows.

Fourth in his high school class (the top boy), he studied only when a course motivated him. ("The same in college—I didn't push for a high average.") He was active in debate, drama, and student council.

Oak Park High, which had produced four other Quiz Kids, was proud of its favorite son. Wrote one of his teachers in the *Journal of Education*: "A Wednesday never came that some of his classmates didn't remind us that we must all listen to Jack that evening. Never once did I hear anyone call him a 'smarty.' "

The school paper published Jack's lengthy reports on the Quiz Kids trips and played up his victories. "All this success would have turned a lesser person's head," one article ran. "But Jack stayed his old self—affable, hard-working, and sincere."

"I didn't like the ballyhoo and notoriety," Jack grimaces. "Every time I won, it was in the paper. It was a bit embarrassing. Even after I was off the show, wherever I went, somebody found out. I used to think it was an invasion of privacy. I didn't want to be known as 'the Quiz Kid.' "

At school, he says, he was teased a lot, referred to as "the brain," and expected to know everything . . . "although I must say, it didn't bother me much. My teachers didn't draw attention to it. All in all, it wasn't a great cross to carry. Possibly there was a danger of feeding one's ego, becoming something of a phony. People would think you knew all the answers, but you knew it wasn't true."

Jack "didn't feel that different" from his peers. "Gerard passed for the prodigy. The rest of us were just a bunch of intelligent young people who had memories like glue.

"My parents always thought I had a rather blase attitude One time I put the war bond in my shirt pocket, and it got into the washing machine."

He accepted the discomfort of being in the public eye as the price for "a mind-enlarging human experience." Everything about it engaged his lively interest: the other Kids ("I didn't regard them as competitors, maybe my parents did"), the staff ("wonderful people"), seeing the control room, being on the radio, traveling, meeting celebrities. ("On the train to Los Angeles, I told a joke that Jack Benny laughed at.")

On a deeper level, Jack believes, being a Quiz Kid gave him "a certain self-confidence and fostered the love of learning—respect for the man who knows what he's talking about. *Do you know the answer or don't you? Where are the facts?*"

Fourteen years after his graduation, he discussed that point with Harve Bennett Fischman and Cynthia Cline when the three were recalled for a bout with the New York Quiz Kids. "We all agreed that on the program you just had to know details. But it wasn't trivia. It was things people thought they ought to know but didn't, and they were glad we knew them. No one expects children to have the wisdom of the ancients. They feel it's wonderful if a child learns his lessons, and that's what we were doing.

"Knowledge was good, but it didn't help you lead a better life or make moral decisions or face a crisis."

Jack's crisis came at Harvard: a confrontation with what he perceived as a pervasive and dogmatic secularism.* When he arrived in Cambridge in 1944, on partial scholarship, he was a government major, still intent on a foreign service career. He made the Dean's list "by the grace of God and my notes." But he found himself at odds with the skeptical Harvard ethos. "There were professors who openly derided any religious belief as superstition. They were fighting the old battle of religion versus Darwin. That battle has been over for years, but a lot of people don't realize it."

For Jack, there was—and is—only one truth. "The same God Who created the world and science is the God we approach through religion. For me, the story of evolution is the way Creation occurred. Anybody who believes that the Book of Genesis is talking about seven days of twenty-four hours— It's poetic language. When I was teaching English in Ethiopia, where you have a backward Church, an uneducated clergy— it was 1957, when the first Sputnik went up, and we could look up and see it. My students said, 'Our priests say the world is flat because the Bible says, Go preach the gospel to the four corners of the earth.' And I said to them, 'What have we just been studying?' 'Figures of speech . . . . Ahhh!' They got it."

Feeling himself an outsider at Harvard, as he had to some extent in Protestant Oak Park, he clung to his religious upbringing. "If you've never had to defend your faith, you find yourself, as an adolescent, rebelling against what you've been taught. But if you're engaged in the battle with your peer group—My rebellion was not directed against the Church, but against the secular structures, and still is. I think the Church is the only place where you get any sane answers."

Before he could fully come to grips with the angst his Harvard environ-

---

* In New Haven, about the same time, another brilliant young Catholic with different political leanings, William F. Buckley, Jr., was having a similar reaction, later documented in *God and Man at Yale.*

ment aroused, he was drafted. He went into the service the summer after his freshman year, two days before the atomic bomb was dropped on Hiroshima. G.I. Jack, who had itched to fight the Nazis, instead found himself seeing the ''seamier side of army life'' as a quartermaster managing a post exchange warehouse near Frankfurt.

The utter waste and destruction he saw in postwar Germany sharpened his hunger for a moral order. ''I don't think there's ever been a novel or movie that really caught the spirit of the occupation, the total effect of madness . . . what it was like to live in the midst of ruins with very little food, the flourishing black market, the immorality of soldiers and civilians, the breakdown of society. It was very sobering . . . the beginning of a process of reflection which led to posing ultimate questions and seeing the futility of politics without a moral base. It was the beginning of the resurrection of my desire to be a priest.''

He found positive aspects to soldiering—discipline, drill, teamwork, following orders—that foreshadowed his decision four years later to submit to the Jesuit vow of obedience. ''It's a challenge to surrender the thing we hold dearest: our own will. When you are part of an enterprise, cooperating with others, you necessarily have to sacrifice some of your own opinions and desires. If you feel the group is doing good work, doing God's will, that is your career decision: to join and do whatever you're asked to do.''

He had returned from the army to a Harvard campus where he felt more than ever beset by antireligiosity. Not having gone to Catholic schools, he felt himself on weak ground; he needed to study Christian philosophy. He resolved to leave ''the greatest university in the world'' to seek an amalgam of faith and reason: ''You can't live on two tracks.''

So he transferred to Georgetown. While taking scholastic philosophy and theology, well-rounded Jack played saxophone in the college band and organized his own group, ''The Hungry Five''; sang in the choir; was on a champion debate team and won a medal for extemporary speaking. He was vice-president of the dramatic society, senior delegate to the National Federation of Catholic College Students, and a member of a history honorary. He and his friend, ex-Quiz Kid Paul Sigmund (now a Princeton politics professor) drew up a new student council constitution giving students expanded powers.

Intellectually, Georgetown was no Harvard. ''Students argued religion a lot less: 'It's all true, look it up in the book, what's the point, we all believe the same thing.' ''

The urge to link with others who cared passionately about religion finally impelled him to write to the Society of Jesus. ("Of all the orders, they have the reputation of being the most intellectual.") He did the normal thirteen years of Jesuit training in eleven, followed by a year of advanced theological study and pastoral work in Muenster, Germany, and obtained a master's degree in philosophy from Loyola University along the way. He was ordained in 1961 ("a great day"). Ex-Quiz Kid Dick Williams attended.

Jack's primary motive in preparing for the priesthood had been to spread the gospel in a secularized world. In the course of his training, he became more and more concerned about social issues. "The teaching of the Church on social and political and economic questions is not widely known nor implemented," he laments. "It's not even taught in our own schools. The Pope writes encyclicals, and people say, 'Isn't that wonderful' and go on as usual."

His two years of teaching in Ethiopia stunned Jack out of such complacency. Shortly after his arrival in Addis Ababa in 1956, he witnessed a "traumatic" student strike that shut down the Jesuit-run high school. The protest was inflamed by anti-Western propaganda following Egypt's Suez Canal takeover. The students, members of the educated elite, objected to the imposition of manual labor (which they considered beneath them) as a form of discipline, claiming it was racially motivated.

Jack recalls, "I'd begun to get rumblings of discontent, but the headmaster said, 'Don't worry, nothing will happen.' Then on Christmas Day, we were having dinner, and we heard rocks coming through the windows."

Earlier, Jack had gone to a lot of trouble to help the students fix up some broken drums and rusty bugles and had arranged a parade. A couple of days after the strike began, he went into the room where the instruments were kept. "Every drum had been smashed. I was really broken up. Because I felt a warm bond with the students. And I felt the whole thing was unnecessary—a different attitude on the part of the administration could have averted it."

His "Third World experience" was even more profoundly formative than the one in postwar Germany. Living with the proud, mysterious Ethiopians burst the bonds of his culturally circumscribed thinking. Coming face to face with extreme poverty in a country attempting to develop under tremendous handicaps awakened him to the enormous discrepancies between living standards in different parts of the world. He became deeply involved in problems of justice and human rights.

The deity he believes in is an active God Who "cares intensely about what each person is and thinks and does . . . Who is with His people and not remote.'' A God Who created human beings with free will, and Who "takes the time to work out His will" through the moral and spiritual evolution of humanity.

Despite his social conscience, Father John Lucal is no Father Berrigan. His bent is more reflective than militant. While he has participated in spiritual renewal to open himself to relationships and feelings, he remains at heart "an idea person, not a people person."

His training completed on the threshold of the turbulent sixties, he enrolled in doctoral studies at Columbia University. Within a month after another man of the cloth, the Reverend Martin Luther King, Jr., led a massive march on Washington to proclaim his dream of racial equality, Jack Lucal began studying international relations and African affairs and writing editorials for the Jesuit opinion journal, *America.* He also taught a course at Fordham University and delivered conference papers on peace, disarmament, and the ethics of the Vietnam intervention.

Shortly before starting at Columbia, he received a letter from Lou Cowan, who was trying to track down his proteges. Jack's response, perhaps influenced by the ribbing he still endured from time to time, was slow and lukewarm.

Nov. 4, 1963

. . . Lou, I confess that I am not particularly thrilled at the idea of more publicity in re the QK experience. . . . I do think that we all are now to be judged on performance in the world, rather than on youthful precocity. . . .

If there is one point to be made publicly, it is that the Quiz Kids were quite normal boys and girls who have grown up to be solid citizens for the most part in an unspectacular way. This is not to say that I wouldn't like a Nobel Prize, however! Especially the Nobel Peace Prize . . . and I hope that my work as a priest and student of international relations will make me deserve one, even though I remain in the background and never receive it. . . .

Sincerely in the Lord,

Jack, S.J.

"Did I say that?" He is amused. "That sounds like me. . . . Prizes are prizes. I'd like to *do* something that was worth the Nobel Peace Prize. I wouldn't care if I got the prize or not.

"I think I was a little more optimistic about the possibilities of bringing

peace to the world in 1963 than I am today. I've seen the workings of
international organizations. The wheels grind so slowly. So much blah-
blah-blah.''

His firsthand experience with international organizations came after
seven years of trying to write a dissertation on the subject. The project,
spanning the entire history of the Church's involvement in world affairs,
''got too large''—he wrote five hundred pages and was only up to 1926.
After seeking approval several times to narrow the scope, he became so
exhausted and ill that his superior advised him to drop it. ''I had to do
something more active, get away from the typewriter.''

So in 1974 he was named to the Vatican's United Nations delegation.
He organized a World Day of Peace, was instrumental in reforming the
UN Charter to give observer states a bigger role, and monitored disarmament discussions. The high point of the year, for Jack, was his
speech on nuclear nonproliferation, presaging the Pope's 1976 condemnation of the arms race.

His work at the UN tempered his thinking about ''when and where the
Church might have an influence and where it wouldn't.'' He is impatient
with politicians who ''pay lip service to Christianity'' but divorce its
ethical teachings from their day-to-day decisions. ''I think our Western
view that puts the world over here and God over there without any interaction is schizophrenic. Everything I've been working on is to see how
this interaction can take place in a practical way.''

Jack had been at the UN a little more than a year when he was tapped
to administer SODEPAX, an ill-fated effort at Catholic-Protestant
cooperation toward social justice. SODEPAX (Society, Development and
Peace), a Geneva-based joint committee of the Holy See and World
Council of Churches, had been created in 1968, in the flush of ecumenical
optimism. By the time Jack came to the helm, enthusiasm had cooled,
and budget and staff were skeletal.

He organized workshops, met with officials and activists, and arranged
a colloquium on theological approaches to the challenge of the 1980s. But
he encountered resistance to interference with local churches and felt the
strain of serving two masters. It became clear that SODEPAX wasn't
going anywhere. But Jack still believes the endeavor had great symbolic
value and remains committed to Christian unity as a long-range goal: ''I
don't see it around the corner.''

When the project was terminated, he assumed the traditional Jesuit
seat as religious liaison at the International Labor Organization. He is
excited about the opportunity to contribute to the development of inter-

national labor legislation. His responsibilities include keeping an eye on activities of Catholic workers' groups and analyzing Pope John Paul II's ground-breaking 1981 labor encyclical, which denounced subordination of human effort to the profit motive.

Jack views both laissez-faire capitalism and atheistic Communism as unacceptable alternatives, each locked into the "obsolete" notion that work takes priority over the worker. "We need something in which there's more power to the people—more self-management, more democracy, much more equality of wealth. Something perhaps so new that we don't know what it is yet."

He expounds on the need for a "Copernican Revolution" in the thinking of world leaders in the same methodical, comprehensive way that he discoursed years ago, on the radio, on the responsibilities of living in a democracy.

"We have to live together, to understand one another, and to organize our life on planet Earth, which more than ever is becoming one global economy and political system." He sees the United Nations and its subsidiary agencies as evolving toward a rudimentary world government—"not the kind in Washington or Bonn" but some sort of loose confederacy. "The question is when and how, and whether it will be in time to prevent a nuclear holocaust. The world can become one with justice and structure and genuine community, or it can become one jungle in which everyone is shooting at everyone else."

Utopian? He denies it. "The flag-waving nationalists are the hopelessly unrealistic fools—they think we can go on living as we did in the nineteenth century. The search for security through more weaponry is a snare and a delusion. Two superpowers that are remarkably similar are strangling each other to death and endangering the future of the human race."

Would God let that happen? "Mmmm. I've thought about that, and who knows? Never try to predict what God will allow." He laughs. "Never."

Whatever catastrophe he fears for humanity, whatever frustration he finds in combatting shortsighted apathy, Jack Lucal is at peace with himself. "I definitely feel I have been called to work in the international field." Unlike some of his brothers, he does not chafe under the demands of his vows, and he has had no serious midlife doubts. "I don't think it's wise to look back too much. Whatever you're doing at the moment is the most important thing."

He keeps in touch with the ecumenical movement by living at an international conference center outside Geneva operated by the World Council of Churches, and serving as Catholic chaplain there. The celibate life is not easy. "You feel very much the desire to have a family. The feelings of loneliness tend to come when you're bored or in between things, or things aren't going well. But if you are dynamically absorbed in something, then it's a possible thing."

Satisfaction comes in teaching, writing, saying mass, preaching, finishing a report, attending a meeting, and in raising people's consciousness, "very slowly, little by little." Yet with age, he also is aware of opportunities missed, of limitations.

He sits back, after lunch, sipping a Heineken's.

"I don't think I've accomplished much. I still feel that I'm beginning. We have an awfully long training—I was thirty-six when I finished, and then I went for my Ph.D. . . . "

Despite an impressive five-page resume, Jack Lucal feels, "I could have done better. I could have finished the dissertation or written this article or that book. I'm not one of those people who can just sit and work and work and work. I get nervous indigestion. I've felt very much not being able to do, physically, all I would like to do."

His memory is not what it was. "There's a loss of innocence. We say, 'That's not important,' or 'I've seen that before.' Because we're not really interested, the element of wonder goes out, so we don't remember. When you're young, you're not able to distinguish what's more and less important, so you tend to remember it all."

His wide-ranging curiosity has been, he feels, a mixed blessing in adult life. He wishes he had focused more. "I was intellectually a wanderer. I've noticed that people who produce are usually specialists." Although his French is good enough for writing articles, reading mysteries and watching Parisian quiz shows, he would like to be more fluent.

He does not feel he has lived up to his Quiz Kid expectations—expectations that gave him "a boost" at the time.

"When I was little," he laughs, "I used to tell people I was going to be the Pope someday. I suppose that what I'm doing now *is* somewhat unusual, but most people don't know what it is." He laughs again. "Becoming a Jesuit puts limits right away. You're not going to be President of the United States."

He pauses, emphasizing the point. "I felt when I entered the order that I was sacrificing something—the possibility of becoming famous." He speaks slowly, deliberately. "But I wanted that. I reached a point where I felt that self-seeking ambition was wrong. Fame, glamor, glory—all of that was to be rejected.

"I used to think it was evil. Now I think it's neutral. If you can use it to help other people, fine. But it's a temptation, like wealth. It's not money but the *love* of money that is the root of all evil." Being part of a structure that regulates the way he expends his time and energy as well as money ("Nothing I have is really my own") gives him "a wonderful feeling," a liberation from the tyranny of aspiration.

"I don't have to worry about whether I rise to the top. I don't care. I've never been a superior nor desired to be one. That would be a distraction from what I really want to do: work for justice and peace."

It might be tempting to say that Jack Lucal's world is a sheltered one, that he took the easy way by renouncing the struggle to "make a name for himself." Tempting, but not true. For Jack's work is as demanding as a corporate executive's, as far-reaching as many statesmen's. Rather than releasing him from worldly pressures, his vocation plunged him into the great issues of our time. In responding to what he saw and experienced, his intellect and vision forced him into the fray. How ironic that he, who put all his gifts at the service of God and humanity, still doubts that he has given enough!

The evolution from Jack Lucal, Quiz Kid, to Father John Lucal was, in retrospect, all of a piece. For him, victory and renown never were the point, any more than grades were the point of study. What counted was intrinsic worth. Jack Lucal, in that simple, right-minded America of the early 1940s, regarded "Quiz Kids" as an opportunity to begin what became his life's work. In a *Quiz Kids Magazine* essay on "What I Would Like To Be When I Grow Up," he wrote:

> . . . I believe the world needs more spiritual guidance . . .
> Certainly men who dominate the destiny of others should not forget
> that righteousness and material success work together!
>
> I hope to obtain a superior education so I shall better understand
> the problems confronting leaders. I shall hope to win the respect
> and confidence of anyone I meet anywhere . . .
>
> Radio is powerful, so I hope to be able to convince my listeners
> that religion, whatever theirs may be, is not a Sunday habit but
> something to be lived and enjoyed, something to make us all
> happier whether we are rich or poor, humble or great. . . .
>
> This may sound presumptuous, but if I do have a divine
> calling I shall work hard to accomplish all these things. . . .

Margaret Merrick: Polio Victor

Margaret was always delightful—full of wit and life.
    —Ex-Quiz Kid Richard Williams

*A little saucy . . . Sometimes people who have a slight defect
compensate by being more outspoken.*
    —Ex-Quiz Kid Joan Bishop

One thing made Margaret Merrick stand out from the other Quiz Kids:
her crutches.

It was more than a dozen years before the Salk vaccine. Infantile
paralysis was a dreaded scourge. From the time the sidewalks began
sizzling in June until the end of the last heat wave, epidemics felled thousands each summer. How the virus spread was anybody's guess. Many
parents kept their children away from the crowded public beaches. No one
knew whether it made any difference.

President Franklin D. Roosevelt was America's best-known polio
victim. Margaret Merrick, for a time, may have been second. "The Quiz
Kid with infantile paralysis and an Irish spirit," a Des Moines radio
columnist called her. "Spunky" was Joe Kelly's term.

Margaret came on the show in July, 1942, two months after her
fourteenth birthday and barely a year after her polio attack. Accustomed
to minding two younger brothers and a baby sister, she took us smaller
Kids under her wing. I picture her leaning on crutches, smiling cheerfully, a sly sparkle in her eyes. Black hair pulled back from her broad forehead. White Peter Pan collar peeking from a plain wool sweater. Sensible
saddle shoes.

She was the 111th Quiz Kid. More than half her predecessors had been
girls, but few had racked up enough points to stay on the show. "Are the

gals short on gray matter?'' asked *Quiz Kids Magazine.* ''They make the grade in the preliminaries but falter before the mike. Maybe they're just shyer than the boys.''

Margaret Ann Merrick was neither shy nor short on ''gray matter.'' In twenty-one months, she made forty-five appearances. ''All-round answer girl,'' she was (even for a Quiz Kid) a voracious reader, gobbling two hundred books in three months. With Margaret aboard, I no longer was the lone female in the traveling crew. Uncomplaining, she tailed the group on walking tours and, in Washington, mounted the Capitol steps, counting each one to lighten her laborious climb.

In Des Moines, newspapers hailed her as a returning native. Her mother had grown up on a farm in Oskaloosa, Iowa; her father—a veterinarian and creator of Dr. Merrick's Sulfodene lotion for dogs and cats—had been in practice there when Margaret was born, the year before the Crash. Shortly afterward, the family had moved to a seedy neighborhood near the University of Chicago.

In those days, people hardly could afford medical care for their children, much less their animals. The eggs a farmer would offer Andrew Merrick for his services were useless to pay Parke Davis' drug bills. He gave up his practice and went to work as a stockyards inspector.

By the time the Depression hit bottom, there were five mouths to feed, and Dr. Merrick had a drinking problem. The children were farmed out to relatives: Margaret, at six, to an uncle and aunt in Ohio. She arrived at Christmas and soon was skipped out of first grade, having taken instantly to reading.

As the economy picked up, her family reunited and moved to Chicago's western suburbs. Andrew Merrick, fighting his liquor habit, joined newborn Alcoholics Anonymous and built an animal hospital in Brookfield. His wife, Dorothy Santee Merrick, was nurse, receptionist and bookkeeper. A committed Quaker, she taught the children the value of truth and integrity and raised them in her husband's Catholic faith. Margaret attended parochial schools until she entered the public junior high in tree-shaded Western Springs, where her parents bought the modest Colonial house in which her widowed mother still lives.

In 1941, after Margaret's eighth grade graduation, polio struck. Her parents were in Charleston when they got the news; they drove straight through to the hospital. She was paralyzed almost from the waist down, and one arm was temporarily affected. The shock may have had one salutary effect. Within the year, her father stopped drinking for good.

For her first Quiz Kids broadcasts, she had to be carried up to the dais.

Four months later, she waved at her crutches and said, "For Christmas I want to get rid of these." Her public was pulling for her. In a dramatic remote interview, she spoke with Sister Elizabeth Kenny, whose new method of treating polio victims with hot packs was achieving remarkable results in Australia. "Don't give up hope," Sister Kenny told Margaret.

In September, 1943, the Quiz Kids went to Washington, D.C. As they sat in the Senate gallery, Illinois' Scott Lucas paid tribute to them, and Majority Leader Alben Barkley read into the Congressional Record his hope that someday several of them would grace that distinguished body.

Margaret has no recollection of that. What she does remember is that she stumbled on a hotel carpet and fell, permanently injuring her left knee and ending her hopes of walking unaided.

"I was in a great deal of pain for months afterward. I still can't straighten that leg. At that time it was very bad, very bad. But thirty-eight years later, it's not so bad."

"You get used to anything," I murmur.

"That's right. Or else. And I don't care for any of the 'or elses.' "

My rendezvous with Margaret Merrick Scheffelin, Ph.D., is in a cocktail lounge at Chicago's O'Hare airport. Educational consultant, mother of eight and grandmother of four, she is en route from her California home to meet with U.S. education officials in Washington.

I find her in the powder room, having divested herself of the extra outfit "packed" under her gray flannel suit. (She travels light to free her hands for crutches.) The dark colleen is gone. Slight of frame, this Margaret has graying, close-cropped hair and a translucent, lined face. But there still is the prim white collar and a familiar glint in the hooded eyes.

The look remains no-nonsense. At fifty-two, she wears practically no makeup or jewelry. In her lapel, an Air Force stickpin. Her husband, Edward J. Scheffelin, is a retired career officer, their youngest daughter a cadet.

Margaret moves to a table with surprising speed, using a light, elbow-high metal crutch to balance her braced left leg. (The "not-very-good-looking" brace allows her to manage with one crutch most of the time.) In a small shoulder bag, ready to deliver to Washington, are her reviews of federal funding proposals from institutions that train people to work with handicapped children. The bulk of her time is spent as program evaluation and research consultant to the California Department of Education, compiling annual reports on how well the state meets its special education commitment.

A Fulbright grant took her to the University of Hamburg for half of 1980 to study employability of the deaf-blind (''the most debilitating handicap I can imagine''). She lectured in three languages in West Germany, England, and Belgium and visited her eldest daughter, married to a German. Next destination: Japan, to facilitate Fulbright exchanges and meet another daughter, an army captain in Korea.

Co-author of a monograph on learning disabilities, she leads workshops, does private consulting, serves on professional advisory boards. And she makes televised appeals for polio vaccination.

''Every chance I get, I tell parents: 'Immunize your children. Prevent them from becoming disabled.' I had to get my immunization the hard way.''

When paralysis hit, Margaret was thirteen and a ''complete tomboy.'' Short but sturdy, she played ''everything there was'' with her brothers and their friends. Her nose had been broken by a thrown bat.

''I was never interested in doing a lot of the things that girls typically did. I liked to be active. I was a pretty tough kid. I'd grown up in a very tough neighborhood.''

Her homespun speech has a mannish twang. ''One morning I got up and started to go to the bathroom, and as I got out of bed, I fell. I didn't have any strength in my legs. No warning. No headache, no nausea, no fever, no nothing. Just get out of bed, and all of a sudden, you collapse on the floor, you can't move. That is not a pleasant feeling . . . not a pleasant feeling.''

As she relates her ordeal, she frequently shifts to second or third person, detachment and Irish humor masking emotion. She is a participant-observer. (''I've always been one of those. Somewhere up in a corner, over the left shoulder or the right.'') Alternately professor and stand-up comic, she at one moment cites psychological studies; the next, makes faces, imitates voices, gesticulates, delights in her own jokes. She is onstage.

''I had been reading, naturally, and I says, 'I think this is polio.' The doctor says, 'Well, it might be, but it might not be, and don't think about it.' Doctors never tell you anything.''

''So,'' I remark, ''you were the first to diagnose your case?''

''Naturally! What else could it be? That was the beginning of the great polio epidemic that summer. They were trying to make iron lungs as fast as they could. So many people had to be in isolation wards that after three

weeks, if you had any place to go, they kicked you out of the hospital.''
She whispers. ''Because they needed your room for somebody else. It was
that bad. It was really awful.''

So Margaret came home. Her nurse thought of the idea Sister Kenny
later developed, to reduce the pain by laying on steaming hot blankets.
''A-a-ahh! I'll never know whether it helped or not, but everybody did
what they could. There was no real cure. Once y'got it, y'got it.''

In September, when her friends were starting high school, she went
into a rehabilitation hospital, the HDCC, Home for Destitute Crippled
Children. ''The kids used to call it the Home for Damn Confounded
Children.'' A teacher came around once or twice a week to help her keep
up with her schoolwork. ''So, flat on my back, I scribbled away.''

When she got out three months later, she was on crutches. ''I could
raise one foot over a pencil. That was as far as I could move. My folks
asked me whether I wanted to go to Spalding School for crippled kids,
which meant a long bus ride to Chicago and probably not a very challenging curriculum. . . . ''

''Crippled kids'' sounds jarring today, but Margaret shuns euphemism. ''I don't care what y'call me, I still can't walk without my
brace and crutch.'' She laughs. ''I think the airlines had a good idea.
They call people by whether they have a seeing problem, hearing
problem, or walking problem.''

Despite her ''walking problem,'' Margaret's decision was to rejoin her
former classmates at Lyons Township High School, a three-story structure with four thousand students and no special services. The school did
try to arrange her schedule to minimize stairs, until her senior year, when
she took college-level courses given on the third floor. She hiked up and
down, dragging her books behind her.

The story is told with verve, almost gaiety. Finally I ask: Didn't she
have moments of depression or despair?

''Months! What do you mean, moments? Months! If you don't feel
rotten, you are emotionally disturbed. First of all, they don't know
whether you're going to *live* or not, until they see whether you can
breathe and whether it's going to spread.'' She mimics, '' 'Oh, Mrs.
Merrick and Dr. Merrick, your little girl may never walk again. On the
other hand, she might. We don't know.' That's the prognosis.

''Now for the kid inside the body, that is not a very happy thought. It
would be one thing if, let's say, I had been Elizabeth Barrett Browning,
who was very happy to lie on a cushion and be waited on and not go
anywhere. But not me! I was always very proud that anything I wanted to

try, physically, I could do. I didn't have a bicycle—we were too poor to afford one. I used to see people on skis, and I'd think, *Oh boy, that'd be fun.* There were a lot of things that now—glunk!—I wouldn't be able to do." She repeats softly, "Wouldn't be able to do."

At dancing school, she had been "a very popular partner. But when you can't move very well, you can't dance. You can't even walk fast. You can't climb trees. On the ice, you gotta creep. A little paper clip on the floor is a disaster to somebody on crutches.

"When you're thirteen, you're making up your mind about who you are in life. You have one set of views about yourself, and then all of a sudden, circumstance intervenes, and that view . . . doesn't work anymore."

In the rehabilitation hospital, she was so depressed that she refused to eat for days, giving in under the threat of the intravenous needle. She could have no visitors of her age; the memory of that loneliness still rankles. Only her mother could come every day.

White-haired Dorothy Merrick sits on a faded couch in her faded living room full of timeworn furnishings and books. She cranks up a big, old-fashioned music box; its pensive melody underscores her reminiscence. Affected by a slight stroke, she speaks slowly, but her memory is clear. Her solid strength mirrors Margaret's.

"Once we were on a radio program, and somebody asked to what I attributed her success. I said, 'Family and her faith in God.' We tried not to cater or treat her specially; it was just a matter of fact. We forced her to go out." Despite the tight family budget, "her brothers made her go to shows with them, which they loved to do, because then they got to go.

"A few years ago, one of my friends told me, 'Dorothy, I used to think you were just awful with Margaret, making her do things and go places. Now I realize that was the best thing in the world.' "

One night, when Dorothy reached menopause, she started crying at the dinner table for no apparent reason. "Mother," said Margaret, "all the time I had polio, I've never seen you cry."

Dorothy pauses, remembering, "I did it at night. After she was in bed, I would get in the car and drive and cry by myself for hours."

At school, Margaret found herself unable to re-establish her friendships. "Your friends are used to you one way," she explains. "It's like an adult when somebody dies. What d'ya say? What d'ya do? My eighth grade friends were the popular kids. They went out on dates, they were in sports, they were the cheerleader types. I couldn't dance, couldn't cheerlead, couldn't go out for any sports. The Margaret that had been was the Margaret that was no longer.

"Luckily there was a group of girls who had other values. They were nice to be with. We could talk about things. They didn't date, they weren't popular. All of them are now successfully practicing adults, and some of the eighth grade friends have made spectacularly unsuccessful marriages."

At the end of her freshman year, out of the blue, came a call inviting her to try out for Quiz Kids. "They were hard up for girls," she explains. "Nobody was bringing any forward."

One of the Quiz Kids staffers involved in the girlpower search was Joan Brown, who had been a counselor at a camp Margaret attended at nine. ("That was BP—Before Polio. *Years* before!") Unaware of Margaret's physical impairment, Joan remembered her as "The Demon Reader."

"That wasn't really my nickname," Margaret chuckles. "I think it was Miggy the Piggy, 'cause I wasn't very neat. I have marvelous memories of that camp. . . . Asphalt roads—when you went barefoot, you'd sink down and leave your prints. It was warm and sticky. You couldn't get lunch unless you had a postcard written to your folks. They collected 'em, too, the rats!

"There was a teeny-weeny library in a tent, and it had some things like *The Bobbsey Twins* and perhaps some that were a little more intellectually stimulating, but not much. I read every one of those books three or four times under the covers at night with a flashlight."

So, five years later, Joan Brown called the camp director to track down a child she remembered only by her first name. The director came up with Merrick, and Joan checked all the suburban directories until she found it. "That's how desperate they were," Margaret chuckles.

"I'd never listened to the show. I thought, *God, if there's anything I don't need right now, it is to be on a radio show that says, 'This is a smart kid.' I'm not a kid, I'm four-teen. Practically over-mature!* But I thought, *What's to lose?* Filled out the dumb form, went down and auditioned.

"Goodness! Talk about pushy parents! The families were either trying to calm the kids down or get 'em bucked up or have them recite things like the list of Presidents. Even then, I could see the difference between a family that says, 'Well, if it's going to be fun, go ahead and do it,' and a family that says, 'Now remember—even if you fail, we will still *love* you!' Ugh!''

Margaret found the audition and the show itself "a piece of cake." She did no special preparation. ("How could I? I was reading all the time anyway.") As "all-purpose utility infielder," she played the field. Math problems were her greatest challenge. "Those math whizzes would always—just like my husband, he's like an abacus—figure them out ahead of me. And they were always right. They really knew." Once she beat Joel and Richard to a solution; it was one of her proud moments, her mother recollects.

Margaret recalls a not-so-proud moment. "We were asked to think of ordinary expressions that had strategic metals in them. And I thought of 'lead in the pants.' Joe Kelly about blushed over, and I could see that the staff was going cross-eyed. Then I thought of another one—thank goodness, I've repressed it now—but I didn't say it. Because it was a family show. Some of the things I could think of might have been funny, they might have counted as a point, but I didn't say them because they weren't nice.''

To Margaret, "the Quiz Kids show people were like a family of cousins you go to visit on Sunday. I remember the staff flying around, getting everything ready, being nervous, nervous, nervous. I had put on shows at school, so I knew what live shows are. Something's gonna fluff. You never knew whether guest artists were going to cancel out—travel was so difficult in those days. If people didn't have a car, or didn't have gas rations, or couldn't get a cab, or the train wasn't running, it was tough.

"I thought Joe Kelly was wonderful. He was a genuine person. I have met a lot of phonies in my life—I had met a lot of phonies by the time I was fourteen. And he was not a phony." She chuckles about how Kelly "neatly didn't see the hand waving down at the end when he could tell it was going to be another wild guess.''

In contrast to her fondness for her Quiz Kids associates, meeting the famous did not impress her. Vice-President Henry Wallace? "A preoccupied man. Later I found out why. He was thinking of running for President, undercutting Mr. Roosevelt." Senator Scott Lucas? "A pontificating windbag—never a heavyweight in the thinking category.''

She thought more kindly of Mamie Eisenhower, whom the Quiz Kids visited in her apartment at the Wardman Park Hotel, where Margaret suffered her fall. "A nice lady. She had cookies for us, and she showed us things the general had sent—a hassock of Moroccan leather—not because he was *the general,* but because he was over there and could send things back. She showed us pictures of her son. She treated us like visiting people, not radio celebrities. She found out what we were interested in and listened.''

Margaret denies fitting in the ''famous category'' herself, even though she received letters from all over the country. As a Quiz Kid, she came in for some razzing. She softpedaled her intellectual ability and still does. She has no use for showoffs, and she takes care not to be one.

''I still bump into people who say, 'Margaret, somebody told me you were a . . . whiz kid?' Or they say, '*I* remember the Quiz Kids show. My folks used to sit us all down around the table, and every time a question came up, they would look at us and say, "Canyouanswerthat?" And then one of you smart-alecks would answer it. And I always thought to myself, *I wish this program had never been thought up, and if I ever meet 'em, I won't like 'em,* but I like you—I can't figure it out!' ''

She laughs. ''I don't usually publicize it, any more than I publicize anything else I've ever done, because I'm not a 'here I am' sort of person. Also, I've learned through the years that it's considered one-upmanship.''

Her being a Quiz Kid meant very little, she claims, to her schoolmates. ''So you can sit and answer questions. Big deal! Everybody does that all day long in school.'' She grins. ''It didn't reflect discredit on the school by any means, but it wasn't like winning the football championship.''

Although she excelled academically (in eighth grade, her reading level had gone off the chart at twelfth-grade-plus), she insists that others did equally well. ''There was always somebody who was better in math or better in English or this or that. I never thought of striving to be out ahead of everyone else. I was not one of those child prodigies who read the encyclopedia at eighteen months.'' Having skipped a year made her feel, if anything, behind rather than ahead of her peers. From second grade on, she had struggled with handwriting, and her classmates were wiser about games and non-book knowledge.

Busy at the animal hospital, Dorothy Merrick paid no special attention to her daughter's mental ability, just as she refused to coddle the physical disability. ''I didn't have a laid-out plan to go by,'' Dorothy says. ''I let her go her own way.'' Her father, too, was occupied with making a go of the hospital, working seven days a week and operating at night.

Her brothers showed no jealousy, although one, John Merrick (now a veterinarian) recently confessed to Margaret that he had tried out for the show and never told her about it. The boys, according to their mother, ''had as much potential, but they could do other things, while she would sit and read.''

"My world and my family's did not revolve around Quiz Kids,"
Margaret explains. "That was a once-a-week thing. We made it a family
outing—our only family activity of the week. My folks took us to Alle-
gretti's Restaurant. Oh, I loved that place. My sister, too—she was about
four. Boy, she liked that spumoni ice cream!"

Margaret remembers one time when photographers came to the house
and wanted her sister to get in bed in the middle of the afternoon, so
Margaret could pose as telling her a bedtime story. "*No way* did she
want to fall for that! We had to sweet-talk her every way we could to
convince her that she was going to be able to get up."

The publicity had no effect on her family life, Margaret maintains.
"Remember the circumstances of the selection. *They* came to *me*. The
family who might have seen a bright child as a li'l star which could reflect
well on them didn't exist in my case."

The bonds were part of her motivation for continuing; in her family's
circumstances, $4,500 "could mean the difference between being able to
do some things and not." (Eventually she used part of the money for a
down payment on a house.) This was a girl who had drawn her own paper
dolls . . . who still remembers finding a dime in a crack. ("It bought two
loaves of bread.") With her Depression-bred "Waste-not-want-not"
mentality, she was "absolutely awestruck" when the Quiz Kids visited a
mansion that had white carpets.

Much as she enjoyed being a Quiz Kid, Margaret insists the experience
had no impact on her later life. "We would reminisce about that as much
as anything else. No more than." Her scrapbook and the charm bracelet
she received as a graduation memento gathered dust in the Western
Springs house until her mother sent them to her a few years ago. She has
told her children very little; the subject has not come up, and "it
wouldn't mean anything to them."

I press her. As an educator, wouldn't she expect such an unusual
experience to affect a youngster's development?

"Think about the age at which it happened. At fourteen, I knew that
even if I stayed on every week, it would be over in x-number of months.
But now think about somebody who was five years old and was on the
show for six years. Whew! You're talking about their whole childhood. I was
fourteen chronologically," she adds. "I was thirty-four in life's pressure cooker. Polio! That was a big sink-or-swim happening."

In her mother's view, though, "Quiz Kids was a wonderful thing for
Margaret because she missed out on so much in high school. She may not
realize it, but it couldn't help but give her a lift."

To Margaret, the wartime climate put the program in perspective. In 1942, the year she became a Quiz Kid, senior boys at her high school were going off to war. "The thing I remember most is something that was very, very deep in my feeling at the time, and that was when we appeared at the Bethesda naval hospital. Meeting Mrs. Eisenhower was nice, so what? When we saw these people that had been out fighting the *war,* I said to myself, *Here I am, a kid. I haven't done very much at all, compared to what these people have been doing.* Any effort we could put out to encourage people to buy bonds, support the war effort, visit a hospital, do something for a veteran—Don't gripe about rationing, think about what *these* guys have been through."

Once she tried to help by knitting scarves for soldiers. But her stitches were so uneven that she had to unravel the yarn and give it back. "So it was really a patriotic pleasure to be able to do something [as a Quiz Kid] that I could see some *results* on."

Patriotism has shaped Margaret's life. The Quaker's daughter married a military man, a World War II bombardier veteran and reserve officer she met at Ohio State. For the next two decades, she followed Ed Scheffelin from post to post. They have lived in some twenty-five towns and owned twelve homes before their present ranch house in Carmichael, California, near Sacramento.

Since they settled in the Golden State in 1968, Margaret has been the chief breadwinner. "Scheff" developed high blood pressure and a heart condition from too much high altitude flying. He takes care of the house and the acre of grounds. Role reversal? "I don't like terms like that," Margaret bristles. "My husband says everything the Scheffelins do, other people latch onto."

In the early years, she leaned on him financially and emotionally. "He deserves a great deal of credit for what I can do today." Although concerned with feminist issues ("I have always found more discrimination because I was a woman than because I walked around with crutches"), her number one precept is "Marry the right man."

Conscious of her handicap, Margaret knew that Mr. Right had to be "somebody who understood people for themselves, somebody with extremely strong character, somebody who was not a kid, somebody who was kind. I had figured out what I wanted, and when I saw him, I said, 'This is it!' "

Narrowing her career choice was not so easy.

As a child, she had wanted to do everything she ever saw anybody else do. One day she hankered to be a physical education teacher, the next day a chemist, the next day, to race motor cars. "At that time, there were not many careers open to women. But my mother and father never said, 'There are some things you won't be able to do because you're a girl.' I had never been artificially limited. Well, polio is not an artificial limitation."

When high school guidance counselors "shook their collective heads," her mother took her to a vocational clinic. The recommendation was architecture. "That sounds good," said Margaret. Despite Ohio State's reluctance to admit a woman in the engineering school, she enrolled there in September, 1945.

"Colleges and universities were bursting with returning war veterans. In the dean's welcoming address, he looks out over this tremendous expanse—four hundred of us, six women—and says, 'All right, men! Take a look at the man on your left! Take a look at the man on your right! Then take a look at yourself, men! Because one of you is not going to be here next year.' "

She laughs. "No mention at all of its being a mixed group. Now, to show you what things have come to—From time to time, I get a bulletin from Ohio State, and they are very proud that now about 30 percent of their entering class are women."

Disenchanted with her architecture professors' penchant for discouraging originality, she switched to foreign languages. (She is proficient in four.) An honor student and class officer, she dropped out at nineteen to marry. "In those days," she explains, "if a couple was getting married, usually the man had a job, the wife stayed home, kept house, started a family." Although she still intended an eventual career, she was tired of school and needed a break. "I had never been on my own. I went from home to a dorm. I knew nothing of survival skills."

Scheff, too, dropped out temporarily when he was recalled to active duty. In 1950, they were living in a trailer in Albuquerque when Margaret brought their two baby daughters for a guest Quiz Kids shot while visiting her parents.

She became an intermittent student, taking her education in small doses whenever her peripatetic life and parental obligations permitted. She wanted a large family ("I like kids") and decided to become a teacher. With limited financial resources and apparently unlimited energy, she reviewed textbooks while nursing babies at two o'clock in the morning, proficiencied out of as many courses as possible, and arranged her schedule around her husband's and neighbors' babysitting availability.

Polio had turned her into a planner. ("If it's going to take me ten minutes to get upstairs and ten minutes to get down, and I have only twelve minutes, there's no way I'm going to do it.") She didn't always know what she was planning for, but followed each path until it led to the next, making use of whatever chances came her way.

By 1952, she had accumulated three preschoolers and a bachelor's degree from the University of Albuquerque and had begun teaching night school English and math. Five years and two children later, with number six on the way, she was working toward a master's in special education at the University of Illinois, where Scheff was assigned to the Reserve Officers Training Corps.

Her career choice was pragmatic. "Teaching was a trade I could take from place to place, something I could do with two crutches and six children." She did not count on her husband for perpetual security, realizing she might someday have to take care of him. While rearing her children, she built credentials and a work record so she could support them if necessary.

And teaching came naturally. She had guided youngsters all her life: first her siblings, then her own. Polio and motherhood had instilled patience, and travel had acquainted her with diverse people and places.

Her concentration on special education came about by coincidence. At Illinois, she needed money to pay a babysitter so she could take a required course. A professor told her a $400 scholarship was available for taking another course, on mental retardation. The more she read in the field, the more fascinated she became. Here was a place where competent teachers were really needed.

Degree in hand, Margaret began working full-time. She supervised English instruction for foreign service personnel in Lackland, Texas, then ran special education programs for bilingual children in San Antonio.

Back at the University of Illinois in the mid-'60s, she won a fellowship and got her doctorate in special education and psychology. In the midst of her studies, she gave birth to her eighth child, an Rh baby. Transfusions saved him from being irretrievably retarded.

She took an appointment as assistant professor at California State University before shifting to consulting work. The evaluation program she now heads for the state is, she says, unique in the nation; teachers themselves assess what goes on in their special education classrooms, rather than relying on outside experts. Pupil placements are reviewed periodically to make sure programs match individual needs, ''rather than having a child stacked like a book in the archives.''

Margaret's values are rooted in the forties: work, family, country. Although more financially comfortable than ever before, she and Scheff live simply. She tries ''to leave things a little better and happier than I found them.''

As in her childhood home, the children have helped raise each other. ''My husband and I have always believed that everybody should pull his own weight in the world. Each person had jobs to do and did them.'' Careful organization was the key to shepherding their outsize flock through what could have been a bewildering succession of moves. ''I don't think stability is geographical,'' says Margaret, who herself was uprooted at an early age.

She has no patience for might-have-beens. She deals with what is. ''People have a certain number of hours in the day. I fritter away very little time in useless complaining, and I don't like it when anybody does. It serves no useful purpose. With the children, my husband and I haven't had the kinds of social lives some people have had. We haven't gone on long vacations. We have very little in the way of physical monuments to show. We put our time and energy into the family.''

Under the ''Scheffelin bill,'' each child was guaranteed four years at any state-supported college. Besides the daughter living in Germany and three in the armed forces, a fifth girl is a landscaper. Two sons are in engineering. The youngest boy, still in high school, is doing well (like his dad) in the stock market.

''We have always told the children this is their life. Each one is different.'' Her child-raising philosophy? ''Every child is 'special.' Understand the particular job *this* child has to do in growing up and making a place in the world. Help with that job. Don't *do* that job!'' Parents, too, are individuals, she adds: ''Look after yourself. No one else has that job.''

How would she rate herself as a mother? ''You'd have to ask the kids. I'd say I've been good enough.'' With only one son left at home, she is suffering from ''withdrawal symptoms.''

She still is a great reader, as are her brood. (''I have probably given away eight thousand books through the years.'') She was kicked out of a speedreading course because she already could read 1,800 words per minute. (''But that's not real reading.'') She even can read upside down, a trick she picked up in deciphering the folded bottom end of her father's morning *Tribune* at the breakfast table.

She is not so fond of television, though she stayed up for the Watergate reruns. She preferred old-time radio shows like "Inner Sanctum," that "let you use your imagination" to most of the current TV fare.

With Margaret, ideas are the life of the party. Her interests are eclectic; she resists ruts. "I'm still alive, so I haven't fulfilled my goals. I want to see the year 2001." Her latest aim, crystallized by her Fulbright stint, is to educate Americans about the revolutionary advance represented by the European Economic Community. She has written newspaper articles praising the West German system of free postsecondary education and urging businesses to form disabled employees advisory committees. She is active in a Harry S. Truman Club to recruit able political candidates and is toying with a shot at elective office. Recently, she has been appointed to the Defense Department's advisory committee on women in the services.

As a woman, she is realistic about the progress she has seen and what remains undone. "We won't reach the millenium until all-male preserves like the Bohemian Club are closed down. And when the attitudes that come with setting up that kind of business-social club are gone, I hope women don't turn around and do it back."

It is ten minutes to her departure. She lets me help put her bags on her shoulders but insists on taking the steep flight of stairs from the lounge to the gate on her own.

Three days later, I see Margaret again on her way back to California. She has stayed overnight at her mother's home, and I drive her to the airport. She hobbles up the embarkation ramp, clutching a small heirloom rocker her mother has given her for a grandchild. She refuses assistance; if anything should happen to the rocker, she will be responsible.

I comment on her agility. She shrugs.

"On dry land, without paper clips to slip on, I do pretty well."

Richard Williams: All-American Boy

December 26, 1941

Dear Mr. and Mrs. Williams:
I have heard Richard on the Quiz Kids program ever since he first appeared on it, and I don't think anybody else can touch him by miles. I don't know how you have done it or how he does it, but I am convinced that . . . you have produced the most wonderful boy in the world. If I had to cast a ballot for the American parents who have done the best job in this generation, you would get my vote hands down. All the Quiz Kids are good, but . . . Richard is in a class by himself. . . . I'd give everything I have to be the father of a son like Richard.
      —Anonymous fan

"Richard was first, Harve second, and Joel and Ruthie tied for third . . . "

That was how the score generally went in the Quiz Kids' wartime heyday. The supporting players might vary, but Richard Williams' name almost invariably led the rest.

He was the "super Quiz Kid," the one many of his colleagues acknowledged to be smartest of all. At the time of his December, 1945 graduation, he had been on the program a record 212 times in five years and probably had been on more trips than any other Kid. Six years later, Joel Kupperman and Lonny Lunde, then among the top regulars, named him Quiz Kid of All Time.

Yet on his first broadcast, two months after the show began, ten-year-old Richard answered no questions at all. He was too bashful to raise his hand more than a couple of inches, and Joe Kelly never noticed it. Given a second chance, Dick overcame his timidity and made the winners' circle for thirty-eight consecutive weeks.

The show's first mathematical wizard, he did instantly, in his head, calculations many people wouldn't tackle with pencil and paper. At a children's hospital in Buffalo, he mentally totaled a barrage of numbers the young patients threw at him, while the superintendent, set up as a foil, stood by making helpless scratches on a note pad.

As often is the case, his mathematical gift was accompanied by a musical one. Richard had perfect pitch; he made the highest score in his home state of Indiana on the Seashore musical aptitude test. When the Quiz Kids staff learned he could play the piano, they devised a stunt that he performed the first time in a movie short. He would play "Tea for Two" or the opening bars of the *Moonlight* Sonata ("pieces I knew so well I could do them blind," he says) while working algebra problems like this one:

> *Joe Kelly:* Suppose you have a pair of balances that are out of balance. You weigh an object on one side and it weighs ten pounds. You weigh it on the other side and it weighs 40 pounds. What is the true weight? . . . . Richard?
>
> *Richard:* Twenty pounds. The error on one side would be inversely proportional to the error on the other. The relationship of the false light weight to the true weight would be the same as the relationship of the true weight to the false heavy weight. Let x equal the true weight, and you have the algebraic equation, 10 is to x as x is to 40. So x equals 20.

On a personal appearance in Gary, Indiana, near his home town of East Chicago, eleven-year-old Richard was confronted with a huge blackboard containing 64 horizontal and vertical columns of numbers, in geometric progression from 1 to a 19-digit figure. The question: "Suppose each digit represents a grain of corn placed on an enormous checkerboard. How many grains of corn are there?" In two minutes and ten seconds, he came up with the solution: 18,446,744,073,709,551,615.

Richard was "not just a human adding machine," as C.J. Bulliet of the *Chicago Daily News* observed. Always alert, when asked to estimate how many vessels would be repaired at a California shipyard between Pearl Harbor day and December 7, 1944, at the rate of one every sixteen hours, Dick remembered to adjust for the fact that 1944, a leap year, would have an extra day. Soldiers sent him their artillery problems to work out, and breadwinners wrote seeking help with their income tax. (He himself in 1941 paid $385 in taxes on his $3,900 Quiz Kids take; at the time, he was getting a 36-cent allowance, of which 10 cents went into the Sunday School collection.)

In sixth grade, he was studying analytic geometry with a tutor, alongside his fifteen-year-old brother Glenn; two years later they were into calculus. ("Glenn would have been brighter than I as a Quiz Kid, but he was too old,'' Dick later told Sally MacDougall of the *Chicago Herald-American*.)

What made Richard Williams special was not just his astounding facility with figures but his span of general knowledge. As Larry Wolters of the *Chicago Tribune* wrote near the end of the show's run, Dick was ''regarded by many as the best all around kid the Quiz Kids ever turned up.''

He was particularly sharp on geography and current events. He could locate most cities, mountains, and rivers, and could name the boundaries of virtually every country. (Once, when his parents gave him an atlas, he found that two tiny nations had been omitted and returned it to Rand McNally, which admitted the error and sent him a replacement.) He and his brother followed the daily battle reports and recorded the changes on large *National Geographic* maps posted on their bedroom walls. As the Nazis overran a country, the two boys would dash to the stationery store to buy a packet of the vanquished nation's stamps. (''Speak of being unmoved by the plight of Europe!'' Dick laughs.) Near the war's end, fourteen-year-old Richard wrote for *Quiz Kids Magazine* a series on ''Our United Nations,'' couched in mature phraseology and vigorous style.

Quiet . . . self-effacing . . . modest . . . unassuming . . . unspoiled . . . such words jump out again and again from contemporaneous descriptions of Richard Williams. Fellow-Quiz Kids remember him as elegant, kind, serious, warm. Fair of face, with an even voice and disposition to match, he answered the most difficult questions with an air of effortless grace. He was the soul of Protestant probity, the favorite of clergymen and retired schoolmarms. On the annual Christmas program, he would deliver an original prayer with gravity and a touch of a quaver.

''Richard will be a great man,'' said his Congregationalist minister, ''because already he is a great boy.'' No prissy paragon, Dick liked sports shirts and Laurel and Hardy, and disliked getting up in the morning. Quiz Kid Harve Bennett Fischman, his best pal on the show, referred to him as ''Lamby-Pie'' because of the huge quantities of meat and potatoes he put away. The two boys, near the same age, occupied adjacent rooms on trips, played chess on the train, and pulled pranks.

Dick's smile was broad, and his eyes (as *Quiz Kids Dictionary* observed) seemed ''to have a permanent sparkle, as though he were always enjoying some private joke.'' Margaret Merrick Scheffelin recalls, ''His face would never crack up; he never gave away a punch line.'' (When told that Fred Allen's wife Portland had been born in the city of that name, Dick quipped, "It's a good thing she wasn't born in Schenectady!")

He was, as Ed Simmons of the Wade Advertising Agency said, "a born nice kid." Colleagues were deeply impressed with his unobtrusive courtesy to Margaret: he always would get a chair for her and help with her crutches.

Even at twelve, he had a plentiful supply of aplomb, as Harold Hadley of the *Philadelphia Bulletin* remarked. Asked to compare Portland's feminine population with Seattle's, tactful Dick responded that he had seen pretty girls in both cities. When ten-year-old Carol Peterson interviewed him for her radio column in *Everywoman's Magazine,* she asked what kind of people he liked best. "I thought he would say somebody like Einstein," she wrote, "but instead he looked at my carrot top and replied 'Redheads!' So you see, he figures out other things besides arithmetic problems."

As he passed to the older end of the Quiz Kid spectrum, he became the group's elder statesman. For most of us, the rule was "All's fair . . ." Not for Dick. Taking candy from babies was not his style. When wee Joel Kupperman began invading his mathematical domain, Dick became unhappy enough so that his mother complained her son wasn't getting a fair shake. But he magnanimously deferred to Joel on the easier problems that obviously were meant for the younger lad. On one such occasion, when Joe Kelly called on Richard first, he said, "Joel is smaller than I am, so why don't you let *him* answer it?" The studio audience applauded the gesture. Joel, however, had misheard the problem. Dick, instead of coming out with the right answer, told the little boy where he had gone wrong and let him refigure it.

Joel, in turn, revered the senior mathematician. Once, after Dick had gone through a particularly intricate solution, guest quizmaster Eddie Cantor responded, "Are you kidding, Richard?" Joel instantly piped up: "He wouldn't kid you. Richard's right. He's always right!"

I, too, was a beneficiary of Dick's gallantry.

> Richard won heavy applause when he credited Ruthie with having given the correct answer, although Kelly did not hear her and was about to award Richard the points for it.
> —*Boston Globe,* February 21, 1944

Once, in the Quiz Kids office, Dick happened to pick up a book called *Peculiarities of the Presidents,* which, he found, contained many of the historical tidbits Harve was noted for knowing. Dick bought a copy but never intruded upon his friend's bailiwick.

Richard Williams was, in sum, a born diplomat. And that is exactly what he became.

I have caught him between assignments on a muggy August day in Chicago. Back from two years in Canton as chief of the first United States consulate on Chinese soil in three decades, the fifty-one-year-old career political officer is about to move up to second-in-command of the ten-times-larger Hong Kong consulate.

Dick Williams, as he prefers to be called, is (as Joan Bishop affectionately describes him) "a little man with a big head"; but he remains anything but bigheaded. In faded green tropical fatigues, with umbrella dangling and arms held stiff at his sides, he resembles an Alec Guinness character. His features, despite a receding grey hairline and gold-rimmed bifocals, are startlingly unchanged. The old boyish amusement dances in the blue eyes. He laughs a lot, usually at himself. At lunch, he takes a second roll: "One of the gummy ones, please. I've been pigging out since I've been back."

His speech is cultivated, but leavened with an occasional "Bullshit!" He talks with what he confesses is "boring slowness". . . an almost compulsive effort to find precisely the right answer. Throughout our day-long conversation, he analyzes the course of his life with the relentless thoroughness with which one can imagine him approaching an intelligence dispatch.

"My first interest in the foreign service came from another Quiz Kid, Jack Lucal, who was considering going into the State Department. That was the first time I ever heard of the foreign service, and from the time he mentioned it, it always stuck in my mind as an interesting thing to do . . ."

Dick Williams' name originally was sent to the Quiz Kids office by a teacher in the East Chicago schools. He received the questionnaire just as he and his family were about to leave for a Canadian fishing trip, filled out the form in a last-minute rush, and mailed it from Tomah, Wisconsin, where they stopped for lunch. The hurriedly-completed application gave little indication of what distinction he would attain; in fact, it was so sketchy that Roby Hickok later said "sheer mental magic" had made Joe Bailey, the Cowan office manager, pull it out of the pile.

On that fateful day when Dick's missive was wending its way south-ward while he and his family sped in the opposite direction, the four of them occupied themselves by playing quiz games, a pastime they fre-quently enjoyed. His mother would read off the questions from a quiz book, and everybody would put down answers and compare scores. Dick, being the youngest, usually came in last.

"I suppose intellectually we were very competitive," he muses, "but not in the keeping-up-with-the-Joneses ways."

Today his mother, Clara Petersen Williams, widowed since 1959, still lives in the simple stucco bungalow where she raised her boys. Sitting in her sunny living room amid Oriental art objects brought back from visits to her younger son's diplomatic posts, eighty-year-old Clara has a vista of the corner where he played long ago with the neighborhood pack. She chuckles as she recalls the time a friend brought over some out-of-town guests and pointed Dick out among the boys playing ball. "They couldn't get over it—they thought he'd be in with a book."

Dick Williams' clan were East Chicago people. Clara was born there, and her husband David—a kindly man, as reserved as his wife is plain-spoken—grew up in the community. Dick's grandfathers, Welsh and Danish-German immigrants, labored in steel and chemical plants. None of his grandparents went beyond eighth grade . . . "but that doesn't mean they weren't brilliant people," Clara adds. (One of her cousins, Howard Petersen, drafted the Selective Service Act of 1940, served as assistant secretary of war, and became head of a Philadelphia bank.)

Dave Williams, a civil engineer, was a partner in a family firm, Williams Brothers and Miller, which manufactured oil and gas burners. Clara, before marriage, had been private secretary to the chief engineer at Inland Steel. She did church and charity work, played pinochle with her boys (the loser having to do the dishes), heard their prayers at night, and made them do chores like lawnmowing, weeding, and cleaning the basement. After Dick's Quiz Kids graduation, she was named Ideal State Mother of 1946.

In that blue collar Hoosier mill town of sixty thousand, where a big night would be going to Hot Dog John's after a movie, a boy as pre-cocious as Richard Williams was bound to stand out. When he was five, the local newspaper ran a headline, "Dick Williams Is Headed for the White House." (He eventually got there on special assignment—answering President Lyndon Johnson's mail.)

After he became a Quiz Kid, East Chicago declared a Richard Williams Day. Broadcasting from his school, the Kids competed against a panel of local dignitaries, including the principal and Dick's uncle, all decked out in caps and gowns. When Dick graduated from the show at Christmas, 1945, the program was beamed from his own living room, complete with tree and carols. His gift was an unabridged dictionary, which he still has.

Dick regarded his acclaim as no big thing. "My parents were bright people, my brother was a bright person, and they treated it as though they were not impressed by it."

Nor had his easygoing parents worried when he did not speak until two and a half. Baby Dickie kept his counsel, taking everything in, then suddenly burst forth with a full-blown vocabulary. A year later he was reading: first picking out words he recognized from his building blocks, then breezing through a primer his dad brought home. The tyke began poring over his eight-year-old brother's school books, studying the maps in Glenn's geography text, and perusing *Time* magazine. In nursery school, he would read fairy tales to the other children.

"My grandfather," Dick remembers, "would take me around to see his old cronies, and they would perch me up and get me to read to them." His first arithmetic lessons were his grandpa's showing him how to keep score in rummy games and add up restaurant checks.

When the boy was about seven, his father taught him some basic algebra. "Dad would be shaving in the bathroom, and I would go in there and sit on the toilet seat with a piece of paper and a pencil, and he would say, 'x plus $2y$ equals 9, $3x$ minus y equals 7.'" On family trips, following his brother's lead, Dick would keep elaborate ledgers of mileage, number of telephone poles passed, and other such vital statistics. Upon returning home from one summer vacation, he reported having caught 231 inches of fish.

Dave and Clara Williams, unsure of how to handle their boy wonder, took him three times to the University of Chicago Laboratory School for testing. At four and a half, he showed a mental age of nearly eight and an I.Q. of 165, which four years later had jumped to almost 200—the highest score the university psychologist ever had encountered.

Dick still can picture one of the questions on the first test. "There was a circle with an opening, and they said, 'This is a ball park, and you've lost your ball. Trace a path to show how you would go about finding it.' I drew a spiral all the way to the center. The only question I did badly on—they showed me a series of pictures of women, and asked me to pick out the pretty one, and every time, I picked out the ugly one. My father said that was because I was used to my mother!"

The psychologist advised regular kindergarten placement plus special enrichment. The East Chicago schools did their best to cooperate, allowing Dick to take typing, French, and piano while his companions struggled with reading, spelling, and arithmetic. Later his parents hit on the idea of math tutoring for both their sons.

By the time Dick was in third grade, the schoolwork was so obviously too easy that his mother took him back to the University of Chicago for more tests. The Lab School offered him a scholarship, but his parents decided against it because of distance. On the university psychologist's advice, the boy was skipped, to his total surprise.

"My school life was quite different before that time and after," he recalls. "I remember being very popular in the first years of school." When the class chairman was elected, the nominees would be sent into the cloakroom so they could not see who was voting for whom. When Dick's name was called, he could hear the chairs and feet shuffling as practically everyone in the class stood up to vote for him. "I think they admired a bright child at that age, and also I was very secure with that group. But that changed as soon as I was double-promoted."

Sports, in fourth grade, became more important, and while Dick enjoyed playing, he was not particularly athletic. He found himself at a disadvantage with the older boys. After he became a Quiz Kid, in sixth grade, he was away from school on tour half the time.

His mother and teachers thought the Quiz Kid experience helped Dick—who had been so retiring that he blushed when called upon in school—to develop more poise and self-assurance. "The pupils are back of him 100 percent because he never makes them feel he is one bit different from them," one of his teachers wrote in the *Journal of Education.* His publicity recited the litany of adjustment signs: sixth grade patrol boy, eighth grade student council representative, head of the high school debate club, actor in school plays.

But Dick himself, looking back, believes being a Quiz Kid may have intensified his shyness. "I didn't really have a normal school experience. I think we were kind of freaks, at least in the school I was in. Maybe if I had been somebody like Harve, a more forceful and outgoing person— But for an already shy kid . . . "

He remembers a high school party at which he overheard a girl telling the hostess, "People say he's an awful snob, but they're wrong, he's very friendly."

"She was talking about me," he says. "I think that says something about the way a shy child can be perceived 'This kid is a super-brain, therefore if he doesn't pay attention to me, it's because he's snobbish.' "

He did have three or four very close friends in the debating society. "Just before I left the Quiz Kids, we made a trip to Hartford, Connecticut, and while there, I got a letter from this debate group—news of what was happening. I can remember being just flooded with delight. I was overcome by the knowledge that this group of people my age had gone to the trouble to write me that letter. I must have had an awful lot of inferiority feelings about being a Quiz Kid, that I didn't expect people would do a normal, human, warm thing like that."

Only in retrospect, however, has he become aware of these feelings. "One of the things that has struck me is how much more reflective my children are than I was as a teenager—than anybody was in those days. Growing up in the thirties and forties, you just sort of accepted the way you lived."

Years later, when Dick was an adult, his mother raised the subject of how he felt about the Quiz Kid experience. "She said to me that she and my father, as they looked back, were concerned about what it had really been like and what the lasting effects had been. And she said then that if they had realized it would become the kind of thing it did, they might have reflected more about whether they should put a child through that. When we started, it just never occurred to them that it would be more than a quite limited and casual experience. And within a few months, the show itself was a considerable hit, and I and they were much more involved than they had ever dreamed.

"My response to my mother's question was offhand and quick and positive, because I didn't want to make her feel bad. I knew that in reality, my own feelings were much more mixed, but I couldn't sort them out and articulate them."

Today, Dick Williams, is, on the whole, glad to have been a Quiz Kid. "It's almost the 'you only go around once' kind of feeling. It was a unique experience with some really quite marvelous things that I'm just very glad to have done. Wonderful Manhattan! How thrilling it was for somebody even from Chicago to go there!"

One lesson Dick learned from his Quiz Kid travels was that "there's nothing magic about being a star." He found Eddie Cantor "obnoxious —a total neurotic. If any of his staff suggested something, he jumped down their throats. He also had no interest in children." Harry Truman did show an interest in the Kids, and so did Fred Allen and Jack Benny, whom Dick found "warm and affectionate." (He has memories of rehearsing for the Benny show at the comedian's lovely Beverly Hills home and of the swimming pool surrounded by orange trees.) But Mary Livingstone "did not radiate warmth," and Benny's daughter Joan (whom Harve later dated in college) seemed, in Dick's eyes, "spoiled beyond belief."

He remembers the artificial Hollywood children's society he observed at Joan Benny's and Jane Withers' birthday parties. "Those were both pretty awful. We came away feeling, *Poor little rich girls.*" The Hollywood moppets "were all brought in cars, and they sat around this table of very expensive things, this catered party, and they were all brats." At the Withers party, Dick smiles, the "countrified" Quiz Kids looked on as the birthday girl and her friends did the conga, the latest dance craze. "We had never been anywhere where things of such sophistication were done."

What had a far more profound effect on Dick than meeting stars was his contact with fellow-Quiz Kids like Jack Lucal. "I think if I had not been a Quiz Kid," says Dick, "very likely I would have ended up doing something like engineering or science. Quiz Kids had a very heavy emphasis during those war years on international events and politics, and most of the regulars were interested in the social sciences."

At the time, both Dick and his brother wanted to be engineers like Dad. (The family's idea of a "hot evening's sport," reported *American Magazine,* was "to sit at the dinner table and figure out the cubic content of the Taj Mahal, and then devise for it a method of low cost heating.") Charles F. Kettering of General Motors and Harvey Firestone, Jr. of Firestone Company showed the two youths through their laboratories and told them to come back when they were ready.

Glenn did become an engineer, and Dick also worked in that field for a few years. But of the two interests he had picked up early in life from his big brother—math and geography—the latter turned out to be the stronger. When Glenn was drafted in 1943, Dick let the calculus lessons languish. "I just wasn't that interested on my own." At the University of Chicago, where he enrolled at sixteen (after finishing high school in three years), he found his one physics course with Edward Teller, father of the hydrogen bomb, "downright boring. Even the grad students didn't know what he was talking about."

The U of C in those postwar days was "a liberation" for a lad who had traveled all over the country but had gone to high school a block from home. (He had turned down a full scholarship to Exeter because it was too far away.) Afterward he would go on to study engineering at Purdue and business administration at Harvard, but Chicago he regards as his alma mater. "The others are schools I went to, but that's the one I was inspired by. It was an opening to a whole world of ideas I had never experienced before.

"As I think about life in East Chicago, Indiana in the 1930s and early forties, it was a very narrow horizon. Quiz Kids certainly widened it, but the basic thing was, everybody was so conscious of religion and national background. I was very, very Protestant. I do not think it was ever a matter of deep conviction. I behaved conventionally—I really did what I was told! My parents were rock-ribbed Republicans. We were for Alf Landon in 1936. My brother said he was twenty years old before he realized it wasn't the same thing to be a Republican as a Congregationalist."

At the U of C, Dick became a New Deal international liberal and remained so until recent years. ("All labels are off these days, aren't they?") And he "fell away from the church . . . not only because I didn't have religious feeling. I also was appalled at the supineness of the Protestant churches over what had happened to the Jews. If on as clear and horrible a moral issue as you'd ever have, they had not stood up and screamed, then they just didn't seem to me worth paying attention to.

"The University of Chicago made me aware of that whole spectrum of things: the Nazis, the plight of the blacks, what the U.S. had done to the Nisei during the Second World War. . . . It was a very ethically charged place to be."

Socially, too, his first college experience was a breaking away from the part of his life East Chicago represented—"all the nineteenth century pieties." His second year, he moved into a fraternity house and began smoking and drinking. "I partied a lot. It was a really joyful time."

And a release from Quiz Kid notoriety. With a common name, it was relatively easy to fade into the crowd. "I didn't tell anyone about it. If someone found out, I was embarrassed—I didn't know how to handle it." Van Dyke Tiers, another brilliant ex-Quiz Kid, was on campus at the time. Dick remembers that they would pass each other without speaking.

Always a top student before, Dick let down a peg at the U of C, throwing himself into fraternity life and becoming vice-president of the Student Union. When he went on to Purdue, an easier school, he was able to pull A's and qualify for engineering, literary, and journalism honoraries while at the same time working his way up to managing editor of the student newspaper—a feat he regarded as a way of proving himself to his fraternity brothers, "those who were different from me, who were not bookish intellectuals."

Richard Williams today is a highly efficient and respected foreign service officer at a grade just below the top. His salary is about $60,000 plus free overseas housing and a generous pension plan.

Though his advancement has been fairly rapid, he sees little likelihood of reaching the highest career level, an undersecretaryship. "I have not risen far enough. There are people who get to my rank as much as five or even ten years earlier. To get to the very top career jobs, probably by my age you would already have been an ambassador to a small country."

Promotion in the State Department, with its old boy network, can depend on connections and luck at least as much as on ability. But one of the reasons Dick Williams has not progressed faster is that his early ambivalence regarding his career choice led him at one point to leave the department for five years.

To follow his father and brother to Purdue's engineering school had been the path of least resistance for a young man still uncertain of what he wanted to do. He had taken his MBA, thinking it would be useful in either the family business or the State Department. When he finally entered the foreign service in 1956, one of the top two in a class of eighteen, he was "stuck" in the budget office of the State Department, compiling requests for allocations. "That was my reward for having done a master's in business at Harvard."

Three years later, he was a lowly vice-consul in Hong Kong. When his parents and brother, on a world tour, stopped off to see him, Dick was becoming discouraged. "I think the fact that I was shy and unassertive is part of the reason I did not advance more rapidly," he explains. "I don't have that problem now. I've made speeches and hosted people. . . . It's like becoming a Quiz Kid—after you did it awhile, it was no strain."

In his early State Department years, his efficiency reports labelled him as "quiet." Now he has learned that "people have got to be forceful in seeking good jobs, and not just trust the system to find you the best thing."

The "restrained assertiveness" he perceives to be optimal for State Department success is, of course, what he projected as a Quiz Kid. "But there the path was laid out for you. It was made clear in what way you had to be assertive. You were not left to find it out for yourself. I think that, as a result of the set of mind induced by Quiz Kids, when, afterward, you did not get automatic recognition for work well done, the disappointment was great and not, in my case, really acknowledged at the time. I had a moderate amount of depression for a number of years that flowed in part out of this experience and also out of normal things that happen to people, like deaths of fathers.

"My father's death was a crucial event in my life. The Chinese have a saying, 'You are not really a man until the death of your father.' " David Williams had a fatal heart attack eighteen days after returning from his world tour, and Dick came home to join Glenn in the family firm—something he had told his dad he wanted to try. But with Dave gone, the business faltered, and the attempt to salvage it proved disastrous. Dick got out and was being groomed for a high-level executive career at Commonwealth Edison when, in 1965, he finally concluded that diplomacy was his best suit.

One reason it took him so long to return to the State Department was that he had to wait for his Chinese wife to obtain U.S. citizenship.

Dick had met Jane Hsueh-chen Khuo when he arrived in Hong Kong in 1958. The daughter of a wealthy tobacco trader, she had fled northern China when the Communists took over and was teaching Chinese at the consulate. "And so," he says, "she was my teacher." They became engaged, and after he returned to East Chicago, he sent for her.

He pulls out his wallet and shows me pictures of Jane and their attractive teenagers, Marc (a freshman at Oberlin) and Maria. In a way, he admits, the marriage was a continuation of his rebellion against convention: "Certainly in marrying a Chinese there were elements of the desire to show that the races were equal." When his brother wrote to him in Hong Kong, asking whether he had thought through the problems a mixed marriage would bring, Dick replied, "I think that would be a very immoral reason not to marry."

Clara Williams also had misgivings until she got to know the bride-to-be, who stayed with her for six weeks before the wedding. "I wondered if it would affect the children," says Clara, "but it doesn't seem to at all. Marc said the other day when he was here, 'I think I'm very lucky because I have both backgrounds.' "

Dick today is frank about the difficulties of reconciling conflicting child-rearing practices. "You meet as internationalized adults. Differences may lend enchantment. But when you have the first child, you're thrown back to the pattern *you* were raised in." He smiles. "So now I'm back in the 1930s in East Chicago, Indiana, and she's back in the 1930s in Tianjin, China. Americans encourage a child to be independent; Chinese, quite the contrary. Most of the chips are on the American side, because you are living in an American subculture. If you want your child to grow up to be a coping, successful American adult, it will not do to teach him to be excessively deferential to authority.

The basic idea that people have to grow up to spread their wings and get away from their family and think for themselves—that's all American.''

By 1968, when Dick returned to Hong Kong after a White House staff assistantship, he was approaching forty. He had decided to pursue a China specialty and had taken a year of language and cultural training. He was beginning to feel a stronger sense of direction, confidence and awareness of "the unwritten rules of how you get ahead in the foreign service."

The four years in which Dick Williams headed China economic reporting at the Hong Kong consulate coincided with the later stages of the Cultural Revolution, when the Mao government was relentlessly eliminating all traces of "imperialist influence." Since the United States had no embassy in Peking, Dick's unit was responsible for reporting to Washington on mainland developments. His reports helped lay the groundwork for the historic visits of Secretary of State Henry Kissinger and President Richard Nixon that led to resumption of diplomatic relations with China. However, Dick is careful to disclaim anything more than peripheral involvement. "Kissinger was very secretive; those things were very closely held at the White House level. We did not know that Kissinger had been there and that Nixon would go until it was announced."

Similarly, when he was rotated back to Washington to head intelligence research on northeast and southeast Asia, he had no idea what impact his analyses—which reached the Secretary of State and sometimes even the White House—were having on U.S. policy.

"In Washington, no matter whether you're the Assistant Secretary, even the Secretary of State, you're no more than one piece in this huge decision-making complex. Even as President—what astonishes is how little you can really do. But it is very interesting to participate."

In August, 1979, Richard Williams became U.S. consul-general in Canton. It was the high point of his career to date and the culmination of those years of diplomacy in which his "inputs" had played an inde-terminate part. Once again, he made headlines. Vice-President Walter Mondale flew in for the formal unveiling of the consular seal, and the new ambassador, Leonard Woodcock, came down from Peking. "I had to do all the walk-through with the advance party. It was quite a splash."

Then there were the quiet satisfactions of creating an "efficient, happy post," assisting American business people, and helping Chinese reunite with relatives in America. "To open a post is a very rare thing, and you have a very tangible sense of accomplishment when you've done it. In intelligence research work, you can't point to 'this report did this' or 'that report did that.' But in this case, there is now a fairly good-sized U.S. government office operating that wasn't there before. I *did* that." He laughs. "So that's nice."

In a children's atlas that his father gave him when he was seven, there was a picture, which Dick still remembers vividly, of people living on sampans in Canton, China. "That book started my interest in geography and really in the world. And that I should in the end have lived in Canton is very curious."

Going there was "a leap into the unknown." The economic progress and political liberalization since the end of the Maoist era had left Canton still rather primitive. Dick and his family lived in a penthouse apartment in the hotel where the consular office was temporarily housed due to lack of office space. The children's schooling was by correspondence; Dick made time, despite the press of duties, to help them with it. Food was "terrible"—greasy and dull. There was no place to go, except, every few months, to cosmopolitan Hong Kong; the family's first stop would be Lindy's, for a corned beef sandwich and dill pickle. "Then we'd go back to this austere place seventy-five miles away. But one of the kids said, 'Well, Hong Kong is wonderful, but in Canton we are the king and queen and prince and princess!' They lumped that together with the Quiz Kids thing as being a special condition of mine."

Dick got his children to study Chinese history for a month before the family's grand tour of the country, discussing a chapter with them each evening. "Maybe this harks back to Quiz Kids," he laughs—"I always wanted my kids to do constructive things. I always wanted to drag them off to museums."

But in the vast museum that is China, the highlight of the tour ("one of the most moving experiences" of Dick's lifetime) was his wife's first meeting with the family she had not seen since she was nineteen. Her parents were dead, their thirty-room mansion had been broken up into as many apartments, and some of her brothers and sisters had been consigned to labor camps until the political climate liberalized.

Dick describes the reunion with a rare display of emotion. "We were swept upstairs to the apartment, and everybody was perched around this tiny room, about twenty-five people, but the oldest sister was not there. We were still talking as strangers, and everybody was a little uncomfortable. Where was the oldest sister?

"Then suddenly we hear her steps on the stairs. She comes into the

room and''—his voice breaks, his lips tremble, and his eyes moisten—
''she and my wife step toward each other and . . . she is a very motherly
type . . . she held out her arms and said in Chinese, 'Thirty years! Thirty
years!'

''And my wife and she—'' his voice breaks again—''embraced each
other and everyone in the room cried, just for a few minutes, and then we
all kind of pulled ourselves together and the emotional reunion had taken
place. We were a family.''

Shortly after, family members individually and quietly—not wanting
the others to hear—began talking about their troubles during the Cultural
Revolution. One of Jane's sisters described how her husband had been
paraded in the streets and two of her children sent away to the hinter-
lands. Dick said to her, ''You've really had an awful time, you've really
suffered.''

''Oh, no,'' she replied instantly, ''*we* didn't suffer. There was no one
who died in our family.''

With Dick's characteristic empathy, the event struck emotional chords
in him. ''There are so many awful things that have happened to people in
our century. You know, starting with the Quiz Kids time—there were
people on the program who were refugees. And some of my closest
friends in high school were Jewish, as well as most of the people who
were travelling with us on the show. For a long time after that, I thought
that as far as the politics of your time are concerned, you could have only
one traumatic experience, and for people of my age it was what the Nazis
did to the Jews. What has happened in China is an experience of the same
profundity.''

He pauses to reflect. ''I think part of why that reunion had such
resonance for me was that I grew up in a quite wonderful family in the
1930s. My mother was one of eight children, and they all lived in East
Chicago. And we used to have these mammoth Christmas and New
Year's parties. We had this all-embracing kind of extended family that
almost doesn't exist anymore, which meant a lot to me then. And the
Chinese still have it. The Cultural Revolution tore it, but to some extent,
at least, it is still there—particularly when they all came back to receive
their long-lost sister.''

This is a man whose currents run far deeper than the serene gentility
he displayed as a Quiz Kid. His compassion, rooted in the ''squeaky-
clean'' values of his childhood Protestantism, blossomed with exposure to
divergent strains.

Richard Williams—idol of my husband's Jewish high school crowd who aimed to pull A's without seeming to try—turns out to have been strongly attracted to Jews: "I think of them as being very achievement-oriented. Like me.

"You know," he remarks, "something about Quiz Kids suddenly rings a bell. I have noticed that my son seems able to accept with equanimity that he won't be the best in something, and I couldn't have done that. I guess I have been driven in a way that I haven't been conscious of."

At this stage, though, he no longer feels "terribly" compelled to be number one. "Of course, in some respects I suppose we all want to be at the top. But as I look back at the last twenty or thirty years, the interest of the job is really the main thing." Until the 1960s, he observes, "there was greater respect for the people at the top, whatever they were *really* like. I don't think any of us feels that any more. So today you have to define what matters to you in terms other than whether or not you get promoted."

His rejection of "society's standards" is linked with his impressions of headliners he has seen at close range these past few years—impressions that echo his reaction to celebrities he met as a child. In Canton, he played host to visitors like Walter Mondale, tennis champion Jimmy Connors, and opera star Roberta Peters. Such contacts, says Dick, "left us all, even the kids, with the feeling that these were not people qualitatively different from ordinary people . . . that it was not a transforming, or necessarily satisfying experience to go to the top of your field."

As a man who believes he was a child prodigy and who was regarded as one of the most promising youths of his generation, does he feel he has fulfilled his potential? A brief pause, then a decisive "Yes."

"I really almost think it's not a meaningful question. I don't think we *have* definite potentials. I might be ambassador to China instead of deputy consul-general in Hong Kong. But as I've just said, that kind of external definition of success doesn't convince me any more. You've got to define the standards internally. So I guess I don't know how to answer except to say that I am satisfied.

"It's partly a matter of age. The things they say in pop psychology books about being more your own person in your forties and fifties are really true."

Still, he would like to become an ambassador. Or perhaps a deputy assistant secretary. What he finds most satisfying about State Department work is "living in foreign places—trying to get deeply into what it's like there and to convey that information faithfully back to your government.'' There is also, on Washington assignments, the fascination of being close to the making of policy.

His other main satisfaction is parenthood, which he considers ''one of life's major experiences.'' The conflict between the pressure of work and his desire to spend more time with his family is one he has felt keenly.

''In Canton, our life was not our own. In Hong Kong, it will in many ways again not be our own. That's what you invite when you get successful in anything. State Department life rewards workaholism. Somehow it can become all-consuming. And when you're fifty years old, you ask yourself, *What the hell am I doing all this for?*''

For relief from his intellectually demanding work, he enjoys ''something mindless'' like playing Chinese checkers with his wife and daughter, though on long nights in Canton he ''finally'' read *War and Peace.* His reading rate has accelerated because of the need to go through vast mounds of material. ''After a while, I find it difficult to slow down and savor the style of something.''

Dick does not believe in the existence of ''superintelligence''— mental abilities beyond the normal human range. Although his memory, as a child, was described as near-photographic, today he does not feel it is extraordinary. His real strength is logical analysis, a capacity that has been as valuable in his diplomatic work as it was in solving math problems on the Quiz Kids show. Unlike Joel Kupperman, who has criticized the program's encouragement of quick, superficial answers, Dick finds no incompatibility between independent thinking and glorification of the remembered fact.

In those days, he points out, ''*Everybody* knew more facts than anybody does now. Truly, in the television age, attention is fragmentary. I was laughing at a party with some other middle-aged people, and I said, 'You know, I feel sort of wistful that when I die, there will be no one left who knows three verses of the ''Star Spangled Banner'' and four verses of ''America the Beautiful.'' '

''I think we were at the tail end of the historical era when it seemed the number of facts in the world might be finite, so it was worth trying to absorb a good many of them. But—oh, I think it goes too far. On TV last night, they mentioned that the weather in Iowa was such-and-such, and my son said, 'Where is Iowa?' '' He laughs. ''I think that's miserable, not to know where Iowa is!''

Patricia Rope, a Washington-based China consultant, is one of the many friends Dick has accumulated in moving from post to post. She sees him as "very strong-willed and assertive . . . willing to state his opinions on anything. He's noted for writing wry cables and has a very insightful sense of humor. He's a Renaissance man—more rounded than a lot of people who don't know about anything except what's going on in Canton province. Certainly he's one of the brightest people in the department.

"Dick is a very resilient person. I remember talking with him about the Quiz Kid thing, and thinking, *God, you're really normal considering what you've been through.*"

In November, 1980, ex-Quiz Kid Peter Reich, then a *Chicago Tribune* writer, did a piece on his old radio associates. The article, accompanied by a photo in which Richard Williams appeared, went out on the wires and eventually found its way to the Canton consulate, where someone posted it on the bulletin board, circling Dick's picture in red with big capital letters, "THE BOSS."

Dick laughs about the incident: "No more hangups!" That realization had struck him a few years earlier when, at a Washington dinner party, friends asked him what being a Quiz Kid had been like. He described for them the January, 1941 New York trip, "when we went, as we did so many times, on the Commodore Vanderbilt train, which left Chicago from the La Salle Street station something like three in the afternoon and then early the next morning you woke up and you were going down the Hudson. And there were a whole bunch of newspaper reporters, and they took our pictures perched around the locomotive.

"So, coming in on a train which no longer runs, we were met by representatives of newspapers which no longer exist and then we went in a motorcade down to City Hall to meet a mayor, who was—Are you ready for this? —Fiorello LaGuardia! I mean, can we have been alive when LaGuardia was alive?"

He laughs. "Maybe that was to some degree a cathartic experience. I realized that I no longer felt embarrassed, that it was nothing to feel embarrassed about. It seemed like a different epoch of human history."

We are at dinner. Over a bottle of wine, I remind Dick of a comment he made at fourteen, when a newspaper reporter asked him about the pitiful life and death of William Sidis, the phenomenal prodigy of the preceding generation. Dick said that Sidis, unlike himself, had been forced too much, and added, "I'm sure I'll be perfectly happy."

Dick laughs. "That's a lovely line. That was very upbeat, wasn't it?"
"So I want to know," I ask, "are you?"
He laughs again, then stops abruptly. "No. It doesn't exist."
"I don't know whether there's anything perfectly anything anymore,"
I respond.
"I've thought of that, raising children," he says. "When we were little, you went and asked your father a question, and he gave you an answer. There was never any problem. But when my kids come and ask me a question, it doesn't seem there *is* any clearcut answer."

Five months later, Dick writes from the Hong Kong consulate:

This is truly challenging work—directing and editing political and economic work on China at this most interesting time; briefing and hosting Cabinet members and Congressmen and other VIP's; supervising about 160 Americans and 300 Chinese . . . . Along with it there is great material luxury and deference.

Certainly by any normal standards I am quite a considerable success. . . .

On reflection, I think that the Quiz Kids experience seems to have produced in me standards of success so high as to constitute a difficulty, making adult attainments which for most people might be amply fulfilling seem less than fully sufficient.

Harve Bennett (Fischman):
Born Showman

Harve was the personality boy. He had a lot of charm,
a sense of theater.
            —Rita Duskin

He was certainly very smart, but he also had that smart mouth . . .
a certain irreverence. I liked his style.
            —Ex-Quiz Kid Patrick Conlon

Harve Bennett Fischman was the Quiz Kid graduate the others voted "most unlikely to fail." The prediction came true . . . after what Harve calls a twenty-year gap.

Today Harve Bennett (he dropped the Fischman two decades ago) is probably the wealthiest and most powerful ex-Quiz Kid, the only one of the top regulars listed in *Who's Who in America*. As an executive television producer, he earns in peak years $450,000. ("More than the President of the United States—that gives me a bit of a shock.") For ten weeks in the late 1970s, three of his shows ("The Six Million Dollar Man," "Bionic Woman," and "Rich Man, Poor Man") were among the top five in the ratings. But he keeps such a low profile that, he smiles, "When I walk into a room nobody knows who I am."

"Rich Man," which received the 1976 Golden Globe award, four Emmies, and nineteen other Emmy nominations, launched a new form: the mini-series, to which Harve returned in 1979 with *From Here to Eternity*, starring Natalie Wood. His twice-Emmy-nominated "Mod Squad" broke new ground in the sixties with a black leading character and social themes like youth alienation, drug addiction, and race relations. Also an Emmy nominee was *The Sam Shepard Murder Case*, a made-for-television film.

In 1981, Harve persuaded Ingrid Bergman to come out of retirement for what has been called her finest role, in the $4 million Paramount Prime Time docu-drama, *A Woman Called Golda*—hailed by the Christian Science Monitor as "something more than an extraordinary TV movie." His first feature film, *Star Trek II: The Wrath of Khan*, for which he was co-writer as well as executive producer, has won critical plaudits for recapturing the human qualities of the original television space fantasy. Other projects: an NBC series, "The Powers of Matthew Star," and a revived "Quiz Kids" program hosted by Norman Lear on CBS cable television.

On the "Quiz Kids" show of our youth, Harve Bennett Fischman was number two. Eight months younger than his pal Richard Williams, Harve almost invariably finished second in the standings as well as in their traveling chess matches. ("It's hard to play chess with a mathematical genius," he says.) Dick was the Quiz Kids' fair-haired boy; Harve was that redhead with cheek. Dick was a WASP; Harve, a Jew with a Semitic surname that his father refused to let him drop when he went on the show at ten.

"I didn't like the name," Harve explains. "I felt it labelled me (in a society that was more label-conscious than it is now) as a certain cliche: Jewish and therefore smart. I felt outside. It would have been wonderful to be named Richard Williams. Intuitively I knew that people were hearing my name on the radio, and they couldn't see me, and they would have given me more credibility without the preconception my name would create."

Growing up in a Polish south side Chicago neighborhood, Harve had been beaten up a couple of times; once a bucket of whitewash had been dumped on his head. "Remember, we were at the height of the anti-Semitic crisis overseas . . . the Bund . . . Anti-Semitism in public places was more rampant than ever before or since. Being Jewish was constantly a defensive posture. When Roby Hickok, in her press releases, described me as that freckle-faced kid with a shock of Huckleberry Finn hair, I thought they were selling non-Jewishness."

Looking back, it seems strange to think of Harve as an outsider. Everybody's "boy next door," he got to do things other boys hardly dared imagine: writing for newspapers, interviewing movie stars, shaking hands with Presidents.

"Harve Fischman would be easy to meet," wrote Wauhillau La Hay of the *Chicago Sun*. "He has the nicest grin . . . and doesn't act or look particularly smart. Intelligent, yes, but not so darned intellectual."

He was a stocky kid, with a weakness for pop and candy, who disliked asparagus and mushy movies. A sports enthusiast in striped tee shirts, who played fullback on his grammar school football team, spent summer days at the beach, set pins at a bowling alley, and, on train trips, initiated the rest of us Quiz Kids into the joys of All Star Baseball games. A history buff with 176 I.Q. who looked as though he'd never cracked a book in his life but who (as reporters quipped) could toss off dates as if they were footballs and knew more about Presidents' wives than most men know about their own. A slick wordster, who had a pun or wisecrack for every occasion.

It was mischievous Harve who put the rest of us up to turning a Canadian ship stateroom into a chamber of horrors, dousing the lights and throwing wet towels at unsuspecting entrants. Impulsive Harve who decided we should have a marshmallow roast in the fireplace of his New York hotel room and discovered too late that the draft had been bricked up. Popular Harve whose teacher wrote that he never bragged, was not the least bit conceited, and entered into everything with 100 per cent interest. Smooth Harve who, as he grew into his teens, became a bobby-sox heart throb, with fan clubs across the country embroidering his name on sweaters and mobbing him at personal appearances. Bold Harve who, on a bet, kissed Jinx Falkenberg (the first actress he met in Hollywood) and wired his father, Yale Fischman, at his Chicago law office: "Don't you wish you were me?" Devilish Harve who once was suspended from high school for firing a gun (with a blank cartridge) during a play rehearsal.

There was patriotic Harve, who collected six hundred keys for scrap metal salvage, contributed twenty history books to the U.S.O., and urged the nation's schoolchildren to "go easy on shows and candy and chocolate sodas and put that money into [defense] stamps and bonds instead." Hammy Harve, who wrote and emceed a vaudeville routine we Kids performed at bond rallies. Unflappable Harve, who once pinch-hit for Spencer Tracy as featured speaker at the last minute. Glib Harve, who, when a woman buying a bond asked him to predict when the war would end, deadpanned, "More quickly, madam, since you've bought this."

His sly sense of humor came from his mother, Kitty Fischman, who had thought it a good gag to name Yale's son Harvard. Harve used to explain how his monicker got shortened: "Can you imagine the neighbors' reaction to 'Oh Yale, where's Harvard?' "

On "Quiz Kids," Harve pronounced his first name with two syllables. Now he insists on "Harv" with a silent "e."

"It might have been because of the play *Harvey*, with the six-foot rabbit. Suddenly the name became a series of jokes. It got the connotation of a weird person, a milquetoast.''

The name is not all that has changed. The trim fifty-one-year-old television producer, facing me across the dim-lit table for two, bears little resemblance to the ''older man'' who once signed my autograph book, ''From your QK sweetheart.'' The red hair is now grizzled, the dimples deeply etched. There is disciplined strength in the thin-lipped jaw, quiet irony in the canny eyes.

Success personified, this man who has a phone in his 1978 Mercedes . . who once owned show horses and an airplane . . . eats a twenty-five dollar steak dinner, wearing a knit shirt and slacks. He speaks softly but, like one of his boyhood heroes, carries a big stick; his, a code of personal responsibility that brooks no excuse.

On my previous Hollywood visit, with my family, seven years back, he was an expansive but inscrutable behind-the-scenes host. Tonight, just returned from a rare five-day extended weekend in Hawaii, he is tired. In the process of his second divorce, he seems contemplative, almost melancholy: a man to whom I still am drawn by his intensity. A measurer of moments, he bandies no words. Deeply introspective, he withholds little. Master of illusion, he allows himself none.

''Quiz Kids kept me frozen in childhood. At the end of Quiz Kids, I was a national figure. Then the attention stopped. It took me a long time, years of therapy, to redefine my purpose, to realize that I was pursuing an applause addiction.

''Until I reached a level of visibility again, until I began rising through the ranks to prominence in my business, was the better part of twenty years. It was like starting over.''

When stern Yale Fischman is asked to what he attributes his son's success, he fixes me with an incredulous stare. ''You must be kidding! That's what he set out to do.''

Yale and Kitty live in a condominium in the shadow of the Twentieth Century Fox studio, where Yale was comptroller for a while after the family moved to Los Angeles at the end of Harve's Quiz Kid days.

Gentle, diminutive Kitty remembers the afternoon her boy came home from Bradwell School and announced his intention to apply to the Quiz Kids show: ''I laughed, but he said, 'No, I want to. My teacher said I should be one, and I've got a good chance.' '' Filling out the application he spilled a whole bottle of ink on it and then rubbed the paper with eradicator until it was parchment thin. (Roby Hickok later said that was what had caught the staff's eye—it looked like a holy scroll.)

The ten-year-old had made up his mind to apply when he saw the Quiz Kid baby, Gerard Darrow, lecturing on ornithology at a school assembly. Harve wanted some attention, too. When he listened to the show, he found himself answering most of the questions. "And," he explains, "since the reward for answering the questions was standing on the stage of my school, it was an easy connection to make. I thought I was better than Gerard. I had been a totally outstanding achiever."

Harve had been brought up with the standard expectations of a middle-class Jewish youth. His parents were proud of him, but never overawed. After all, Yale—the Hasidic-raised son of a Russian-born carpenter—had managed to become a lawyer and a CPA ("The crowning achievement in the life of my sainted bubby," Harve smiles). And Kitty (the former Kathryn Susman), granddaughter of a Torah scribe, had been the youngest girl reporter in the United States, writing her first story for the *Chicago Times* while she was still in high school.

After Harve was born, Kitty continued working part-time but quit when he was four. "I wanted to be a mother instead of a byline," she explains. "Coming home and seeing that little face waiting for me was more than I could stand."

My mom's a steady lady
Who keeps me in a whirl
For since I wore three-cornered pants
She's been my pin-up girl.
    —Harve Fischman, age fifteen

Savoring his wine, Harve ruminates, brows furrowed.

"I was very mother-attached. Father was a figure who arose earlier than I did and came home after we were through eating.

"My relationship with Kitty now is terrific. But my mother had a sadness about her. . . . " He sighs. "She covers it in social situations, as do I, with a certain gaiety. One of the things that was conveyed to me in childhood was that I became mother's comforter, and that role made me important. When she went off on assignments, this whole relationship was disrupted . . . like losing a function. Once she went to Cincinnati for a couple of days. Just left me bereft."

I am trying to connect this Harve with the fun-loving one I thought I knew. "What were you so sad about?"

"Being alone, I guess . . . helplessness . . . "

"Did it help when she stopped working?"

"No . . . somehow I felt responsible."

Reflecting on his childhood attachment to his mother, he recalls how both Golda Meir and Ingrid Bergman have written of the pain of having to pry little hands from around their necks when they left for work. But he has come to believe that the most important thing is the parent's self-fulfillment. "Maybe the English have the right idea [with their nannies]. There has to be something, somewhere between the kibbutz system and the total raising of children by a mother, that has to do with encouraging independence early on. Separation from the mother is the ultimate act, and the preparation for it need not be delayed. Whatever the forces between my mother and myself, the fact that I was so dependent upon her company I look upon as something I had to grow out of, rather than cherish."

The upbringing of Harve and (later) his nine-years-younger brother Ruel was Kitty's job. "She was the loving mother," says Yale. "I was the disciplinarian."

Kitty threw herself into motherhood with all the relish she had poured into reporting. "Every day in the development of a child is a new experience," she wrote, years later, to Roby Hickok Kesler. "And so much fun. One watches each step and nurtures the interests."

Harve talked in complete sentences at ten months. When one of Kitty's friends began cooing at him in baby talk, he came back with "What did you say?" When he was three, his mother encouraged him to dictate letters to her, helping him sharpen his vocabulary, organization, and natural punchy style.

His interest in history first evidenced itself when, looking through one of his father's old grade school texts, he pointed to a picture of Confederate and Union soldiers in battle and announced that they were enemies—he could tell because their hats were different. Kitty began reading aloud to him from a book called *Boyhood Adventures of Our Presidents*. At a birthday party, she recalls, "all the children were asked to do something. I was amazed when he stood up and said, 'I will recite the Presidents of the United States.' He did, and won the prize."

He learned to read in three weeks, after starting school. One day his father came home and found him on the floor, pawing Yale's favorite U.S. history book. Yale was furious, but his anger dissipated when he discovered that the boy had read half of the thick volume and knew it cold.

Kitty made a game of looking up information and testing her son on quiz books. And it just so happened that the quiz book the Cowan office manager, Joe Bailey, pulled out at Harve's interview was Kitty's favorite one. Harve knew it backwards and forwards but had the intuitive sense to fake a few wrong answers so Bailey wouldn't ask him, "Have you read this book?"

When Harve got the call to go on the show, Kitty remembers, he danced all over the house. First time out, he tied for top honors. But on his fourth broadcast, he reflects, he went "absolutely flat."

"I remember thinking gibberish, saying gibberish. I remember the question, 'Give the name of an author whose last name is the same as an animal.' My mind said Charles and Mary Lamb, and I raised my hand and said, 'Charles and Mary Beard.' And Joe Kelly said, 'Uh, what kind of animal are you talking about with a beard?' and I said 'Charles and Mary Beard,' thinking I was saying 'Lamb' and wondering why he was so dense. I'll never forget that night. It was as if somebody had erased all my coordinated memory cells."

Most of the time, Harve's memory cells worked just fine. He informed the nation that President Arthur had owned sixty pairs of pants, that Tyler had sired fourteen children, that Taylor had died from eating cherries and drinking cold milk, that Madison weighed less than one hundred pounds, that Coolidge had been sworn in by his father, that Van Buren had been the first President born in the United States.

His favorite period was the Civil War. A five-foot portrait of General Ulysses S. Grant on horseback stood guard over his bed, surrounded by tacked-up *Time* magazine covers. When the Quiz Kids challenged four U.S. Senators to a match, Harve and Senator Carl A. Hatch of New Mexico disagreed over whether Richmond had been the scene of a Civil War battle. Harve said no, and a Richmond newspaper publisher called in to say he was right.

"Will the Senator yield?" asked Harve.

"I do more than yield—I abdicate," Hatch replied.

One of Harve's greatest thrills was a four-hour visit with Vice-President Henry A. Wallace: talking, laughing and playing checkers. ("Vice-Presidents in those days had nothing else to do.") Harve admired Wallace's book, *Century of the Common Man,* and Wallace promised to send him an autographed copy.

A few weeks later, just as Yale Fischman was leaving for work, the doorbell rang. Yale called upstairs, "Harve, there's a package for you."

"Who's it from?" Harve yelled back.

"H. Wallace in Washington."

Harve smiles as he relives the moment. "I said, 'Dad, that's the Vice-President!' and he said, 'Oh, my God!' and sat down . . . slowly." There was the book, in a brown wrapper addressed in Wallace's own hand.

Harve had his less triumphant moments. When six Quiz Kids, as a publicity stunt, took an Air Force cadet test, he was the only flunk— he fell down on the math. His spelling, too, was atrocious.

Once, before a rural audience, the Kids were asked what kind of bull they would buy for a dairy farm. Ten-year-old Harve put his foot in his city-bred mouth when he said, "I didn't know bulls gave milk." What followed was, Harve recalls, "the biggest laugh I've ever heard."

At first mainly a history specialist, he broadened his reading to compete with generalists like Richard Williams and Jack Lucal. In five-plus years, before he turned sixteen, he made (according to news sources) 180 appearances.

The correct figure, he insists, is 212, the same as Dick's. "I kept track," Harve says, "by marking down X's."

"Quiz Kids" gave Harve what he craved. Not money (he "thought of it as paper") nor, precisely, fame. He "wanted to be famous at school." He "ate it up." Unlike some of us, his gregarious personality and his concentration on macho subjects like wars and sports enabled him to "be a brain without seeming like one." His proud classmates often came down to the broadcasts.

Trauma struck when his principal (for whom having two celebrated Quiz Kids in his school was a dream come true) double-promoted Harve. He was about twelve.

"There," he tells me, "I ran into 'Who dat?' Coupled with the fact that I was physically behind. I lost my edge in sports. Overnight I went from shortstop to right fielder, from a starter to a kind of benchwarmer. And it was exactly at the time when all those postpubescent, pre-adolescent changes begin. I noticed girls, but girls did not notice me."

"I always thought of you as a ladies' man," I protest.

" . . . I had a terrible crush on *you.* . . ."

"When I was nine?"

"I think so . . . somewhere between eight and ten."

"Too bad I lost it," I smile. "We were 'engaged,' weren't we? Whose idea was that?"

"Probably Roby Hickok's. There was capital to be made."

In high school, Harve again hit his stride. He dated girls his own age, wrote and acted in school plays, appeared on Junior Junction, a teen-produced radio show, and hosted the *Times*-WLS Quizdown. And he wrote a regular teen column for the *Times*, his mother's old rag.

As *Time* magazine said (in profiling him upon his Quiz Kid graduation), he had claimed his birthright. When Harve was born, his mother had nicknamed him "Scoop." She wired her old city editor: "Can you use a good newspaperman?" The editor wired back: "I sure can!"

"She told me that, early in life," Harve remembers. "That was my princedom and my curse. When you are two and three and four years old, and you know you are destined to be a reporter for the *Chicago Times*, a child mind says, *How do you do that?* I remember verbalizing that to her: 'How do I get to be a reporter?' . . . 'Don't worry, you will.' That was a very mysterious answer. It used to worry me."

At their first Quiz Kids anniversary, when the Kids dressed as their ambitions, Harve came as a newspaperman. Two years later, he broke into the Fourth Estate.

A GRAND AND GLORIOUS FEELING!
Quiz Kid Writing his First Article for Paper Realizes an Ambition!
by HARVE FISCHMAN

Hurray! Today I am a reporter!

Maybe you folks out there don't realize the glamor of the newspaper business, but to me it is a world I have dreamed about for the last 12 years. It is a world of laughs and tears, triumphs and failures; it is history in the making.

I consider myself a very lucky guy to jump in one promotion from assistant-assistant editor of the boys' page of the Bradwell Life . . . to a reporter for the Evening Bulletin. . . .

—*Philadelphia Evening Bulletin*, March 20, 1943

Harve went on to do guest columns for some twenty-six metropolitan papers, several of which invited him to come back. In each city we visited, he reported the "inside dope" on the feats and frolics of "Dapper Dick" Williams, "Rippling Ruth" Duskin, "Jumping Joel" Kupperman, and "Hungry Harve" Fischman.

Summer of 1944 found fourteen-year-old Harve covering the

Republican and Democratic conventions for the *Times* and the Blue Network. He "loved the hustle and bustle"—meeting the bigwigs he recognized from the pages of *Time*. ("I still have an uncanny ability to walk into a room and spot the newsmakers.")

Harve wrote to every political personage he met. His loose scrapbooks ("I'm not an archivist") hold replies from House Speaker Sam Rayburn, Senate Majority Leader Alben Barkley, Governor Harold Stassen and many more . . . including a March 30, 1945 note from Harry S. Truman.

The newly inaugurated Vice-President who would, within the month, become Chief of State upon Roosevelt's death, had spent half an hour with the Quiz Kids in his office a few weeks before. When Harve reminded Truman that he last had seen him at the Democratic convention, the Veep remarked, "You were looking at a man who didn't want the job."

In November the Quiz Kids again saw Truman, this time as President. And this time they were ushered in and out of his office so fast that Harve barely had time to make a few mental notes for his high school paper. He did notice a large horseshoe over the door, and he wrote: "I could not help but think it was symbolic of the large part Lady Luck has played in his career."

The *Times* twice sent Harve to Hollywood to interview young cinema stars like Elizabeth Taylor ("hubba"), Margaret O'Brien ("She plays a mean game of gin rummy"), Shirley Temple ("very sweet and VERY pretty . . . and she STUMPED me!") . . . and, of course, Quiz Kid comrade Vanessa Brown. Harve interviewed "Van" (as he called her) on a remote pickup for a Quiz Kids broadcast, and the two of them played a bit of the balcony scene from *Romeo and Juliet*.

By the time of his next west coast trip, a year later, Harve was a Quiz Kids graduate with a confirmed crush on filmdom. His eye was no longer on the press room but on the soundstage.

> . . . though this place is hard, like many of the people who dwell in it, it is the place for any and all ex-Q.K.s with big ambitions and a long line of fast chatter. Any comers?
> —Harve Fischman, *Ex-Quiz Kid Resume,* August, 1947

Two things effected the change in his boyhood aspirations: a movie camera he had been given at twelve, which became his visual diary on Quiz Kid trips, and the Quiz Kids experience itself. "Quiz Kids brought me," he reflects, "from a bourgeois, non-show-business family into the excitement of something which has since become my life. I loved watching Forrest Owen with his stopwatch, Curly Reynolds the engineer, all the backstage stuff.

"I didn't really want to be a star reporter after I had tasted radio and the broader medium. But I still wanted to be a star."

Harve's many Quiz Kid-related activities made him the linchpin of his family. ("A false emphasis on the child as king.")

His baby brother Ruel, nicknamed Sparky because he was born July 4, was trotted out for occasional Quiz Kids appearances beginning at age three. The night before the tot's debut, his mother overheard him praying, "Please, God, make me a good boy, and, if You can, try to listen to me tomorrow night on the Blue Network."

Harve treated his kid brother like a roly-poly pet. "Harve has always been a great brother," says Ruel, a forty-two-year-old bearded philosopher-professor-turned-screenwriter. "I was included in everything. He taught me to play ball, got me my first camera, showed me how to edit film. Being nine years ahead, he was always doing things that were very exciting to me. He still is."

In 1978, Harve enticed his brother to Hollywood from a dead-end teaching job in St. Cloud, Minnesota, after the younger man's divorce. The two have worked together on several projects, including the new Quiz Kids program.

"Harve's a remarkable genius," says Ruel. "The thing he's best at is taking something that doesn't quite work and making it snap together in the editing process. Subtle little changes: a second here, a second there, throw a little sound over at this point. And everybody says, 'How did you do that?' Absolutely brilliant. He can do in a four-hour session what most people would do in three weeks.

"He has a masterful story sense. Here are five, six, seven creative intelligent men sitting around in a room, and you've got a good premise but you can't quite make it work. And suddenly he'll jump up and start pitching the story at you the way it's supposed to be. It's beautiful."

Harve leans back with an after-dinner cigarette. "I think of going from childhood to adulthood as moving from one end of the camera to the other."

His first and last movie acting offer came just as he graduated from

Quiz Kids. He was to play Jimmy Stewart's son, a basketball player, in a Robert Riskin/William Wyler production, *Magic Town.* But an eighteen-month stagehands' strike postponed shooting until Harve outgrew the role. "That was the end of the acting instinct."

Near the close of his Quiz Kid days, a euphoric Harve had told Evelyn Bigsby of *Radio Life,* "As I look at the future, I feel like a boxer standing in the ring waiting for the opponent's next move, his next chance . . . whatever may come, I'm ready!"

What he did during the next two decades might make impressive reading on some people's resumes. But to Harve, his post-Quiz Kid period was "a classic letdown." He had to prove himself all over again.

At UCLA, where he majored in theater arts and film, he soon found that being an ex-Quiz Kid meant no more than last month's audition notice. Setting his sights on a directing career, he plunged into a variety of activities, on and off campus. Besides acting in college productions, writing drama reviews, and helping out in his parents' motel, he had his own local television show; wrote and directed industrial films and Jack Bailey's Hollywood Sound Track; and, as a senior, did the original book and direction for a full-scale live musical revue about a time machine that snarls up history. It was the most elaborate varsity show that ever had been attempted at UCLA, with a cast of 120 and a hilarious filmed sequence. The floodlit premiere was a heady night, complete with real stars alighting from chauffeured convertibles.

> *It's Time You Knew* comes as a breath of Airwick-refreshened air . . . in its very conscious omission of corn, cliche and broad comedy. It all boils down to the commendable attempts of writer-director Harve Fischman to appeal to the audience's intellect and finer sensitivities. . . . The television scene . . . was truly a gem. The audience just howled.
> —Phil Babet, *Campus Theater Spotlight,* May 8, 1952

Then, another letdown. "Life is a series of bigger and bigger ponds," says Harve. "The trouble was, the people out there didn't know what you had done—they hadn't been around to see you do it."

After spending a couple of years in the service, doing rehabilitation work with war criminals and editing a newspaper at an army prison, he migrated to New York with his first wife, Joan Harvey, an aspiring actress who had taken her stage name from his given one. She hoped to break into Broadway, he into television directing. But by the time they reached Manhattan, the bulk of the TV industry was shifting to the west coast.

Harve landed his first job as production assistant on CBS's "Frankie Laine Time," not through Louis Cowan, then network president, but through Garry Moore, with whom the Quiz Kids once had done a bond rally. In the next five years, the young comer moved up to associate producer for the Robert Q. Lewis and Red Skelton shows and producer for Johnny Carson. He directed commercials, did free-lance television writing, and produced CBS specials, such as the Pillsbury Bake-off and Miss America pageant. (He had an "uncanny knack" for winning the betting pool on who would be crowned.)

But variety shows and spectacles were not what Harve had in mind. Aiming for drama and comedy, "the big leagues of television," he returned to the west coast alone in 1960 as Harve Bennett. The breakup of his marriage and the name change occurred at a critical juncture following the start of therapy. His wife, a fresh-faced sparkler he had met at UCLA, was the daughter of leftist parents who were targets of the Red scare.

"I really married my wife's parents," Harve explains. "It was my first exposure to political activism, and since it touched on things I had believed in, in my Rooseveltian youth, I was highly influenced by it. I grew up as a child who idolized the Russians; it was easy to do, given my ethnic origins. While I was a Quiz Kid, I interviewed Ludmilla Pavlachenko, a Russian lady sniper who killed 309 Nazis and didn't count the Rumanians. She embraced me. I have a picture of her; she looked like one of my fat cousins."

With the onset of the cold war, he continues, "Having been imbued with the propaganda from 1939 on, it was very hard to accept that the good guys were now the bad guys. I was therefore ripe for any political statement which reaffirmed my essential belief that there need be no conflict with the Russians. I was so taken with this, and my parents were so nervous, that it sort of pushed me over. I married to get out of the house, to embrace people I thought brave and upstanding, people who were fighting the blacklist."

The marriage fell apart when "times changed politically, and that which bound us together was no longer important." Harve began to see in his actress wife a counterpart of his own childhood "need to hear applause"—at a time when he was growing toward *But what am I worth? What can I do? How do I achieve excellence?*

"The psychological drive that makes people want to act makes them self-centered. They're children, as Hitchcock has said, in an arrested state of development—looking so deeply for approval as to be not quite in touch with their own feelings."

He has shared these reactions with former child star Jackie Cooper. "You learned both as a Quiz Kid and as a child actor to rely on certain devices that please people outside of yourself . . . your parents and your audience. And then you're no longer in that place, and you try your winning ways on people who look blankly back at you, and you find that all those things that made you cute at ten or twelve or thirteen—your freckles and your dimples and your quick wit and your ability to make up poems under pressure—don't mean diddly out there. The loss of those devices makes you feel frightened and alone.

"I believe in Erich Fromm's concept that what we are ultimately afraid of is the acknowledgment that death is inevitable. That we come into life separate, not of our own will, and exit life not of our own will, and we are therefore alone and frightened. We reach out beyond that, by identifying with real or imaginary more powerful forces: groups, audiences, religions. In my case, I think national attention made me feel unalone, and when that was withdrawn from me, I found no immediate understanding of why I felt left out."

Feeling that his marriage had drawn him away from California, where he really wanted to work, he resolved afresh to storm the Hollywood barricades. "In effect I was saying, 'This time I'm going to do it *my* way.' And so, the original inquiry I had made of my father when I first went on Quiz Kids—'Dad, could I drop my name?'—became something I now wanted to do for myself. I was rational enough not to live in the past. The retention of my name would have connected me to the very source of pain. That was over, obsolete. Having been a radio Quiz Kid meant very little in the areas I was going into ten years later.

"I did not want to be taken as a wunderkind. I wanted to be Harve Bennett, who had certain skills, taken for what I am. I was expressing my adultness: *I wish I had done this when I was ten. That was my will that was not expressed. It may be late now, it may even be foolish now* (since I already had a half-career) . . . *Screw it! I'm going to start over . . .* "

For a couple of years, he was out of the entertainment business, selling mutual funds to survive. "It was a very closed shop, and I was at a level very long in supply and short in demand: associate producers, live production specialists at a time when film was taking over. I wanted to be in film more than anything, but had few film credits except for college work."

One day he knocked at the door of KNXT, a CBS outlet, and was hired to produce a local morning show. The same year, 1962, he remarried; his new wife, pert, raven-haired Jane Fitzpatrick, was a non-practicing

Episcopalian who worked for two years as a radio engineer and rode in horse shows.

Harve's big break came the following year, when an old college chum, Bert Nodella, head of program development at ABC-TV, plugged him in. Harve "went into his office as second in command, and three years later was top man at the network."

The keys to his success at ABC (and afterward) were, he believes, political astuteness, "nonparanoia," honesty, and a genuine liking for people, without regard to rank. "The very openness and vulnerability that probably made me seem a little bit naive," he says, "also made me the repository of trust for high office. In a society that is untrusting, a bright person who is moderately able *and* trustworthy has got to succeed. Doors open because people are so relieved to see somebody they can take at face value."

But his rapid rise to vice-president in charge of all ABC programming left him unsatisfied. "As a network executive, I was an editorial traffic cop; I supervised the work of others. The thing about a network job is that you can fail but you cannot succeed. If a show makes it, the credit goes to the producer. If it fails, the network executive gets the criticism. I would frequently make enormous contributions to shows like 'Peyton Place,' 'Batman,' 'The Fugitive,' for which I was on staff salary, while other guys were making a lot of money and getting a lot of fame for doing the same thing as producers. Obviously, sooner or later I was going to be a producer."

The last show he helped develop at ABC was "Mod Squad." He was so vitally involved with the pilot that executive producer Aaron Spelling asked him to leave the network and produce the series. But to be a producer, Harve says, "you also have to be a writer, because there's a scarcity of good writers in Hollywood. So if you're going to produce a successful show, you'd better be able to write it yourself, or rewrite the work of others." He was forced into that situation when a writer let him down; in four days of round-the-clock work, Harve came up with what was pronounced "a great script."

"I vividly remember the feeling: *Hey, I can do this!* I had crossed a line. I had a trade. I could go anywhere and make a living, because I now had a particular skill that was marketable, that depended only upon me, my mind, and a typewriter. From that point on, I had this sense of career, of knowing exactly what I wanted to do. That feeling didn't come until more than twenty years after Quiz Kids."

As a three-year hit show veteran and award-winning script writer, Harve stepped from ''Mod Squad'' into an executive producer's chair at Universal-TV. Six years later, he broke with Universal over distribution of the profits from his hugely successful, long-running ''Six Million Dollar Man,'' and moved to Columbia in partnership with Harris Katleman. His three years there yielded (with the exception of *From Here to Eternity*) mainly minor products, most notably ''Salvage 1'' with Andy Griffith. In late 1980, he switched to Paramount, eager to ''get back into more challenging stuff,'' like *Golda* and *Star Trek II.* Swamped with work, he goes from project to project, almost without design; ''they just seem to be there when I'm ready.''

In retrospect, he now sees, his ''miscellaneous secondary and tertiary jobs'' during those two post-Quiz Kids decades were ''totally preparational'' to the work of an executive producer, television's chief of staff. ''It would be stupid of me to say that I was floating around for twenty years. I wasn't . . . any more than a writer floats when he's growing up, accumulating life experiences. I'm very comfortable in this environment because I spent three or four years on the line. I've managed hysteria. Once I did an auto show in Detroit with twelve cameras, and a literal riot of two hundred thousand people knocked out half my cameras, and I had a show to get on the air. We re-edited and shot and faked the situation from midnight until seven in the morning.''

''This environment'' is the control room in which Harve Bennett stands, chewing gum, supervising the taping of four ''Quiz Kids'' episodes in a single weekend. Here there are no hesitations or doubts; he exudes energy, vitality. His is the final authority, his the alert, organized, almost computer-like mind that takes in problems and spews out a course of action. He is the one to decide, on the spot, whether a segment must be retaped because Quizmaster Norman Lear's ruling has been challenged or a contestant's points incorrectly totaled. Line producer Kay Bachman admires Harve's aggressive leadership but finds his instinctive sureness somewhat exasperating: ''He doesn't need my input. He knows. And he's right.''

His, too, is the voice of the unseen announcer (''the acting instinct again''). Originally, when he proposed the revival to Lou Cowan and Cowan's son Geoffrey in 1976 (a month before Lou's death), Harve was toying with the idea of being emcee, but he recognized that Lear would lend ''tune-in value.''

His initial hope, and Geoff Cowan's, was that a program celebrating knowledge might capture viewers surfeited with the ''Gong Show''—''the television wasteland.'' A network market did not materialize, so Harve and Geoff, after co-producing ''Quiz Kids'' for a few years in Toronto and Boston, went for the narrower cable audience. The show has been nominated for top honors for children's cable programming.

Why has someone who for a long time was bitter about having been a Quiz Kid resurrected the show? ''In a sense,'' Harve says, ''it's why does somebody who was edgy about being Jewish do *Golda*? The answer is, to affirm that it was a good rather than a bad experience. My final feeling about Quiz Kids is that it was very positive for me, that it created problems that have taken some time to work out, but that I might have had the same problems if I had been a teenage baseball whiz (which is what I really wanted to be) who then didn't make the major leagues. It introduced me to show business, glued together the instinct for an audience, got me known. I trade on it in subtle ways to this day. It gave me my first taste of what it was to communicate on a vast scale, as opposed to . . . me and Mom.''

Standing in back of the control room, watching the current Quiz Kids field questions, he murmurs the answers, keeping his own internal scoreboard. Associates are hard put to come up with a history question he can't handle. Yet he confesses to a nagging awareness (even in the old days) of ''faking it . . . being taken for brighter than I was.'' It's a relief, he confides, when nobody says, ''Yes, but please explain . . .'' As he told Marcia Smilack of the *Boston Globe,* ''My particular smarts are not the same smarts as academic smarts entirely, or, God knows, Einsteinian smarts.'' What he has is agility under fire, a talent for ''tap dancing through life.''

''Just yesterday,'' he tells me, ''I addressed a Star Trek convention extemporaneously for an hour and a half, and the group gave me a standing ovation. Friends said, 'Why haven't you run for the Senate? We've never seen this side of you.' And I said, 'Guys, this is what I used to do as a Quiz Kid all the time.' ''

Star Trek is Harve's first foray into the film world he originally hoped to enter. He still has a yen to direct a motion picture, but credentials as a television producer, the role to which he gravitated by chance and early experience, do not readily translate. (''Why should they use me when they can get Steven Spielberg?'')

One of his idols is David Lean, who directed Harve's favorite film, *Bridge on the River Kwai*. Lean, when asked what he wanted out of life, replied, ''I like to tell a good yarn.''

"I guess that said it for me," Harve smiles. "I like telling stories. In feature films, the director tells the story with a camera; in my business, I tell it with a typewriter. I love the process that goes from the blank page to watching something on the screen." His chief skill is adaptive: "taking something that's unformed, partially formed, or misformed, and changing it into something else."

He finds "enormous satisfaction in doing something well that a lot of people try to do. I suppose," he muses, "if I had been a big league baseball player, I would probably have the same feeling. Except I can do this until I'm eighty. And probably will."

Money figures only marginally on his scale of values. "The more you make," he finds, "the more complicated your life becomes and the more you pay for goods and services you wouldn't otherwise buy." What turns him on is work that, "because of its creativity, is more like play. Next to work comes tennis." One knows, without asking, that he is good at it.

Sitting in the soft dusk of his rented Bel Air ranch house, Harve recalls how novelist James Jones' widow kissed him after the screening of *From Here to Eternity* and said, "Jimmy would have been proud."

The tasteful dwelling with its pegged oak floors, massive fireplace, understated furnishings and large plants has the feel of a place that is merely occupied. (With eighteen-hour working days, Harve's home life is extremely limited.) But there are some personal touches. A director's chair with his name on it, standing against the glass-walled backdrop of the San Fernando Valley. In the bedroom and small adjoining office, a "Rich Man, Poor Man" montage . . . photos of Harve smacking a tennis ball and Quiz Kid Harve, age eleven, hand upraised . . . a framed certificate from the Quiz Kids Hall of Fame.

The five-bedroom home in Malibu where he and his wife of sixteen years raised their twelve-year-old son and ten-year-old daughter is on the market. For two years, since the failure of attempts to save the marriage, Harve Bennett—who, as a tot, hated to see his mother leave the house— has lived by himself. The separation was amicable; he sees his children about twice a week.

A marriage, unlike a piece of videotape, cannot be made to work by the quick press of an editing button. One senses what it cost Harve Bennett to accept defeat.

"It's the typical story," he says, "of one person whose life revolved around work and another who was not being fulfilled. I had been through my midlife crisis and she was going through hers, and we came out in different places. Now I'm in a *real* crisis—having to deal with being absolutely alone.''

He deals with it by throwing himself into work. When he comes home at night, he may have three scripts to read. He watches television for professional purposes or as a bedtime placebo. (His all-time favorite is Sid Caesar's ''Your Show of Shows.'')

Since his marriage broke up, he has resumed therapy. (''Every engine needs a tune-up.'') He finds relaxation in his own form of meditation. ''My personality is oriented toward performance, knowing answers, being on top of things. To just let go and say, *I have no thoughts in my mind and nothing is expected of me,* is very calming.''

Sometimes questions intrude . . . questions about meaning, purpose, value. ''I find there are no answers to those questions, so I have been able, much of the time, to throw the questions out. I think these are parental questions that come from our manufactured concepts of what's expected of us.''

Does he consider his work art or craft? ''Pop art. I used to call it craft, but I stopped being so hard on myself. I think it is probably snobbish to say that if something is on a mass medium, it is therefore of lesser value as art.'' In a way, he says, ''what I do is like a dog act. . . . But I used to think that way about 'Quiz Kids,' too. Now I look back and say that not many kids in America could have done that, and it was *not* a dog act.''

Once he was ''very concerned'' about the ephemeral nature of his work; now, he feels, ''It matters not. It is possible that 'Six Million Dollar Man' will run for a generation after I'm gone, which amuses me but hardly makes me feel like Michelangelo. I don't believe in immortality, so I don't need it. Doing good work—the pursuit of excellence—has come to be, as it was for John Kennedy, all there is.''

A blend of tough and humble, this man who struggled to the top regards himself as a democrat in the Jeffersonian sense. What he admires in Golda Meir, as in Abraham Lincoln, is the common touch: greatness that never loses ''the sense that you are among others.'' He paraphrases Bergman's final lines as Golda: ''The task is the thing. I did what had to be done, and someone will come after me and do better.''

Of all he has done, he is proudest of ''Rich Man, Poor Man''—an ''unqualified smash'' that harked back to the outlook of the forties. ''It exemplified the American Dream: the classic Henry Fonda hero, overshadowed by people who make it financially, who represents the heart of gold—the outsider who is really the insider.'' Much of his work (including ''Six Million Dollar Man'' and ''Bionic Woman'') falls, Harve says, into the broad tradition of Frank Capra's *Mr. Smith Goes to Washington:* modern morality plays about goodness and patriotism— the ordinary person become extraordinary. What might be called a Quiz Kid syndrome.

Harve's last Quiz Kid year coincided with an historical watershed: the birth of the atomic age, which climaxed the Industrial Revolution and introduced a new scientific-technological epoch. ''It marked the beginning of the breaking up of family and social values as we had known them. After that, nothing would ever be the same.'' And so, he muses, ''I had a larger malaise: standing much applauded in the old world and suddenly finding myself facing a new kind of world, precisely when I was losing that sense of belonging that had characterized my childhood.'' A dominant theme in his work is the attempt to reconcile those two worlds: technology at the service of traditional virtues.

With age, he has grown more conservative, more uncertain. ''As I heard a dear friend, Dalton Trumbo, say a month before he died, when he was being honored for his courage in standing up to the blacklist: 'I have come to believe that there is not very much in this world, maybe nothing, that is worth dying for.' Which I thought was the essence of growing older. I can conceive of sacrificing my life to protect those I love. Beyond that, I have trouble defining what other values are worth laying down my life for.''

Yet in *Star Trek,* which may be Harve's own midlife statement, he has created a fantasy in which classical ideals and noble self-sacrifice triumph in a futuristic world. Reflecting on the film, many months after our interview, I remember his wistful remark: ''Sometimes I feel disoriented and, like Miniver Cheevy in that famous poem, yearn for days of old when it was much simpler, when Mom and Dad told us what to do. We can't go back to that now. But I think we would like to.''

Vanessa Brown:
Our Favorite Actress

She presents a touching portrait of thoroughly sincere, trusting innocence . . . that makes the adolescence of a Jennifer Jones seem corny and that of a June Allyson seem like a pampered midget's.
       —Manny Farber, *The New Republic,* September 19, 1944
       (reviewing Vanessa Brown's performance in *Youth Runs Wild*)

She was gorgeous.
       —Ex-Quiz Kid Patrick Conlon

"Quiz Kids" was little more than a whistlestop for Vanessa Brown, a fourteen-year-old stage actress who made a handful of appearances on the program in 1943, in transit to Hollywood. But her publicity constantly accentuated the Quiz Kid angle. "RKO started playing it up," she says, "and it just snowballed."

Look picked Vanessa, at eighteen, as one of four future female stars, along with Elizabeth Taylor, Ann Blyth, and Jane Powell. Vanessa never quite reached the first rank, though she played important roles in close to twenty motion pictures, notably *The Late George Apley, The Heiress,* and *The Bad and the Beautiful.* B-movie fans may best remember her as Jane to Lex Barker's Tarzan. Onstage, she toured as Katharine Hepburn's sidekick in *As You Like It* and starred for two years on Broadway with Tom Ewell in *The Seven Year Itch.* She was Barry Nelson's "favorite wife" on the "My Favorite Husband" television series. On radio, she worked opposite Ray Milland, Vincent Price, Lee J. Cobb, Walter Pidgeon, Herbert Marshall, Mark Stevens, Ronald Colman and Joseph Cotton. She was honored by two stars in the pavement of Hollywood Boulevard and has been listed in *Who's Who of American Women* and *Foremost Women in Communications.* She even had a song named for her, a bouncy Muzak standard.

Yet she says, "To this day, I'll come into a room and somebody'll say,

'Oh, the Quiz Kid!' I met Orson Welles at a party, and he said, 'I'm bright too, you know!' ''

Lovely, dimpled Vanessa, with heart-shaped face, high cheekbones and Viennese glow, made more of a name for herself, more quickly, than any Quiz Kid regular. But it is a name that will not be found on the Quiz Kids roster. Then, she was Smylla (Smee'la) Brind. "My father put some letters together, and Smylla came out," she used to explain. When she got to Hollywood the film moguls euphonized Smylla first to Tessa, then Vanessa, a name Mervyn Le Roy of Twentieth Century-Fox salvaged from the discarded title of a Garbo picture.

"He knew I hated it," she says, "and he wasn't used to people hating what he created. Ten years later, he'd say, 'Still thinking of changing it?' It was traumatic. Any alteration of the self—makeup, eyebrows— was not moral. Now I've made a bridge: Smylla, Vanessa, either way it's me."

When I close my eyes, thirty-eight years slip away. Her enunciation has the same cultured yet cherubic quality it did on the Quiz Kids show. What has been called a chameleon accent, adaptable to any role.

Vanessa in the flesh is another matter. The svelte young pinup who was *Esquire*'s Lady Fair—whose 118-pound, 36-23-36 form graced *Life, Cue*, and *Cosmopolitan* covers in 1953, when *The Seven Year Itch* was a Broadway sensation—has gotten, frankly, fat.

The magazine covers hang in the hallway of her informal ranch home overlooking Los Angeles' San Fernando Valley. *Life,* she laughs, was a nip-and-tuck affair: "Stalin died that week, but the Russians held back the news for two days. By then I was already on the cover and the *next* girl got bumped!"

She may have lost her figure, but not her sense of fun. Fifty-three-year-old Vanessa Brown still is the vibrant, wholesome charmer Roby Hickok once likened to a "beautiful Swiss milkmaid." When Vanessa is amused, which is often, her cheeks blaze and her eyes crinkle with child-like delight.

Every nook of the sunny yellow home is crammed with two decades' accumulation of unmatched furniture, books, papers, art, and music. Vanessa's second husband, Mark Sandrich, Jr., is a composer-director-producer. The Cassini gowns and Claire Potter Oriental persimmon pajamas Vanessa modeled for *Life* now hang in their twenty-year-old daughter Cathy's closet. "See—" the practical mama brings out the pajama outfit to show me—"It's a very good cotton, and she fits it."

"She doesn't fill it out like Mom did," interjects seventeen-year-old David.

Vanessa came up in Hollywood at the same time as Marilyn Monroe. With a 169 I.Q. and strict old-country upbringing, Miss Brown was hardly the standard celluloid sexpot of that era. Though *Cosmo* proclaimed, "Her Brains Didn't Get in Her Way," she maintains that her reputation as "Hollywood's IQtie" cost her some jobs. Demure Vanessa, who appeared on *Look*'s cover at sixteen with unadorned sweater and unpainted face, later stooped to an occasional provocative pose to prove that a girl with a good head need not be an egghead. "In Hollywood," she told *Life*, "having a mind is all right if you conceal it behind a low-cut bosom."

First she did some girlie shots, tame by today's standards, in black lace bra and panties, which brought indignant protests to the helpless Quiz Kids office. ("I didn't know how terrible it would be until after they talked me into it," blushes Vanessa.) Then she made headlines by suggesting that she should pose in the buff "for a happily married photographer," so as to get in character for the seductive model in *The Seven-Year Itch*. Thousands of photographers reportedly volunteered, and it even was rumored that the pictures had been taken. Vanessa later explained, embarrassed, that the whole thing had been a joke and that the "happily married photographer" was her (first) husband, for whom she had indeed posed—back shots only. Nevertheless, the army newspaper *Stars and Stripes* dubbed her Miss Cheesecake of 1952, a favor she repaid by mailing the G.I.'s one from Lindy's.

Asked in an interview by Oliver Curtiss, "What happens to a Quiz Kid who grows up into an auburn-haired beauty," she replied:

> You do anything to convince people you're not some sort of intellectual monster. You draw the stage-door johnnies who are always bringing red roses, and you love it. It's wonderful to have people think you're normal, and I don't ever want to hear about being a Quiz Kid again.

At twenty-five, midway through her run in *Seven Year Itch*, Vanessa Brown was the hottest thing in New York. She was earning in the $75,000 bracket and had been picked by commentator H.V. Kaltenborn as one of 1952's outstanding women, along with Princess Margaret of England. ("Who is this Margaret Rose?" another actress wondered. "Is she in the theater?" Without missing a beat, Vanessa cracked, "Of course! She's playing at the Palace.")

Katharine Hepburn hailed Miss Brown as the one young Hollywood actress sure to achieve greatness on the stage. But Vanessa headed back to tinsel town and another plum: "My Favorite Husband." After that, relative obscurity. When she surfaced in 1967 in the film *Rosie*, she played a "roundish, weak-willed sister." Since then, she has done two television roles: in Norman Lear's "All That Glitters" (1977) and on General Hospital (1979-81), as an overweight mother attending Richard Simmons' reducing clinic. ("One of the joys" of that assignment was losing twenty-six pounds in Simmons' real-life exercise program.) The weight crept up on Vanessa, who always had a weakness for sweets, during the child-bearing-and-rearing years, when she was not before the camera.

Popular idols have been known to pay a bigger price than some extra pounds. Perhaps the real point about Vanessa Brown is that she was smart enough to survive.

Back in 1943, when Quiz Kids plucked her for a guest spot on the panel, Austrian-Jewish Smylla had been understudying the refugee girl in *Watch on the Rhine* for nearly two years. The role was a fitting one. The Viennese beauty had been evacuated to Paris at five, then to America at nine, by a father astute enough to keep his wife and only child a step ahead of the Nazis. They left for New York, with the few possessions they were able to bring, in March, 1938, just as Hitler was marching into Vienna.

It took Smylla a mere three or four months to become conversant with English. Soon she was reading Dickens and Dumas, as she worked her way through the alphabet on the library shelves. Her quick ear for language came from her "Papa," who knew eleven—most of them, including Chinese and Sanskrit, self-taught. He tutored her every morning to help her retain her French and German.

Radio appearances on a junior movie review panel led to the invitation to join the cast of *Watch on the Rhine*. She was crushed when her parents made her turn down the role because it would have meant missing school, but producer Herman Shumlin offered to let her understudy instead. The show opened on her thirteenth birthday. By the time the road tour began, her parents relented and took her out of school. She got classmates to send her their notes and, on her return, she passed her exams at Hunter High School for the gifted.

"Quiz Kids" tapped her just before the play left Chicago. "When we met her backstage, we were immediately captivated," wrote Roby Hickok. Smylla placed first and made additional guest appearances in the ensuing months, when we Quiz Kids were in New York and again when she was on her way to Hollywood. She wowed listeners by answering riddles posed in *francais* and *deutsch* and translating Hitler's speeches and Napoleon's letters.

"I wanted to be on the show terribly much," she says, "even before they came to the theater and picked me. I used to listen to it and had already filled out a questionnaire. I guess I wanted to show that I knew a lot. I've always been competitive, ambitious to succeed. Less so now. Mark has shown me another side of living—taking time to enjoy the moment."

Vanessa once joked that she wanted to earn her doctorate because her parents were Ph.D's "and I don't want to be the only one who isn't."

Her mother, Anna Butterman Brind, was an Adlerian psychologist and ardent Zionist, who had met her husband in a Hebrew seminar in Vienna. Baby Smylla was the guinea pig of the circle around Alfred Adler. "They all followed my progress," she laughs. "They measured me like they measured everything else."

Her father, Nah Brind, a man of few words but many talents, was an Orthodox-Jew-turned-unbeliever who had hiked across the frontier of his native Russia at the start of the 1917 Revolution. He translated all of Dostoevsky's works into German, wrote for French papers, acted in the Yiddish Theater, and, after coming to New York, contributed to the Jewish *Daily Forward*. Eventually he got a counseling degree and, with his wife, helped found the first Psychodrama Institute of California, after the family moved there to launch Smylla's movie career.

Only in later years did she become aware of her parents' "enormous contribution" to their field. Her consciousness was of the "rigors and joys" of growing up within the "tight family unit" in which she lived until her first marriage at twenty-two—impressions she described in a monograph after her parents' deaths:

> . . . As I remember my father—his was a stern, austere, quiet, and
> somewhat remote personality. Getting a word or an opinion out of
> him took monumental patience that was rewarded by rare aphorisms.
> . . . Yet he loved jokes and puns and, according to his friends,
> took great pains to set them up.
> My mother . . . was a very forceful and beautiful woman, who

was able to be supportive of people. . . . To the outside world she
was a dynamo: vivacious and charming. To her inner circle, father
and me, she could be very stubborn and difficult. . . .She was
very ambitious, but her ambitions were not merely personal—they
extended out to her family and to those whom she befriended.*

"My mother was a very pushy woman," says Vanessa. "She was
always talking about how brilliant my father was. So naturally, I wanted
to be brilliant." Achievement ran on multiple tracks. As a child, besides
being a top student in accelerated classes ("the accepted standard in our
house"), she played the piano, sang, painted, won a newspaper short
story contest, and wrote, directed and acted in school plays.

Her theatrical career had begun at seven, in Paris, when her father—
then writing subtitles for European releases of American films—had her
dub a little-girl role. Then, in New York, he coached her for radio
auditions using a reading from *Song of Bernadette*.

By the time she actually played Bernadette on "Hollywood Startime,"
she was an up-and-coming young Hollywood actress. Her mother had
initiated the movie bid (realizing the big money was there) during the
Watch on the Rhine tour. She took her daughter to agent Paul Kohner,
who, struck by the girl's resemblance to Ingrid Bergman, sent photos to
David O. Selznick. The producer agreed to sign Smylla if she could get to
movieland on her own; the Quiz Kids bonds helped pay the way.

On loan to RKO, she won immediate plaudits as the teenage lead in
Youth Runs Wild—though, as one review noted, it was hard to picture
the wholesome fifteen-year-old doing any such thing. After that
promising start, she jumped from studio to studio until Mervyn Le Roy
decided to groom her for stardom.

"My mother," she says, "didn't have terribly much influence along
the way, except she was on the set until I was eighteen, and she made a
lot of my clothes, and her values were stamped on me."

Tired of talking, Vanessa suggests a swim in her neighbor's pool,
where she works out daily. "I can do forty laps. My uncle taught me; he
said I could have been an Olympic swimmer."

Exercise is part of her survival formula. In college days, she sometimes
played tennis with Charlie Chaplin's wife, Oona O'Neill, at the Chaplin

---

* Vanessa Brown, *In My Father's House*, 1975, in the archives of the Yivo Institute,
New York City, N.Y., p. 1-a, 1-b.

home. "Charlie would entertain whoever was waiting to play. That was kind of what you were invited for, to be the audience for friend Charlie. One Sunday afternoon he did an imitation of a Thai opera, which is like a soap opera and takes forever. He enacted all the characters, and he was the audience eating oranges, and he did it all in gibberish, like a Thai sing-song, but you understood everything.

"There were maybe two of us, and he was doing it for us, and that was it. It was fantastic. Real magic. If it had been on film, it would be a classic."

With Vanessa, unlike Chaplin, acting was not a compulsion but "a nice way to make a living"—something she "fell into," did well at, and found she enjoyed.

She was star-struck in a different way. She had a hankering to be an astronomer, loved math and physics. But when it came time to register at UCLA, her father advised her against trying to combine those courses with movie work, so she majored in English. "I figured he knew what he was saying. There was always an absolute quality about him."

Nor had she been given any real choice about whether to go to college. "It was in the air that I had to go. I didn't see what it was going to do for my career. I think a lot of it was a waste of time."

She enrolled at sixteen, a year after her film debut, and kept on working straight through college, juggling classes and cast calls, getting up at 5:30 A.M., doing homework on the set, and eking out a B average. She was not particularly choosy about her roles. As she once told *Theater Arts,* "An actor who works constantly eats in the same way." She "took a big ribbing" at school when she did *Tarzan.* "My intellectual friends said, 'My God, what you won't do for money!' I needed the job, I had to pay the rent."

UCLA knew her as Smylla Brind, and that is how she signed her movie reviews for the campus paper, the *Daily Bruin.* But Smylla's reviews came to an abrupt halt after she panned *I've Always Loved You* (later renamed *Concerto*) but averred that the female lead, Vanessa Brown, would "bear watching." Her editor, Frank Mankiewicz, hit the ceiling: "If you still want to work in the industry," he warned her, "I suggest we not run this." She switched to book reviews. ("They were safer.")

For a long time, her *Bruin* associates and her professors were the only ones privy to her double identity. Not until a large picture of Vanessa Brown appeared in the *Los Angeles Times* did her campus friends recognize Smylla as the face they had seen on the cinema screen.

Friendship was something of a hunger for a girl who had moved around
so much. "Every damn time you had to start all over again." When she
was naturalized in 1943, the year she went from Quiz Kids to Hollywood,
she felt glad because "now I would belong, I wouldn't be an outsider."

Her immediate acceptance by the regular Quiz Kids played a big part in
her warm feelings toward the brief experience. "When I first met the
Kids," she tells me—"Dick, Claude, you, Joel—I felt more comfortable
than with any other kids I knew at that time. I guess you respond to other
people being bright." Traveling with *Watch on the Rhine,* she had
helped other youngsters in the cast with their studies. "I was doing a
girl's homework for her, and she was going bowling with the boys. I was
so mad! I didn't *want* to go bowling, but I wanted to be asked."

When we Quiz Kids came to Hollywood late in 1943, Vanessa already
was there; we visited her on the set. When she made good as Agnes in
The Late George Apley, some of the Kids sent her a gigantic card. Later,
touring in *As You Like It,* she met Dick Williams in Boston and spent a
"marvelous" fall day with me at Northwestern, renewing our
acquaintance. "I still remember how the leaves looked, red and yellow,"
she tells me. "I was proud and happy that you were going in for
journalism. I felt maternal—I had an interest in your future."

Years later, when she was in Boston for the opening of one of Mark's
plays, Claude Brenner gave her a party. Now, coincidentally, she lives six
doors from Harve Bennett on a winding drive which, Harve says, "we
are thinking of renaming Quiz Kids Alley."

In Hollywood, with its evanescent associations, friendships tend to be
fleeting but the bonds can be deep. When Vanessa first arrived, Shirley
Temple greeted her at a party and took the neophyte under her wing.
Later, when Vanessa made her splash in *Seven Year Itch,* Shirley came
backstage. "We congratulated each other on our good fortune," Vanessa
recalls—"on having nice husbands. I haven't seen her since. Those of us
who are from the wars of growing up in this town congratulate each other
on having survived emotionally. When Marilyn was with Yves Montand,
I said, 'Marilyn, you look so happy!' and she said, 'So do you!' "

Vanessa and Marilyn Monroe first met in a dance class at Twentieth
Century Fox. Vanessa showed the "new girl" around, answered her
questions, told her what coaching was available. "Marilyn wanted to
improve herself, and I tried to help her because she was very nice and

didn't know where to go. I was never a starlet like Marilyn," she stresses. "As a starlet, you're not considered an actress but a piece of cheesecake. You have to go to a lot of junky events where they snap your picture in a backless dress."

When Marilyn died, Vanessa (at the suggestion of a mutual friend, actress Jean Peters) went to CBS, where she had a contact, to make sure the news hawks didn't write "a lousy obit."

"I wanted to have her treated with dignity. Those of us that come from those years were part of a family. You felt kind of responsible for each other."

Vanessa doubts the sex goddess intended suicide and blames the studio executives for her death from an overdose of sleeping pills. "They made millions off her and never cared about the results. When she finally got to psychiatrists, it was very late. She had a drive to become a somebody because she was born a nobody, an illegitimate child. She was alone at the mercy of these mentors. She went from man to man because she didn't know any better. She didn't have the background I had, the parents who understood something.

"I didn't ask much guidance from my mom and dad. I'd already gotten it. Morality was like the salt at the table. But it's hard. You're forming your first crushes, and they're not the boy next door. At sixteen and seventeen, you'd have a director who'd be very interested in you, and you'd know he was married, and you'd wonder what's the nature of his interest, and yet you'd be fascinated by his conversation. There were a lot of tight squeaks that I was very agile in getting out from under."

One situation from which Vanessa adroitly extricated herself was an unwanted marriage proposal from Sam Goldwyn, Jr., when she was hardly more than eighteen. She simply told the elder Goldwyn about it, and he shipped his son to England.

Her first marriage, four years later, was to Dr. Robert A. Franklyn, a plastic surgeon ten years her senior, whom she prefers not to discuss. "A man with positive opinions," as *Cosmopolitan* characterized him, he took over guidance of her career. It was he who encouraged his bride, fresh out of college, to cultivate a sexier image, replacing her sweaters and skirts with decollete gowns.

"All brides are beautiful, but Vanessa was one of the loveliest," warbled the September, 1950 *Ex-Quiz Kid Resume*. "Vanessa writes intriguingly that she hopes to come to Chicago this year 'in one of New

York's finest plays of the past season, with one of the greatest stars in the world today, by one of the best playwrights in the world.' "

The play was *As You Like It,* the star Kate Hepburn, who chose Vanessa to play Celia to her Rosalind when Cloris Leachman left the cast. "I went up to read for her," Vanessa remembers, "and she said, this forbidding lady: 'You think you're smart, you Quiz Kid, you! What did Shakespeare mean by the phrase, bearded like a pard?' (I was startled that she had read about the Quiz Kid stuff—I certainly hadn't mentioned it.) And I said, 'Leopard . . . bearded like a leopard.' It was a guess, a *wild* guess. And she says, 'By golly, yes! You *are* smart!' "

Vanessa considered herself Hepburn's protege and later named her daughter Cathy after the older actress. "She is absolutely fantastic. She lets you get close, but only up to a point. I used to tease her—as near as you could come to teasing her. She went to great lengths not to hear about reviews. In Chicago, she had a curtain in front of her dressing room, and I walked slowly in front of it and read the notice, the part about her, out loud. And then you heard this piercing voice: 'Tell that girl to be quiet!' "

In a huge red leather scrapbook with "Vanessa Brown" imprinted in gilt letters on the cover, there is a picture of herself and the great lady, bedecked with precious gems. Vanessa recounts how she lured camera-shy Kate into posing for a March of Dimes benefit, a traveling show of famous jewels. "Someone called me and said, 'Miss Brown, we under-stand you have great influence with Miss Hepburn'—first time I'd ever heard that!—and did I think Miss Hepburn would take a picture with the ruby necklace that Essex gave [Queen] Elizabeth?" Vanessa said since it was for a worthy cause, if everything could be set up to take the pictures quickly, right after the performance, she would see what she could do to persuade Kate.

"I said to her, 'I've got something to tell you later.' She was like a child. All through the play, she would say to me, 'Psst! Psst!' Finally she has this very fast change, and she whispers 'Come here! Now! You must tell me now!' " Vanessa had so whetted Kate's curiosity that, when she told her what was wanted, the grande dame agreed to pose . . . but only on condition that Vanessa come along. "So they gave me the Hope diamond to wear, and these enormous diamond rings on both hands."

Heady with the success of *As You Like It,* Vanessa began angling for a shot at Broadway. ("My ex-husband thought that would be a good idea because things were slow in Hollywood.") In 1952, she landed the lead in George Axelrod's comedy, *The Seven Year Itch,* produced by Elliott

Nugent and Courtney Burr. She got a boost in the competition for the part of the wholesome temptress when Burr happened into a tavern where patrons were watching Vanessa on "Twenty Questions." "I slayed everybody in the bar with some answer about chicken liver. And I had a movie running in New York called *The Fighter*, with Richard Conti and Lee J. Cobb, and there was a huge slinky picture of me, five feet tall, in a black satin strapless, embracing this semi-naked fighter, in front of the Mayfair Theater, off Broadway. But the clincher was that I asked Axelrod, 'Did you write . . .' and I gave him the name of this obscure pocket book, which was his first book. He was absolutely enchanted."

Nugent told *Cosmopolitan* that he had been warned about Vanessa's Quiz Kid reputation but found her intelligence "an asset, not a hindrance. She studied the play . . . so thoroughly that she brought depth of character to her portrayal." Nugent recognized that Vanessa had just the right mixture of innocence and allure. Critics agreed: "Exquisite as a wild violet" . . . "Fascinating, even fresher than the average daisy" . . . "Delightfully giddy" . . . "A joy to watch" . . . "A perfect performance."

But Axelrod was not so pleased with an interview Vanessa gave the *New York Journal-American*, expressing the quaint hope that girls who saw the play would be warned away from married men. "George Axelrod didn't mean to write a message play," she laughs. "He was furious with me."

Vanessa left *The Seven Year Itch* in 1954, after six hundred performances. Her husband was interfering. "He got into a fight with the producers over money, and he was threatening to sue. It got sticky. I was very tired. And I was starting to wonder, *what next?*"

Sam and Bella Spiwak had written a play for her, *Festival*. But she turned it down, signed with agent Norman Brokaw (even though there was no specific role in the offing) and returned to Hollywood. "I figured I was in a big hit, and that was it. I couldn't see myself in another play and another magazine cover. The fact that I was an enormous success really bothered me. I'd made it—I didn't see where else you could go. Had I been oriented as an actress, I might have said, *In another part I'll perfect this or that.* I had never envisioned myself as a Broadway star. It was a great part, and I loved doing it, but it didn't make sense to keep going that way.

"I wasn't very content in New York. My marriage was finished, and I hadn't settled down. I wanted to come home. Maybe I wanted to go back to Hollywood and try to make that kind of success there. I'd had good parts, but never the kind I had in *Seven Year Itch*—sexy, witty . . . But I didn't go about it very cleverly. I didn't have any jobs once I got back.''

Stage success does not automatically translate to cinema stardom, she points out. ''Angela Lansbury is now going from play to play to play. Bacall can't make it back.'' Vanessa tried to buy movie rights to *The Seven Year Itch*, but Axelrod chose Billy Wilder, who cast Marilyn Monroe in the part Vanessa had created on the stage. (''The picture was miserable. It was not Marilyn's fault. The direction was heavy-handed. The delicacy of the encounter was what the play strove for. But if you lay it on with a trowel—'')

''My Favorite Husband'' was a lucky accident; Vanessa happened to have tea with a CBS executive just when Joan Caulfield had dropped out. The show was in its third and last season. ''There was not much push behind it,'' says Vanessa. After that, there were lean years for the ingenue (then nearing thirty) who once had chirped that she wouldn't believe a slump if she saw one. She did some single television spots and summer stock and tried to start a repertory company with William Saroyan and others, but Saroyan pulled out and the project foundered.

When she met Mark Sandrich at a dinner party, he said he might have a script for her. Instead, the thirty-one-year-old bachelor married her. Mark pulled her off the merry-go-round she had ridden since childhood. On their second dinner date, between mouthfuls, he announced that the last thing he would do was to marry an actress. ''I figured he meant that,'' Vanessa smiles, ''and I was very much in love with him. So I turned down a lot of television and a movie or two. And then after a few years, I didn't get any offers.''

''I think she was relieved,'' says Mark, ''that I didn't care whether she acted or not.''

Vanessa is in the kitchen. At the battered grand piano, fifty-three-year-old Mark, balding and baggy-trousered, has been playing one of his compositions.

He and Vanessa, he tells me, were contemporaries at UCLA but never met there. He never saw her onstage, doesn't remember what he thought of her films, and, although he was a Quiz Kids fan, never heard her on the program. Her brains do not intimidate him: ''There are a lot of bright people.''

Mark smiles as he recalls how his determination not to marry an actress evaporated. ''You make these rules, and then you meet a girl, you fall in love, and you get married." He hadn't wanted to get involved in "the terrible ego problems actresses have. If they don't get a job, they feel personally rejected."

His wife, he says, was no exception. But problems in the early part of their twenty-two-year marriage worked themselves out, as competitive Vanessa absorbed some of her husband's calm. By the time she started making the rounds again, looking for acting jobs, she felt quite at ease.

"It doesn't matter whether I get the job or not," says Vanessa, "and I've gotten over the fact that it's a smaller part. I have fun, catch up with other actors I haven't seen in awhile, and enjoy whatever the routine is that you have to do."

She regards "the good family life" she and Mark have created as one of her most satisfying accomplishments: "I feel very useful." Both Cathy (a UCLA English major) and David have shown some interest in the entertainment industry, but their parents have tried to steer them to something steadier. "Unless you've got a burning, unshakable drive," says Vanessa, "plumbing is better business."

She touts her children's honors and achievements like any proud mama. But her son's high school graduation freed her ("I celebrated inwardly") to focus again on her own career—one which, through the years, has taken on different and deeper dimensions.

"Survival," says Vanessa, "means you're still a total person." Her total is the sum of many parts. Her father's daughter, she is multifaceted; she has blossomed in writing, broadcasting, civic affairs and art.

Her serious side began coming to the fore during the troubled period in New York, during *Seven Year Itch*. At twenty-five, Vanessa—whose whole life had spun on fast forward—already was in the throes of what amounted to an unusually early midlife crisis. The dissolution of her first marriage was jarring: "I didn't believe in divorce, but it was necessary." Meanwhile, she was seeing a therapist and having long talks with friends like drama critic George Jean Nathan. "He was the closest to being able to explain why I was feeling so bad. The advice was 'Keep going, keep writing, and you'll live through it.' "

Already she had sold three stories to the *New York Daily News*. She completed a play, *Europa and the Bull*, and collected a pile of rejection slips. "In the American theater," she told *Cosmopolitan*, "the accent is on youth. I'll have to prepare for the time when I won't be in demand. An actress gets old and some people don't want to see her. But a writer improves with age, like brandy.''

Later she would write in the *Los Angeles Times* that the conversations
with Nathan

> . . . effected a rebirth within me. I was ripe for it. He helped give me
> courage to heed my inner direction once more.
>
> The blocked path where I had stumbled opened. Again, it was
> the search and perfection of one's inner expression in whatever form
> one chose. No longer the emphasis on the external trappings of
> ''reaching the top.'' Rather an infinitely more exacting, and never-
> to-be-fulfilled task, the pursuit of one's personal destiny. . . .

In 1956, the same year she and her first husband finally split up and her
repertory company closed, she went to the Democratic convention as an
alternate delegate for Adlai E. Stevenson. She produced and co-hosted a
radio program on election issues and made a television documentary on
the hydrogen bomb and nuclear fallout.

She first had worked for Stevenson in 1952 and had invited him to
Seven Year Itch the night of Eisenhower's inauguration. When he came
backstage, she struck a pose and held up a sign she had painted,
''Stevenson in '56.''

''The only question is,'' said the defeated candidate, ''what shall I run
for?''

He was, Vanessa remembers, ''very low. He was pleased that someone
would think he wasn't finished.'' She still believes he would have made a
difference as President. ''I liked the direction he seemed to be pointing us
in, which was greater than ourselves.''

After Stevenson's 1956 loss, she continued as Los Angeles media
liaison for John F. Kennedy and for Robert Hutchins' Center for the
Study of Democratic Institutions. She also did extensive research and
lecturing on automation, in cooperation with Labor Secretary Willard
Wirtz—a far cry from the days when she had spoken to college students
about ''Sex on Broadway.'' But she became disenchanted with Hutchins
and his heavily-funded program (''I don't think he was in touch with
people or real ideas'') and disgusted with a Democratic leadership that
could neither balance a budget nor keep a poverty program afloat.

While she was doing media contact for the Democrats, she met Edward
R. Murrow, who exerted ''a deep moral influence'' on her. ''He was
discouraged about the way CBS was handling the coverage of news. Yet
he felt it was his duty to continue as long as he could. He had a mission: a
belief that if people were informed, they would do the right thing. It had

purpose and direction. It made what you did every day make sense, rather than just adoring yourself or worrying about the lines on your face.''

One of the people she dated during that period was Frank Sinatra. ''One evening we talked about science—he knew a lot—and he said, 'I've never had an evening like this.' His yearning, strangely enough, was to conduct music. He gave me a record, his first conducting record. He had that same feeling for excellence, wanting to do something that will stay as a monument, which as a performer you don't have.''

In 1962, three years after her remarriage, Murrow—by then at Voice of America—hired her to do interviews with political leaders like Stevenson, Robert Kennedy, Eugene McCarthy, and Arthur Goldberg. She spent eight years as a low-paid but dedicated writer, producer, and correspondent, at a time when her children were small and she ''needed an outlet,'' and went on to do economic reporting for National Public Radio. Her interviews covered such figures as Walt Disney, Zubin Mehta, Dr. Benjamin Spock, Danny Kaye, Louis Nizer, and Dr. William Pickering, and subjects ranging from labor relations to solar radiation to SYNCOM, the first communications satellite.

Her most rewarding VOA program was about an inexpensive food supplement put out by the Meals for Millions foundation. An American teacher traveling in Mexico heard the broadcast and ordered the powder for 5,000 starving Indian orphans. ''So my program fed the kids. It was something concrete—something you could touch that came from the talking.''

For Vanessa, the interview technique is a way of getting comfortable with people. Even back in her early Hollywood days, she would buttonhole established stars and pull out an ever-ready pad and pencil.

Utilizing her accumulated contacts and her ever-fattening diaries, she has written personality profiles and book reviews for the *Los Angeles Times* syndicate, *National Review,* and other publications, and has done newswriting and camera work for KTLA, a local television station. She is collaborating with her agent, Don Schwartz, on a book about his method of teaching acting; developing a radio series; and producing pilots for a television panel on career guidance. She does readings for Jewish benefits and has been honored by Bonds for Israel, B'nai Brith and Hadassah.

As an artist, she has had a one-woman showing at a Beverly Hills gallery. She does commissions and experiments with string painting. ''You turn on some music, go blank inside, and it comes out.''

She works at being relaxed, living in the here and now. ''Each day I start out with a calendar and try to finish the projects I'm on. If not, something else happens along the way, so it doesn't really matter. I'll do the best I can—nobody can do better. There's nothing I feel competitive about now. But,'' she adds, ''it'll come again. It's not dead.''

Vanessa is completing rewrites on *Claire—A Love Story*, a novel ''of self-discovery and development.'' The precis has a familiar ring: a young woman in her early twenties has gone from parents that sound suspiciously like the author's into the arms of a ''fairly standard overprotective ogre'' whom the heroine divorces after going into analysis. She has two affairs and ends up with a movie producer husband, a sort of ''nice Joe Mankiewicz.''

Autobiographical? ''Do you think I would *tell* you that?'' Vanessa bridles with (mock?) indignation. ''Of course it's not!''

Mankiewicz, who directed her in *The Late George Apley*, once predicted that Vanessa Brown would be a great star. ''If she doesn't become great in pictures,'' he said, ''she will some other way, as a painter or dancer. Something is going to burst forth from that kid.''

Much has burst forth from Vanessa Brown. Yet now and then, one senses this normally ebullient woman retreating to some private region of self-doubt. When I compliment her on her writing style, her eyes cloud with an uncertain stare, and I recall a story she has told me: Once she asked Ronald Colman, ''How do you know if a take is good?'' and he said, ''After all these years, I still don't know.''

A performer looks outside for affirmation. For Vanessa, *Seven Year Itch* made her feel that she was a comedienne; ''Quiz Kids'' told her, *Yes, I am smart.* The child who, in Paris, wanted to be first in her class so she could get a ceremonial kiss from the mayor grew into the young woman who sought her accolades from audiences. . . . who won the prize, then found it empty.

Primed to perform, Vanessa Brown now plays herself. The single-minded drive of a Chaplin, a Hepburn, a Marilyn Monroe, is not her natural style. She found the narrow track of ambition too confining, the spotlight stifling. She says of Marilyn: ''The attention I had during *Seven Year Itch*—that's what she had tons of. She probably felt what I felt, triple, every week: I need to be quiet, to withdraw from conversations, to have somebody to whom I can say, 'I don't feel good' or 'I'm excited' or 'I can't fall asleep.' ''

Even Hepburn has expressed ''terror'' at the thought that she has spent her whole life in the theater. In a 1982 interview with Mary

Cantwell, the great Kate compared herself to a fox chased by hawks. ''I don't think I've used my intelligence as much as I could have,'' she said. ''I think I could have amounted to something that would have interested me more. . . . I'd much rather have been a painter or a writer. . . . When you're an actor, really you're trying to please people, aren't you?''

Having glimpsed the limits of glory, Vanessa has chosen inner growth, valuing plaudits from respected friends. Like Carl Sandburg, who scribbled on a restaurant menu after she read one of his poems at a gala affair: ''You be artiste. Many good people besides me love you for what you are, a demure and swift child of god.''

In a retrospective piece on Sandburg, published in the *Los Angeles Times* after his death, alongside her portrait of him, Vanessa recalled a memorable conversation in 1959, when the poet had been her houseguest:

> Carl had been taken by my paintings, as very strong abstractions.
> He was trying to tell me something profound; important; intense and personal. And all that stays with me now is an inchoate feeling of ''Have faith . . . have courage . . . strong feelings . . . force does overcome you . . . stay with it.

In her art—the watercolors with their delicate, Chagall-like hues, the bright free-form string paintings, the shadowy oil peopled with mysterious, watching eyes—she probably expresses her inner being most directly. She signs her paintings Smylla. . . . ''That's my name.''

"Quiz Kids" producers (from left) John Lewellen, Louis G. Cowan, and Rachel Waples Stevenson.

Movie stars and Quiz Kids compete before an audience of servicemen at the Hollywood Canteen. From left: Ruth Duskin, Gerard Darrow, Susan Hayward, Joel Kupperman, Joan Leslie, Richard Williams, Jinx Falkenburg, Harve Bennett Fischman, with Quizmaster Joe Kelly at the microphone.

Assistant Program Director Eliza Merrill ("Roby") Hickok enjoys a laugh
backstage with Ruth Duskin.

Father's Day with the Quiz Kids. From left: Richard and David Williams, Ruth and Boris Duskin, Gerard and Joseph Darrow, Harve and Yale Fischman.

Sitting in for the Quiz Kids on Mother's Day are, left to right: Frances Brenner, Clara Williams, Rita Duskin, and Bessie Darrow (Gerard's aunt). Behind them: Claude, Richard, Ruth, and Gerard.

Joe Kelly presides over another Mother's Day grouping. From left: Sheila, Marcella, and Pat Conlon; Naomi, George, and Rose Cooks; Mark, Alma, and Mike Mullin; Sara, Harriet, and Joel Kupperman.

A post-war Quiz Kids panel relaxes before the show. Lonny Lunde is at the piano with (from left) Pat Conlon, Ruth Duskin, and Joel Kupperman.

Lonny Lunde

Naomi Cooks

Singing with Joe Kelly, from left: Naomi Cooks, Pat Conlon, Joel Kupperman.

The television era brings a new sponsor and a new group of young faces. From left: Janet Ahern, Frankie Vander Ploeg, and Harvey Dytch, along with older regulars Sally Ann Wilhelm and Pat Conlon.

Harvey Dytch is nuzzled by Tracks, the pup he was given on the show.

Joan Bishop sings in the Chicago Opera Company's production of *Manon* in 1945.

A reunion in New York in 1956: Richard Williams, Joan Bishop, and Gerard Darrow.

Actress Vanessa Brown appears on the covers of *Life*, *Look*, and *Cosmopolitan* and as Esquire's Lady Fair.

photo by Caren Goodman

Author Ruth Duskin Feldman today.

photo by Ruth Duskin Feldman

Joan Bishop Barber and her husband, John Barber, look over a Quiz Kids scrapbook.

Energy consultant Claude Brenner.

Jack Lucal, S.J., is headquartered in Geneva,
Switzerland.

Diplomat Richard Williams.

Margaret Merrick Scheffelin poses with her mother, Dorothy Merrick, in 1972.

Producer Harve Bennett

Vanessa Brown today is an artist, writer, and journalist.

photo by Ruth Duskin Feldman

Lon Lunde today, composer by day, lounge pianist by night.

Pat Conlon is now pursuing an acting and directing career in New York.

photo by Ruth Duskin Feldman

Naomi Cooks Mann poses with an oversized pencil from her newest venture, a store called Think Big!

Computer programmer Harvey Dytch with his wife Meredith.

Joel Kupperman: Math Whiz

February, 1942. A letter printed in a large, childish hand arrives at the Quiz Kids office.

Dear Sir:

I am five years old but I play with numbers. I can do 99 or 98 times any number up to 100 in my head . . .

I can do like 1/2 of 3/4 or 2/8 of 5/6 of an apple. I know if sugar sells for 6 cents in one store and 9 cents and 11 cents in other stores, the average price is 8 2/3 cents.

. . . I know a little geography, too. Like about the hemispheres, how many continents, their names and what is N.S.E. and W. of the United States.

I like numbers best. It is fun to fall asleep, counting 6 plus 6 equals 12. 12 plus 12 equals 24. 24 plus 24 equals 48. 48 plus 48 equals 96. 96 plus 96 equals 192. 192 plus 192 equals 384. 384 plus 384 equals 768. 768 plus 768 equals 1,536.

I would like to be a Quiz Kid. I am not as good on numbers as Richard, but I am pretty good . . .

Love and kisses,
Joel Kupperman

P.S. My grandfather has teeth that he takes out at night but he is smart.

February, 1982. On the television "Password" game, the word is "Joel." Guest Bill Cullen gives the clue "Kupperman." The young woman contestant draws a blank. When the game is over, Cullen explains that Joel Kupperman was one of the most famous Quiz Kids. "Boy," he adds, "does that date me!"

For those old enough to remember, "Joel Kupperman" still carries a special mystique. He is the one ex-Quiz Kid whose name almost invariably follows the words, "Whatever happened to . . . " For years after the show ended, people would ask, "What was Joel Kupperman *really* like?" As ex-Quiz Kid Patrick Conlon says, "Joel was the quintessence of what they were selling on that show. He summed it up."

Joel Jay Kupperman began summing it up on "Quiz Kids" when he was not quite six. At his audition, he was asked to multiply 24 by 98. "Dat would be 2,352," he replied instantly. Joel was the toothless dynamo who "lisped in logarithms," as John K. Hutchens of the *New York Times* put it. He was called "Superman Kupperman" by *Coronet* magazine and "Midget Euclid" by *Time*. He could mentally square 999,000 and do quick cube roots of six-digit numbers. Peering out of shatterproof horn-rimmed glasses, he did his lightning computations with the help of "secret tricks"—shortcuts he said he had figured out himself, such as rounding off to the nearest zero before multiplying, and then adding or subtracting the difference. He figured in his head, he once explained, because when he was "young" he had had trouble writing.

At a Philadelphia war bond rally, Joel was asked to estimate the turnout. "I don't make estimates," he coolly informed Harold Hadley of the *Philadelphia Evening Bulletin*. "I calculate correctly."

One thing he calculated was his own income tax. And (on one broadcast) Fred Allen's. "I don't see what all the fuss is about," the *New Yorker* quoted the little boy as saying. "Just a little simple addition and subtraction. And multiplication."

Nor was he fazed when Joe Kelly posed the following problem: "A circle is eight inches in diameter. Inside the circle a triangle is inscribed, and inside the triangle another circle, and inside the circle another triangle, and so on until there are five circles and four trianges. What is the area of the innermost circle?" After some hemming and hawing, Joel came up with the unwieldy fraction 50 2/7 over 256 square inches. Kelly, who had "11/56 of a square inch" on his card, regretfully pronounced a stunned Joel wrong. But after the broadcast, hundreds of irate letters from mathematicians poured in, pointing out that the two answers were equivalent—Joel simply had not reduced the fraction.

The boy's mother, Sara Kupperman, described by the *New Yorker* as "a small, somewhat worried-looking lady," claimed there was no family precedent for her son's precocity: "I just don't know *how* it happened." The child had his own explanation: "It's a gift God gave me. But I know how to use it."

Joel did not begin to walk and talk until eighteen months old, and he learned to count not long after. His father, quiet, gentle Sol Kupperman, an engineer with the city waterworks, had a fine head for figures himself. "He first realized that he had a fellow-mathematician in the family," according to the *New Yorker*, "when he saw that his infant son, instead of chewing the beads on the side of his crib, was using them as an abacus." At three, the tot was adding and subtracting. At four, he could total his mother's grocery bill faster than an adding machine and once caught the grocer shortchanging her.

"That amazed her so much," *Time* deadpanned, "that she wrote a child psychologist for guidance. The advice was to leave the boy alone. His parents say they did. They do not explain how he found out how to solve cube roots."

Sol Kupperman bought his son a set of arithmetic books. Joel wrote to the publisher: "You made a mistake in an answer on page 123. . . . 3,136 divided by 8 equals 392 not 492. I am five years old . . . "

Joel and his dad had a daily fifteen-minute numbers workout before breakfast; the little boy delighted in these sessions. He was forever pestering his kindergarten teacher with problems. One day he asked her, "How much is 5/6 of 6 plus 49 plus 12?" Then, before she could catch her breath, he told her the answer. "You should be a Quiz Kid!" she exclaimed in exasperation. Whereupon little Joel went home and wrote his letter to the Quiz Kids office.

When he went on the program in March, 1942, he was the youngest Quiz Kid yet. At that point, though, he knew very little besides numbers. By the time he returned six months later, his reading had widened, and so had the topics of his morning discussions with his father; now he could answer questions on literature, history, and current events.

What Joel needed on those early broadcasts, and for many that followed, wrote Roby Hickok, "was a microphone strapped to his chest. Too often he was under his desk when he wanted to answer a question." He would kick the chair legs, fidget with his knees, rub his head, and rock back and forth. A technician had to stand by him, thrusting a mike within range of his mouth.

The child's proclivity for perpetual motion became legendary.

"Engaging Joel in conversation," Fred Allen once said, "is not unlike talking to a vine. Every time you turn around, the vine has grown out of earshot. You say something, and the next thing you know, he has clambered up your vest front and down your spine." (Joel said he was sorry for Allen because the comedian was "awfully dumb" about numbers. The two kept up a correspondence, and at Allen's request, the boy sent him the next tooth he lost. Allen wrote back that he was keeping it on his desk and leaving "little pieces of candy and meat around in case the tooth gets hungry.")

Interviews with Joel had to be conducted while he was climbing over chairs, standing on his head, popping up like a Jack-in-the-box, or running off (with his distraught mother in hot pursuit) to get a deck of cards to play with the nice reporter.

In Portland, where Joel and I emceed the auditions to select that city's Quiz Kid, Jeanne Yount, a local scribe, wrote: "He's as hard to keep track of as a wire-haired terrier and he dashes about investigating his surroundings with the same friendly curiosity." When the older Quiz Kids, Richard Williams and Harve Bennett Fischman, climbed Wahkeena Falls, Joel was not far behind; his mother caught him halfway to the top.

On the train to Philadelphia, after pursuing a photographer's flash bulb under a seat, the six-year-old came up and bumped his head on the chessboard Dick and Harve were playing on, sending the knights and bishops flying. Joel promptly burst into tears. "Every night he prays to God to make him good," his mother told a *Bulletin* reporter, "and then the next day something always happens."

When we Quiz Kids visited the *Chicago Tribune*'s farm near Wheaton, Illinois, Joel "took a running dive into a large manure pile," reported the *Trib*'s Gail Compton. "Bouncing up and down, he shouted, 'Yay, look at me. I'm playing on a hay stack.' "

He was a "human coilspring in overalls," wrote Larry Wolters in *Coronet*—a "mighty mite of the mike" with "black, sparkling eyes and a brain that works like ack-ack."

Joel's tongue did not work so fast. He talked, as the *Bulletin*'s Harold Hadley put it, as if he never had swallowed his morning oatmeal. Hearing him spit out an answer was a cliffhanging experience. For instance, there was the time he tried to explain the circumstances under which a naval enlisted man would rate a one-gun salute:

> In his tiny voice he piped up, speaking very slowly, appearing never to deliver a word until he had carefully inspected it:

"Ah-h-h-h—wea-ull—ah—when he fallths a-board the wat—you see-ah—they give him—the *one*-gun tha-lute in the na-a-a-vy —you—see—when he fallths o-o-o-ver—board they give him— —the *one*-gun tha-lute—which ith—which ith"—a long pause, a chuckle, and a loud, clear triumphant shout of victory—"*the thig-nal to fith-h-h 'im out!*"
—Jerome Beatty, *American Magazine,* August 1943

Joel's mother warned him against taking up too much air time. The next week he cut himself off abruptly, explaining, "That wath only a thynopthith. My muvver told me I've been talking too much."

It was his refreshing outspokenness, as much as his astounding way with figures, that made Joel the public's favorite. There was no knowing what would come out of that mushy mouth. When asked, "Which city is nearer the equator, Tokyo or Chicago?" Joel answered, "Tokyo," then shouted, "And Frank Knox, Secretary of the Navy, promised to *bomb* it!"

When we Quiz Kids lunched at Paul Revere's house with all his living descendants, Joel expressed disappointment: "What I really wanted to see were the descendants of Paul Revere's horse."

When Harve and I began talking about being "engaged," Joel got into the act:

"It's pretty informal, of course," admits Harve airily, "but there's an understanding."
"Yes," put in Ruthie, "There hasn't been any announcement."
And Joel piped: "Except by me."
—*Boston Traveler,* February 18, 1944

He could be adamantly close-mouthed, though. At seven, he played a small part in a Universal film, *A Chip Off the Old Block,* with Donald O'Connor. The script called for Joel to show off his knowledge about how to do cube roots in order to get admitted to a military academy. Roby Hickok, who accompanied Joel and his family to Hollywood, described in her book a scripting conference with the producers and the writer, Eugene Conrad:

Joel had escaped outside, after meeting the big shots, and was trying to catch butterflies when I corralled him and brought him back to the conference.
"Tell us, Joel, about your secret trick in getting cube root," the producer asked him.

Joel did a reasonable facsimile of a cartwheel . . . and answered: "I can't tell, because it ith a thequet."

"I mean we want to know for the picture . . . " continued the producer.

"But I thaid it wath a thequet," Joel explained. "If I told, then it wouldn't be a thequet."

The men looked at Joel unbelievingly. . . .

"Maybe," I suggested . . . "maybe these men would promise not to tell."

Joel thought it over and looked at me from between his legs. "No," he said. "It'th a thequet and people don't tell thequeth."

It looked as if it were just as well we hadn't unpacked yet.

"Don't you want to be in the movies?" one of them asked.

"Not very much," answered Joel. "Do you want to know something? My front tooth here—well, it-th about one-twelfth loose." He walked over and showed it to the producer, who looked, and felt.

Mr. Conrad looked too. "I won't tell, Joel, about the cube roots," he said. "I've kept a lot of thequeth, I mean, secrets, in my life. I cross my heart—hope-to-die that I won't tell."

After much urging on the part of his father, Joel made the rounds and made each one promise not to tell. It was a unique privilege—watching that august Hollywood group solemnly cross-their-hearts-and-hope-to-die. . . . *

Later Joel told his Quiz Kids pals that making movies was a snap: "All you have to do is learn some words and then say them while they take your picture." The director and crew who had to film the scene—with Joel scratching his knees, bumping into furniture, knocking down a stepladder, and constantly darting out of camera range—found it somewhat more difficult.

Joel's incentive for cooperating was that he was getting five cents a day from his father (eight cents for good behavior) toward a $1.60 toy boat he wanted to buy. (He had no idea that his salary actually was $2,000 a week.) Back home, on the radio broadcasts, his parents gave him a penny and a marble for every question he answered right (double for good deportment). He saved the pennies to buy chocolate-covered maple nut ice cream bars.

The "baby miracle," his parents and older sister Harriet lived in a

---

* Eliza Merrill Hickok, *The Quiz Kids* (Houghton Mifflin, Boston 1947), p. 131.

"spick-and-span" two-family building on Chicago's north side, as Jerome Beatty reported in an *American Magazine* feature later condensed in the *Reader's Digest:*

> Parents who are searching for a formula that will help them rear Sister or Junior to be as smart as a Quiz Kid will not get it from Joel's parents. They have followed no system . . . and there are no books on child psychology in their library. . . .
>
> Mr. and Mrs. Kupperman are their children's best friends; all four spend a great deal of time together.
>
> The Kuppermans have never indulged in baby talk, and have always taken great care to answer every question the children asked. . . .
>
> Mrs. Kupperman is a quiet and efficient disciplinarian, although Joel's table manners still give her sleepless nights. Joel keeps his clothing, toys, and books neatly put away when he isn't using them; since he was three he has made his own bed, he and Harriet set the table for dinner, and he is in bed before 7 o'clock.

Sara Kupperman, concerned about the effect on Harriet of all the attention Joel was getting, sought advice from Vanessa Brown's psychologist mother, who told Mrs. Kupperman to play up Harriet's own abilities as much as possible. Harriet was put on the show occasionally, and her parents went to great lengths to buy her duplicates of Joel's gifts.

Before Joel became a Quiz Kid, his mother, a former teacher, had consulted school authorities, who told her that without question he should go on the program. His parents took pains to shield him from his publicity, and at first he was totally oblivious to the stir he was causing. When the studio audience applauded, he would join in, not realizing they were cheering *him*.

He was unimpressed with marks of fame; in Hollywood, he declined to cross the street with his sister to see the footprints of movie stars in the cement outside Grauman's Chinese Theater. What excited him was that he lost "woose" teeth in twelve states. He brought toys along on the trips and seemed interested mostly in playing with stray dogs and collecting picture postcards. (Fans sent him thousands of the cards, which his mother hid and doled out a few at a time.)

Joel's sorrow in touring was having to leave Lassie, his beloved black Scottie. "Instead of 'Lassie, come home,' I bet she's saying 'Joel, come home,' " he told Lois Kay of the *Memphis Press-Scimitar*. In Youngstown, Ohio, with Joe Kelly's permission, he gleefully yelled, "Hello,

Lassie!'' into the mike. (''Lassie, it was learned later,'' wrote Roby, ''was completely overcome with joy.'')

The youngest Quiz Kid was very much a child. When, in Indianapolis, he was kept up past his bedtime to see a magic show, he responded to reporters' questions by burying his sleepy head in his mother's dress. At a Philadelphia cafeteria, he ordered two hot dogs, two dishes of ice cream, and two glasses of Coca-Cola, but his mother vetoed the order, and he settled for a Coke.

Orson Welles, himself no mental slouch, said of Joel: ''He is as un-affected, as unspoiled, as simple as Albert Einstein.''

In the second *Book of Lists,* among ten ''Prodigious Child Prodigies,'' Joel Kupperman is number seven, immediately following William James Sidis.*

Joel is the one Quiz Kid most generally acknowledged to have been an intellectual prodigy. Says Dick Williams, the show's older mathe-matician, ''Joel Kupperman was probably the most brilliant person we encountered. I think he really was an extraordinary mind.''

''Joel had a mental process that was different,'' ex-Quiz Kid Claude Brenner agrees—''not merely sifting through the mental data bank and finding that this combination of notes is indeed the second theme of the third movement of Brahms' fourth symphony.''

Other Quiz Kids, including Dick and Claude, also exhibited abilities that transcended memory. But unquestionably, for his age, Joel was a standout, not only for numerical manipulations but for general knowledge.

His I.Q. was above 200, and his mental development was the highest that ever had been tested in the twenty-five years of child study by the Chi-cago public schools. By six, he was reading eighth grade history books and had been skipped into second grade; his parents were loath to push him any faster. At his father's suggestion, his teacher at Volta School would give him algebra problems to do when he finished his regular arithmetic assignment, or let him pick out a book from a special shelf maintained for him. By the time he was ten, he was into geometry and had a vocabulary at least ten percent greater than the average adult's.

He was well-adjusted and ''much more normal emotionally and in behavior habits than most children of high mental ability,'' said the

---

* The chronological list was compiled largerly by ex-Quiz Kid Marguerite ''Peggy'' Bangert Thompson, a regular contributor to the Wallace-Wallechinsky books.

Board of Education's child study report, adding, "He is very strong-willed and has difficulty feigning interest in things that don't interest him . . ."

"Joel is a lovable . . . little rascal, glowing with health," wrote Jerome Beatty in the *American Magazine* profile, "a natural leader, champion wrestler in his gang, the boss of his gym class. Supercharged with vitality, he sometimes lacks coordination, like a car with a too-powerful engine."

Strong, husky Joel called himself "a clumsy little punk." At school, he couldn't walk up the aisle without bumping into something. But he was "all boy," as Larry Wolters said in *Coronet*. He loved sports—soccer, dodgeball, baseball, football. An avid Chicago Cubs fan, he worried his mother sick one day when he failed to return from collecting newspapers for a salvage drive; she found him hours later, sitting on a curb, reading old sports pages. He got into schoolyard scraps, the outcome of which he did not always want to talk about. Once he told his mother, "I don't pick a fight, but if a boy looks as if he's going to start one, I say, 'Look out—I'll hit you back first.' " He stopped reading one of his favorite books, *Alice in Wonderland*, when someone told him it was a girls' book.

His teacher reported that he got along well with other children and did not act superior. Apparently at least some of his schoolmates agreed. "I wath elected president of my [fourth grade] class 23 to 22," Joel confided to the *Buffalo Evening News*. "My pals call me Kup. I gueth they don't think about my being a Quith Kid."

But some youngsters did. Howard Sherman, who attended the same school, recollects how Joel would be brought around to all the classrooms to demonstrate his math prowess—causing him to be regarded as "an uppity brat."

"He would pop into the room," Sherman remembers, "take one look at the problems on the board, and give all the answers immediately. He acted like a big star performing some fantastic feat."

Joel's fellow-Quiz Kids and their mothers had mixed feelings about him, perhaps partly because he was overshadowing the rest of us. The antics that made him such amusing copy were not always so funny face-to-face. What might have been seen merely as high spiritedness under ordinary circumstances was magnified under the glare of publicity. He was a rambunctious kid whom his mother often seemed at a loss to control; she would resort to spanking when she and Joel agreed it would "make him a better boy."

He hated to pose for photographs and was given to tantrums. In San

Francisco, he had to be forcibly detached from a game he was playing with me. "Mr. Kupperman," reported the *Chronicle*, "screamed like an eagle. . . . His mother whispered a few words in his ear. . . . He posed." Another time he accused the photographers of not being "good Americans: You say 'just one more' and then you don't keep your word."

He adored Richard Williams, probably because of their mutual affinity for numbers. In fact, even before becoming a Quiz Kid, Joel had named his little red wagon after the older boy. "His way of expressing his affection," Dick remembers, "was to come up and put his hand around my waist and walk around me, around and around and around. Sara Kupperman would not attempt to cope with that—it didn't seem to bother her." Actress Shirley Booth, observing Joel, confided to Dick's mother, "If that were my child, I wouldn't have him on a radio program, I'd have him on a rest farm."

Harve, in a column written for a New Orleans paper, told of an incident that occurred when eight-year-old Joel got on the navy bus that was to take our party on a sightseeing tour.

> "I wanna be driver!" shouted Joel and the unwilling navy chauffeur was shoved aside as Joel straddled the seat. After satisfying an urge to open and close the door, Joel retired to the seclusion of the back seat, while the driver resumed normal operations.
> —*The Times-Picayune New Orleans States,* June 11, 1944

Vanessa Brown, who took a motherly interest in us younger Kids, says, "Joel was allowed to get away with murder. I think everybody that played to his cuteness and precocity was not helping him. Fred Allen and Milton Berle made such a to-do—the kid thinks he's funny, and then he keeps on getting jolts."

Joel got to be something of a wiseacre. When New York columnist Earl Wilson took him (and me) to see Santa Claus at Macy's, nine-year-old Joel rubbed against Santa's whiskers and shouted, "Hey-y-y, Santa, get an electric razor!

"I know there is no real Santa Claus," he added, "When I was about 5½ I figured it out. Your beard is pasted on. Take off your beard, Santa."

In our train games of "Molopiny," as he called it, Joel insisted on playing with the purple piece; losing was hard for him, and he was an easy target for teasing. In the Detroit auditorium where we appeared for the automotive industry's Golden Jubilee, Harve told a gullible Joel that during construction of the building, a workman had fallen into a hollow pillar, which then had been inadvertently sealed with concrete. Joel's response, Harve later reported, was, "Is the man *dead?*"

"The teasing of Joel," says Dick Williams, "was in part a kidding of Sara." If there was a "stage mother" in the Quiz Kids entourage, it was generally agreed to be Sara Kupperman. Fiercely protective of Joel, she was always on guard to make sure he got his due. On trips, she would sidle up to a staff member and confide, "Joel is *so* interested in Thomas Jefferson . . ."

"She made the decisions in that family," says Pat Conlon, "and she was totally absorbed in this stuff."

Once when Sara Kupperman kept Joel in his Fort Wayne hotel room for punishment, Harve and Dick dropped notes from the windows of their own rooms.

> HELP! HELP! I am being held captive by a fiend. Come to the
> Hotel Keenan, Room 347 before it is too late! HELP!
>   Joel Kupperman

When the manager came barging in, he found Joel and his mother calmly playing cards. (Later a new generation of postwar Quiz Kids repeated that trick on someone else, undoubtedly at an older Joel's instigation.)

Unlike Gerard Darrow, the Quiz Kids' first bantam marvel, Joel Kupperman lasted. Ten years, more than 400 broadcasts. Like Richard Williams, Joel did math problems while playing the piano and (in a new wrinkle for television) at the wheel of an automobile simulator. He even held his own against an electric calculator. Said the *Milwaukee Journal:* "Joel has one of the most phenomenal minds and amazing powers of concentration ever uncovered in quiz kid history."

As he got older, some of the problems he did became more complex, involving trigonometry and a bit of calculus. Some combined simple arithmetic with other knowledge—like this question, which guest quiz-master Jimmy Stewart stumbled through, making it sound even more difficult than it was:

> If you multiply the number of states bordering Alabama by the
> number of states bordering Tennessee, subtract the number of states
> bordering Mississippi, and divide the result by the number of states
> bordering Texas, you will have the number of states bordering
> what state?*

---

* The answer, which Joel gave instantaneously: Kentucky, bounded by seven states.

Like Dick Williams, Joel by twelve or thirteen was at home in virtually every field on Joe Kelly's cards. Not as quick as contemporaries like Pat Conlon and Lonny Lunde, he compensated with breadth. If another Kid developed a new specialty, Joel soon was on top of it.

He knew the members of the first Roman triumvirate (but pronounced Pompey "Pom-pee"), quoted from Marc Antony's funeral oration for Julius Caesar, named the islands through which the equator passes, identified musical notes, recognized a Bach ("Back") prelude, and identified the flags of Chile, Greece, and the Philippines. He knew that Tallyrand was the French foreign minister during the XYZ affair. ("You mean Sally Rand, don't you?" quipped guest emcee Milton Berle.) When asked, in 1948, what monarch had just turned Indian, Joel named pitcher Leroy "Satchel" Paige, who had moved up from the Kansas City Monarchs to the Cleveland Indians. He explained that when an object travels at the speed of light, it has no length "because the molecules get packed together." He ticked off the Presidents in office in 1854, 1834, 1824, and 1814 (Pierce, Jackson, Monroe, and Madison).

Joel was not just an answer machine; he had a sense of humor. In Miami, when asked to comment about the city, using football terminology, he cracked, "I've spent a lot of money here and never got a quarterback."

He was independent-minded. At ten, though his parents were Democrats, he turned Republican. A sort of preadolescent rebellion. Meeting Harold Stassen at Washington's Mayflower Hotel, Joel told the perennial GOP hopeful, "You're my favorite politician."

"That's very gratifying," Stassen replied. "By the time you're able to vote, I may be running on the Republican ticket!"

Fame, to Joel, was "a relative term." While he had met many prominent people, he opined, "probably nobody will even remember them fifty years from now."

Once he outgrew the baby stage, Joel became as reserved as he had once been talkative. Gangling and bespectacled, he looked (as ex-Quiz Kid Naomi Cooks Mann puts it) "just the way you'd think a math genius would look."

Naomi, who went to Roosevelt High School with Joel, felt sorry for him: "His name was synonymous for so long with child genius. That's a heavy load to carry. I never had the feeling that he was real happy."

Pat Conlon, a year younger than Joel, had been friendly with him when they were little, but as teenagers they became bitter rivals. "The more Joel went on," says Pat, "the more he was shutting out human contact and getting into the things that yielded success for him. He was not a bad guy, but he had a knack for doing things that would antagonize people. He was very introverted. He had a difficult home life, and it showed. He'd been given all this adulation . . ."

But to little Harvey Dytch, Joel was a protective "big brother" who played ESP games with the younger boy and liked to put one over on him once in a while.

Joel initiated a friendship with Quiz Kid Lonny Lunde when both were about twelve. They shared interests in music (Joel was wild about Haydn symphonies and did a bit of composing), chess, and sports. Before the show, the two would pair off with a pocket chessboard or just talk. On trips, Lon remembers, they would clown around—"climb to the tops of the tallest towers, disappear for a while, get everybody upset." Joel would ride his bike ten miles to Lonny's Park Ridge home to play ball, or they would meet in Lincolnwood and play miniature golf.

Lonny, though six months older, was a year behind Joel in school. "Joel liked to play baseball," Lon remembers, "but he was a lousy player, and it was hard for him to play with the older kids in his grade— or even with kids his own age. I think that played a big part in his social problems. One day he really wanted to help my team, so he won a game for us by getting hit on the head when the bases were loaded."

Joel's friends in high school were serious-minded youngsters like himself who shared his interests in debating, chess, art, music, and books. ("Any of them could have been Quiz Kids," says Lon.)

"He didn't fit in with the mainstream," says a former schoolmate. "He was interested in discovering the world. He thought one should pursue the life of the mind, not girls."

At fifteen, Joel already was a senior and was taking correspondence courses in math from the University of Illinois. The acknowledged dean of the Quiz Kids, he was voted Quiz Kid of the Year. He was by then so blase that, colleague Sally Wilhelm Fullerton remembers, he would "come in at the last minute, throw his coat on the floor, and sit down as if he'd done it all his life." Which, of course, he practically had.

Joel graduated from "Quiz Kids," entered the University of Chicago on scholarship under the accelerated Hutchins plan, switched from math to philosophy, and got his master's degree by the time he was barely twenty. Then it was off to Cambridge, England, for doctoral study, followed by several years of European travel and a sojourn at Harvard, where he wrote his dissertation and met his wife-to-be. He got his Ph.D. at twenty-seven and became a philosophy professor at the University of Connecticut in Storrs. He also has taught on leave at Oxford and Cambridge.

I remember being surprised when I heard Joel had not gone into math. Actually, his childhood ambitions had ranged from baseball player to farmer-with-eleven-children (he wanted to be a good father, too), and in high school he had considered studying law.

Joel, as he grew up, disparaged what he had done on "Quiz Kids" as mere "calculator's tricks." As has happened with other mathematical prodigies, his interest did not lie in higher mathematics. At eighteen (according to David Freifelder, who was with him at the University of Chicago), Joel became excited about philosophy as "the answer to all his problems." Philosophy, like math, employs abstract thinking and stresses order and structure; so the shift was a logical one. Years later, Joel told Robert Lindsey of the *New York Times* that his dissatisfaction with the "fast, superficial answers" encouraged on the Quiz Kids program probably had been one reason for his turning to philosophy.

People who knew Joel at the University of Chicago remember him as a quiet, pleasant young man who did not stand out. There is no picture of him in his graduation yearbook. "He kept to himself," says Daniel Feldman, then a dorm counselor. "He seemed to want to forget his fame."

Friends say that Joel, at a certain point, became angry about "Quiz Kids," feeling he had been exploited. "All that's in the past," he reportedly told his mother the year he went off to Cambridge. "It's only the future that matters." Yet that summer he went on "The $64,000 Challenge" as a music expert and won $8,000, perhaps to finance his European stay.

In later years, he turned down an interview with David Susskind and an appearance on Chuck Schaden's old-time radio show in Chicago. He also refused ex-Quiz Kid Joan Bishop's social overtures. Joan's mother told the *New York World-Telegram*, "None of us have ever heard from Joel at all. He turned out to be the Garbo of our group."

The last time I saw Joel Kupperman was a couple of years after "Quiz Kids," at a memorial service for his father. His mother remarried and moved to San Diego, where his sister Harriet and her family also settled.

Three decades later, Joel's response to my interview request was polite but firm.

> . . . I cannot be helpful, beyond what little is involved in this letter. The whole subject of the Quiz Kids remains a painful one for me. . . . The painfulness . . . has only a little to do with the merits and defects of the program. I do think that the program was entertaining, and that it gave being a bright child a *cachet* that may have been good for education. Our role, however, was that of superior, know-it-almost-all kids; and in America, at any time, that cannot be a comfortable role for a child or an adolescent. I'm not saying that any of us was arrogant, or that we believed in some kind of superiority, but just that that was how we were perceived by millions of children and adolescents our own age. The excessive cuteness and hyperbole associated with the show made things worse, in my view.
>
> Perhaps these remarks seem to be over-serious: after all, it was only a show. But it also was our childhood, and the images we grew up with. I want as little to do with it as possible.

Joel's unwillingness to talk about "Quiz Kids" is sad but under-standable. As Dick Williams said to me, "Poor Joel . . . and poor Gerard. Those two boys more than any of the others were the focus of all that attention and exploitation. You were young, too," he added, "but fortunately for you, Joel came along almost at the same time. He bore the brunt of that. And then, if a family retained its perspective, that was one thing . . . "

In Gerard's case, the Quiz Kids exposure probably stimulated tendencies to affectation that already were present. Joel, however, was just a sweet, energetic, highly precocious little boy thrust into a situation he could not handle. What he must have suffered in making the transition from *enfant adorable* to shy, gawky teenager and then to adulthood is not hard to imagine.

Friends say Joel did go through troubled times. Priscilla Rope, who took a course with him two decades ago, remembers him as an excellent, enthusiastic teacher but painfully shy in a one-to-one encounter. "He would back away down the hall when I tried to ask him a question."

Why didn't Joel Kupperman end up at a Harvard or Yale? According to David Freifelder, a Brandeis University biochemist, Joel got caught in the post-Sputnik fund squeeze that hit non-science departments. "Things were so tight in philosophy that he applied for thirty jobs and had a hell of a time getting one. You practically had to wait for someone to die. He was offered a position at $5,000, while I was offered one at $13,000."

If Joel is not the topmost star in the academic firmament, he is highly respected. In 1973, the year he became a full professor, U-Conn alumni voted him an award for excellence in teaching.

He reportedly has stayed at Connecticut (in part, at least) for family reasons. His wife, Karen Ordahl Kupperman, teaches history there. Described as a "very serious scholar," she credits her husband with giving her patient assistance with her book, *Settling with the Indians*. He in turn, has acknowledged his debt to her for help with his writings.

Besides numerous scholarly articles, Joel is the author of a course guide on *Fundamentals of Logic* (with Arthur S. McGrade) and two other books, *Philosophy: the Fundamental Problems* and *Ethical Knowledge*. The latter is included in the Muirhead Library of Philosophy, a collection of works of such modern thinkers as Bertrand Russell, Henri Bergson, and Georg Hegel. Reviews of his work have been generally favorable.

> Kupperman's first goal is to write real philosophy, not merely to summarize the views of other philosophers. In this he succeeds . . .
> —*Choice*, February 1979

> Although it can be faulted on several grounds . . . *Ethical Knowledge* represents genuine progress in its field. . . . [Kupperman's] argument is quite difficult and will appeal only to specialists in ethical theory.
> —Gordon J. Schochet, *Library Journal*, August 1971

Has Joel Kupperman lived up to his early promise? As a friend says, "If the expectation was that he would grow up to be a computer, no. If you mean, did he develop into a fulfilled intellect who does very interesting work and tries to use his capacities for top-level activity, yes." Joel has chosen to pursue a life of contemplation, service, and solid achievement.

Besides being a conscientious teacher and original thinker, Joel is said to be a devoted husband, the father of two teenage boys. A former colleague says the Kuppermans are a quiet but well-liked couple who enjoy frequent outings to New York or Boston. They are said to have an equalitarian marriage and to share responsibility for child-raising. Joel is described as slim and affable, with dark-rimmed glasses ("He looks his part.'') His speech is normal. He still plays chess in his spare time. Occasionally someone brings up his Quiz Kid past; he does not.

Lonny Lunde: Facile Fingers

I remember Lonny as a lively, attractive All-American
kid who belied that image of the child prodigy.
— Ex-Quiz Kid Naomi Cooks Mann

The Arc: a swank suburban singles joint north of Chicago, crowded
with middle-aged loners on the make. A thin professorial figure sends
cool jazz rippling off the grand piano in the center of the circular bar. The
face (large glasses, small chin) turns up with a quizzical air, as if the Clark
Gable ears are searching, above the clink of ice and the chatter, for the
laid-back beat of a different drummer. This is easy listening—music of the
forties for a crowd that has been there.

"Thanks for the memory . . . " The soloist lights a cigarette, puffs
quickly, rolls out an arpeggio. A deft, sure touch. Subtle, not intrusive.

"What's my name?" he responds to a tipsy heckler. "Lon. Like Lon
Chaney, Jr. And, I suppose, Lon Chaney, Sr."

What is a musical prodigy doing in a place like this?

Name-that-tune time. Offbeat requests. Bills slip into the brandy snifter
atop the piano. There is a music buff in the crowd; he and Lon trade trivia
questions and answers.

The guy is still playing Quiz Kid.

"Who made 'Granada' popular?" a woman queries.

"Caruso," Lon flashes drily.

Just before the break, I send up a request: "It's Been a Long, Long
Time." Lon plays it, giving me no sign of recognition. Then—"One last
question," he says, looking straight at me. "In what Shakespearian play

is the stage direction, 'Exit pursued by a bear'?''

Lonny Lunde, as a boy, struck me as a bit conceited. Perhaps his smooth way of talking gave me that impression, and the characteristic tilt of his head when he played the piano. I remember how nonchalantly he caressed the keys while other Quiz Kids ran around excitedly, waiting to go on the air. Some people were upset when they lost. Not Lonny.

The Lon Lunde sitting opposite me in his suburban Des Plaines family room is a surprise. In contrast to his relaxed stage personality, he seems nervous, self-deprecating, ill at ease. He smokes incessantly. Although he is eager to cooperate, his introspection appears, in some areas, limited; his answers, at times, laconic. A hearing loss suffered in army rifle training gives him trouble in conversation, though not with music. His memory, once deemed ''incredible,'' is admittedly spotty: ''I don't remember anything but tunes.'' He knows more than 9,000.

In a royal blue baseball shirt, sneakers, and shorts that expose bony legs and knobby knees, he looks like a stretched-out forty-six-year-old kid. Except for the Russian Blue cat, we are alone in the quiet brick ranch house. His wife Jane, a secretary, is at work; his son and daughter, nine and twelve, in school. On the mantel are Lon's bowling trophy and a picture of his son's baseball team. The living room of the tract house was remodeled to make room for the fifty-year-old Charles Frederick Stein baby grand Lon has had since he was ten. ''I don't need a Steinway, any more than I need the best sound equipment,'' he says. ''I'm satisfied with this one.''

Unlike Joan Bishop and other musical prodigies who appeared on ''Quiz Kids,'' Lawson Lunde (the name he reserves for his classical compositions) was born into a distinctly unmusical family. His birthday, though, was an omen: November 22, Saint Cecilia's Day, festival of the patron saint of music, and the date on which Benjamin Britten and Hoagy Carmichael also were born. Lon's sole illustrious forebear, three generations back, was a sculptor, Rolf Lunde, one of whose statues stands in an Oslo square. The only known musical kinsman is a cousin in Norway who, Lon has heard, ''does exactly what I do. Pretty much the same background—started playing very early.''

Once, appearing with the Quiz Kids on the Fred Allen show, Lonny told a scripted joke about how he came to play the piano: ''My mother wanted me to study the violin. One night she heard Jack Benny play. Next day I started taking piano lessons.''

The true story has Mozartian overtones.

The first time Lonny ever touched the keyboard was a snowy Sunday morning shortly after his fourth birthday. Rushing into the house after church, he pulled off his mittens and dashed to the piano to pick out the Christmas carols that had been humming in his head all the way home. Within a week, he was playing with both hands on black and white keys.

His talent astounded his parents, who had bought the piano so his older sister Marcia could study. "I'd sit and watch her," Lon recalls. "As soon as I started playing, she quit. I guess I was showing her up."

("It was an awful blow to my pride that day Lonny sat down at the piano," Marcia told the *Chicago Tribune*. I was thirteen years old and had been taking piano lessons for three years. Imagine how I felt when, without even trying, he could play better than I could!")

Lon taps out a fresh cigarette. "My folks took me down to the American Conservatory, figuring they had a prodigy on their hands. The advice was, no lessons until six. So I just fooled around. We had a horrible grand piano, hopelessly out of tune. Having perfect pitch, I learned things by ear in the wrong key. I couldn't reach the pedals, so my dad bought a pedal extension. The guy at the American Conservatory said I was the only kid he had ever seen that instinctively pedaled correctly."

Paging through a book of old standards like "Beautiful Dreamer" and "In the Gloaming," Lonny learned to read music with the help of his sister and his mother, Evelyn Lunde, who played an occasional hymn. His proud father, Arvid Lunde, bought a disc cutter (an invention marketed briefly at the time) to preserve the boy's musical ramblings. The contraption came with a record player, the family's first. Lonny would listen by the hour. His earliest recorded improvisation, at five, was titled, "The Next Sentence"; his first songwriting attempts included "Ashes in the Basement," "Come Out, See the Bees Come Out," "Beach Is for Doggy," and "When the Nuns Walked," inspired by the little Lutheran's first sight of Catholic sisters. A "compulsive collector," Lon still has some of these early efforts—"mostly lousy."

"I don't believe in throwing things out," he explains. "Not because I ever expect my music to be world-famous, but conceivably it could be of value to somebody sometime. One thing I think is wrong with the musical scene is that so much is being lost. There could be some central storage area for scads of commercially unusable tapes: composers fooling around at the piano, great teachers giving lessons. If we'd had tape recorders two or three hundred years ago, we could have a recording of Bach rehearsing his choir or Scarlatti improvising at the harpsichord or Beethoven giving a piano lesson."

Lonny's early lessons were with Edward Gould Hill, an enterprising teacher who came to the Lundes' Park Ridge home. Eschewing beginner books. Hill started Lonny right in on the classics ("The first thing he ever gave me was Solfegietto by Karl Philipp Emanuel Bach, the second was Chopin's Minute Waltz") and soon had him performing at downtown recitals that closed with renditions by Hill himself. That routine lasted about three years, until Hill moved to the west coast.

"I suppose he kind of exploited me," says Lon. "He had me doing stuff like *Rhapsody in Blue,* that was technically beyond my ability. I didn't realize at the time that it was unusual for a six-year-old to be dragged down to the Allerton Hotel to play three pieces for a bunch of society women. Usually I'd break down in the middle, hit a spot I just couldn't do, and the crowd laughed. It was part of the act."

In the long run, Lon believes, Hill's methods probably were beneficial. "I moved along faster than if I'd been plowing through John Thompson's Book One, Two, and Three."

But Hill's star pupil did not give his teacher an easy time. "Sometimes he'd have to drive up to my school to find me, because I'd be playing ball and forget about the lesson."

Lonny played second base in sandlot games he organized. "There was no program like kids have today. I'd be the one to get up a school team and call kids from other schools and try to arrange games which would be played on miserable fields with pieces of cardboard for bases. And we'd find some guy standing around and ask if he wanted to umpire."

Sometimes Lonny would overhear people saying, "He shouldn't be playing baseball—he's a piano player. What if he breaks his fingers?" His parents, though, encouraged his ballplaying.

"The idea of a musical genius appearing in our nonmusical household had us scared," his mother told the *Tribune.* "It may sound silly, but I think we were more pleased to discover his normal interest in sports."

Lonny's father had been a semi-pro catcher and had turned down a professional contract with Grand Rapids of the Central League. "My mother said she wouldn't marry him if he took it," Lon grins. "She thought professional ballplayers were no-good bums."

Lon, whose sister was in college by the time he was in fourth grade, was extremely close to his parents. "My father is the greatest guy in the world," he says. "I've never met anybody like him." His mother (who never finished college) he regarded as the more aggressive of the two. His father, a University of Chicago philosophy graduate, had a "rough time" during the Depression as a low-paid traveling salesman. But things picked up during the war, and by the time Lonny was old enough to remember, his dad had a nine-to-five job selling industrial paints. When Lonny was four, the family moved to an established, prosperous section of Park Ridge.

It was through one of his father's customers, a neighbor of Quiz Kid Van Dyke Tiers, that Lonny was discovered for the program. One evening the eight-year-old played the piano at the home of this customer, who tipped off Van's father that the little musician might be Quiz Kid material.

The call from executive producer John Lewellen came as a complete surprise to the Lundes. "My folks had never heard of the Quiz Kids," Lon chuckles. "They thought it was some kind of crank call. They said, 'We'll bring him down someday,' but they never did."

A month later, Lewellen called back: "Hey, I thought you were going to bring Lonny in."

"You mean it's for real?" Arvid Lunde gasped.

Lonny's start was inauspicious. Unable to match older heavyweights like Harve Bennett Fischman and Dick Williams, he appeared only sporadically his first two years. But at ten (after those boys had graduated), Lonny—a rabid sports fan who devoured statistics like candy—was recalled to serve as a batboy for the annual *Esquire* magazine All-American high school baseball game ("to prove that one may be a mental marvel and a regular feller at the same time," as one sportswriter commented). Lonny toted bats for the western team coached by Ty Cobb*, appeared on "Quiz Kids" in uniform after the game, and finished first.

"After that, I was a regular. I doubt if there was ever a period of four to five weeks when I was not on. I had two specialties that the powers-that-be felt a need for. Usually there was at least one question that only I could answer, involving music or sports. My folks helped me study and prepare, kept me in touch with current events, had me learn the complete list of Shakespeare plays, the vice-presidents, world capitals, things like that."

Lon became one of the top Quiz Kids, appearing 235 times in seven years. He identified as many as nine notes played together, jazzed up a Chopin prelude, and contrived a composition using only the three tones of the NBC chimes. He improvised duets with Victor Borge and Liberace and accompanied Evelyn Knight and Frankie Laine. He rattled off baseball and football facts; once fifteen sportswriters failed to stump him.

---

* Catcher Hobart Landrith of the eastern team, to which Quiz Kid Dean Berry was assigned, later made the majors.

His Bing Crosby drawl and fresh-scrubbed choirboy look went perfectly with the clear voice that warbled "Beneath the Cross of Jesus" on an Easter program. He loved hamburgers and collected stamps, coins, and matchbox covers. On trips, he was the champion crossword puzzle solver and shared gin rummy honors with Joel Kupperman.

"Lonny is a good example of the average American boy . . .Only his interests run deeper than the average boy's," said a Montgomery, Alabama newspaper. "He not only plays Beethoven, Chopin and Tchaikossky between neighborhood baseball games, but composes his own blues songs." As "Hoagy Lunde," he belted out an original swinger called "You've Got Blues, Oh Brother, You've Got Blues" in a skit on the Fred Allen show.

He had turned to songwriting at eight, laying aside an unfinished symphony and other half-baked classical attempts ("I was full of themes and ideas but had no sense of form and craftsmanship"). One rainy day, when his father came home from work, Lonny greeted him with, "Lookit— here's a song I just wrote."

Lon laughs. "He decided I was going to be the next George Gershwin or Harold Arlen. Right away he started to pound out lyrics, and I kept on writing songs. Almost all of them are complete dogs. My dad was a pretty good lyricist, except his thoughts would run back twenty years to what was in vogue when he was a kid. I do the same thing nowadays—I don't keep abreast of what's happening in the pop music world. If somebody were to say to me, 'Write ten songs within the next two months,' they'd come out sounding like fifties rock or forties ballads."

Lonny's dad got a couple of his son's songs published. The first was "My Wonderful Mother," which the boy played and sang on a Quiz Kids Mother's Day show at thirteen. The sheet music ("I think it's out of print—if not, it should be") bore a picture of Lonny in cap and gown.

Another Lunde ballad, "The Chief Quizzer," became a staple on Quiz Kids broadcasts:

> Joe Kelly the Chief Quizzer
> He gives us no chance to relax . . .
> Joe Kelly the Chief Quizzer,
> He makes us come up with the facts . . .
> He throws questions at us, some easy, some hard;
> For our tender ages he has no regard;
> 'Cause he's got the answer right there on his card,
> Joe Kelly the Quizzer.*

---

* Copyright 1947 Lawson C. Lunde.

Partly because of his Quiz Kid repute, Lonny was in demand as a pianist for club and civic functions. By that time he was going downtown for lessons at Chicago Musical College with Dorothy Crost and Dorothy Mendelsohn, a pupil of Wanda Landowska.

Moisse Boguslawski, a "supposedly noted" pianist who had been Joan Bishop's early teacher, urged the Lundes to take their son out of school, hire tutors, and have him devote most of his time to the piano, as was done with David Davis (a Quiz Kid violin prodigy who, as an adult, had a minor concert career). "Fortunately," says Lon, "my folks didn't buy that."

He practiced no more than half an hour a day—"unless something turned me on," he says. "Any kid who practiced eight hours a day would come to hate music."

One thing that turned him on was winning the competition to appear as youth soloist with the Chicago Symphony Orchestra. Fifteen-year-old Lonny played the first movement of Beethoven's Concerto No. 1. "It was a ball—I really worked for that."

"Backstage, before the performance," wrote Jerome Beatty in *American Magazine,* "while his parents were trembling for fear he was going to make a mistake, Lonny calmly sat in a dressing-room listening to a football broadcast on a portable radio he had brought along. When called, he strolled out, glancing casually at the audience . . . sat down and performed without a single error."

Without an error? Lon shakes his head. "Nobody ever does. But I *was* pretty blase, I suppose partly from being on 'Quiz Kids' all that time.

"My wife and I heard this year's finalists. Those kids were marvelous. I don't think I was that good."

"This is how good Lonny is," reported Jerome Beatty when George Schick, who had conducted the boy's symphony performance, made a guest Quiz Kids appearance. "Schick moved his hands as if conducting, one after another, parts from two symphonies, and Lonny promptly named them correctly, told what instruments in the orchestra would be playing, and went to the piano and played the melodies."

In 1951, as Lonny approached sixteen, Joel Kupperman and Sally Wilhelm nominated him for Quiz Kid of the Year, and little Melvin Miles named him one of the Quiz Kids of All Time. Lonny cast his votes for his friend Joel and Richard Williams.

"They were the *real* Quiz Kids. As I remember Richard, any question on any subject, there'd be a good chance he could answer. Harve would have been close. In the later years, we were mostly specialists, kids who

thought quickly, only a little smarter than the average. I don't think most
of us were superintellectuals—I know I wasn't. Looking back, if I hadn't
played the piano, I probably didn't belong there.''

Academically, Lonny got off to a running start, then slackened. He
read early and could have skipped in grade school, but his parents said no
—a decision for which he is grateful. In a high school graduating class of
nearly five hundred, he was eleventh. But his average at Northwestern
University slipped to B-plus. Temporarily off the musical track, he started
law school but didn't do well and dropped out. (''It wasn't for me. And I
was sick of school.'') Now, despite shelves bulging with old books, his
subscription to *Harper's Magazine* is his ''one fling at making the mind
work.''

Although his I.Q. as a child was around 200 (''I'm very test-oriented''),
he says he is not intellectually inclined and generally feels more at home
with truck drivers than with professors.

''My intellectual challenge,'' he says, ''is in knowing everything
about esoteric music. I don't want any other.''

He ''started changing when 'Quiz Kids' stopped. I suppose,'' he says,
''I wanted to be one of the guys, do the things they liked—going to
harness races. . . . One kid I didn't like always came around with a chessboard. Even at Northwestern, my best friends were not the A students.''

His friendship with Joel Kupperman lasted only through their Quiz Kid
days. ''Joel was like no kid I'd ever met. So doggone smart. He
introduced me to history and logic problems. He had a circle of friends
that used to play chess by the hour—he dragged me into it a few times.
With my other friends, I'd be in a conversation, and the kid doesn't know
what he's talking about, and I could straighten him out, but why bother?
With Joel, *he* was the one who was smarter, knew more. I enjoyed being
with him. Today I doubt we'd have anything in common.''

In a way, he admits, when he invited Joel to join his sandlot ball
games, he ''felt good about bringing in a real celebrity.''

''I didn't feel like a celebrity with my friends. Most of my fan mail
came from old people's homes. In my neighborhood, nobody made much
of a fuss. I used to wonder if So-and-So knows I'm on a radio show. If I
had a bad day, somebody might say, 'You were pretty dumb Sunday.' ''

Being a Quiz Kid was ''not a big part'' of his life. ''I didn't think
much about it. Much more was made of me as a piano player.''

In grade school, he was trotted from room to room to display his pianistic prowess. But he feels he had a normal childhood and credits his "very supportive" parents for putting his achievements in perspective. "Modesty was a virtue they stressed from the time I started to play the piano. They hit me with 'Don't think you're all that important.' "

The only thorn in his side was a teacher who seemed from the start to want to put him in his place. "She would read out test results and say, 'So-and-So and So-and-So got 100, which is a lot more than the famous Quiz Kid got.' I could have slugged her."

Lonny never officially graduated from "Quiz Kids"; the show was between sponsors when he turned sixteen. (The following year he was a panelist, briefly, on a sports quiz, "Ask Me Another.") When he came to Northwestern, I was a senior; he knew I was there but did not seek me out. "Quiz Kids" went off the air that year. The public memory died quickly, he says, so he felt no pressure to live up to it. "I live in the present . . . although I am interested in the past."

That interest takes the forms of genealogical research and a basement lined floor-to-ceiling (and even along the I-beams) with keepsakes and garage sale finds: a set of *National Geographic* and *High Fidelity,* Big-Little Books, mysteries (one of Lon's passions), baseball guides, cartons of old clippings, and thousands of records. He spends hours down there taping FM music, trying to record everything each composer wrote, and exchanges tapes with other collectors. He tapes old Quiz Kids shows, when they are aired, but seldom replays them. Once he checked the Chicago area phone books to see how many former Quiz Kids he could find; he turned up very few.

Lon belittles his Quiz Kids prominence. "We weren't somebodies, really, and out there were the people who weren't nobodies. It just happened that we were on a show. To stay on, you just had to answer more questions than two other kids. It took a great deal of planning on the part of the staff to come up with a show that would wow listeners in Podunk, Iowa.

"Listening to the tapes, the questions seem extremely easy to me. Even the math questions. I don't think they'd seem hard to seventh and eighth graders today. On the other hand, I don't think my kids have gotten the depth of education we did. Of course, there's the effect of the thousands of hours of television they watch. We didn't have it, so obviously we read more."

Still, he has "nothing but pleasant memories" of the Quiz Kid experience. He feels it was "good for most of the Kids." Including him.

In his later Quiz Kid years, Lonny Lunde was one of the quickest competitors. But at first, dabbing timid toes in Quiz Kid waters, he doubted his ability to compete.

With his November birthday, he was on the young end of his classroom spectrum and felt more comfortable with smaller children. "I wish my parents had told me to play with kids in my own age group," he says. "That's what I've told my son. If he hadn't been pressured to play with kids who were bigger, stronger, tougher, and smarter, he wouldn't be nearly as good at things as he is."

He encourages his children to compete by playing games with them. "They both knew from an early age that I'm not going to let them win. If they beat me, it's going to be on merit. I tell them, 'If I beat you one hundred times in a row, don't worry, because when you finally beat me, it will feel real good.' "

He also has enrolled the children in Catholic schools. Lon, who discovered Catholicism at forty-four and spends a good deal of time reading theology, believes that his Lutheran upbringing with its "vaguely-stated morality" may have played a part in inhibiting his self-assurance.

"I think most babies born into churchgoing Protestant families develop an early sense of the vital importance of religion but a total confusion as to belief. They're taught an absolute right-and-wrong dichotomy that doesn't square with what they see around them. It puts kids in a bind about whether they're doing the right thing. I think Catholic kids get something that leads to belief in their own ability. The Catholic Church makes no apologies for what it offers—it is the same for a six-week-old baby as a hundred-year-old, rosary-twirling old crone. In my childhood, church was for adults who dressed properly."

If Lonny as a child lacked self-confidence, years of piano recitals and Quiz Kidding temporarily whetted the competitive appetite. "At the time I was on the show, I had the feeling—I don't think I had it a few years later—that *I can do anything*."

At Maine Township High School, he was a versatile and popular achiever, as his yearbook inscriptions attest: "To the best musician and best intellect in the school"; "To a great science fiction fan, pool shark and bowler"; "Best of luck to a guy who got the honors and really deserved them." He was vice-president of the National Honor Society and a charter member of Modern Music Masters, an international honorary. He joined intramural sports, golfed in summer, and was president of a bowling club. He played the viola ("miserably") in the concert orchestra.

Meanwhile, studying composition on scholarship with Vittorio Rieti at Chicago Musical College, Lon at sixteen performed his first serious work, Sonata for Violin and Piano in C Major, at student composers' symposia in Cincinnati and Chicago. Three years in a row, he took top honors in a state high school solo festival; his junior year, when he played Liszt's *Hungarian Fantasy*, one judge wrote, ''He has the promise of becoming a real artist.''

''If I'd wanted to,'' Lon reflects, ''I think I could have been a concert pianist. I don't think I'd be at the top, though. I have a phenomenal right hand, but my left hand has never been concert variety.''

The turning point was his refusal to enter a competition leading to a five-city tour. ''My teacher said, 'You have only one real competitor.' (That was Johnny Covelli, who became a recording artist of sorts.) It would have meant much more work than I was willing to put in. The life of a concert artist didn't appeal to me. I'm a homebody.''

From that point on, Lon Lunde declined to compete musically. He lives and works near where he grew up, remaining close to his parents and married sister. His resume announces, ''Chicago area only—do not travel.''

A *Chicago Magazine* feature on local piano-bar favorites omits Lon Lunde. (''I don't play the Rush Street spots, therefore I don't get much publicity.'') He has played downtown at Maxim's and the Continental Plaza but prefers his own neck of the woods, where parking is easy and the atmosphere likewise. Not an aggressive promoter (''Even on Quiz Kids I wasn't much of a publicity-seeker''), he went for years without collecting royalties on his recorded compositions. (''It doesn't matter that much to me—I'm not very money-hungry.'')

He carries modesty to a point where he finds it difficult to write a resume: ''I don't like to blow my own horn.'' Yet he feels he can hold his own against anyone in town and prides himself on being ''one of the first names given out'' on referral by other musicians.

He has run the gamut from old-style dance tunes with Victor Lombardo to rock with Jimmy Gross to society music with violinist Franz Benteler. He has given buttoned-down backing to comedian Bob Newhart and has accompanied singers like Gordon MacRae and Margaret Whiting. Mostly, though, he works alone in dusky lounges.

Piano playing has been his full-time occupation for only about five years. After college, law school, and the army, he gradually established himself as a performer while holding a string of conventional jobs: account supervisor for General Mills, administrative assistant for a music publisher, sales liaison for a band instrument company. As a public relations stunt for the latter, he did demonstrations with jazz headliners like Cannonball Adderley, Sonny Stitt, and Cy Touff. Summers, he was an orchestra leader at a Door County resort; there he met his wife, a college music major who was waiting on tables.

Finally, as bookings swelled, "the day job went out the window." His parents had tried to steer him into a less "limited" career in law or business. "But I finally came to the realization that this is what I do best. My wife doesn't like my being gone at night, but she's used to it."

He leans forward, long arms crossed. "I was a little bit conscious of coming back to something from childhood. 'Quiz Kids' may have delayed my going into the entertainment business—satiated the desire. When it was all over, it was kind of a relief, and I didn't choose to explore other avenues. Maybe without 'Quiz Kids' I would have been a self-employed entertainer at twenty."

The detour came after his college freshman year, when he switched from music to psychology because he "wasn't learning a thing." ("It was a mistake. Right after that, they had a wholesale housecleaning and got rid of some of the dead wood on the music faculty.") He wanted to stay at Northwestern, close to home, and a liberal arts education had its attractions: "You can go through music school and you don't get the feeling that you're being really educated." (He did arrange music for the famed Waa-Mu show but never got one of his own songs accepted.) Now he finds the lack of a music degree a handicap in promoting his compositions: "Classical music in this country is university-oriented."

In the army, his psychology credential marked him for an assignment supervising intelligence exams that, he says, "my nine-year-old could administer." The task left him plenty of time to work on compositions he had begun at Northwestern. He completed his Sonata No. 1 for Alto Saxophone and Piano, the first movement of which he had performed with fellow-student James Bestman at a graduate recital.

Bestman's teacher, Cecil Leeson, took a liking to the work and recorded it. "Leeson is one of the absolute pioneers in concert saxophone. When he was young, the saxophone was considered strictly a dance band instrument, and he was one of two or three people who were bound and determined to give it respectability. The big Carnegie Hall recital, which was going to be the first all-saxophone concert ever given in New York, was scheduled for December 7, 1941. He showed up, but hardly anyone else did."

Lon's sonata has had two subsequent cuts, most recently with the late Brian Minor, a Leeson protege, on sax, and Lon at the keyboard.

"The other recordings missed the point. The tempo was too slow—it didn't flow."

In his basement, amid the memorabilia, Lawson Lunde, in his baseball shirt and shorts, his back to me, nods, pleased, as he "conducts" along with the Brian Minor recording. *American Record Guide* gives the disc a rave review:

> . . . the music flows lyrically and smoothly, giving occa-
> sional hints of the 20th century influence from composers like
> Poulenc and Ivert, but for the most part is genuinely original in
> content. Lunde writes with a keen understanding of the instrument.
> . . . The composer himself accompanies in brilliant fashion at the
> piano.

"Even though I make my living playing the piano," Lon says, "composing is my main interest. I don't get as much time to do it as I'd like, but through the years I've put out quite a bit. Most of the music I've written has been for saxophone (even though I don't play a note on it), because I've known several saxophonists that wanted music. This thing sells fairly well."

A second Lunde sonata for sax and piano is dedicated to Leeson, who never has played it. "He says it's halfway through a pile of 150 manuscripts, and he'll get around to it in about ten years."

With fifty opuses to his credit, including some choral works, Lon is listed in Anderson's *Dictionary of Contemporary American Composers.* He considers himself "reasonably skilled—from Opus 20 on, most of them are darned good. I love to write for saxophone because you can do anything, and they'll find a way to play it. The unaccompanied sonata I wrote for Brian Minor is fiendishly difficult. No other woodwind instrument can do it."

Minor's sudden death in late 1981 was "a tragic loss" to Lon. "He was probably the very best saxophonist in the country"—and the most active champion of Lawson Lunde's works. "He was in France for awhile, so my music is better known there than here.

"I don't care much for the classical music climate in this country, any more than the pop music climate. The most noted composers are writing things that hardly anybody wants to hear. They write basically to impress other music professors. I can't see any point in that. A guy whose philosophy is very much the same as mine is Alec Wilder. He was a musician's composer—he wrote to fill in gaps, in areas where there are fine musicians who can't find anything to play."

At the moment, Lon is not working on anything. "I like to write for specific occasions. Once in a while, I'll get a real flash, and that's it—suddenly I'm into something. When the kids are in college, I may start grinding out a lot of music. I'd like to have ten records in the catalog."

Does he ever write down melodies on a napkin? "Oh, yes," he nods. He saves the napkins, too.

Music is Lon's vocation, but parenthood comes first. "As of the day my daughter was born, my life's goal was to be the kind of father my dad was and is. Part of why I like this life is being home all day. I think I know my kids better than most fathers. They seem to be such *happy* kids."

With his wife working days, he is the one to greet the children after school and take them to museums and ball games. One of his heavy time commitments is coaching and compiling statistics for their baseball league.

"April took piano and violin for awhile. Recently she spent a lot of time working on a little piano piece I wrote the night her brother was born, 'Lullaby for Alan, Three Hours Old.' But I am not pushing music at all, because I don't think either one of them really have it. They would have to work too hard to be competent, and I would rather see them steered into something else."

He takes a drag on his cigarette. "People ask me if I teach piano. I don't. Now and then my wife has a pupil or two, and I go nuts listening. Either you show an aptitude right away, or forget it—take some other instrument where you don't have to get ten fingers in action at the same time.

"And yet," he muses, "Svyatislav Richter I don't think did anything until he was eighteen years old. He does not have perfect pitch, he doesn't compose . . .all he does is play the piano better than anyone else in the world."

In the cramped living room alcove, Lon plays for me a bit of the Baroque. "Sometimes two or three weeks go by without my playing anything at home. When I do, it's almost always the music of Domenico Scarlatti. I'm just wild about that guy's music. I have it all—555 harpsichord pieces which are very playable on the piano. I slip in many of them on the job. I think it would be fun to do a whole *lot* of classical.''

"The shadow of your smile . . .'' Lon's pleasant croon blends with his flowing keyboard touch.

It is Friday night at Marcia's (accent on the "ci"), a smoky roadside tavern. The chords blend into the pinball racket and the erotic moans of a pair of aging barflies. In front of a red velvet curtain, a huge HOME RUN sign flashes on and off. A sedate couple, shirts hanging over polyester pants, shuffle, out of step, on the dim dance floor.

"Where is Blueberry Hill?'' Lon's corny patter and musical footnotes gradually gain attention.

"Havanagila, have two nagilas, have three nagilas, they're quite small.''

A parade of amateur vocalists troop to the mike. Lon's accompaniment smoothes their mistakes, adapts to any style. A tenor emotes a difficult song, new to Lon. "He's the only pianist in the Chicago area who could do that for the first time with a singer,'' says a woman at the table next to mine. "He's the best.''

A blonde wails "As Time Goes By.'' Someone shouts, "Play it again, Sam!''

Oldies but goodies: "Waltzing Matilda'' . . . "A Shanty in Old Shantytown.'' Everyone joins in. The place is jumping now.

"I've been workin' on the railroad . . . '', "You're a grand old flag . . .'', "Let me call you sweetheart . . . '', "For auld lang syne . . .'', "Heart of my heart . . . '' Lon pauses to listen to the robust chorus, then feigns a sigh: "*In*describably beautiful!''

At the break, he moves easily among the patrons. A few words here, a familiar handshake there, a friendly beer with a couple of nostalgia-happy news hounds who want to know whether the Quiz Kids show was on the Red Network or the Blue.

Lon joins me in a black vinyl booth. "I think I'm pretty fortunate,'' he reflects—''making a living doing the kind of thing I would under many circumstances do for nothing.''

Like golfer Jack Nicklaus, he feels he is "making money for having fun.'' The open mike is his trademark; "regulars'' follow him from spot to spot. "I genuinely enjoy accompanying amateurs. Some, when they start, are really awful, but they keep coming a couple of times a week, and within six months they're good singers. I get a charge out of that.''

Lon's own voice is ordinary. ''It wasn't until ten years ago that I even opened my mouth on a job. The guy who usually sang with this particular band had gotten sick, and I said, 'What the hell, I'll sing.' People seemed to like it. It takes a voice to hold a crowd, and some nights I'm singing nine-tenths of the time.''

He is trying to compile a list of every tune he knows. ''I like getting requests for things nobody's heard for twenty years.''

His greatest satisfaction is ''making people happy—with music or whatever way. A person in my position encounters a lot of deeply troubled people. Some entertainers tune them out. I try very hard to help.''

While he doesn't care for television (''The last show I was hooked on was Perry Mason''), he is ''absolutely addicted'' to Pac-Man. ''Someone in the dining room asked me to play 'Happy Birthday' when I had my best game going,'' he laments.

He rises. ''Well, to work.'' His slender frame ambles up the aisle toward the piano and the blinking HOME RUN sign. He pauses and looks back at me, over his shoulder.

''Any requests?''

Patrick Conlon: Anchor Man

*Pat was my first real crush. I remember his wit. He had the
sharpest, quickest mind. He could recall anything
he had read. It was hard for him to fit in. I had that
problem too.*
— Ex-Quiz Kid Sally Wilhelm Fullerton

I thought Pat was a little too competitive. But so was I.
— Ex-Quiz Kid Lon Lunde

Patrick Owen Conlon has a strong Celtic edge to his voice and the look
of a leprechaun. Slightly hunched in tan trench coat and feathered
Tyrolean hat, he guides me through Manhattan lunch hour traffic to his
favorite theatrical hangout. There is a piercing intensity in his clear blue
eyes. A lock of longish hair straggles across his forehead. The strawberry
blond beard, flecked with gray, adds distinction to his high-boned face.

A dozen years ago, he chucked a safe berth teaching college theater in
Chicago to try for a New York acting-directing career. Never married, he
lives alone in a West End studio apartment in the ''actors' ghetto.''

Most of his professional credits are in dinner theater, stock, and cruise
and touring packages. He has directed everything from Chekhov to Neil
Simon, including two off-Broadway productions: *Crystal and Fox* (1973)
and *Once More With Feeling* (1978). But his real passion is acting, and
the work is chancy. A couple of years ago, for ten weeks, he was both
directing and acting in *A Funny Thing Happened on the Way to the
Forum,* grossing $600 a week. Between times, like many theater people,
he takes what he can get: stage managing, casting, even telephone
answering and office work. ''If I can survive,'' he laughs, ''I'm doing
okay.''

Pat laughs frequently, the robust merriment of one too smart to take
himself too seriously. His masculine tones ring with boyish exuberance;

his opinions tend to the superlative. His run-on answers call to mind the times Joe Kelly tried to stop him from adding fact after superfluous fact.

"I'm forty-three years old. I'm an actor. I *love* to get in front of audiences. I love to entertain them, I love to hear them laugh. If it's a serious thing, I love to do that too. I love that communication. I always did. I did when I was on the show."

"The show" means "Quiz Kids." He counts his performing career from the day he donned cap and gown at six.

It was 1943, the height of the program's wartime popularity. By the time he turned sixteen, ten years later, other stalwarts like Lonny Lunde and Joel Kupperman had graduated, and Pat (at his mother's suggestion) was asked to stay on as "anchor man" to answer questions muffed by the predominantly peewee panels. He racked up more total appearances than anyone but Joel: 385, if the near-infallible Conlon memory serves.

He and his mother have a running dispute on that point. "Mother will go to her grave insisting that I was on the show more than Joel."

"Pat downgrades himself." His mother, Marcella Conlon, shakes her curly gray head. "Being humble is very good in some areas, but not in show business. When he's trying out for a show, he doesn't put down half his credits. People have known him for years and not known anything about his background. Not just being a Quiz Kid—he's done enough other things, he doesn't need that."

Porcelain-faced Marcella, a wisp of a woman, sits quite still, hands folded primly, in the corner of a sofa in her fastidiously-kept pink and green velvet living room. The widow of F. Patrick Conlon, a prominent Chicago trial attorney, she is as well-preserved as her historic Beverly neighborhood, a southwest side bastion against creeping blight. The handsome white-shuttered house with its columned portico has been the family home since Pat was eleven.

His younger sister Sheila, a sometime theatrical producer, round-faced and ingratiating, sits cross-legged on the floor. "I think Patty has the idea," she chimes in, "that he doesn't have to pick up a phone—that sooner or later his abilities will be recognized. Life isn't like that, unfortunately."

When Marcella praises her son's dramatic talents, she speaks from more than a mother's vantage point. An aspiring actress in her youth, she turned to drama teaching as more practical. She produced school and community shows while Pat and Sheila were growing up, then headed the theater department at a Catholic girls' high school for twenty-five years.

Marcella fed her children Shakespeare with their pablum and took them to plays almost as soon as they could walk. (Pat remembers seeing *The Tempest* in New York with the Quiz Kids when he was seven: "We got to go backstage and meet the actors in their costumes and makeup. I was enthralled.")

Leafing through Pat's Quiz Kids scrapbook, Marcella pauses at a picture of her angel-faced speck of a boy looking over a lineup of assorted-sized shoes. "When Patrick first came on the show," she explains, "he was always kicking the mike, so they made him take his shoes off. But he wouldn't do it unless the others did. Claude Brenner was so embarrassed —his sock had a hole, and his big toe was sticking out."

Marcella—herself a "prodigy" who was admitted to the University of Illinois at fourteen—had listened to "Quiz Kids" religiously from its inception, when Pat was only three. "The show fascinated me," she says. "Having gone through a childhood where reading was my love, I could appreciate these youngsters and the fact that they had such charm and grace."

Although Pat assumes his mother "got the ball rolling" for him, she insists a neighbor must have been responsible. "By that time," she explains, "little Patrick's brains had become the subject of conversation." He was rattling off Shakespearian monologues and, at his kindergarten graduation, delivered the Gettysburg address, complete with gestures.

At barely a year old, he had spoken in full sentences and reportedly knew a hundred nursery rhymes. At two, he could recite poems he had heard once. At two and a half, he could spell words like *idiosyncracy*. He followed his mother around, begging for stories and asking questions.

"Our reading times were a delight," says Marcella. "Often we would act out what we had read—the three witches in *Macbeth*, or *The Little Lame Prince*—so the love of reading and the love of acting grew together. Sometimes he would attempt to write a little scene, and I would go over it and make suggestions."

Soon Pat was working up his own productions, assigning parts to playmates and to his little sister, who preferred to play with her dolls. "You don't know anything unless you know about Shakespeare," he told her.

A month after his Quiz Kids debut, an audience of 1,200 cheered when six-year-old Pat identified a soliloquy from *Macbeth* that stumped a panel of business executives. At nine, he matched wits against actor Maurice Evans.

At benefits, he would (as Sheila puts it) "do his Bible bit," ticking off the genealogy of any Biblical name someone called out. He traced Jesus' antecedents back to Adam, spewing out some ninety names in less than two minutes. "He could do it for Moses, too," says Marcella—"He was nondenominational." It was a challenge he set himself, she says, when he came across the lists of *begats* in the Good Book. "Today he can take a script and memorize it in one evening, while some other poor actor is racking his brain for two weeks."

"I am absolutely cursed with a good memory," says Pat. "I really do not know how to forget."

What one needed as a Quiz Kid, he says, was not so much intelligence as recall. "There were people who were none too bright, and they did very well if they could remember certain things. Most people could do that if they schooled themselves—they're just lazy. A thing happens in their head, and they let it fall out."

Showing creative intelligence was actively discouraged on the show, he says, "because if you answer the question that comes *after* the question, you're delaying things, and the commercial won't get on in time. I've come later to know what creative intelligence is, and to meet people who have it. I think I can hold my own, but I'm certainly not at the top of that spectrum. I have to work very hard at it. 'Quiz Kids' and the things we had to do in school—that was easy."

Even as a youngster, Pat had more respect for thought than for surface knowledge. At twelve, on the program, he quoted a verse he had learned in school.

> How few there are who really think
> Among the thinking few,
> How many never think at all
> But only think they do.

By that time, the "quick-thinking Irish lad" was applying his phenomenal memory to history, current events, sports, and science. He knew the periodic table of elements and could name the American vice-presidents in order. Astute Marcella coached her boy on strategy. "She knew all the moves they could possibly come up with," says Pat. "I got to be a trained killer."

> Pat raised a hand at the start of every question and one almost
> could see his mind working. Then when he really had the answer,
> he would wave the hand furiously.
> —*Kansas City Star,* May 11, 1947

Like his hero, Harve Bennett Fischman, Pat occasionally generated complaints about his brashness. Once, he remembers, he ''absolutely had to'' correct Joe Kelly when there was a mix-up on his card about which were the fourth and fifth Presidents. ''Something all Quiz Kids knew,'' Pat laughs, ''but nobody else really cares—and why should they? Most people don't know who the President is now, let alone in 1800!''

''There was one period when Pat was beginning to act a bit cocky,'' Marcella remembers. ''His father took care of it.''

Bright, jovial F. Patrick Conlon was a strong but subtle influence on his son. ''I was blessed,'' says Pat, ''with two parents—I couldn't tell you which was the more intelligent. It's dead even.''

Pat in many ways tries to emulate his lawyer father. ''I read one of his final summations once. It was one of the most eloquent things I have ever seen.''

Popular F.P., as he was widely known, was president of the Illinois Bar Association, had political connections, and liked to help young lawyers get started. ''If my husband had pushed even a little bit,'' says Marcella, ''I think Pat would have been a lawyer. But we were in agreement that the children had a right to choose their own vocations. They both chose theater.''

The Conlons were a close-knit family. ''Big Pat'' saw to it that his children wanted for nothing. A sportsman, he took his uncoordinated son to ball games but did not push him into athletics. A fine baritone, in demand for attorneys' functions, F.P. would gather his family around the piano in the evening to sing Irish ballads.

Sweet little Sheila, vocally gifted, made her Quiz Kids debut at four, singing a selection from *Rigoletto*. She appeared with Pat from time to time until, at nine, she turned shy and declined to answer a question. ''Why don't you ask my brother,'' she told Joe Kelly—''he could answer it better.''

''I made up my mind early,'' Sheila explains, ''that Pat was the brain of the household. I went off in other directions.''

Sheila was a social butterfly; Pat was (as his mother puts it) ''the kind of youngster who would worry something to death until he found out about it.''

''As to the height of Goliath,'' writes Patrick Owen Conlon of Chicago, ''the person who said it was eleven feet was wrong. According to I Samuel 17-4, Goliath was six cubits and a span in

height. A cubit is 18 inches, a span nine inches. So David's opponent was nine feet nine inches tall. I am nine and I am going
to be a detective when I grow up. . . . '' Note: Pat is one of the
famous Quiz Kids, a fact he modestly refrains from mentioning
in his letter.
— *Chicago Herald-American*, 1947

When Pat was a little boy, he told reporters he wanted to be a super-
sleuth by day and an actor by night. On our cross-country train rides, he
initiated murder games in which he had us all combing the washrooms for
the body. In Austin, Texas, he was sworn in as honorary sheriff and wore
his badge proudly while searching for mysterious clues that never led to a
culprit. "I am on the side of law and order," he announced.

Today Pat laughs when reminded of his Sherlockian tendencies. "In a
way, you're a detective if you're in theater, because you have to detect
meaning." Over lunch, we are discussing Ibsen's *The Wild Duck*,
which I have seen the night before. The play, directed by Arthur Penn, is
at Brooklyn Academy of Music, where Pat picks up money as stagehand,
usher and jack-of-all-trades. The program sums up the theme:

How much truth is too much? This tragi-comedy pits an ardent
idealist against a household built upon lies.

The play is one of Pat's favorites, and the issue engages him deeply.
"Everybody says Gregers is the villain. Not necessarily so. He is very
understandable, from his point of view. I think the actor should key up
more on that driven quality that people in Ibsen have. They are single-
minded and obsessed. They have a mission, and they will accomplish it.

"Dr. Stockman, in *An Enemy of the People,* is quirky and odd. He's
never going to be one of the crowd. But he happens to have the right on
his side, and that's very powerful, even though the whole town turns
against him. The guy's going to suffer, they're going to throw stones
through his window, but he doesn't care."

The connection is irresistible. "I'm curious," I put in, "about your
love for Ibsen and the person who is an oddball and outcast—"

As always, Pat divines the question before it is asked. He laughs conspiratorially. "Well, we all had to live with it, Ruth!"

Pat is as uncompromising, in his way, as an Ibsen character, his
passion for truth bred by the constant effort to find the right answer. He
places minor events by their precise dates. "Exactly!" is one of his
characteristic expressions.

Once, he recollects, in a high school English class, someone misquoted,

"Music hath charms to soothe the savage beast." Pat piped up, "The word is *breast.*"

The other students howled, thinking they had caught the Quiz Kid in an error. Finally the teacher had someone look up the quotation . . . "and of course," Pat smiles, "they had to acknowledge that I was right. And then something crystallized for me, which is called the curse of being bright." He laughs. "Wouldn't you think they would be happy to learn the real fact? But it wasn't that way at all. They were absolutely furious. They wouldn't talk to me. That's when I realized that people don't want the truth. In fact, they hated it when it came from me. I have learned to bite my tongue a lot of times. But you know, to this moment—they were wrong, that's all there was to it. It comes back to haunt you in terrible ways, but that is how I feel."

Although his mother and sister claim he was popular as a boy, he remembers being singled out as a Quiz Kid from the start. "Kids can be very cruel about this kind of stuff. I was punished for being smart, for being on the show, for making money every week. I wasn't doing anything terrible to them—I was just doing what I was told to do, and trying to do it as best I could."

He got along better with adults than with other children and came to look forward to seeing the Quiz Kids staff members and especially Joe Kelly. ("He treated me like a real person, not just a piece of meat that was out there to answer questions.") But the adult who had the most profound effect on Pat was Harry S. Truman, on whose Vice-Presidential lap he sat in March, 1945, at the age of seven.

"He wasn't the way adults usually are to kids—they put on a phony smile and say, 'How old are you?' and these goofy questions they think you should ask a kid. When you meet an adult like Harry Truman—here's somebody who's really interested. He was still the same person as when *he* was a kid. He listened, he responded, he had a hell of a good time . . . and a month later, Roosevelt died, and he became President of the United States. I'd never met an adult like that before. I was simply filled with joy that there could be such a person. And then I knew it could happen, and I didn't have to worry about it anymore."

Pat's early school showing was, he says, not particularly illustrious. Although his mother believed he already could read, because he had memorized everything she read to him, he found that "printed words on the page didn't make sense" until his second grade teacher worked with him individually. Then he promptly went from the bottom of the class to the top.

He recalls having done little better than average on a first-grade I.Q. test because of his poor spatial vision. Later he scored "something like 143" on a group test and (his mother says) "way up in the genius category" on an individual test. "I found out," he explains, "how to take tests—to answer what they're likely to ask."

By eighth grade, he had skipped two semesters, the most Marcella— feeling she had been pushed too far herself—would allow. By then he had more or less come to terms with the Quiz Kid stigma and was "practically running the school." He rang the bells, worked on the paper, was the leading actor, received the Outstanding Student award, won an oratory contest, and represented Fort Dearborn school at a downtown luncheon with the mayor.

Then, at Calumet High School, he had to run the gauntlet again.

Cook County Judge Kenneth Gillis, who eventually became his best buddy, remembers: "Someone said, 'I hear Pat Conlon, that Quiz Kid, is coming to Calumet. When he gets here, we'll pants him.' "

In that depressed area, where most kids did no more than get through high school, "the Quiz Kids thing was a big liability," Ken explains. "It made him look sissified, un-macho. It was nearly impossible for a Quiz Kid to make friends. And his mother produced PTA musicals. That was another part of his prominent existence."

As Pat saw it, "Calumet High School in the 1950s was a citadel of mediocrity. Nobody did much. They didn't want to do badly, but they certainly didn't want to do well. Even the athletic teams. They won and they lost, they won and they lost. Right in the middle, just like the Eisenhower years."

Pat was off the chart in both directions: way up in academics, way down in sports. He dreaded going to gym and felt very much alone. "If others didn't make the first move, I probably wouldn't. And by this time, my weekends were all tied up for me."

There were two Quiz Kids shows now—Friday nights on TV and Sundays on radio—plus the *Sun-Times* "Quizdown" on Saturday mornings, which Pat hosted starting in eighth grade. Some weekends he pulled in $250. ("Not bad for a twelve-year-old.") His sweetest reward was spaghetti lunch with his father atop the Stevens Hotel. But he was annoyed when strangers would stop at the table and ask for his autograph. "I realize now that people aren't doing it to bug you—it really is a compliment. Sometime I may luck into a TV series or something, where that can happen to me again, and I would know what I was getting into. But when you're a kid, you don't.''

Pat, as he came into adolescence, was beginning to rebel inwardly against Quiz Kidhood. While he enjoyed playing the game (''Once the light went on, I took off like a racehorse''), after seven years it was becoming old hat; and he began to feel the show was causing him much more trouble than it was worth with people his own age.

He never told his mother how he felt. ''I guess,'' he explains, ''I sensed that my being on the show was important to her.'' Important, as well, to the staff members, who, Pat realized, counted on him to balance the little mites ''who could be cute and lisp and giggle but really were not good players.''

''Everybody assumed this was going to go on,'' he says. ''It never occurred to me that I could put a stop to it. I felt I didn't have the power to say no.

''The actual doing of it, I didn't mind that much. I understood instinctively that nobody's interested in your problems when you're in a position to entertain people. And afterwards, the problems don't seem quite so terrible. My hero, Moliere, actually went on once when he felt like dying. I sort of understand what he must have felt.''

Weighing the pluses and minuses, Pat is glad he was a Quiz Kid and would encourage his (hypothetical) child to do such a thing—''if the interest was his.''

For the most part, he says, it was a positive experience that gave him an early understanding of how the business works.

The pleasure he found in being part of a group of people coming together and cooperating to produce a show, each with a particular task to do, has stayed with him. ''I very much enjoy working in theater in any capacity. Naturally, I'd rather be on the stage than ushering or selling tickets. But I've learned that I enjoy that, too, because there are things you can do to turn a bad experience for people into a good one.'' He feels no comedown in doing menial work.

''I never thought of myself as somebody special. Obviously, other people did, and that was a problem for me.''

His trials strengthened Pat for the individualistic path he follows today. ''At that particular point in your life, it's very important what the crowd decides. You want to be just another kid. But I suppose in the long run, it's much better that you go through an experience similar to mine, because after all, you're only going to be a teenager for a few years.

"My parents all their lives were different in certain ways; I understood that this is a lonely way to go, but it can be done. My mother was at the top of her class in the days when girls were supposed to pull back. She brought this up to me all the time." His father took many *pro bono* cases and gave away much of his income. "He would stop dead in his tracks and help a stranger, with no reward other than knowing he had done a good deed. I saw him do it a hundred times."

Pat smiles as he tells of his grandfather, John Cornelius Conlon, a man whose thick Irish brogue belied his New World birth. The old gentleman would come over every Saturday, pockets bulging with quarters, and would throw them in the street like confetti for the neighbor children to scoop up. An oft-told household tale concerned the "seedy-looking fellow" who once approached Grandfather Conlon in a bar and offered to inscribe his fine gold watch in return for drinking money. Companions jeered that the watch was gone for good. But the barfly brought it back at the agreed time, etched in a beautiful script. "Grandfather Conlon didn't say a word to the guys at the bar," Pat grins. "He just showed them the watch. That's all he needed to do."

What really "took the curse off" of being a Quiz Kid for Pat was the advent of Sally Ann Wilhelm. He has been dropping bits of the story all afternoon. Finally he spills it, over a second glass of wine. "Ah, the long lost and never forgotten Sally Wilhelm. . . . ."

She was from Elkhart, Indiana, homes of Miles Laboratories, makers of Alka-Seltzer. Sales promotion manager Oliver B. Capelle, who emceed a local Quiz Kids show there, took an interest in her, and, at eleven, she was promoted to the Chicago-based network program.

The daughter of a railroad conductor, Sally was studying ballet and wanted to be a musical comedy star. "A child of unearthly beauty," as she was described in *Reader's Digest,* she had long curls pulled back with barrettes, and a wide, innocent smile, perfect for television closeups. She was as delicate and ladylike as Pat was aggressive.

"At the beginning, she was really not that good," he says. "She was on because of the sponsor's influence. But she got to be quite excellent."

With the double radio and television appearances, Sally estimates she was on the program more than two hundred times in five years, the all-time female record. She remembers the satisfaction she felt when she passed up Naomi Cooks, the only other girl who came close to my mark.

By the time Sally was fourteen and Pat fifteen, she was commuting the hundred miles from Elkhart almost every weekend. The two paired off during the half-hour waiting period before air time. "One thing led to another," Pat smiles, "and it became apparent that we liked each other. . .a lot." That was the year, Pat says, that the Quiz Kids staff "got so desperate" for a live audience for the radio show that they took it around to schools, taping the program in front of the assembled students. "They had worked things out with my school so I got excused because I was doing something for 'education.' " He laughs. "And I would go down to the LaSalle Street station and wait for Sally's train to come in, and then she and her mother and I would go to the school and do the show. And as things developed, those moments I would spend with her—and they were very few—were indeed very, very nice and much looked forward to. The high spot of my week."

Sally's surname was the same as that of a baseball pitcher, Hoyt Wilhelm, and knowing how the Quiz Kids producers' minds worked, Pat alerted her that eventually there would be a question concerning that. "It was a running gag between us—which of us would be first to answer." But when the time came, he impulsively ceded the question to her.

Once, not realizing the mike was live, he confessed his love to her on the air. "We were arguing about some point that had come up during the show (Joe Kelly was going on about something, and the music was playing), and I prefaced the thing, 'You know I love you . . .' or words to that effect. I felt like a dope."

Pat's romance with Sally "turned everything around."

"I was really depressed," he remembers. "I'd been on the show nine years, really tired of it, didn't have any friends. I was not enjoying life at all. And then there was *that*. And once that happened, then everything else—I met some people I really started to like. A bunch of friends in the tag end of my high school days."

Pat Conlon calls Ken Gillis his "soul mate"—his "very best friend in the whole world." They last saw each other in 1977, when Pat was in Chicago.

The gentle jurist and I are having a drink in a suburban bar. "That's a pretty lofty title they laid on you people—Quiz Kid," he says. "You'd better be awfully good to live up to that. When I met him, Pat was breaking away from that pressure."

To Ken, Pat was "just the guy sitting across the aisle in trigonometry.

He wasn't superior or aloof. He didn't go home and read all the time.''
Neither of the two boys was a jock, but both were big White Sox fans. ''I
still have some favorite seats I call Conlon's Corner,'' says Ken—
''way out in left field in the foul zone.''

Ken, who later got his law degree from the University of Chicago, had
been born of uneducated parents and had gone to a grammar school that
was ''a nest of hillbillies.'' At Calumet, he had friends in the sound crew
that maintained the audiovisual equipment, and he and Pat hung out in
the crew's headquarters. Ken ran a roulette game at lunch hour, and a
horse racing pool. ''I think Pat won that. We used to go to the track. We
pitched pennies Friday nights on 84th Street.

''Pat wanted to be a regular guy, shake the Quiz Kid image. He liked
the guys that went out drinking beer, riding around in cars, chasing
girls.'' Ken remembers one time when Pat was kissing a girl in her
basement. ''She was really built. She was wearing an angora sweater—
it drove him crazy.''

Ken points out Pat's graduation picture and the accompanying blurb in
his 1954 yearbook.

> ''Jocko,'' Ring Committee, Film and Reel, Junior Honor, Stage
> Hand, Temulac (yearbook) delegate, ACCL (All Calumet Civic
> League) delegate, senior year intramural sports, Latin Club, PTA
> variety shows, National Honor Society.

''Jocko'' was the sound crew's nickname for him, after umpire Jocko
Conlon. Pat became an unofficial crew member, running the projector
and swaggering down the hall with an empty reel and a counterfeit pass.

Sometimes the whole gang came down to the Quiz Kids studio and
mouthed wrong answers from the audience. Once they posed for a picture
in caps and gowns, mugging with racing forms and knives. Ken
remembers following the Quiz Kids up a narrow back stairway to the
dressing room. ''Naomi Cooks was right ahead of me, and I commented
to Pat on her nice ass. Maybe I brought the Quiz Kids down to earth for
him.

''He once kissed Sally Ann in that dressing room.''

After ''Quiz Kids'' ended, Pat and Sally went separate ways: she to
Taylor University in Indiana, he to Illinois, where he majored in radio-
television and joined his father's fraternity. One New Year's Day, he
drove out to Elkhart through a blinding snowstorm, and a couple more

times after that. Then Sally transferred to Northwestern, where Pat was working toward his master's degree in theater. They dated for awhile and then stopped.

"In those days," Pat explains, "girls were very much into getting married when they got out of college, and I was nowhere *near* the point where I could consider that. Obviously she was, because she did get married a couple of years after all that came to an end.

"I think girls in those days were victimized by expectations that have changed for the better. I'm really happy that I've lived long enough to see that happen. But I certainly could have done much worse than Sally Wilhelm. I still have a Christmas card in which she said she loved me."

Sally Ann Wilhelm married Hugh S. Fullerton, a small-town newspaper publisher. Their home is in Hastings, Michigan. They have an eight-year-old daughter.

Sally was a featured dancer in Northwestern's Waa-Mu show and took a master's degree in English, with honors, at State University of New York. She has taught high school English, given dance lessons, edited her husband's newspapers, and worked in a brokerage house and in a bank's trust department. Currently she runs a federally funded alternative education program for dropouts and delinquents. "I fell into it," she says. The editorial work "got to be repetitive. I'm the kind of person who doesn't like to do anything twice."

She views "Quiz Kids" as "an early high." It "made some of the stuff that came later seem anticlimactic" but gave her confidence that "there's almost nothing that, if I put my mind to it, I couldn't do." The experience, she says, "awakened a lifelong interest in all areas of inquiry—a stimulating, enlivening impetus."

But, like Pat, she found herself socially isolated. The time she spent commuting for the show set her apart from her classmates, and so did her interests—ballet and Shakespeare. In retrospect, she feels, "if I had tried a little harder to be part of the group, I might have been successful. I didn't realize I had to make compromises."

Sally remembers Pat fondly. She says religious differences were a barrier. "I'm an Episcopalian, and he said he would never consider changing religions."

Pat has come close to marriage several times but always has pulled back. "Marriage and family life," he says, "as I saw it, growing up in the forties and fifties, seemed like a very unfortunate situation that most people seemed not to be really enjoying. The people in the marriage are usually very nice people. They're just in some kind of a prison that they don't understand.''

Nor does he understand ''the great desire to have children.'' But he does regret one of the women that got away, a drama student of his at St. Xavier College. What held him back was the yen he felt for other women. ''Replaying it now, I'd say, yes, possibly you could commit yourself to somebody and let the other attractions do whatever they were going to do. But I didn't know that then. That's one of the lies that used to be promulgated.''

Pat taught at St. Xavier for five years (meanwhile heading a resident cafe company on Chicago's south side) before going back to Northwestern for his doctorate. He found frustrations in teaching in an all-girls' school and (thinking back to his mother's experiences) preached liberation to his students ''long before Betty Friedan wrote her book.''

''The only thing those girls cared about was the next mixer at Notre Dame. Some of them had very good minds, if they would have gotten them to work on something.''

Pat directed more than fifty college productions at St. Xavier, Roosevelt College, Northeastern Illinois State University, and in Northwestern's summer ''Cherubs'' program. Robert Schneiderman, former chairman of the Northwestern theater department, who taught Pat directing, remembers him well: ''He was an excellent student; he earned his A's. He knew how to bring out the best in people. I always had confidence that he would be a good director.''

What influenced Pat to make the New York move was his romantic involvement with another former student who was planning to make her bid for Broadway. And he was becoming disenchanted with educational theater. ''You can kid yourself that you're in theater, but the fact is, you're in *education*. There are people who've had forty-year careers doing really bad work, because they're not commercially accountable to anybody. I wasn't interested in being in the environment where that happened. And at a certain point, I summoned up the strength to give up the sure thing and take a chance.''

First came a year of therapy with Loyola University Professor Roderick Pugh. ''Best money I ever spent! Not only because of his insights, but because of who he was. He had achieved great things for a black kid growing up when he did.''

Pat's parents opposed his psychotherapy. ''This is very Irish,'' he says, ''the tendency to sweep things under the rug. What you push out the door comes back through the window. When you're Irish, sometimes it comes out as comedy, which pulls the pain out and gets you some laughs and recognition. I had built up certain defenses to make life livable for myself, but I saw that those were self-defeating, and I was a very unhappy person.

''What it boiled down to was what I was never aware of when I was a kid: that you have in life the power to say *no*, if you choose to exercise it. At a certain point, I decided to change things. And I did it.'' He pauses. ''I really feel I did.''

> Liberty consists of giving each individual the right to liberate himself, each according to his personal needs.
> —Henrik Ibsen

''What I'm doing now,'' says Pat, ''is what I chose to do. There's nothing I have *ever* enjoyed more than acting a role in front of a live audience.''

An equity actor, he has never yet appeared on or off-Broadway, though he has done a fair amount of out-of-town repertory work and a few television roles. In-town jobs, when he can get them, generally are done in dinky attic or bar theaters with hard seats, in out-of-the-way, sometimes unsavory neighborhoods. At the moment, in a west side church basement, he is in rehearsals for Brendan Behan's *The Hostage*, playing his namesake, the lame old Irish caretaker.

''I am the luckiest actor in New York to get the opportunity to play Pat in *The Hostage*, and for the second time yet. I wish my father could have seen me. Grandfather, too. I've really called on my experience with those men.''

An actor he admires is E.G. Marshall. ''He plans and asks questions to prepare himself for any individual moment. I've heard that Orson Welles said to him, 'You're the only person I've ever acted with that actually thought on the stage.' ''

''Very often,'' he adds, ''you'll hear actors bitching that the playwright is wrong about something . . . even when the playwright is Shakespeare or Chekhov or Ibsen. The effrontery of people to stand up and say that Moliere didn't write the scene right! It's *you* who should be working hard to find out why the thing should work.''

Pat's total acting training consisted of two courses at Illinois and one graduate course at Northwestern, where he played in *The Seagull* and

Richard II. Robert Schneiderman, who directed him as Bolingbroke in the latter, characterizes Pat's performance as "straightforward, with little natural flamboyance. A brusque, dry delivery."

Pat feels he improved when forced (by the lack of male students) to act in his own productions at St. Xavier. "It's like tennis. Nobody gave me a lesson, and eventually I got to know how to do it."

He also appeared in some of his mother's school shows, once as Henry Higgins in *My Fair Lady*. "The role is perfectly suited to me, so I will probably get the opportunity to play it again. I would *love* to have Mother play Higgins' mother, because"—he chuckles—"all we'd have to do is play our real relationship. Henry Higgins will get off on things—nobody can stop him, because that's what interests him at that particular moment."

His own lifestyle, he admits, "seems amazingly wrongheaded," viewed from the outside. Marcella, who fed his early theatrical appetite ("She created a monster") has accepted his decision with pride. "But to her, it's hard. When people are into things like where's your next dollar coming from, and what about your pension—It does take some getting used to. I was not a kid when I came here. I was thirty-two years old."

One thing that eased the plunge was that sister Sheila already was on the New York scene.

"Little Miss Chubbins" (as her doting daddy used to call her), who got over her early shyness and accumulated some fifty Quiz Kid appearances, grew up to be an intrepid promoter with an ingenuous "Who, me?" air. Like her brother, she gave up a chance to marry, preferring to give show business a whirl. Unlike him, she has used her Quiz Kid background to get her foot into several doors. She has sung leads in musical comedies across the United States and Canada, co-hosted the Jim Conway show, lighted stages from Carnegie Hall to Dublin, and done theatrical booking, casting, and public relations as well as producing. Her mentors and clients include Imogene Coca, who steered her into theater ("she was a big fan of Patty's"), and Carmel Quinn.

"Look to the Rainbow" is her philosophy and her favorite song; she sang it in her first professional job while still at St. Xavier, where she studied theater under her brother. "I have the bad grades to prove it," she laughs. "He used to come down to the lounge after me. He was a wonderful teacher—always open to students, night and day. And he was very fair."

As a child, bubbly Sheila idolized her big brother. "Still do, in a lot of ways. I really thought he was *it*. I used to follow him around, tried to go with his friends." She loved going along on Quiz Kids trips. "We had experiences that other people never get in their whole lifetime . . . having a band meet us when we got off the train . . . I remember when we went to Duluth, the police whisked us off with sirens going and took us to an ice cream parlor that was closed, and said we could have anything we wanted.

"I was so taken with the celebrities that came on the show," she tells me. "I sat around there with my autograph book, while you people had to do all the work. And then my mother and father took us out to dinner afterward, and the ride down by the lake and all—it was just an adventure."

When Pat came to New York, the roles were reversed. "He was over to my place one evening. I fixed dinner, and we were having a glass of wine, and I said to him, 'You know, Patty, I really think we'll have to find a play of our own and get it and you direct it.' This was really funny—*he* was listening to *me*."

Ill luck has dogged her efforts.

Through her mother's best friend, she wangled an introduction to Sam Spewack and talked him into letting her produce his *Under the Sycamore Tree*. "He took a liking to us because of my youth and the fact that I wanted to jump in and do it." She lined up Melvyn Douglas and Imogene Coca, who agreed to a Broadway comeback after a thirteen-year absence. But Spewack died in the midst of negotiations, and his wife Bella proved recalcitrant.

The headlines, though, gave Sheila the momentum to get the rights to Brian Friel's grim Irish drama, *Crystal and Fox,* from his agent, Audrey Wood. "I hounded her for two years. After she and Mr. Friel finally gave in, we went out to dinner, and she said to Patty, 'I want you to know, young man, the reason you have this play is because your sister was so persistent. She wore me down.'"

Crystal opened April 23, 1973, the anniversary of William Shakespeare's death, at the McAlpin Rooftop Theatre off Broadway. The cast included Rue McClanahan, who went on to television stardom in *Maude,* and a newcomer, Brad Davis, who later caught the *Midnight Express.* "It was a marvelous, beautiful show," says Sheila. "Patty got all sorts of great notices for his directing. Both Mr. Friel and Miss Wood said this was by far the finest production of his play, and we were very proud of it. It was the very best both of us had to offer."

Reviews, for the most part, were good to excellent. ("Brilliant acting . . . magnificent company . . . highly engrossing . . . a strange harsh work but fascinating.") Pat was both praised for eliciting "laudable performances from the entire company" and (he recalls) panned for "appalling permissiveness."

But the show closed in three weeks, the day before Pat's birthday. "I think if we'd gotten more funding," says Sheila, "we could have ridden it out."

Much of the original backing had been obtained through their father, who had solicited pledges from his many friends. He died suddenly, just after the rights to the play came through. Most of the investors pulled out, and Sheila had to raise $75,000, fast. The remnants of the Quiz Kids bonds, found in a safe deposit box after the funeral, helped.

Though devastated by her father's death, Sheila had promised him to keep going. ("On his birthday," she recalls, "the show was running, and Patty said, 'I think we gave him his best present this year'.") But a year and a half later, after producing cruise ship packages with Pat, she collapsed from nervous exhaustion and went home to mother. The three of them worked together on a 1977 Chicago production, *Compliments of Cole* (Lois Nettleton, Ann Jillian), which closed abruptly when (according to Sheila) the musical director took off with all the arrangements.

Meanwhile, Sheila and Pat developed a proposal to co-host a Quiz Kids revival, but Lou Cowan preferred Harve Bennett because of his television production experience.

Hope springs eternal in the theater business. Sheila has irons in the fire: a revival of *Cole,* a summer theater. Pat has prospects of directing *Forum* again, a show he has done several times. And he goes to "cattle call" auditions where being allowed to get all the way through his piece is a triumph.

"In theater," he says, "you're dealing daily with rejection. That's the nature of the business. You can quite literally go from rags to riches within a second, and back again."

Pat thinks he could do well as a talk show host or theater critic, but for now, he intends to pursue what he is doing. "I'm confident of my ability, if I get the opportunity. We'll see . . . as my father always said."

The next time I pin Pat down is for lunch, two months later, shortly before his May birthday. He is a Taurus. So was his father and, he tells me, so are Joel Kupperman and Naomi Cooks. "Bring your heavy armor when you go to Taurus Convention! They're slow to anger, but when they do, it is really like a charging bull.''

At our first two meetings, Pat was in uniformly good spirits. Today I glimpse a darker side. He objects to my tape recorder and bristles when questioned about discrepancies between his mother's version of events and his. (I recall his description of his father: ''A very mysterious person. He didn't tell you anything he didn't really want you to know.'') He is irritated about having to put up with ''overdirection'' in *The Hostage*. (''I'm not into disobeying instructions, but I understood it better.'') He looks forward to a discussion of *In the Jungle of Cities* at Brooklyn Academy, and is prepared to do battle with ''anyone who considers that Brecht didn't write a good play.''

Lunch is hurried; Pat has to get back to his office job. As I watch him stride off into the Manhattan traffic, hair flying in the wind, something Ken Gillis said comes to mind: a prediction that Pat may yet hit it big, as some character actors do late in life. ''He's got sheer, dogged determination. He wants to do it, and I don't think he'd be happy at anything else.''

And I recall Pat's comment about how he licked his isolation in high school: ''We Tauruses are the slowest starters in the world. While everybody else gets off to a start, we're trying to figure out what's going on. But we're also the best finishers, because at a certain point, if you haven't beat a Taurus, you can't.''

Epilogue.

> Marcella Conlon, starring in Victory Gardens' acclaimed *Close Ties*, is winning applause for her portrayal . . .
> —Irv Kupcinet, *Chicago Sun-Times*, February 1, 1982

Fate has tapped Marcella Conlon in the shape of a former student who remembered her when problems arose in casting the key role of an aging matriarch. Marcella won the part, her first professional one in nearly half a century, and made it shine.

Sheila, who calls to tell me the ''inspiring'' news, is associate producer on a Rue McClanahan film to be shot in Yugoslavia. Pat, who has come in for his mother's opening, is coordinating subscriptions for a medical journal and doing a ''very telling'' role in a play about drug abuse for schools and churches.

And so, the curtain still is up.

It would be easy to call Pat Conlon misguided, or even foolish—a man pursuing a boy's dream. But there is an inner strength to Pat; the strength, at last, to be himself. As Sheila says, "He has integrity. He's trying to be a better human being. He works at that all day every day."

To Pat, all the world's a chessboard. "We all know the moves, and we find different ways of playing. And that's part of the fun."

Naomi Cooks: Literary Light

Very creative and imaginative.
—Ex-Quiz Kid Patrick Conlon

The pig-tailed darling of the show.
—*Charlotte Observer,* January 15, 1949

The kind of little girl anyone would love.
—*Cedar Rapids Gazette,* Sept. 5, 1948

Naomi Cooks became a Quiz Kid when she was eight and I was twelve. Although I still had four years to go, I had withdrawn from the trips and combed out my pigtails; the role of cute little girl needed filling, and Naomi was a natural. Other wee lasses came and went, but none sparkled quite so brightly nor lasted so long.

Tiny, apple-cheeked, dimpled Naomi, in pristine pinafores and bow-trimmed braids, was everybody's valentine . . . "the kind of personality that jumps through the microphone." She had a crisp baby voice, a gremlin giggle, and a startling air of assurance. You could almost hear her grin.

"This 53-pound bundle of energy," said a publicity release, "blew into the Quiz Kids classroom June 30, 1946," the night Harve Bennett Fischman graduated. Her parents had responded to an ad for female applicants, and Naomi had made such a big hit at her initial audition that a special delivery letter arrived at the Cooks home in the middle of the night, asking her parents to bring her in again. Naomi chalked up some 120 appearances in the seven years before the show ended, and probably traveled more Quiz Kid miles than any other girl but me.

Once the Kids were asked why there were more boys than girls on the program. "Girls are shyer than boys," suggested Sally Ann Wilhelm. "No," said Naomi, "boys are shyer."

Naomi was anything but shy. At the height of a coal strike, the *Washington Evening Star* reported, the Quiz Kids arrived in the nation's capital "led by a beribboned eight-year-old and her doll. . . . Naomi Cooks . . . tilted back her red bonnet and let go at John L. Lewis. 'I don't like him because he won't give anybody coal and pretty soon our radiator won't work.' "

"Naomi does all right for herself," a Montgomery, Alabama newspaper observed, "for beneath her daintiness beats a heart full to overflowing with mischief and tomboyishness. She has a subtle way of starting all sorts of trouble, then sitting back and relaxing as though she didn't know what it was all about." She was fond of dropping popcorn down Joel Kupperman's and Lonny Lunde's backs when they weren't looking.

She had an impudent mouth. In Washington, she took one look at the chairs in the House of Representatives and asked, "Why don't they have desks to write on, like the Senators have? They CAN write, can't they?" When someone remarked that nobody could catch up with Joel in the math department, Naomi replied, "Well, Einstein has. The question is: Has Joel caught up with HIM?"

Naomi's department was literature; she lived in the library. Her devotion rested with impartial favor on *Little Women* (which she read at least four times), *Tom Sawyer* (three times) and Shakespeare's *Hamlet*. She could, as a Toronto newspaper exclaimed, toss off quotes "from almost any play written by the bard." She knew her Bible and mythology, too. When Joe Kelly asked the panel to think of mythological punishments that would be "a lot worse than staying after school," up piped eight-year-old Naomi:

> Well, one of the punishments of Hercules was—when he killed one of his friends in a fit of anger, his father was told that he could put any punishment upon Hercules, and he was sold into slavery for three years and made to dress like a woman . . . and SPIN . . . and things like that . . .
>
> And Loki, one of the Norse lesser gods, talked too much, and he had his lips sewn together—(Giggles)
>
> *Kelly:* That's fine, that's fine, Naomi . . .
>
> *Naomi:* And one of his OTHER punishments was something like that of Prometheus, but he was chained to a rock and a serpent was hung above him, and deadly poison kept on dripping from his jaws onto his face. But his wife would come and hold a bowl under it . . . but when the bowl got full, she had to go and empty it . . .

Kelly: Yes-s-s, yes . . .

Naomi: So it got on his face every once in a while.

Kelly: Yes, naturally. Well, thanks, Naomi.

Naomi never got nervous. Not even when, at nine, she pinch-hit for vacationing Joe Kelly; after all, she said with gusto, "I have the answers on my cards." When her mother, Rose Cooks, began getting cold feet about her impending Mother's Day appearance, Naomi told her, "You will not get mike fright, Mother, unless you want to."

The little girl studied drama and wanted to be an actress—"if it doesn't interfere with being a housewife and mother." She impersonated literary characters, gave droll imitations of Gracie Allen, Jimmy Durante, Red Skelton and Tallulah Bankhead, and starred as "Fifi La Cook" in a hilarious skit on the Fred Allen show. At twelve, on the Quiz Kids television program, she did the balcony scene from *Romeo and Juliet* with John Carradine, entirely unrehearsed and from memory.

In 1954, the year "Quiz Kids" ended, she won first prize in the Illinois "Voice of Democracy" high school oratory contest:

> . . . I am a great idea, and my voice and message have been heard
> down through the centuries . . . sometimes softly, and sometimes
> with much greater force. I lift my voice, and I speak up for
> myself. I speak for Democracy.

Naomi's flare for words became apparent by the time she was nineteen months old. She repeated her mother's telephone conversations with the doctor, spouting terms like "tonsillectomy," "streptococcus infection," and "oleum percomorphum," a cod-liver-oil-type preparation the tot took with her orange juice.

At two, egged on by her older brother's example, she read off the billboards she saw from the car window. "She's a Quiz Kid," Grandpa Cooks would say.

Naomi came from bright but not highly cultured forebears. ("I don't remember a lot of books around the house," she says.) Her father, Julius Cooks, son of a Russian-Jewish peddler and grandson of a blacksmith, wed Rose Miller, daughter of a Warsaw tailor, nine months before the Crash. Julius put himself through John Marshall Law School at night, selling for Armour & Company; but during the Depression, lawyers were pushing carts, so he stayed on at the meat-packing house and worked up to branch manager, later practicing law for a few years. Rose skipped a year and a half of school but never went to college; she was a legal secretary before her children were born. Naomi grew up in a four-room apartment in her grandparents' building on the north side of Chicago, sharing a room with brother George until she was fourteen.

Julius and Rose Cooks were awed by their precocious imp. At six, Naomi astounded her mother by picking up a volume of Shakespeare and reading from *Othello*. ("I was frightened," says Rose.) By the time the child was in third grade and a Quiz Kid, her parents were at a loss how to handle her education. "Teachers would send her on errands," says Rose, "or let her monitor the kindergarten class, just to keep her out of their hair. The assistant principal told us we should teach her to do housework and cooking. At the library, she was picking out adult books, and the librarian wouldn't let her have them."

Rose took her daughter downtown to the Board of Education for testing. When she returned a few hours later, she was told, "You have an amazing child."

The experts at the board's Child Study Bureau did not divulge Naomi's I.Q. but did say she was reading at high school level. They advised that she be allowed to read whatever she wanted and that she learn a language. Soon she was rolling off phrases *en francais*. When asked, on "Quiz Kids," how she would greet Puss in Boots in his native tongue, she first cracked, "I'd say 'Meow,' " then purred, "*Je suis enchantee de faire votre connaissance.*"

The child study experts also advised that she develop manual skills. She quickly taught herself to type and knit. "If you can read, you can do anything," she told her mother. Not just a bookworm, she bicycled, roller skated, swam, and enjoyed baseball as well as hopscotch.

By the time she was eleven, she had skipped three semesters and was in eighth grade. She traded her braids for bangs and a perm and got invited to parties just about every week. She had, as a Quiz Kids release put it, "more poise, charm, and personality than most women have at thirty."

At thirty, Naomi Cooks Rattner was an English literature instructor at City College of San Francisco, wife of a lawyer and mother of a two-year-old. Seven years later, still teaching, she had split from her husband and had done course work toward a Ph.D. at Berkeley, when Merla Zellerbach of the *San Francisco Chronicle* profiled her as a former Quiz Kid. "I'd like to forget my nefarious past," Naomi sighed, "but it still comes back to haunt me."

Yet five years later, her response to my letter was enthusiastic.

Your book sounds like a great idea—though the world seems to have changed so very much in the past decades that it's difficult to imagine that smart kids were once such a hot entertainment item.

I'm on sabbatical from my long-time teaching job at City College, trying to finish my dissertation on 19th-century novels. (I refer to it as ''the book,'' since I feel too old still to be working on a dissertation, but want to avoid the possibility of having my obituary report the death of ''world's oldest surviving graduate student.'')

My new husband, Bruce Mann, is a securities lawyer, involved with high-technology companies like Genentech. My daughter Jessica is almost 15, a freshman at San Francisco University High School after 10 years at the French-American Bilingual School and a summer in France. My son Joshua is almost 10 and in fourth grade at French-American. Bruce has three marvellous children (married daughter 23, 19-year-old son at Vassar, 16-year-old son at Exeter), and we will soon all be off for two weeks of skiing at Squaw Valley. We all get along so amazingly well that we practically sound like ''The Brady Bunch.''

Let me know when and where, and I'll ''tell all.'' I mean, it's impressive to have someone request an interview!

By the time I catch up with Naomi Cooks Rattner Mann, six months later, her life has taken another new turn.

''I just took a big leap. I held my breath and quit my tenured teaching job of twenty years to go into business. I had been thinking about making my great escape for some years, and when I got married last year— Bruce travels so much, I didn't want to miss out on all those goodies.''

She and a friend, Margot Parke, are opening a boutique featuring larger-than-life objects: six-foot pencils, giant alphabet blocks, and the like. The shop, on Geary Street off Union Square, is to be an outlet for a New York pop art line that Naomi and Bruce discovered on one of his business trips, when they wandered into a little Soho gallery. ''It was like going through the rabbit hole in Alice in Wonderland,'' says Naomi. ''Suddenly here was this magical world of stuff.'' Later, she was complaining to Bruce that she hated the thought of going back to her teaching job when her sabbatical ended but ''certainly couldn't quit'' until she had something else to do. He suggested she buy a piece of the Soho business and open a west coast branch.

The name of the venture is Think Big!

''Margot and I see this as a stepping-stone,'' Naomi explains. ''We're learning to market and merchandise and build up a business. I think if three years from now we had four or five branches and were grossing a million and a half dollars a year, we'd say that it was a modest success. We could probably do even better.''

Petite and chic, Naomi radiates energy and self-confidence. With frizzy hair, gold jewelry, tweed blazer, knickers, silk blouse, and burgundy leather briefcase slung carelessly across the seat of her Volvo station wagon, she is the image of the New Woman, yet somehow reminiscent of F. Scott Fitzgerald's ladies. Brisk and businesslike but elegantly sexy. There is a gleam in her eyes and a cock of the head. At forty-three (''and aging rapidly''), she is as facile-tongued as ever: ''Words are my province.'' She speaks with a mixture of conviction and amused detachment, caressing each well-turned phrase.

She is a firmly transplanted Californian. ''California gets into your system. Life is easy. When Bruce and I go to New York, all our contemporaries look pale and overweight. On the other hand, some of our children are a little *too* mellowed out—they haven't had any cold winters of the soul. They expect the breadfruit to drop off the trees.''

A day-in-the-life-of-Namoi is like trying to capture quicksilver. A stop at the soon-to-open shop to inspect incoming merchandise . . . lunch with Margot . . . . on to Margot's house for a business conference . . . . home to Namoi's to deal with cleaning woman and children . . . . then out to dinner with Bruce. ''This is a slow day,'' says Naomi.

She fairly gushes with excitement about the challenge and variety of her new entrepreneurial role. ''It got to the point in teaching where I could hardly bear to get up in the morning. I long ago solved all the problems, and it just stopped interesting me.'' For Naomi, teaching was an extension of Quiz Kidding. ''Teaching is theater, and I'm terrific in the classroom. It's a way to get applause. And it gives you something you didn't have as a Quiz Kid: when you're good, you're in total control. It's a real power trip. But I started losing it in the last few years . . . like having a show run too long.''

Naomi ''fell into teaching,'' she says, ''as a lot of women did who were reared in the fifties.''

She ''had a feminist orientation from Bryn Mawr, but never really acted on it.'' When she graduated *magna cum laude* at twenty, she had no idea what she wanted to do. She toyed with the idea of going to law school, then returned to Chicago because she had a boyfriend at Northwestern, and accepted a fellowship there for a combined master's degree in English and teaching. (Her father thought the credential would be good to have.) A year later, after writing "some sort of phony thesis," she had her degree and a job at Niles Township High School. The following year, she and her bridegroom were California-bound.

She originally saw her first husband as someone who wasn't going to walk the straight and narrow. "I didn't want to stay in Chicago and have two babies and move to the suburbs. I wanted to see the world. He promised that, but he didn't deliver. He wanted to live on a houseboat in Sausalito, and of course we never did that. We came out here and lived the most narrow kind of life.

"I was sort of adrift in my twenties. Once I got married, I thought, *Well, everything will just take care of itself.*" She laughs lightly. *"I'll work at some job or other until I have a child or until (dot-dot-dot).* When I came out here, I sort of fell into this opening at City College. I should have headed right for Berkeley or Stanford and finished my Ph.D. I could have had any job in the world—everything was wide open here."

By the time she decided she wanted to go for the doctorate, her husband was starting his own law practice, and she was loath to give up the financial security of her teaching position. "And by the time I went to Berkeley for my Ph.D. in 1973, it was too late to get a good academic job in the Bay area."

When her children were young, she arranged her teaching schedule around their naptimes and took them to the playground in the morning. She would meet a friend there at 9:30 every day. "Sat on a park bench, went home, made lunch for the kids, went to work. And then I'd grade papers all night and start all over again the next morning. I don't know why I thought these kids had to be in the playground every morning."

She had steady help, and if the kids were sick, she could take a day off. "I wasn't running high-powered business meetings. Some of my friends think I'm such an ardent feminist, but I wonder—now that I'm married to somebody who has a real go-go career, I don't know if a household could sustain two of those. I don't think you can have the focus that kind of really top-flight career requires and still be wondering if somebody's got his lunch money and if this one is going to get to ballet on time."

Naomi's determination to break out of her first marriage was influenced by her involvement in developing a women's program at City College. ("There I was with two little children, and I was plotting my escape.") She saw her decision to apply for a National Endowment for the Humanities grant, so she could go to Berkeley for doctoral studies, as "paving the way to changing things. I'd been in neutral for a long time. I still remember the day I went to enroll. I felt like a totally different person. I was distancing myself from my husband.

"I think people of my age group marched lockstep into marriage without knowing who we were. The idea was that you didn't need to be a somebody yourself if you were growing up in the fifties, but you had to marry a somebody. And my first husband turned out to be not the right kind of a somebody for me. I'm much more of an extrovert than he is and much more into the material world. He thinks he is a spiritualist, and I make no such claims."

When the marriage foundered, Naomi returned to work, put aside her dissertation, and began looking for ways to supplement her income. With a friend, Deanne K. Milan, she wrote a college composition text, *Forms of the Essay: The American Experience*. "I had never published anything, but I knew I could write. It didn't do badly. It sold about fifteen thousand copies the first year and eleven thousand the second, and it's still selling."

She began remodeling homes. "It happened accidentally, as most of the best things do." The divorce had left her with "a wonderful old house" to sell. "I bought another one that was just a colossal wreck, but I thought I could do something with it. And in a year, somebody offered me three times what I'd paid for it. So I did it again."

Conscious that her father had limited his career by avoiding risks, Naomi went all out. "I did all the things my brother and father told me not to do. I borrowed money up to the hilt. I figured I didn't have much to lose and I had a lot to gain. And I was lucky. When I made my first $100,000, my head was spinning. It was a real kick to make a lot of money at one fell swoop, what it would have taken me five years to make teaching. It gave me an exhilarating sense of power. And after that, my brother has not given me any advice about how to handle my financial affairs."

Meanwhile, Naomi had been living for a while with a professor in Berkeley. "I had a marvelous relationship with this man for a number of years, but we were not meant to live happily ever after. We were too different." Living with this professor, she began to realize that she was not temperamentally suited to the "seedy academic life."

"I have lots of reasons why I didn't have a high-powered academic career, but I think the main reason is that I'm not cut out for it. I'm too worldly. I didn't want to do it unless I could do it first-class."

Nor does she consider herself an intellectual. "Academics are very good at spinning things out. There are a lot of four-hundred-page books where the kernel is one paragraph. I find that irritating. In the world of business, where money is at issue, you don't have the leisure to talk, talk, talk. You want to get to the point and go on to something else.''

She did intend to finish the dissertation, but just when she took her sabbatical for that purpose, she met and married Bruce Mann and spent so much time traveling with him that she hardly touched the paper. ''I tell myself I will do it someday—it bothers me, like an untied shoelace. But you know, I got bored with it! I had solved the problem in my head, and I didn't want to sit in my room with my typewriter any more.''

Meeting Bruce completed Naomi's metamorphosis. At forty-five, he is a managing partner in the three-hundred-member law firm of Pillsbury, Madison, and Sutro (''one of the five biggest and most prestigious firms in the country,'' she says proudly). When a friend offered to introduce them, Naomi's first reaction was, ''Forget it—this is a three-piece, button-down corporate lawyer. We'll never make it through to dessert.'' Bruce, in turn, expected Naomi to be a ''hippie professor.''

''And of course,'' she laughs, ''we hit it off immediately, and through him I entered a world of *big* business. He takes companies public, and works with venture capitalists who do $10 million deals. These people are extraordinarily intelligent and creative, quick and exciting to be with, compared to the second-rate academic job I had and the kind of people who get stuck in that world.''

Naomi's desire to leave her teaching job was tied in with her disenchantment with the ideals of the sixties. She and her first husband had been active in the peace movement and ''the whole liberation movement of all peoples,'' and he had been involved in public service litigation. But as time went on, Naomi began to see City College as ''a nice blue-collar urban community college that got ruined by the Great Society.

''I was teaching in an environment that was becoming a blackboard jungle right before my eyes. I was shocked to see the financial scams that were being run by various minorities who were getting paid to go to school. I was looking at classrooms filled with dope addicts and welfare mothers who would show up once in every ten times, but collected their checks. I didn't want to be a part of that. And that's another reason I'm interested in business: the marketplace is more efficient than government, and it works.''

The enrollment in Naomi's course on the modern novel had fallen to eleven people out of a college of fifteen thousand. ''And this is a *hot* course. People who teach literature of the eighteenth century don't even offer those courses any more. It's very hard to tell your black students that if they don't learn this kind of English, they're not going to make it in this society. Because their leaders are telling them something else. They major in black studies and go right out again, no further ahead.

"Even at Berkeley, undergraduates are really ignorant. You have to explain the significance of the French Revolution and who Wordsworth was and that the world didn't start in 1963 or '64, when the Beatles came to New York."

She became disillusioned with women's studies, too. "The women's literature course got taken over, the way the movement did, by lesbian-Marxist-feminists. I didn't want females of a different persuasion telling me that my whole lifestyle was antithetical to theirs. I've always liked men, and I never thought of a particular man as my oppressor. I feel very strongly that it wasn't my ex-husband's fault that I didn't pursue my own goals. I saw my obligations in a certain way. He never made me do anything."

Naomi always has been drawn to highly intelligent, driven men. ("There have been no ski instructors in my life.") Bruce, she calls "really brilliant. He's got the quickest mind of just about anybody I ever met. He couldn't stand to be with somebody who couldn't keep up. My husband got into a dominoes tournament, and he'd never played dominoes before, and he won—he does not allow himself to lose. We all play games in our household, very competitively. I'm a super Scrabble player.

"People say, 'Don't you wish you and Bruce had met earlier, you're so perfect for each other!' I don't think we would have been so perfect twenty years ago. We were different people—we were striving for different things. I'm my own person now."

As talkative as she is, there is one subject Naomi generally avoids, even with her closest intimates like Bruce and her partner Margot: the question of "Quiz Kids." Only to the Berkeley professor, in the context of her marital crisis, did Naomi open up and unload her feelings about her past. She resents "presumptuous strangers" who buttonhole her at cocktail parties.

"I have really squelched that," she says. "I never wanted it following me around. What do you do when you're a middle-aged ex-Quiz Kid? Your days of glory ended at sixteen—what is there to look forward to?"

Yet she is inordinately curious about my project and about our com-patriots' doings. She suspects that some have had "so-so" careers: "Being smart is not all it takes to be a success. I have an excuse for having been at a third-rate junior college," she adds—"I'm a girl."

Margot, who used to listen to "Quiz Kids" on the radio, also is full of questions, though she twits her friend by claiming to be unimpressed. As I help the two of them carry cartons into their unfinished store, Margot turns to me and says drily, "She was a smart little brat. I think you would have gone over better on television."

"I *was* on television," Naomi responds, a bit piqued, as she critically eyes a window display that announces the coming opening. She moves a huge paper clip here, adjusts a mammoth memo pad there, then stands back to survey her handiwork.

Naomi thinks of her Quiz Kid experience as passive: "not something I did, but something that happened to me." Her memories are vague . . . but then, she also has trouble recalling the title of her book. "*Something, Something, Colon, The American Experience.* This is really dumb. You see, I do put things behind me."

In her essay on "Why I Should Be a Quiz Kid," Naomi wrote: "I really don't know why, except that it would please my mother and father."

"My father," she says, "hasn't in worldly terms ever been a tremendously successful man, but he's very lively, and everybody loves him. He's happy with his accomplishments and the way he's lived his life, and he approves of just about everything I've ever done. My mother is a very intelligent woman with a lot of energy and talent, who never directed it at anything. I think she was kind of a show biz mother, although she would deny it. My being a Quiz Kid may have been a sort of highwater mark of her own career."

Over Welsh rarebit and sourdough bread at Rosebud's, an elegant English pub with paneled walls, Naomi explains to Margot why she was put on the Quiz Kids show. "I was brought in to be the ingenue to Ruth's star, because she was getting too old to be the cute little girl. It was a pretty tough role to cast. To find a smart girl who was personable and *performed* was hard, because the performers were twirling their batons and tap dancing and singing their way to fame and fortune, and what did they need 'Quiz Kids' for?"

In the beginning, Naomi says, "it was fun. We traveled in wonderful Pullman cars, made appearances on Fred Allen's show. . . . I loved all of that. It was all the things I like in life." But later she began trying to "get away from being little Naomi"—making "Quiz Kids" a forbidden topic. "I didn't like that to be who I was. It was clouding everything else I was doing."

Her discomfiture surfaced in seventh and eighth grades. Having been skipped, she was only ten or eleven, and being small, she looked even younger. "I wanted to start looking like a teenager, and my mother (she really *was* a show biz mother in this!) still wanted me in little plaid dresses with bows behind my back. And it was a real fight to get those damn pigtails cut off!"

Her parents took her off the show in summers so she could go to camp. But she resented the one time when she had to come home in mid-season "for some Quiz Kid event." (The "event," according to her mother, was the Republican National Convention; Naomi and Joel had been asked to do a writeup. "Afterward," says Rose, "Herbert Hoover sent her an autographed picture. She probably has it hidden away in some dark closet. That's Naomi!'")

The time came, in high school, when (Naomi says) she told her parents she wanted to stop being on the program. "My mother was very much opposed to that." Rose remembers no such conversation. "I don't think Naomi ever put her feelings about 'Quiz Kids' into words. I think she thoroughly enjoyed it, for the most part, but she never wanted to talk about it."

Naomi admits that she was ambivalent and not very assertive. "I guess I wanted to keep on doing it, as long as it didn't interfere with the rest of my life." Growing up in a family that was not open about emotion, she learned early not to reveal her feelings. "My whole posture when I was growing up was, 'Everything's fine.' "

Brother George, who was put on the show a few times, was less tractable, says Naomi. "He thought it was a crock! He was a real spunky kid. He wasn't going to read a book he didn't feel like reading. My brother," she adds, "is an extremely successful, intelligent person, but he was never a successful student. It may well be that he turned away from all that because there was so much heat on me."

"I was a wise guy," says George Cooks. "I screwed off in school."

Glib, affable George, four years older than his sister, is a graduate of Roosevelt University's business school. He started in the mail room at Spartus Corporation, a clock manufacturing company, worked his way upt to president, then went out on his own as a manufacturer's repesentative, importer, and consultant.

His Quiz Kid specialty was old-time automobiles. Once, on television, he identified a 1909 Brush lent by the Museum of Science and Industry. At the end of the telecast, the car was cranked up, and Joe Kelly and the Kids hopped in and rode merrily off.

"Why was I on the show?" says George. "Because I was Naomi's brother, pure and simple." His mother, he says, wanted him on. "I felt it was a gross pain. It was not my thing—it was Naomi's thing. To me, it was more important to be with the guys." The strong-willed siblings developed an intense rivalry when both were in high school but are on good terms now. George remembers Naomi's having to "work very hard" to keep up socially with her older classmates. He recalls tearful arguments at home, when she insisted on wearing lipstick and going to dances. "Naomi was a super young person thrown into a set of circumstances—She had a lot of catching up to do. I wouldn't want it for *my* children."

"I spent my high school years," says Naomi, "trying to show that there was more to me than all this elusive brainpower. I was very popular. I made that my sole aim in life.

"I was walking a fine line," Naomi explains. "The square people ate in the cafeteria. The hotshots went across the street to the local cafe. I had friends in that lunchroom, but I never ate there. That would have been death for me. Because across the street, people smoked, they had a juke box. I wasn't going to identify myself with the people who were square."

Naomi believes her zeal to overcome the "overpowering" Quiz Kid image had long-lasting repercussions. "I don't consider myself as well-educated as I ought to have been, given my intellectual talents. I think 'Quiz Kids' got in the way of that. I think I would have been a better student, more focused and directed and career-oriented, if I hadn't been trying so hard to live down being a smart kid."

Live it down . . . but not too far down. She graduated from Roosevelt High School as salutatorian. "I didn't want to be number one, and I fixed it so I wouldn't be. I took a whole year of typing and shorthand. My counselors were egging me on to take advanced courses, and I was really resisting." Although Naomi admits she has a "real good mind," she never regarded herself as truly outstanding . . . "and being a Quiz Kid didn't make me think so either." Being a top student was not difficult, she says, in a "not-very-good" public school. "And I liked school. I was a closet scholar."

At Bryn Mawr, she gave herself up to her "natural tendencies" and

became "a real grind." ("You couldn't survive there without
working.") It was a small school, far away from home, all women. "I
could be the best student I wanted to be, never take my nose out of books,
and be somebody else every weekend. It was easy to be a smart girl,
because they were all smart girls, and that's what you were supposed to
be. It was a new situation, and my past wasn't trailing me. I was fourth in
my class and covered myself with glory."

At Bryn Mawr, she was encouraged to think, interpret, and analyze.
But there were few requirements outside her major, English literature.
Looking back, she wishes she had been made to challenge herself more.
"I pursued the course of least resistance. I never went beyond second
year high school math, and I never took physics. I know two languages
well, French and Italian. I've read every novel that was ever written in
English. And I studied history. Everything else was what they made me
take."

Although in high school she had been active in debate, drama ("I
don't think I had much talent"), and newspaper—"all very verbal stuff"
—she dropped those interests in college. "It was more of being a Quiz
Kid, in a sense. But that was the bind it put me in: I didn't want to do
that any more by the time I was an adolescent, but there weren't a lot of
other things I felt I was really good at. I didn't decide to turn a corner and
become a nuclear physicist or concert pianist.

"I went on talking. And being cute. That was what I was on that show
for. The Shakespeare was definitely secondary."

For a long time, Naomi was angry about her Quiz Kid experience.
Now she has "a more-or-less ho-hum attitude." She acknowledges her
ambivalence: "When I was counting up the money that was enabling me
to go to private camps and college, I would have said I was very glad, and
then there were times I would have said, no, I'm sorry, because I took
certain directions I wouldn't have taken otherwise."

Her anger stemmed in part from the feeling that she was exploited—
though "in the most nonmalicious way."

"We were getting those lousy $100 bonds. I wonder what kind of
money that show was generating? We should have been paid *ten* times
that. I could have been a rich woman today!" Exploitation, to Naomi, is
"manipulating children to do something they don't want to do, even if
you think it's for their own good." But, she adds, "if I said to my
parents that they participated in this exploitation, they wouldn't under-

stand what I was talking about. My mother must have gotten a tremendous amount of gratification out of my being on the show. My father is an easygoing guy—as long as he didn't see any harm in it, he wasn't going to object.

"And they weren't *truly* show biz parents. I mean, when *Miracle on 34th Street* was being cast, the producers wanted to fly my mother and me to Hollywood, and my father put his foot down. I could have been Natalie Wood! I never knew about it until it was all over."

Naomi "wouldn't *think* of" letting her own children do anything like "Quiz Kids." ("They don't need the hundred dollars a week.") "I don't think kids have to be 'normal.' To differentiate yourself from the crowd is highly to be wished. But it's *how* it happens, and when, and whose choosing it is."

Her child-raising philosophy is laissez-faire. Her children learned to read on their own, as she did, at an extremely early age. "I never taught my children anything, I haven't made lists of books for them to read. There are times when I wish I'd made them take music lessons and all that. I've kind of let them drift."

With her parents, she has discussed very little about her reactions to the Quiz Kid experience. "Except I remember, ten or twelve years ago, saying, 'I didn't like it much when I was in high school,' and my mother saying, 'It was such a wonderful opportunity, and all those wonderful things we got to see and do, not to mention those hundred-dollar bonds . . . ' And my mother used to keep those damn scrapbooks around, and she'd want to show my friends, and that drove me crazy. If you talk to her about it, she'll claim that never happened. She'll say, 'What? Who, me?' "

Of all the Quiz Kid mothers, Rose Cooks was one of the last I would have picked as a show biz mama. I remember her as good-natured, relaxed, enthusiastic, and a bit bewildered by the whole thing. Exactly how she comes across today.

In the curio-filled living room of the brick bungalow she and her husband bought when Naomi was in high school, Rose—lively and alert despite recurring cancer*—talks of her daughter almost with reverence. "If Naomi does anything, she does it right. You can never keep her down. The amazing people like her are gifted, truly. Things are easy for them. They see things in another light."

---

* Mrs. Cooks died on Mother's Day, May 9, 1982, eight months after our interview.

On a lace-covered table near the leaded-glass windows lies a copy of Naomi's book. The inscription on the flyleaf is from ''Your daughter, the author.''

In the bedrooms hang pictures of Naomi and George in Quiz Kid regalia and an original cartoon signed ''To Naomi with love and kisses from her fans, Joe Palooka and Ham Fischer.'' On a shelf, a miniature piano from Liberace. Naomi's scrapbooks are here, as is her Bryn Mawr diploma. Rose drags out boxes of pictures, mementos, childishly scrawled poems, and clippings. ''Naomi was always getting in the papers,'' smiles her mother, who loved to get her in them.

As for the Quiz Kid experience, Rose says, ''I don't think it hurt her—or any kid—if the parents had the right attitude. We weren't stage parents pushing our child. We didn't care that much. I was glad when she could collect a bond for her education.''

Rose describes her daughter as ''high-principled.'' She shows me a maxim her own third grade teacher wrote in her autograph book:

He lives most who thinks the most, feels the noblest, acts the best.

''I always tried to live up to that,'' she says, ''and taught it to my children. Julius and I were interested in Naomi's making the most of her abilities and becoming a person, and I think she has.

''Life goes on. . . . She has kids to take care of, now this new venture. Quiz Kids, Schmiz Kids! I get pleasure from my grandchildren.''

In Margot's dining room, Naomi shows me the Think Big! samples. A row of five-foot-tall Crayolas. A toothbrush large enough to be a back-scrubber. The Prince racquet to end all Prince racquets. A $500 screwdriver. ''People who are scaling down the detail of their environments, who are going minimalist or high-tech find that these things look very fresh. I have a house full of antiques, and this stuff looks great. It's the contrast. Any time you distort perspective—''

The product is an ''expensive toy,'' but Naomi is not playing games. ''We have a lot of friends whose wives have little boutiques that are open by appointment only, and are tax losses. I'm certainly not doing that.'' At the same time she recognizes, ''I could never have quit my job at City College if I hadn't gotten married to somebody who was financially secure.''

Much of what Naomi says rings a bell with me. Having grown up only a few years ahead of her, I can understand where she is coming from. Yet her forthright materialism jars me. "When we were young," I begin, "there was a sense of idealism, especially surrounding the Quiz Kids. We were supposed to be representatives of American values—"

"Well," she laughs, her arm sweeping across the roomful of oversized objects, "here it is!"

Seriously, she says, "I did all that. It's a combination of trying to realize those illusions and being disillusioned. It's a female issue, also. We grew up in a fairly repressive time for women, and 'Quiz Kids' may have reinforced that. You and I were successful as Quiz Kids because we were tuned in to what people were looking for: little girls who were smart and cute but not *too* smart, who did what we were supposed to. Now, I always had a hidden sub-life where I did what I wanted. I was not always such a nice little girl with clean hands and white gloves. I was involved with a couple of men before I was married. So I didn't buy all that privately . . . but I certainly bought it publicly."

Though Naomi was competitive—even aggressive—as a child, self-assertion did not develop until much later. "I got into a marriage that was not particularly satisfying, and I tried to make it work and to do all the things a good wife is supposed to do, until I got fed up. I don't think that's any way to raise a girl. I think more delineation of personal goals— What I've learned is that you can be creative and successful in a lot of different ways. Including financially. And women have been discouraged from doing that."

Making business calls from Margot's living room, Naomi tosses off terms like "managing the float" as readily as she once recited the balcony scene or juggled sixteen novels for a literature course. "People have asked us, 'Do you have any retail training?' What would I need that for? I didn't understand cost accounting and double entry bookkeeping, so Bruce brought me a book and said, 'Read the first chapter, that's all you need.' It was very simple.

"Short of brain surgery, I don't think there's anything I couldn't do. I'm not put off by things. But I've done things that I don't think are hard. Maybe that's the secret of success—choose what you're good at."

Naomi feels "Quiz Kids" may have encouraged her tendency to "get by on shallow things" because she was used to a superficial kind of success. "I do a lot of things okay, but I don't bother to get expert at them." She recalls the time her daughter, then about six, came home and looked at her report card—it was all A's except one—and said, "The teacher was mistaken. I was excellent in that, too."

"To get a B without working," Naomi explains, "means, *If I wanted A's, I could get them.* It's a way of not challenging yourself. You just tell yourself, *I am who I am. I'm very good at everything, and teacher was mistaken.* Or, *the world is mistaken*—" she laughs—"*I'm really superior!*"

The house Naomi lives in is one of the gems she redid. A twelve-room Old English brick in Ashbury Heights, above Haight Street, with red geraniums on the steps, window seats in the dining room, and a view over rooftops to the Pacific and Golden Gate Park. The house was condemned two years ago, when she bought it for a $200,000 song.

Naomi, Bruce and I are having a before-dinner cocktail in the sitting room; some of their offspring hover around the doorway. "They know why you're here," says Naomi. "Bruce must have told them. They're going to ask about it later. I've never really talked about it with them. It's so hokey from their point of view."

"No, it's not," says Bruce. "Jessica would be getting higher grades and would be much more willing to say she likes school if she didn't feel that she couldn't measure up to her mother. The image is that of a great television-radio star, and that's obviously something she can't compete with."

Bruce is trim, good-looking and understated in a quietly expensive herringbone suit. In contrast to Naomi's vitality, he talks softly and slowly, with unpretentious authority. Naomi holds his hand while we drive to a Japanese restaurant. As we sit shoeless, partaking of exotic specialties like raw fish with horseradish, Bruce questions Naomi about her aversion to having people ask her about "Quiz Kids": "How is it different from the president of a major corporation wanting to meet Jack Nicklaus or John McEnroe?"

"Well, I'll tell you," she replies, "I've never been interested in meeting anybody like that. I wouldn't cross the street to watch the President's motorcade. I have no interest in celebrities whatsoever. Because I was one. And it's tinsel.

"Another thing I discovered today," she continues, "is why I hate for people I don't know to get close to me. I think it's because of all those people who used to crowd around and ask for autographs. People don't realize what an invasion of privacy it is. I find it physically painful."

"That was part of your social contract," Bruce points out.

"When you engage to be a celebrity," says Naomi. "But we didn't engage, we were amateurs. I think a little self-denigration was built into that: *You're very smart, but you're just a normal kid.* There's something very American about the whole thing. *You're great, but not too great— you're just like the rest of us.* You had all the notoriety of a child star without the perks . . . and you weren't getting rich, you were only getting famous. I'd rather be rich without being famous than famous without being rich. Unless it was for something like winning the Nobel Prize, or writing a great book. Not just being a cute kid with pigtails.''

At this point, Naomi's bottom-line assessment of her Quiz Kids experience is ''sort of neutral.''

''I think—and I can't prove it—that without it, I might have developed more assertively, been more successful, discovered part of myself earlier. But I see positive aspects too. Given the lower-middle-class family I was in, I wouldn't have been exposed to so much so early. Maybe the drive does come from that, in fact. I saw a whole world! The Cowans' duplex on Park Avenue—I thought that was a nice way to live in real life, not just in the movies. I also remember not being bowled over by it. And I think that's something I gained from 'Quiz Kids'—maybe it matched some natural tendency in myself. I never fiddled with the wrong fork for long; I just looked and picked up the right fork and went on.''

Think Big! opened a month after my visit and promptly sold out its initial stock. A local television station ran a segment on people who had redone their homes in Think Big! motifs. Now Naomi is exploring additional franchises. Says her brother George: ''She became an entrepreneur overnight.''

Naomi Cooks, the great escape artist, has flown one coop after another: from conventional conformity to sexual freedom, from marriage to divorce, from academia to commerce. The Quiz Kid of the 1940s became the boy-chaser of the fifties . . . the activist of the sixties . . . the feminist of the seventies . . . and now, the executive of the eighties. A woman imbued with a strong drive to achieve, she is bright enough to perceive where her culture bestows its rewards and to bend her gifts in that direction.

Years ago, Naomi's mother had her Quiz Kid key mounted on a charm bracelet. ''Last year,'' says Naomi, ''when gold was selling for $950 an ounce, I took a lot of old gold stuff that I never wore—things my ex-husband had given me—and sold it all. It's probably melted down, and the Quiz Kid key may indeed have been among that stuff.''

Harvey Dytch: Dino Mite

*Harvey Dytch is one of the most promising youngsters
ever to appear on the Quiz Kids program.*
—*Open Road,* September, 1950

Buck-toothed Harvey Dytch, cute as a chipmunk, had sleepy eyes, ragged bangs, a lisp, and a propensity for filibustering. When he started out as a Quiz Kid, in 1950, at age six, he had to sit on two fat Chicago phone books to reach the mike. His specialty was animals in general and dinosaurs in particular. He made more than seventy appearances on radio and television in the program's last four years.

Harvey was one of the small fry who graced the television show practically every week toward the end. Neither he nor any of those other little ones attained the notoriety of a Gerard Darrow or Joel Kupperman. The "wow" factor had diminished, and being a Quiz Kid was no longer such a feather in the cap. The panel resembled a row of bow-bedecked kewpie dolls. Two of the regulars, pompadoured Frankie VanderPloeg and wide-eyed Janet Ahern, did modeling.

Janet is candid about the qualities that got her on the show: "I was an adorable little curly-haired blonde who spoke sweetly and wasn't afraid to speak up. I also had a lisp. My father swears they had me on for comic relief." When asked what she would do first thing in the morning if she lived on a farm, city-bred Janet replied, "I would do just like I do at home. I would get out of bed and go peepee and then wash my hands." The camera immediately cut to Joe Kelly, who was holding his head in his hands. "Well," he said, "it's great to know that Janet gets a good start in the morning."

Janet's specialty was opera, but she "had no interest in it," she says. "They picked it for me so I could answer something, as no one else on the panel knew anything about opera."

Frank, who specialized in astronomy, also was popular for his unconscious humor. "Are you married, Frankie?" Joe Kelly once asked him. The five-year-old solemnly replied, "No, but my mother and father are." Though he played the saxophone on the show with Tex Beneke, Frank claims he had no childhood talents that could not be achieved by many or most other children. "My saxophone playing," he says, "was probably not any better than that of any other kid whose mother made him take saxophone lessons." Being a Quiz Kid, for Frank, was "just something I did, like going to school or eating or sleeping."

Quiz Kidhood had become almost run-of-the-mill. Mutton-curled Brenda Liebling (who followed her older sister Rochelle onto the panel at the age of four, after calling out an answer from the audience during an audition) never told her friends she was on the show, and none of them realized it until her picture appeared in the paper during the quiz scandal.

But Harvey Dytch's first two Quiz Kid years, before Alka-Seltzer relinquished sponsorship, were a heady adventure. Then, the television show was new and riding high. His father, Harvey, Sr., wrote the letter that got his boy a tryout, and within seven months, the Chicago lad, who had never traveled before, was flown to Philadelphia (his dad's home town) to dedicate a section of the zoo. He was greeted at the airport by Pandora, the prize chimpanzee, and whisked by police escort to the mayor's office.

"Do you want to know anysing about animals?" demanded the little chatterbox. "Ask me somesing." Then he dumbfounded a group of gaping functionaries with a lecture on how dinosaurs became extinct "fifty hundred million years ago":

> "The flesh-eating ones," said the pug-nosed, freckle-faced
> youngster, "were the tyrannosaurus and the allosaurus and the
> other ones were the brontosaurus and the diplodocus."
> . . . He continued . . . wagging [his] forefinger. "First, the
> plants changed to charcoal, and the plant-eating ones died. So
> there was nussing for the flesh-eating ones to eat. So the flesh-
> eating ones starved of meat, and therefore they, too, would die."
> —Theo Wilson, *Evening Bulletin,* Aug. 16, 1950

Harvey and his mother, Lucille, had the governor's suite at the Belden Stratford Hotel and the protection of a private detective. They went to a

Phillies ball game and to Valley Forge and had a personal tour of the Franklin Institute Museum, where Harvey got to sit in an airplane cockpit and drive a 350-ton locomotive down a stretch of track.

When they got home, Mrs. Dytch received a letter from the curator of the zoo: "We all marveled at the fact that you have managed to keep him a real boy. He has none of the common traits of 'child prodigies.' "

Harvey's two most exciting moments before the camera were on his seventh birthday, when he was presented with a cocker spaniel puppy, and a year later, when a wealthy Texas rancher gave him a horse. Nationwide contests to name the animals brought in hundreds of thousands of entries. Harvey chose "Tracks" for the pup (because it made tracks through the house) and "Dynamount" for the steed (a reference to his beloved dinosaurs). Unfortunately, Dynamount proved too spirited for the boy to ride and once kicked his father in the forehead.

Harvey's passion for dinosaurs had been kindled at three by a trip with his father to the Field Museum of Natural History. The tot was fascinated with the skeletons and dioramas and murals.

He would repeat anything his mother read to him, and learned to read by following along; he was especially fond of *National Geographic* and anything about nature. At Hibbard School, he would go to the library while the rest of the class pored over Dick and Jane. He worked his way through the card catalog, reading every book on animals he could get his hands on. Once he was asked on the show, "Why would a shark dentist soon run out of business?" Without a moment's hesitation, Harvey gave the answer: "Because sharks keep getting new teeth."

On other broadcasts, he reeled off the names of the prehistoric periods in which tyrannosaurus reigned (Jurassic, Triassic, Crustacean) and sketched the giant beasts while describing their features. Once, at the circus, he was approached by a boy who recognized him from television. "How do you spell Caribbean?" the heckler challenged. "I can't," Harvey admitted, "but can you spell allosaurus?"

A "regular boy," he also liked football and baseball; his favorite players were Bob Rush and Andy Pafko of the Chicago Cubs. His main complaints about being on "Quiz Kids" were having to wash behind his ears and put on scratchy suits and having to scramble with the older Kids for a cap big enough to fit his large head.

He talked about becoming a scientist and explorer—"the kind that looks for bones in Colorado." When Joe Kelly asked the Quiz Kids how many children they would like to have, eight-year-old Harvey replied, "None. If I go to Africa and I have a baby, the baby might die of a sickness. If I were on safari," he added, "a baby certainly couldn't be born there."

Harvey Edward Dytch never went on safari. Nor has he had any children. He has had, in his words, "a checkered career" since his quiz days ended at ten.

At sixteen, he graduated from Von Steuben High School as salutatorian and National Merit Scholar finalist. But he dropped out of the University of Chicago twice, bummed around San Francisco for almost a year in the early 1960s, spent four years in the Navy, finally graduated from college at twenty-eight, started graduate school, and dropped it. He is now a computer programmer on a cancer research project, earning in the upper twenties after a recent raise. He has gone through periods of intense involvement in philosophy, Oriental religion, and atonal music, before returning to his original interest in science.

Thirty-eight-year-old Harvey explains why he remains childless after a dozen years of marriage: "I feel that having a kid requires a real commitment. I'm too selfish—there are certain things that having a kid would mean giving up."

A stocky man with a broad, youthful face, he sits quite still at the end of the couch, hands folded. He speaks hesitantly, earnestly, but almost expressionlessly, groping for words. It is hard to picture him as the energetic lad who admired the leopard for its ferocity and fearlessness. At home on a Sunday afternoon, he wears faded jeans, jogging shoes and an open shirt, torn at the hem. His light brown hair is tousled.

He and his wife Meredith, a $20,000-a-year architect for an interior design firm, live in a nondescript brick three-flat a mile east of Chicago's Albany Park area, where he grew up. The tiny front grass patch is overgrown with bushes. The bay window in the living room overlooks houses with asbestos siding and sunflowers.

When I first called Harvey, he was reluctant to be interviewed. "I don't know if I want to go through all the publicity again." Normally he avoids discussing his Quiz Kid background. "I have to warn Meredith sometimes about telling people. Here I am involved in computers, and having been a Quiz Kid, that types you as a certain kind of person—an egghead. People think you just do equations and study."

His feelings about the Quiz Kid experience are "completely mixed." Although he enjoyed it at the time, he has repressed most of the memories. He mentions, as have others, the fun of traveling, getting to do things he wouldn't otherwise have done, and the money that helped him through college. He loved his visit to the Bronx zoo—petting a tiger, playing with the cubs. But when asked whether he would let his children (if he had any) be Quiz Kids, his answer is an immediate no. "I would want them to develop the way they wanted to develop, without being set apart and having a role thrust upon them."

His difficulties, unlike Claude Brenner's or Pat Conlon's, had little to do with teasing or social rejection. ("After a while, kids forget about that—they know you from everyday.") Rather, the problem centered on his self-image. "I'm not sure if it made other people look at me as different or if it made me look at myself as different," he explains, "but I've got a feeling that things wouldn't have taken quite the same track had I not been on the show. I think it tended to make me associate in school with the *real* eggheads. Afterwards, I've bent over backwards to become normal."

With a 136 I.Q., he does not regard himself as "superintelligent." "There are a lot of brighter people around, who can pick up on things more quickly and are sharper than I am. At least now I feel I can admit that to myself. I've learned that intelligence is not the be-all and end-all. I'd rather be around nice people."

Harvey's early view of himself as an intellectual was bound up, in his mind, with skipping as well as being a Quiz Kid; he was double-promoted twice. "I guess I was glad at the time—I knew it was an honor. All these good things. Here I was, getting special attention and proving myself." He remembers wanting to be Quiz Kid of the Week (the top scorer on the TV show), and sometimes he was.

His parents were unaware of his ambivalence and expressed surprise when he told them later. "They did what they thought was best for me," he says. Harvey describes his parents as bright but not intellectual. Lutherans but not frequent churchgoers, they lived in a predominantly Jewish neighborhood, in moderate circumstances. His father was a self-made man who never finished high school. ("He was very proud that I was on the show.") Lucille Dytch, with a master's degree in education, was assistant principal and eighth grade teacher at Chappell School. While Harvey and his little sister Gail were growing up, the family lived with their grandmother, who helped raise the children.

Gail, a tiny, spirited blonde, appeared on "Quiz Kids" at five, frolicking in skits and commercials. But she hated the question-and-answer part. "It was very traumatic," she laughs. "I couldn't stand the pressure."

Gail laughs often and hard. At thirty-five, she is still petite and baby-faced, sunny and vivacious. Shapely in designer jeans and V-necked sweater, she serves me coffee on Whitehall china. Her suburban home in Highland Park, Illinois, is white brick and stucco, with statuary, stone bench, and pink petunias. Two small scuffed gym shoes stand guard outside the door. Pictures of Gail, her lawyer husband Howard Schaffner (her childhood sweetheart), and their eight and ten-year-old daughters are prominently displayed in the dining room.

In contrast to her brother, Gail's whole life is wrapped up in her children. A former kindergarten teacher, she intends to stay home until the girls are in college. "My life is my house and my kids."

When the older girl, a gymnast with Olympic potential, was profiled on television, Gail worried about the effect on her younger one. "I thought, *Here it goes again—my poor baby.* I keep looking for signs of jealousy or hurt. I think it made me very insecure, my brother being a star. People would say to my mother, 'Oh, I didn't know you had a daughter too!' "

Gail resented Harvey's horse—the fact that he took riding lessons and she didn't. "It may have been because I was too young—that was my parents' stock answer." Once a wealthy man took Harvey and some of the other kids to a museum, and Gail was left out. "I decided it was because I wasn't smart enough."

In high school, a counselor said to her, "Why can't you be like your brother?" While Harvey was a top student, except in gym, Gail was athletic and gregarious but barely managed to pull C's. "Not working up to potential," her teachers always said. Then, at National College of Education, she made the dean's list. "I think," says Harvey, "she did much better after I started becoming a black sheep."

"I was a complete misfit," Harvey says. "I used to pick friends who were outcasts. At grammar school graduation, I was practically forced into taking somebody out, and I think that was the one date I had, even through high school. I guess the social climate was such that I felt intellectuals didn't date. I used to feign non-interest."

He did not begin going out with girls until he entered the University of Chicago, where "everybody was intellectual." There he met his wife at a party; they married after he got out of the Navy. "Meredith was kind of an outcast too. She had a difficult childhood."

Meredith cheerfully agrees. "I was the odd one out, because I was always reading." Short, plump and lively, she has come in from the dining room, where she has been going over some of their favorite Laotian recipes. "All these books are mine," she says, pointing to the shelves that flank the mantel.

Harvey went through "a long period of not reading very much," he explains—part of the anti-intellectual turmoil that beset him in adolescence. As a youngster, he had striven for grades. "I felt there were a lot of expectations I had to live up to. Then, in college, I became disgusted with competitiveness. I didn't like the way it made me feel about other people. I like an atmosphere in which people are working for the same goals."

Then, too, he adds, "being thrown into this big pond with all these people who were very capable intellectually, maybe I was a little bit worried that I wasn't going to be top of everything. I suddenly found out that I couldn't get good grades in college by doing nothing. So I decided the easy way was not to compete at all, just not try. When I did leave school, I was failing. I wasn't going to any classes."

Leading up to Harvey's quitting college were several years of floundering and rebellion against his early typecasting as a future scientist. In high school, he felt he was expected to do a science fair project, even though his interest was shifting to music. His project on "A Mathematical Analysis of Melody" (nominated for a youth achievement award and exhibited at the Museum of Science and Industry) was an attempt to bridge the two interests. But his discovery of music and the humanities was steering him into "a turbulent uncertainty about my direction."

His exploration of classical music began after reading, in high school English class, a story based on a scene in the opera *Siegfried*. He went to the library and listened to some Wagner records. "I was just bowled over."

He had never heard much classical music at home. "I'm sorry I didn't —I might have perfect pitch now. People I've known that had it have always had early exposure to music. I think it's a matter of letting your whole being become deeply involved with a particular sound, which you can do only when you're very little."

In high school, he took up the French horn. ("He said trumpet players are a dime a dozen," his mother remembers.) He played for shows throughout the city and thought seriously of a musical career. "That was a source of contention with my parents," he recalls. "This whole business of music they saw as going towards a very unrealistic future, whereas science was bright and rosy."

He started college as a physical science major, thinking of a career in nuclear physics, but after one semester switched to philosophy. "I felt the important thing that would really help people was not progress in making TVs and atomic bombs."

He had begun delving into philosophy in high school, asking himself ultimate questions. "I convinced myself that God didn't exist, and I really became upset. Once you decide that, a lot of things fall apart. I was reading Dostoevsky's *The Brothers Karamazov*, and I felt that there wasn't anything solid anymore: 'If God doesn't exist, everything is permitted.' "

In college, having "broken somewhat free" of his middle-class home with its Judaeo-Christian moral base, he began searching for an alternative source of form and meaning. But he quickly became disgusted with philosophy as "an intellectual word game." Still seeking structure, he changed his major again, to music theory and composition. He had begun "fooling around" with the piano and attempting to write music in high school. "Here's something that appeals to you on both an intellectual and emotional level, and you don't quite know why. I wanted to know how that worked."

He also immersed himself in Oriental religion, studied Chinese, and wrote haiku. "I think Buddhism is concerned about people. A lot of the things that I've read, particularly in Zen, appeal directly on a very gut level to what I feel. I do believe that there is a higher reality, but maybe this is it . . . right now."

Heavily involved in his spiritual search, Harvey cut classes and neglected his assignments. His memory of the sequence of events is fuzzy; he believes he may have been put on probation or even terminated at that point. He started for Mexico with friends, but their car broke down in Bloomington, Illinois, so he got on a bus to San Francisco. "I wanted to put some distance—and I'd heard it was a very interesting city. A friend of mine was very big on the Beat writers, Kerouac and Ginsburg."

In San Francisco, he did odd jobs and lived in "strange places." ("I was letting things ferment in my mind.") He waited tables in a boarding house in exchange for a room and meals, put up television antennas, and scrubbed up in a beanery.

"I guess I had enough of that, so I came back to Chicago. My parents had been very upset, pleading with me to come back."

"He said it was time to come home when the public library wouldn't give him any more books." Lucille Dytch shakes her head, mystified by her son's wayward ways. "Then when he went back to the University of Chicago, he had to pay more than $100 in fines for books he hadn't returned and records that had been warped by leaving them on a hot register. I guess bright kids are that way. Money doesn't mean much to him. To this day—Abbott Laboratories offered him $2,000 more than he was getting at his present job, and his boss more than matched it. Now he wonders how much sooner he could have gotten a raise."

Mrs. Dytch, retired after thirty-five years in the Chicago public schools and recently widowed, lives in the faded green clapboard cottage overlooking the secluded shore of Fox Lake where Harvey spent his boyhood summers. She, not Harvey, has his Quiz Kid scrapbook. She recites her son's honors and achievements. "Harvey's very humble," she says.

Harvey quickly dropped out of the University of Chicago again and joined the Navy, becoming a sonar technician. The work—repairing electronic gear and tracing submarines by means of sounding devices— required mathematical aptitude and a sharp ear. "One of the things I loved," he says, "was that you got to listen to the sea at night."

The destroyer escort on which he served made a transatlantic voyage. "It was my first contact with Europe—a real eye-opener. There's a different smell in the air; the sounds are different."

In the Navy, he began feeling better about himself. "I guess I had put enough distance between me and the intellectual thing. It was removed enough in time so that nobody knew me as a Quiz Kid. I met a lot of people I would have had no chance of meeting in high school and college. Everybody knew I was smart, and I got along with them. It was on a different basis—not competitive. I started reading science and taught myself calculus. I became interested in fluids and how they moved and was amazed to find out how little I really knew about it."

When he got out of the Navy, he persuaded the University of Chicago to readmit him as a geophysical science major. ("I was careful to tell them I'd matured.") He graduated Phi Beta Kappa three years later, working summers as a bus driver to put himself through, and won a fellowship for graduate study. But once again, he decided he'd had enough of school. ("Those graduate students are tremendously competitive.")

Having taken a programming course in college, he joined the

university's cloud physics laboratory, using computers to study effects of urban pollution on weather. But to go further in meteorology would have required an advanced degree.

Now he is chief programmer for a cytocybernetics project at Chicago Lying-In Hospital. He heads a team of a dozen researchers working to develop a machine that will do quick, accurate, automatic diagnosis of pap smears. "Teaching" a computer to distinguish between normal and malignant cells is, for Harvey, a "very appealing combination" of math, logic and creative thinking. "To do a well-structured and well-thought-out program is a certain kind of work of art." He believes artistic and scientific creativity are closely linked. "Creative activity in the arts means a certain openness to new things, being able to see things in a different way and to make leaps of imagination. That's certainly a help in the hard sciences too."

Eventually he would like to do something involving computers and music. "I'd like to take an orchestral score and put it in front of a TV camera and have it played back. Or conversely, have somebody sit down and play the piano and have a score produced from that."

He is seriously studying piano, practicing and improvising two hours a day—a discipline he was unwilling to impose on himself in his youth. He finds pounding the keyboard a great way to relieve tensions and let out emotions. "I'm a person that tends to keep things bottled in." At one point he tried counseling but did not find it helpful.

He feels "much more relaxed" about himself now. "I don't feel the expectations are there so much, except insofar as I put them there. I do set goals for myself, but not in a competitive sense. I've learned to accept the fact that I have to work hard if I'm going to do something hard."

Although he has "come to appreciate the things money can do," he has no interest in earning a lot of money—"as long as we can live reasonably okay." What does matter to him—just as he told a *Chicago Daily News* reporter at fourteen—is having a job that interests him and in which he feels he can do some good.

Does he ever feel, having been a Quiz Kid, that he should be doing something more spectacular? "Occasionally that ugly head rises. When I went back to science, after coming out of the Navy, my parents thought I was going to be an adult prizewinner. Occasionally I do feel some drive to achieve like that. But I'd rather just do a good job and let the chips fall where they may.

"I could be studying every night and pushing myself to accomplish a lot of things. Maybe the fact that I had the experience with the show helped me to see that I didn't really need to do that.''

Paradoxically, he also admits to a certain resentment that he is not one of those people who are ''always on.'' ''Maybe being on the show cut off that possibility for me, made me look upon that kind of person and attitude in a way that made it distasteful to me.''

When asked his greatest accomplishment, he cracks, ''Surviving the Quiz Kids.'' And yet, he is not sorry he was one. ''I am who I am because it happened that way, and there's no way to unravel it.''

Harvey Dytch is the Quiz-Kid-in-spite-of-himself. His speech is simple, his attitude self-effacing, but his curious mind and intense interests give him away. He is a seeker after knowledge—but not just from books. ''I learn about life from meeting people. I feel I'm constantly learning by going on living.''

He still has a soft spot for dinosaurs. He shows me a large model of a plesiosaur that his wife gave him and animatedly discusses the current theory that dinosaurs were warm-blooded and ''may be living amongst us today in the form of birds.''

I have one final question for him. ''Do you still feel 'different'?''

He smiles. ''I feel I'm asymptotically approaching normalcy.''

The reference is to a straight line and a curve that come closer and closer together but never meet.

. . . And the Rest

The Quiz Kids saga, with its cast of hundreds, cannot be concluded without a glimpse at what became of some of the other characters in the story. I sent questionnaires to approximately 130 ex-Quiz Kids apart from the principal ones I interviewed, and 69 responded:* 37 men and 32 women.

The sample does not pretend to be scientific; it consists, as Margaret Merrick Scheffelin put it, of those I could find who were willing to talk. Because the only lists extant are from the show's first six years, the sample is heavier on that vintage; all but three respondents are in their forties and fifties, and about 60 percent have hit the half-century mark. Most became Quiz Kids between the ages of twelve and fourteen, as was usual in the program's early days; a dozen started as young as four, six, or eight. More than 60 percent appeared fewer than five times; a third, only once. (Eight of those were out-of-town contest winners.) Eleven returned at least twenty times.

These ex-Quiz Kids have made ripples far and wide since their first splash on the Chicago show. They have spread from coast to coast and all the way to Hawaii (Arthur Reinwald, partner in the Honolulu law firm of Hoddick, Reinwald, O'Connor and Marrack). Their occupations include

---

* Participants and their occupations are listed in the appendix.

real estate broker (Shirley Bersadsky Goldman, a member of the Million Dollar Club, who was New Orleans' Quiz Kid) and CPA (Ronald Weintrob), but the biggest clusters are in education and the professions.

As a group, these ex-Quiz Kids are achievers. Many of their resumes bulge with honors, professional awards, publications. Thirteen are in Marquis *Who's Whos*—seven in *Who's Who in America,* three in *Who's Who in the World.*

Their present status and accomplishments are not necessarily related to their degree of Quiz Kid success. A few cases in point:

• James Dewey Watson was co-winner of the 1962 Nobel Prize for Medicine for the discovery of the structure of DNA, the reproductive basis of life—a breakthrough that set off a wave of biochemical research and opened possibilities for genetic engineering, production of synthetic insulin, and cancer control. Director of the Cold Spring Harbor Laboratory, he has held research fellowships at the University of Copenhagen, Cambridge's Cavendish Laboratory, and the California Institute of Technology; has taught at Harvard; wrote two books, *The Double Helix* and *Molecular Biology of the Gene*; won the 1977 Presidential Medal of Freedom, Carty Medal of the National Academy of Sciences, Eli Lilly Award, Albert Lasker prize, and others; and has received honorary degrees from ten universities. (Three Quiz Kids appearances—he "failed on the Bible." As he once told Lee Edson in a *New York Times Magazine* interview, a "six-year-old Jewish girl"—I shudder to think he must have meant me—knew more about the Old Testament. His sister's explanation, though, was that he lacked audience appeal.)

• Richard Lieb, Emmy-winning arranger-conductor of "Sesame Street," does Muzak and other commercial arranging and was bass trombonist, composer and arranger for the Kai Winding septet, Radio City Music Hall Orchestra, and Johnny Carson's "Tonight" show. (Two Quiz Kids appearances, once playing a harmonica duet with guest artist Larry Adler. "A quick lucky shot," says Dick. "I didn't expect to get on in the first place, so I wasn't surprised at not lasting.")

• Dr. Richard E. Sedlack is chairman of the clinical practice committee at Mayo Clinic, equivalent to chief of the medical staff. (Three Quiz Kids appearances, the third on a program honoring the 4-H Clubs of America with the secretary of agriculture as guest. Asked how he would like to live on a farm, Dick frankly expressed his view that farms were not fit habitation for man or beast. "That superb bit of diplomacy did me in," he says.)

• David Nasatir has been a sociology professor at Berkeley, UCLA,

California State and other universities, a consultant to national governments and international organizations, and Senior Fulbright Scholar in Brazil. (Three Quiz Kids appearances. When Joe Kelly asked the Kids to go through some complex mathematical manipulations to determine the position of the hands on a clock, Dave raised his hand, before Kelly finished reading the question, and gave the correct answer: twelve o'clock. "Unfortunately," he recalls, "Jolly Joe asked me how I had arrived at the answer, and, innocent little kid that I was, I told him. I had noticed, I said, that the questions always appeared complicated but actually were very simple. I assumed, therefore, that the answer was going to be something like twelve or six, and if it wasn't the one I chose, I'd simply say I had made an error of two in my division. I got the call right after the show saying that they wouldn't be needing me for a while.")

The Quiz Kid women in the survey have combined marriage, parenting, and careers to a degree remarkable for our generation. All but two have been married; all but four are married currently. (Two more are in the process of divorce.) All but two are mothers, in most cases with two, three, four or more children; some are grandmothers. But only eight list their occupations as housewife, homemaker, or "domestic engineer." All have been gainfully employed, in most cases full time—sixteen (half the group) throughout their adult lives; four more, except when their children were young; and the rest, before and/or after child-raising. While most have gone into traditional women's fields such as education, health, social work, and music, there also are a doctor, a lawyer, an information systems analyst, a bookstore owner, and two college administrators. Nancy Wong Nelson, who appeared on "Quiz Kids" once, is preparing for the ministry after having been a member of Rutgers University's education faculty.

Joanna Tyrny Noncek, another one-shot Quiz Kid, never went to college but worked her way up from nursing assistant to hospital department supervisor in Barrington, Illinois, meanwhile producing five children and six grandchildren from her thirty-five-year marriage.

Sydel Finfer Silverman Wolf, the youngest of seven children, does not consider herself gifted and appeared on the program only twice. But she has applied her organizational and practical skills to a lifelong academic career. The mother of two, she is head of the doctoral program in anthropology at City University of New York. She has had three research fellowships, has been appointed to many national panels, and has had one of her books picked as "outstanding" by *Choice*.

Rochelle Liebling Kahan, who made thirty Quiz Kids appearances, is a Jill-of-two-trades, both of which run in her family. Granddaughter of a professor at the Vienna Conservatory of Music, she was giving piano recitals and making orchestral appearances at five. She has soloed with the Chicago Symphony and other orchestras, concertized, and won many awards. She switched to law (her father's profession) to support her husband through medical school, and became active in women's rights issues. Since the birth of her nine-year-old daughter, Rochelle's professional interests have returned to music; living in Houston, she gives piano lessons and is a member of a duo-piano team, Kahan and Trawick.

Sharpshooter Ann Bokman, a junior riflery champion who appeared on the show three times, also has set her sights on a variety of targets. She was doing postdoctoral biochemistry research when she married Dr. Thomas G. Akers. She followed him to Egypt, where he did medical research for the Navy while she taught at Cairo American Collˈge, and then to Tulane University. Versatile Ann has combined homemaking and child-raising with scientific writing and editing, teaching handicapped children, and nutritional research, and now (thanks to a newspaper article revealing her Quiz Kid past) helps produce a Varsity Quiz Bowl for public television.

Coming as they did from nonaffluent homes, these ex-Quiz Kids as a group have done well financially, but not spectacularly so, perhaps because few are in business. Most earn between $30,000 and $60,000; seven, mainly lawyers who are partners in large firms, $100,000 and up. Median income for the men is $52,000, for the women (fewer of whom are in the remunerative professions of law and medicine), $32,000.

One reason median income is not higher is that many Quiz Kids remained in the relatively low-paying academic world, where they had had considerable early success.

Seventy percent of the respondents had their education accelerated, usually in grade school. There is no clear verdict on the wisdom of that course; generally speaking, the benefits of advancing quickly and avoiding boredom were offset by the social penalties. As Sydel Finfer Silverman Wolf says, "It always made me feel like the smartest but most socially backward of my peers." C. Harker Rhodes, Jr. (a partner in the Chicago law firm of Sonnenschein, Carlin, Nath and Rosenthal and a board member of the Chicago and Illinois Bar Associations) got his juris doctor degree from the University of Chicago at twenty-one and, he says, "spent the next thirty years wandering about, trying to fill in the things I imagined I missed." But Sally Wilhelm Fullerton, who never skipped, sometimes wishes she had.

The most extreme acceleration was reported by Richard A. Freeman, now a stockbroker and assistant branch manager for Bear, Stearns and Company in Atlanta. He graduated from grammar school at ten, high school at twelve, and the University of Chicago at fifteen. The effect? He says simply, "It enabled me to become an attorney at twenty-two."

All but two of the group have bachelor's degrees, in some instances, more than one; sixteen have professional degrees; twelve doctorates; and sixteen more have at least one master's degree. Nearly half mention membership in Phi Beta Kappa, Order of the Coif, and other honoraries, high class rank, graduation *magna* or *summa cum laude,* or other academic distinctions. More than twenty won scholarships and fellowships (in some cases, several) to schools like Harvard, Yale, Oxford, Cambridge, Berkeley, Stanford, Wellesley, Chicago, Columbia, Northwestern, and Michigan, and grants from institutions like the National Science Foundation, National Endowment for the Humanities, and U.S. Public Health Service.

Elinor Smith Miller has had a string of thirteen such stipends, including a Fulbright. A French professor, translator of two books, and chairman of the arts and letters division of St. Mary's College of Maryland, she has been self-supporting since she was fourteen, never took time off from work to have her four children ("I had them on weekends and at spring break"), and once was so strapped that she had to use her two Quiz Kids bonds to eat.

As far as could be determined, there are no Rhodes Scholars in the group; but Alan Stamm (counsel to the Los Angeles law firm of Long and Levit, arbitrator, municipal judge pro tem, and a trustee of the Center for Law in the Public Interest) was a Rhodes finalist.

Twenty-three of the respondents, including nine women, have taught in colleges, universities, professional schools and seminaries, and several besides Watson have done original research.

Dr. C. David Jenkins, director of sociomedical sciences at the University of Texas and president-elect of the American Psychosomatic Society, has directed investigations of cardiovascular disease and hypertension for the National Heart, Lung and Blood Institute and has done research and consulting for the World Health Organization, American Cancer Society, American Heart Association and others. He is author or co-author of nearly one hundred articles, chapters and monographs, has lectured extensively in Europe, and has devised the Jenkins Activity Survey for Health Prediction. Because of a five-year, $2.3 million study he directed on effects of stress on air traffic controllers, he was featured in *People* magazine during the 1981 strike.

Another scientific frontiersman is Dr. Joseph Bogen (formerly Joe Tietz, the Cincinnati Quiz Kids contest winner), now clinical professor of neurosurgery at the University of Southern California and consultant to New Hope Pain Foundation. He has done major research in several areas, notably human split-brain studies at the California Institute of Technology. He has eighty-three articles, book chapters, and reviews to his credit and is writing a book on *The Other Si₂ of the Brain*.

Of the eight respondents with published books, the most prolific is Paul E. Sigmund, professor of politics at Princeton University, with ten volumes (most recently, *The Overthrow of Allende and the Politics of Chile*), followed by David Freifelder, Brandeis University biochemistry professor, with six titles plus eighty-seven scientific papers, and Richard Frisbie, award-winning Chicago communications consultant, with six books and four hundred magazine articles on a wide variety of topics.

One of Dick's volumes, *It's a Wise Woodsman Who Knows What's Biting Him,* is reminiscent of his Quiz Kid specialty: snakes. "Keeping snakes as pets was somewhat frustrating," he recalls, "because they were so good at getting away. I lost a Florida rat snake once in the Goodman Theater, and as far as I know, it's still there." He says he "might have become a naturalist if I had happened across the right major in the college catalog." Instead he "drifted into journalism." His career exemplifies the versatility characteristic of many Quiz Kids, spanning newspaper work, advertising, editing, public relations, and audiovisual production. After seven years with the *Chicago Daily News,* he got into corporate sales promotion, then "drifted" (again) into an ad agency, winding up as creative director for Campbell-Ewald before going out on his own. He was editor-in-chief of *Chicago Magazine,* helped launch the National Satellite Cable Association, serves as president of a cooperative of forty-three suburban libraries, and numbers among his clients McGraw-Edison, Capital Cities Communications, Hertz, Brunswick, and R.R. Donnelly & Sons. The urge to pick up snakes-in-the-grass reasserts itself from time to time; once he brought one home in a paper sack, to the great surprise of his wife and eight children, who were expecting a bag of ice cream.

Most of the other ex-Quiz Kids have continued to pursue their early interests, vocationally or otherwise. For example, Harry L. Sebel, Jr., whose specialty was pure-bred dogs, became (in addition to a financial consultant) a breeder-exhibitor and dog show judge in Dallas. Bible expert Ronald Youngblood is now a Baptist minister and professor of Old

Testament at Bethel Seminary West in San Diego.

The majority have been active in community as well as professional affairs. A prime example is Betty Swanson Upjohn, an early regular on the show, who started her journalistic career as editor of the *Ex-Quiz Kid Resume* and went on to become women's editor of the *Kalamazoo Gazette*. A pillar of her community, she has been honored by two service citations. She organized a volunteer center, launched a nature center, was president of the Kalamazoo Service Club and Junior League, and chaired a $16 million endowment campaign for Kalamazoo College, of which she is vice-chairman of the board of trustees. Now, as owner (in conjunction with her husband, Burton Upjohn), of a real estate investment firm that constructs offices for triple-A-rated companies nationwide, she is the first woman in 110 years on the board of the First National Bank and Trust Company of Michigan and its holding company, First American Bank Corporation. She also does public relations work for her husband's Parkview Hills planned residential development, which has been featured in national magazines for its ecological balance. "Because of our success in business," says Betty, "we have been able to make a real difference in the quality of life for this community."

Robert W. Haller, Fort Wayne, Indiana's Quiz Kid and now an attorney there, is president of the American Lung Association of Indiana and has served as president of the Fort Wayne YMCA and Kiwanis and lieutenant-governor of the state Kiwanis, as well as holding offices in the Lutheran church. He won a Distinguished Flying Cross and other military medals and received the 1979 Sertoma Service to Mankind award. Yet he calls his endeavors "small scale" and says, "I have probably missed opportunities to be of service."

Some of those involved in government and politics include: Dean Berry (partner in the 280-member Cleveland law firm of Squire, Sanders and Dempsey), who has been a councilman in Rocky River, Ohio and is a Republican county committeeman; William F. McHugh, a U.S. Labor Department administrator in San Francisco and recipient of three superior performance awards; Charles F. Vihon, who was bankruptcy counsel to the House judiciary committee and worked with seven other government agencies before going into private practice and now consulting in Stamford, Connecticut; Verne W. Vance, Jr., the Omaha Quiz Kid, who (prior to entering law practice with the ninety-member Boston firm of Foley, Hoag and Elliot) was an official of the Agency for International Development, and has served as chairman of the Massachusetts Advisory Council on Education and alderman of the town of Newton; and Frank

VanderPloeg (little Frankie on the Quiz Kids television panels), who besides being a partner in the Chicago law firm of Hopkins and Sutter, is chairman of Project LEAP—an anti-vote-fraud organization—and author of an attorney's guide to Illinois election laws.

Only fifteen of the respondents feel their participation in the program directly affected their careers, but in some cases the impact was powerful. Paul Sigmund says his single appearance as Philadelphia's Quiz Kid cemented his commitment to high academic standards and led to a Fulbright scholarship, his present professorial position, and "a fulfilled life." He has put political theory into practice as consultant to UNESCO, AID, the Peace Corps, the U.S. State Department, and the platform committee of the 1968 Democratic National Convention.

Marjorie Bruce Runnion, a southern Illinois girl who managed to get herself on the show twice while visiting in Chicago the summer she was fourteen, believes her Quiz Kid credential helped her win a postgraduate fellowship to the London School of Economics. She also found it "a great asset" in seeking her first journalism jobs. ("I still have friends who have great faith in my intelligence because I was a Quiz Kid.") Marge spent nine years as a *Life* reporter in New York, London, and Washington, and currently is an editorial researcher for *People* and a free-lance writer. In addition, she founded and administered a museum and art center in Brattleboro, Vermont and served on the President's Advisory Committee on the Kennedy Center for the Performing Arts.

Marge notes with bemusement that the same determination to solve "seemingly impossible dilemmas" that enabled her to find a way to become a Quiz Kid, even though she lived 250 miles from Chicago, has recently backfired. Her husband, a Vermont newspaper editor, insisted on living there, while Marge chafed at the lack of professional opportunity for her. She found what seemed an ideal solution: working two or three days a week in New York, then commuting back to Vermont. "Then, a year ago, my husband suddenly announced that it was all over, that we had become too 'competitive,' and that he wanted a divorce. So much for determination and perfect solutions!"

"Quiz Kids" also gave a career boost to Kenneth Childers, a Creek Indian sometimes taken for black, who appeared on the show only once with the great Indian athlete Jim Thorpe. Ken became an award-winning architect despite the lack of any formal training. A high school dropout, he got his college equivalency in the Air Force, then worked his way up from office boy in an architectural firm until he finally had his own

eleven-member Chicago office. His firm was responsible for 6,000 structures, from tract housing to industrial parks and shopping centers to
theaters and hospitals, and shared a 1972 American Institute of Archi-
tects award for a school-in-a-park. He was supervising architect for urban
renewal projects and for the Governors State University in Park Forest.
Now semi-retired in Las Vegas, he credits "Quiz Kids" with opening
doors and giving others confidence in him: "I wouldn't trade it for anything."

Warren Cavior, now a New York corporate public relations consultant, says that winning the New England Quiz Kids contest confirmed
his desire for pre-eminence.

"It was a clear validation of my abilities," is the way Barbara Scott
Huszagh, a three-time Quiz Kid, puts it. A radiation therapy technician
before her children were born, she went back to school after her divorce
to earn a master's degree in social work. "Even though I've been a
'professional mother' for thirty years," she says, "I have kept the confidence that I'll have a second profession too."

Appearing on the program was a turning point for Marguerite (Peggy)
Bangert Thompson. For twenty-seven years, while rearing three children,
she has been an English teacher at Wright Community College in
Chicago, where her husband also teaches. Yet, having grown up in a
"chauvinistic" milieu, Peggy might never have gone to college herself,
had it not been for "Quiz Kids." Her family was relatively poor, her
father was not a college graduate, and her mother was "only" a gym
teacher. ("I recall my father once saying that college was wasted on
girls.") Although the thirteen-year-old was on the Quiz Kids show only
eight times, and was so nervous before each broadcast that she couldn't
sleep, the experience confirmed her capacity for academic work and determined once and for all that she would go to college. The established
female Quiz Kids were role models for her: "I found out it was okay for a
girl to be smart."

DiAnne Mathre Thomas, a farm girl from DeKalb, Illinois, parlayed
her six Quiz Kids appearances into her own radio quiz show back home,
and later hosted a homemakers' television show in Champaign, Illinois,
where she got her home economics degree. Now a homemaker herself,
DiAnne counts her quizzing days among the highlights of her life.

However, Brenda Liebling, who became a frequent Quiz Kids fixture at
four and loved it, found having been a child performer "no help" in
trying to break into the big leagues of show business. She has been a story
analyst for Metro-Goldwyn Mayer, administrative assistant at Universal

Studios and research coordinator for television documentaries and specials (Jackie Gleason, Hugh O'Brien); she also danced in the film *Hello, Dolly* and co-starred in a pre-Broadway revival of *The Desk Set* with Shirley Booth. Married to a Houston attorney, Brenda now is midway through law school herself. When one of her two children was picked at school to be screen tested for a Norman Lear TV pilot, Brenda "in no way encouraged her," as, she says, "I feel that 1) a childhood career does not help you have an adult career in the entertainment industry, 2) the adult career is what really counts, 3) an adult career in the entertainment industry is filled with too many frustrations for me to encourage my children to pursue it. I would not, however, stop them if they did it on their own," she adds, "as I believe every person should try to use their talents, if they have any, to the fullest."

Robert Easton, top west coast dialect coach, had a reaction diametrically opposed to Brenda's. "Becoming a Quiz Kid changed my entire life," he says. "As a result of my Quiz Kid experiences, doors were open to me that I could never have anticipated." Bob, who originally planned to be an aeronautical engineer, is known as "the Henry Higgins of Hollywood," and "the dialect doctor." In a single typical week, he teaches an Irish brogue to Gregory Peck, Oxford English to Eva Marie Saint, Louisiana rural to Michael York, a Pacific Northwest accent to Jaclyn Smith, and Eastern Tennessee to Jane Fonda.

The tall, bearded redhead, who has eradicated the Texas drawl he had as Quiz Kid Robert Easton Burke, has also played character roles in fifty-nine motion pictures and some eight hundred radio and television shows. He was Chester's inept brother on "Gunsmoke," Ronny Burns' dim-witted Texas college buddy on the Burns and Allen show, Nancy Kulp's bashful bird-watcher boyfriend on the Bob Cummings show, and Fibber McGee and Molly's next-door neighbor. The "man with a hundred voices" also has written screenplays, taught and lectured, and is working on a book, *Dialects and Diction in Fact and Fiction.*

The product of a broken home and an unhappy childhood, Bob says the Quiz Kids program was "the first really good thing that ever happened" to him.

When he joined the Quiz Kids panel at fourteen, Bob was already six-foot-four and weighed all of 134 pounds ("one of Dr. Sheldon's archetypal ectomorphs"). Shy, introverted, and lacking in self-confidence, the dialectician-to-be had just worked his way out of a severe stammering problem brought on by his parents' bitter divorce and his father's continuing court battle to gain custody of him. To establish his contention that Bob's mother's intellectual permissiveness was damaging the boy, his Phi Beta Kappa father—a bitter, frustrated man—constantly denigrated his efforts. "If I got 98 in a subject," Bob remembers, "he was angry that I hadn't gotten 99. When I got 99, he was angry I hadn't gotten 100. When I got 100, why hadn't I gotten that in all my subjects?"

At his audition, Bob felt he had failed because he could not answer all the questions. "Afterwards I realized the others hadn't done as well as I had, but my father's brainwashing had blinded me to that. I was aware only of *my own* shortcomings. Much to my amazement, several weeks later, I heard my name announced. I was overjoyed and dumbfounded. My first appearance proved to be the most euphoric day I had experienced in my first fourteen years of life. When I answered a question correctly, Mr. Kelly beamed and the audience applauded. After the show, people asked us for our autographs and asked to take our pictures. This was astounding to me. I was actually receiving approbation from people other than my mother and her friends."

With a custody hearing coming up, Bob's father wrote to the Quiz Kids office demanding that he be removed from the show. Bob recalls: "One of the unforgettable phrases was, 'I feel that protracted participation will not be of lasting benefit to the boy.' How wrong he was."

His father lost the custody suit—the judge, it turned out, was a fervent Quiz Kids fan—and Bob continued on the show some sixteen times before he became over-age.

In December, 1945, Bob was one of the Kids picked to go to Washington, where they were introduced on the Senate floor, beat a panel of Senators, and met President Truman, another big Quiz Kids fan. Bob also was thrilled to meet his hero, Captain Eddie Rickenbacker.

The boy could hardly believe his good fortune when he was chosen to be in a comic sketch on Fred Allen's program. "It was the first time in my life I had ever read a script. I had never even dared to audition for a school play, and here I was performing on my favorite comedy show. As I struggled to make the words on the printed page sound natural, I never guessed that I would become a *professional* actor and would actually instruct Oscar- and Emmy-winning actors and actresses on how to deliver their lines. All I knew was that the Quiz Kids show was the best thing that had ever happened to me. I had felt the love of audiences, and for the first time in my life I was developing confidence in myself.

"I realized that my father's assessment of me as a hopeless failure was not a true picture of me but a sad reflection of how he felt about himself.

This insight freed me enormously. It is no exaggeration to say that everything good that happened to me later was directly or indirectly a result of my participation on 'Quiz Kids.' ''

Although no one else has such a dramatic story to tell, almost all the ex-Quiz Kids who participated in the survey, whether regulars or one-timers, enjoyed being on the program. ''It made my aura for six weeks,'' says Ruth Fisher Henoch, a part-time college English teacher. ''It was a moment or two of glory.''

''It made me proud to have a brain and showed me that smarties could be regular kids too,'' says Lois Myna Karpf, a word processor and statistical typist, who was on the program once at age fifteen.

''What a neat thing to happen to an eighth grader,'' says Marie Gleason Vonder Heide, who also appeared only once. ''I was old enough to appreciate being on network radio, and I had never in my life had a hundred dollars.''

''I loved the ego trip,'' says Anneke de Bruyn Overseth, director of development for the University of Michigan's School of Business Administration. (Her parents, however, did not; after four times, they took her off the show.)

About half of the respondents do recall some uncomfortable aspects: embarrassment about giving wrong answers or making *faux pas,* chagrin at losing, resentment of not being called on, the stigma of being labelled as smart, put-downs by teachers, the envy of friends, and the obligatory razzing at school. David Freifelder was ''stared at by everyone, looking for horns,'' and Peter Reich had to fight schoolyard battles after his appearances, to prove he was no pantywaist. And, while some look upon their Quiz Kid background as a conversation piece, others are reticent about discussing it.

Nevertheless, the vast majority feel the experience had a positive overall effect—in some cases, more so than they thought at the time. For Janet Ahern Martin, a television regular at six, being a Quiz Kid made her feel different from her friends and was a continual source of conflict at home. ''My mother was constantly quizzing me on opera. The show took up my whole weekend, or so it seemed, and all I wanted to do was play.'' Yet today, happy and well-adjusted, she feels that being a Quiz Kid gave her a sense of accomplishment and ease in meeting people. When her first marriage ended, she went to work in industrial sales until her remarriage, becoming the company's top saleswoman within three months.

David Smothers, senior editor at United Press International in Chicago, who lost on his one-and-only Quiz Kid attempt, felt "upstaged and shut down" by veteran competitors and suspected some of cheating. Now he boasts of having been one of them. But he notes (poetic justice?) that two of the more prominent Quiz Kids, with whom he went to college, seemed less happy than he. "I felt that the lives of some children were damaged by being Quiz Kids."

Daryce Richman, a child pianist who appeared on the show about thirty times beginning at age seven, was not accepted by her grammar school peers and tried to keep her Quiz Kid status quiet. Now a west coast studio singer, pianist and actress who has appeared on such shows as "The Smothers Brothers," she is "very proud" to have had the Quiz Kid opportunity.

Many—especially those who had limited Quiz Kid engagements—say the personal and social effects were negligible. But others feel the experience made a definite difference: "It made me expect more of myself" . . . "reinforced the image of smartness" . . . "gave me more confidence that I could compete" . . ."expanded my desire for knowledge" . . . "helped me overcome nervousness" . . . "crystallized a commitment to excellence at a formative age" . . . "imparted a feeling of inner worth" . . . "opened up my world."

Several mentioned the benefits of contacts with other Quiz Kids. Says Betty Swanson Upjohn, "I met children who were so much more gifted than I was. It gave me a perspective on my own abilities—something many bright kids do not gain until college."

Scientist David Jenkins, who "generally managed to avoid claiming the identification," says his four-time Quiz Kid status gave him a sort of closet self-esteem during difficult parts of his adolescence. For Julia Marwick Rainer, proprietor of The Book Mark in Northfield, Illinois, her seven appearances came at a gangling period and gave her much-needed acceptance—"it enabled me to have a 'success.' "

Most of the group took their losses pretty much in stride; some recognized that they were less knowledgeable than those who outlasted them. But a few were crushed. "I found the experience painful and humiliating," wrote a contest-winner who insisted on anonymity. "I keep my 'past' a deep dark secret. . . . I have had a happy and successful life, marriage and career. No thanks to QK."

"It's hard being axed when you're seven," says Jonathan Jackson, who says he had "a semi-stage-mama." He felt he had let his parents down—"It helped contribute to my terrible fear of failing. I've gotten over it," adds Jonathan, now an upper-bracket advertising executive with

Ogilvy and Mather and a recipient of the Cannes, Rizzoli and other awards. Unmarried, his advice to parents of gifted children is "Let them be."

Jonathan was an only child. So was Lois Piske Parks, now assistant manager of an export business, who made her sole Quiz Kids appearance at fourteen. "I had a good general knowledge on a variety of subjects— until the mike was turned on," she explains. "Intimidated" by the other Quiz Kids and embarrassed at not doing well, she felt she had failed her school and her parents but was, she adds, "secretly satisfied."

Thirteen respondents—almost one-fifth of the sample—were only children (not uncommon in Depression-bred families). One might assume that their parents would have focused aspirations on them, but most do not seem to have felt any particular pressure. The largest number— twenty-six—were the oldest children in their families. (Psychologists have noted that firstborns tend to be achievement-oriented, and gifted youngsters often are "eldests" or "onlies.")

Whatever the family position, very few felt that their being Quiz Kids made much difference in their family lives, aside from their parents' normal pride and excitement. "The enlightened family didn't make a big deal of it," explains Dean Berry, who appeared about a dozen times. Elinor Smith Miller is one of the few to report exacerbated sibling rivalry: "It stepped up my sister's unmerciful teasing about my being a brain."

Sometimes the sibling situation was handled by giving the brother or sister a chance to go on the show, as in the case of Marlene Richman, whose younger sister Daryce was being played up as a piano prodigy. Marlene, who was in competition with her sister musically, has had a lifelong career in music education and, as a performer, has won awards, contests, and festivals.

Dr. Judith Graham, who was a Quiz Kids regular at twelve, suspects her younger brother may have felt some internal pressure to measure up; he graduated first in his medical school class, while she had been second. Judy is in private counseling practice in Seattle after starting a medical counseling program for the eight hundred inmates of the county jail, where she was the only doctor.

Peer resentment—the most ubiquitous drawback for Quiz Kids— was no problem for lighthearted Judy, a Navy brat who commuted to the show from Des Moines and later from Toledo. Even though she had to be late getting back to school each Monday, she got no flak from her classmates. Being a Quiz Kid, says Judy, rid her of the "need to be like everybody else, that shackles so many teenagers."

Just how confining those shackles could be is clear from the experience of Joan Moy Smith, who made a single Quiz Kids appearance at thirteen. "After it was announced that I would be on the program, older children would come to the classroom door and peer in at me. Some classmates drew away, as if I'd changed. Others were eager to be pals. I didn't enjoy feeling lonely and different, so I stopped answering questions in class. The afternoon before my appearance, the band director, attempting to cheer me up, told me I didn't have to say anything, adding 'It's better to be quiet and thought dumb than to open your mouth and remove all doubt.' So that night, I didn't raise my hand, although I knew several answers. The next day at school, I felt relieved to be treated like an ordinary person again." That experience, says Joan, now an elementary school reading specialist, makes her more understanding of the feelings of the gifted children she teaches.

Certainly these ex-Quiz Kids, as a group, are not ordinary. But almost unanimously, they deny having been prodigies. "I was more likely an idiot savant," jokes Peggy Bangert Thompson. "I barely learned the multiplication table."

"Prodigism," pronounces Ruth Fisher Henoch, "is a disease imposed by parents on otherwise healthy tissue."

Most of the former Quiz Kids say they were merely bright, poised, curious youngsters, who were given extra doses of cultural exposure. "I had intelligent, interested parents, and I wanted to be like them," says Mary Clare McHugh Sanders.

About two-thirds of the group were early readers, either on their own or with the help of parents and siblings. Many, like Dick Frisbie, were astute test-takers. "I could sense the answers to questions even when I wasn't familiar with the subject," says Dick, who won a full scholarship to the University of Chicago by guessing at half the answers on the competitive exam.

Many had "flypaper memories" for "things of so-what value," as Judy Graham puts it—the ability to mentally place a fact on a page and dredge it up on demand. Although some say their memories have declined, Ralph E. Adler, a computer programmer/analyst, still has a "head full of trivia." Dave Jenkins feels his memory and general intelligence have improved with exercise in the competitive field of medical research.

In this television and computer age, the ex-Quiz Kids have not given up their love affair with the printed word. Despite busy careers, the majority still do a good deal of pleasure reading ("almost every time I sit down," says Joan Moy Smith). Most watch television moderately or not at all; when they do, they prefer news, specials and public broadcasting. ("I also sneak a look at *Dallas* fairly often," one admits.)

Marie Gleason Vonder Heide, a former teacher who holds a master's degree, audits college classes for fun. "People can't understand why I want to know things just to know them."

However, these ex-Quiz Kids are not just bookworms. While some are totally occupied by their careers ("work is leisure," says one), many give recreation—travel, culture, and hobbies—a high priority. Most find it relatively easy to make friends.

Although almost all are healthy and energetic, the one area in which many of them do not shine (despite the old press-agent paeans to well-roundedness) is sports. More than two-thirds of those answering the questionnaires, like most of those interviewed, were not athletically inclined in childhood. Some have become more so as adults; favorite activities are swimming, jogging, and tennis. But one-third of the group get no exercise except walking. Says Betty Swanson Upjohn (a la Robert Maynard Hutchins), "When tempted to athletic activity, I lie down until the urge goes away." Warren Cavior's favorite sport is "batting my eyelids at destiny."

Three-fourths of the respondents have a current religious affiliation (nineteen Protestants, ten Catholics, sixteen Jews, and one Unitarian), but fifteen of those are inactive or nearly so. "My religion," says David Nasatir, "is confined to celebrating life. I try to do it continually."

Most of the participants in the survey (unlike some of those interviewed for preceeding chapters) have stable, conventional family patterns. All but six have been married, and all but three of those have children (an average of 2.6). About 80 percent never have been divorced. Several proudly volunteered information about their gifted offspring. Virginia Booze Klages, who has two gifted daughters and one with Downs syndrome, said, "Parents who were pretty smug about intellectual ability had to take a hard look at its value when they had a retarded child. We found love and satisfaction are independent of mental swiftness—if you try."

Aspirations, for most of the group, center on personal growth and accomplishment, enjoyment of life, harmonious relationships, good parenting, service to others, and contributions to knowledge; very few mention wealth or even financial security as prime goals. Rather, their aims are "to live fully," "to do the best I can," "to leave things better than I found them," "to achieve personal strength and serenity," or simply, "to be me."

About one-third of the respondents feel they have achieved their life goals, some to an even greater degree than they had hoped. Others are "still working on it." Many revel in new adventures and challenges. ("There's life in the old girl yet.")

For some, "great expectations" have been scaled down by time and reality. Says Dr. A. W. Haelig: "I wanted to be a great scientist; now I aspire only to be a good physician." Jack Rooney, who had political ambitions in his thirties, is happy as a Michigan State law professor.

Perhaps the most representative is Dick Frisbie's statement, "I have not been as successful as my wildest dreams, yet I have been more successful than anyone had a right to expect." That is also true of Peter Reich. He entered West Point with ideas of being "another Eisenhower or MacArthur" but got so many demerits that he decided he was more cut out for writing. He had hoped by this time to be financially independent, to publish his own newspaper, to write a book, to win a Pulitzer Prize. He has done none of the above. But as a *Chicago American* and *Chicago Tribune* staffer, now with the *Phoenix Gazette,* he has garnered five Pulitzer nominations and thirty major awards, including the nation's top three in his field of aviation and aerospace reporting. He has witnessed history in the making: covered the first moon flight and both Kennedy assassinations, was one of the first newsmen to pierce the sound barrier and set foot on the South Pole, and met every U.S. President from Harry Truman on. "I've done all right," Pete says. "We can't all be Hemingways."

Seemingly most content are those whose aims were not stratospheric. Still as characteristicaly modest as in their childhood are Michael and Mark Mullin, both Quiz Kid regulars at an early age. Mark, an Episcopal clergyman, feels that in becoming headmaster of St. Alban's boys' school in Washington, D.C., he has "achieved more than I thought I would," while Mike, a biological oceanography professor at the University of California, says, "Though I have achieved at least as much professional recognition as I think I deserve, I wish I were a more original thinker on large-scale oceanographic problems."

The women with careers seem generally more satisfied, especially in the empty-nest years, than those without. "When I was younger," says DiAnne Mathre Thomas, "I had notions of being somebody important in government or foreign service. I turned out to be more of an average law-abiding citizen in Hometown, U.S.A. I have not been successful in combining marriage and career. Born a generation too soon, perhaps. (Or is that an excuse?)'' Virginia Booze Klages, on the other hand, says, ''My raised-consciousness daughters would never aspire to my house-wifely existence, but I find a lot of satisfaction in directions that are not salary-producing.''

Eloise Matthies Niwa, like Joan Bishop, Lon Lunde, and Daryce Richman, was a Chicago Symphony Orchestra youth soloist. Unlike them, she appeared on ''Quiz Kids'' only once, but she went on to regional wins in two national piano competitions. Her dream of becoming a concert pianist was laid to rest with the birth of her first child (''and later revived in her''), but she has done much recital work and accompanying, plays regularly with her own trio and with the Chicago Symphony (occasionally as soloist), teaches at DePaul University, and is president of the American Society of Musicians. Eloise feels she has ''the best of many worlds.'' Her professional life is busy, and she enjoys home, family and friends. ''So I guess I've achieved less than I hoped for originally in terms of personal glory, but more than I ever thought possible in the way of complete fulfillment.''

The people who participated in this survey, like those I interviewed, are highly disparate in geographic location, occupation, and lifestyle. Their one link is that they were on a radio or television program thirty or forty years ago. Once public figures to varying degrees, today they are essentially private people. Yet they have responded to my queries with candor and self-insight. After all, for a Quiz Kid, a question requires a straight answer!

As a group, our age span is nearly a generation; our formative influences range from the Depression and the Bomb to postwar affluence and protest. But there seem to be some common threads in our life patterns. Most of us are doers rather than spectators. We tend to be idealistic and eclectic. You are more likely to find us on the ''road less traveled'' than on the corporate ladder. We are perpetually learning. We are not easily deterred. And the end of our stories is still unwritten.

Conclusion:

Reflections on Growing Up Gifted

There is no heavier burden than a great potential.
  —Linus in *Peanuts* by Charles Schultz (United Features Syndicate)

. . . the self is not something one finds;
it is something one creates.
—Thomas Szasz

We Quiz Kids, as a group, have neither fulfilled the highest hopes nor realized the worst fears laid upon us three or four decades ago.

As the most prominent gifted youngsters of our generation, we were subjects of intense speculation. There were those, like Professor Lewis M. Terman of Stanford University, pioneer in research on the gifted, who predicted for us adult success "far beyond the average." Others were equally convinced that we would be misfits and duds.

The assumption that brilliant children were headed for dark futures— a belief perpetuated by the folk wisdom of a fiercely egalitarian America— was demolished by Terman's landmark study of fifteen hundred California school children with high I.Q.s. That study, begun nearly two decades before Louis G. Cowan conceived the Quiz Kids program, continues today. Both the Termites (as Terman's subjects have been dubbed) and we Quiz Kids grew up to be, for the most part, healthy, happy, well-rounded adults doing responsible work, earning good incomes, having stable marriages and larger-than-average families, and making substantial contributions to society. Some have become eminent in their fields.

Today it hardly seems surprising that a group of youngsters selected for quick minds, good looks, and appealing personalities would do well in later life. Yet because as children we were regarded as so exceptional, the question "Whatever happened to the Quiz Kids?" may imply a challenge

The Quiz Kids have surpassed Professor Terman's gifted group in ways that may, at least in part, reflect generational differences. Nearly all the ex-Quiz Kids I was able to contact (see list in Appendix) are college graduates, but only 70 percent of the Depression-educated Termites are. One-third of the ex-Quiz Kids —45 percent of the men and 15 percent of the women—have Ph.D.'s, M.D.'s or the equivalent, as compared with 15 percent of the Terman men and 5 percent of the women.

By the usual occupational standards, the Quiz Kid men are more uniformly successful than their Terman counterparts, whose ranks include some clerks, salesmen, and marginal businessmen. Most of the male ex-Quiz Kids are lawyers, scientists, professors, executives, consultants.

The Quiz Kid women, to a greater extent than the Terman women and most of our contemporaries, have managed to juggle family and career. Only 43 percent of the Terman women were income workers for the majority of their adult lives; at least 60 percent of the female Quiz Kids fall into that class. The figure is more notable in view of the fact that just 52.5 percent of the entire female population, age sixteen and over—including the "liberated generation"—are even now in the work force, according to the U.S. Bureau of Labor Statistics (May, 1982).

and a rebuke. Where are the Einsteins and Shakespeares among us? Or even the Roosevelts and Fords?

Again, a look at the Terman findings is instructive. Daniel Goleman wrote in the February, 1980 issue of *Psychology Today*: "Most of the men and women in the study have passed retirement age, and it now seems clear that exceptional intelligence does not preclude ordinary happiness or worldly success. But neither, apparently, does it guarantee extraordinary accomplishment. Although most of the men and women in the study have done well in their careers, none appears to have achieved the summit of true genius. None has so far been awarded a Nobel prize or similar honor. There are few millionaires among them, and hardly any distinguished creative artists."

Much the same can be said of us Quiz Kids, except that we are not yet "over the hill," and we do boast one Nobel prizewinner—James D. Watson, who was not a startling success on the show. I know of no Quiz Kid millionaires, nor did I turn up any Picassos.

To measure our success by such exalted standards reflects misconceptions that, unfortunately, persist in some quarters: misconceptions that put unrealistic, sometimes self-defeating expectations on gifted youth.

Consider this gem from a newspaper column, circa 1940:

> I have often wondered what happens to Quiz Kids when they grow up. They know all the answers when they are children, and what more is [there] for them to learn?

The idea that anyone "knows all the answers"—much less a group of youngsters who were asked questions limited enough to be resolved with a minimum of dead air time—is patently absurd. So is the notion that such children are "geniuses," "prodigies," or even, necessarily, "tomorrow's leaders."

It is now clear that children can learn many things much earlier than was formerly thought possible, and our Quiz Kid feats no longer seem quite so astounding. Furthermore, many equally or even more gifted contemporaries did not have the opportunity to try out for the show, did not choose to, or did not possess the requisite pep and charm. There was, in fact, no real reason to assume that most of the youngsters who shone on that program would turn out to be anything more than we did: intelligent, able, respected adults leading interesting, useful lives.

The term "child prodigy" once was reserved for the Mozarts and Menuhins: those who, at an early age, produced original work or exhibited accomplishments that would be striking even in an adult. A genius was understood to be one of those rare individuals whose powers clearly transcended the norm: a Newton, a Tolstoy—a "breakaway mind" that propounded a revolutionary theory or created a masterpiece. But as a result of Terman's efforts to de-mystify genius, that term has come to refer to high intelligence as measured by standardized tests. Anyone with at least 140 I.Q. (the floor Terman set for his study sample) became a "potential genius"; and "prodigy" came to mean a child who was precocious—only more so. These days, breathless newspaper accounts of such "geniuses" and "prodigies" still crop up with some frequency.

While such terminology may provide a convenient way to pigeonhole the intellectually well-endowed, it can be misleading in light of the traditional meanings that continue in common parlance. There are approximately two million children in the United States with I.Q.'s of 140 or more. Persons in that range (which would include most Quiz Kids) constitute, according to some estimates, one percent of the population: a "potential genius" for every hundred people walking the streets! Even Terman began to back off from such blanket characterizations when faced with the fact that not all his subjects had enjoyed brilliant careers. (Interestingly, on the other side of the coin, Nobel prizewinners William Shockley and Luis Alvarez reportedly did not qualify for the Terman sample.)

Lou Cowan, originator of "Quiz Kids," understood (as some of our public did not) that I.Q. alone does not a genius make, and that a child who can read at three, identify hundreds of birds, or memorize a long list of Biblical "begats" is not, ipso facto, a prodigy. True prodigies are rare, and are not, generally speaking, found on quiz shows. They are too busy pursuing the intensive training they need in order to advance in their fields—usually self-contained fields like music or math, which can be mastered rapidly without commensurate life experience.

"Quiz Kids" did number some musical prodigies among its roster, including Lonny Lunde and Joan Bishop. For numerical virtuosity, we might nominate Joel Kupperman and Richard Williams. But Joan and Lon chose not to pursue concert piano careers, and neither Joel nor Dick cared to devote himself to higher mathematics.

As Professor David Feldman of Tufts University points out, interest and tenacious commitment are keys to a prodigy's progress. Further, it is not uncommon for a musical prodigy to peak early and drop from public notice, nor for a math prodigy to end up in a different field—few, as they move along, show the inclination or capacity for deep mathematical analysis. And prodigious capability rarely transfers from one field to another.

We have little hard knowledge of what causes prodigies to develop and why they do or do not fulfill their promise. But Professor Feldman's studies suggest that early prodigious achievement hinges on opportunity and cultivation, as well as the right genes. Thus, as Lon Lunde points out, a child living in a house with no piano is unlikely to be a musical prodigy.

Parental handling is important, of course. William Sidis' father set out to produce a prodigy, but young William rebelled against the merciless pressure and publicity forced upon him and spent the rest of his life as a lowly clerk. On the other hand, philosopher John Stuart Mill and mathematician Norbert Wiener (founder of cybernetics, the science underlying the computer)—also "manufactured" prodigies—emerged from prolonged identity crises in young adulthood to make brilliant contributions.

While the out-and-out prodigious failure, the Sidis, is rare, neither do most child prodigies flower into Mills or Wieners. Nor, conversely, do all creative geniuses start as spectacular sprouts. Albert Einstein, for instance, was seven before he could read and did not even speak until four; teachers told him he never would amount to anything.

What, then, determines which youngsters will grow into the giants of their time? What distinguished a Gerard Darrow—who as a boy was a bird-fancier, collected flowers and shells, and carried insects around in his pocket—from a Charles Darwin, who did the same? Or, for that matter, from Quiz Kid James Watson—also a bird buff—whose co-discovery of the structure of DNA has been called one of the triumphs of the twentieth century, the greatest scientific step since the theory of evolution?

There are no pat answers.

It would be easy to say, as with Sidis, that exploitation spoiled Gerard. Branded a prodigy of prodigies, he could not measure up. His family life was hardly ideal, his social and emotional development far from optimum. But neither did he show evidence of the exceptional productive capacity that has been known to transcend a troubled youth. Nor did he do anything, as far as we know, to develop his early interest in ornithology.

Darwin was no child wonder. He was uninterested in his studies and made false starts on two different careers before joining the voyage of the Beagle at twenty-one as a junior naturalist. As his autobiography reveals, he considered his abilities only moderate. He was not, he claimed, quick or clever; he had difficulty following an abstract train of thought; and his memory was so poor that he could not recall a date or a line of poetry for more than a few days. Certainly not Quiz Kid material!

What he did have was a love of science, "unbounding patience," industriousness, and "a fair share of invention as well as common sense." Above all, an open mind and "the strongest desire to understand or explain" what he observed. Like other great thinkers, he had what has been called a "divine discontent" urging him on . . . a combination of inspiration and self-discipline.

Watson's vocation, too, was no cradle quirk. His Quiz Kid specialty, at thirteen, was not science but current events. Only when he read *Arrowsmith* in high school did he begin directing his thoughts toward glorious discoveries. Watson's approach, in contrast to Darwin's, had some distinctly Quiz-Kid-like aspects. A determined competitor, he was out for the Prize; he and Francis Crick won the race to unlock the DNA secret (as Watson's best-selling book, *The Double Helix*, relates) with the help of a little brain-picking, a lot of brashness, and some good guesswork.

One of Watson's graduate students once told Lee Edson of *New York Times Magazine,* "His greatest talent is an uncanny instinct for the important problem, the thing that leads to big-time results. He seems to . . . pluck it out of thin air."

Today's scientific breakthroughs are less likely to come from lone, patient sifters of mountainous data than from "whiz kids" like Watson (whose DNA discovery came before his twenty-fifth birthday). But the essence of such originality still is the intuitive leap.

Educators now believe that creative ability, whether in science or the arts, is one of several kinds of giftedness. Academic aptitude, the sort that intelligence tests purport to measure, is only one variety, and the amount of overlap varies. The Quiz-Kid-type, who has what Professor Joseph Renzulli of the University of Connecticut calls "schoolhouse giftedness" —the memorizer, the solver of puzzles with known answers—may or may not also demonstrate exceptional creative imagination—the ability to formulate a problem in a way that leads to a novel solution.

Whatever our other talents, we Quiz Kids were essentially performers. We were expected to perform better and faster (and with winning appeal) the kinds of tasks children normally do in school. As adults, our forte seems to be, for the most part, more adaptive than original: a Claude Brenner, whose skill is bringing other people's technological innovations to the marketplace . . . a Jack Lucal, who interprets and amplifies the Pope's pronouncements. Certainly there are creators among us: Lon Lunde, the quick-hand-raiser-turned-composer, Dick Frisbie, the "inspired" test-taker who has written six books. But often our vision tends to be (in our own estimate) somewhat limited. As oceanographer Mike Mullin confesses, his contributions to knowledge are "obscure bricks rather than buttresses in the cathedral of science."

Some educational critics believe that the American school (as exemplified by the Quiz Kids model) has stultified the creative spirit— that the Darwins and Einsteins have emerged in spite of the system. Schools, as did the Quiz Kids program, generally reward the tractable rather than the rebellious, the willing more than the strong-willed. Yet the most highly creative personalities often are the least likely to conform. As was stated in *Today's Child,* "The histories of creative geniuses show that the intensely creative child is neither a parent pleaser nor a teacher's joy. He or she may, in fact, be an embarrassment to the former and a threat to the latter."

Current research on the two sides of the human brain may throw additional light on why the best students frequently are not the most original thinkers. Schools (the researchers claim) normally favor left-brain activity —rational, verbal—and neglect or even discourage right-brain development—intuitive, sensory, integrative. But at the highest levels of intelligence, it is believed the two parts of the brain work together; thus whatever dichotomy exists between academic and creative giftedness might be bridged by a greater stress on right-brain functions. "Our present emphasis on the logical mode," wrote Patricia L. Fox in the October, 1979 issue of *The Reading Teacher,* "can produce only imitators, not innovators."

Educators today also are attempting to identify and develop leadership ability, another gift apparently distinct from academic brilliance. It is true that good students (like many of the Quiz Kids) often appear to be leaders in elementary school. But in adolescence and after, allegiance tends to shift away from those who seem to be intellectually too far above the crowd, and toward those who excel in sports and what has been called social intelligence. Thus Dick Williams, who in the early grades was almost a unanimous choice for chairman of his class, became in high school the acknowledged leader of only the few who shared his intellectual interests.

As adults, many former Quiz Kids are active in our communities; but real power is another ball game. Despite the commencement prattle about "future leaders," rarely does the child who gets all A's and shines on standardized tests become President of the United States, or even of General Motors. (A 1977 study by Doktor and Bloom suggests that top business executives tend to think intuitively, rather than in the logical, left-brain manner favored by academicians.) Our national leaders seldom are distinguished for superior intellect; rather, the prerequisites are supreme self-assurance, practical savvy, and manipulative skill. As Justice Oliver Wendell Holmes said of FDR: "A second class intellect. But a first-class temperament!" A Joel Kupperman may be elected fourth-grade class president, but the gold-star-winner or valedictorian is not necessarily the most likely to succeed, outside of academe.

It is therefore noteworthy that very few of the most renowned Quiz Kids—with the striking exception of Joel, who totally spurned his "notorious" past—have followed academic careers, as several of those less prominently featured on the show have done. Some of the latter say their Quiz Kid experience strengthened their commitment to high scholastic standards. Some of the regulars, though, when they got to college, did not strive for the very top grades, preferring to concentrate on learning for its own sake or to devote time to other activities; and a few, such as Lon Lunde and Harvey Dytch, reacted against competitive intellectualism.

Some, bitten by the entertainment bug, remained in that world or returned to it later; others went into applied fields like law, communications, and teaching, as opposed to pure research. But there are few entrepreneurs among us. Having done well in structures not of our own making (school and "Quiz Kids"), we gravitated, as bright youngsters frequently do, to other structures (the foreign service, a religious order, an educational system, a newspaper) that allow considerable but not unbounded initiative.

What influenced our relative success in a world beyond "Quiz Kids" and academia was not so much intellect (a commodity we all have in sufficient supply) but the match between interest and ability, the judgment we brought to decisions, and the determination to carry them out . . . plus, of course, the proverbial little bit of luck.

As Naomi Cooks Mann points out, the easiest way to succeed is to choose what you are good at. For Lon Lunde and Harvey Dytch, it took years of apparent floundering before they settled on music and science, their early strengths.

An important study on the ingredients of success is under way at the University of Chicago. There were no child prodigies among the one-hundred world-renowned mathematicians, concert pianists, Olympic swimmers and tennis players under age thirty-five whose histories have been dissected by Professor Benjamin S. Bloom's researchers. In fact, few of these topflight achievers stood out as unusually gifted at the age of five or even ten. Some did not show as much ability as siblings who started with similar parental encouragement and early training. One thing that made the difference was motivation; an all-consuming will to excel. Fired by recognition and fueled by expert coaching, these young people concentrated on developing their talents, often to the exclusion of social life and other activities. Similarly, among the Terman group, the top achievers were those who, from childhood on, evinced noticeable drive, ambition, initiative, independence and persistence. Those who *chose* a vocation rather than drifting into one.

Of all the Quiz Kid stars, Harve Bennett showed that fiber. The product of a pair of achievement-oriented parents, it was he, not they, who insisted he try out for the show. It was he whom his perceptive colleagues singled out as "most unlikely to fail." And it is he who has in worldly terms come closest to the zenith in his chosen field.

Fundamental to success is the ability to focus on and pursue a goal, as

Harve did. Being well-rounded, as Quiz Kids were supposed to be, some of us have found it difficult to do that. Jack Lucal calls himself an ''intellectual wanderer.'' Joan Bishop is ''honeycombed.'' I never went to graduate school because I could not commit myself to a particular field.

Multipotentiality is a mixed blessing for many gifted youths. Marshall P. Sanborn, professor of education at the University of Wisconsin, cites the complaint of a twelfth-grade boy in the university's laboratory school:

> I have found that if I apply myself I can do almost anything. . . .
> I find an English problem equally as difficult as a physics problem.
> I find them also to be equally as challenging and equally as inter-
> esting. . . . This is why I find it so difficult to decide my place in the
> future. Many people wouldn't consider this much of a problem; but
> to me, this lack of one area to stand out in is a very grave problem
> indeed.
>   —From Hoyt and Hebeler, *Career Education for Gifted*
>   *and Talented Students* (Olympus Publishing Co., 1974)

Versatility can be a plus if combined with judgment and a sense of direction. Claude Brenner started as an aeronautical engineer and evolved into an energy specialist. Harve Bennett, who ''tap dances through life,'' is in a field—television production—where ''tap dancing'' is the name of the game. Margaret Merrick made use of whatever opportunities happened to come her way in the interstices of marriage and motherhood to build a career first as a teacher, then as an educational consultant.

People like Claude, Harve, and Margaret are flexible, able to veer and tack—the kind who are not apt to be blown down by the winds of techno-logical or economic change. That was the sort of smarts one needed to survive on the ''Quiz Kids'' show. In a Darwinian sense, the fittest were those of us whose talents were particularly adapted to success in the Quiz Kid environment; and those abilities, in turn, were sharpened in the process. That we were not necessarily fittest to be opera stars or Nobel prizewinners, Presidents or Popes, should disappoint only the naive.

Yet some of us have a nagging feeling that we should have done more. Having been among the chosen few—the ''best and brightest'' of our time—set us up for a fall. What Harve Bennett refers to as the ''classic letdown.''

In a sense, our easy Quiz Kid acclaim gave us a false view of the world. Those of us who were most celebrated on the show, especially if we started very young, grew up with the impression that we could be winners just by knowing the right answers, being cute and modest, raising our hands, and waiting to be called on. But adult society does not auto-matically reward the quick, the bright, the artistic. Indeed, society does not automatically reward anybody—something some "smart" people never learn. Adults, unlike children, rarely get ahead except on their own initiative, nor profit save by their own effort. The means of doing so are, as Dick Williams points out, less readily grasped than the rules for scoring on a quiz show or shining in school.

Some of us, as often happens with gifted children, became semi-compulsive perfectionists, driven by the need to continue to be best or by the dread of failure. (As Claude Brenner puts it, the feeling of *Am I going to make it tonight?*) Probably, given our personal chemistry and our particular family backgrounds, we would have had those tendencies any-way; as with the chicken-or-the-egg, cause and effect are impossible to unravel. But I do believe the Quiz Kid experience reinforced certain traits, some beneficial, some less so.

I, for one, found it difficult, after my childhood laurels and my parents' lavish praise, to accept life's inevitable disappointments and my own parental shortcomings. While my early success left me (as it did some of my Quiz Kid colleagues) with the buoying but rather irrational feeling that *I can do anything,* at the same time I felt inadequate to meet that impossible expectation. One reason is that the more deeply I went into something, the more distant horizons I could glimpse. In college, I would come out of each examination worried about how I had done—to my classmates' disbelief, since I rarely fell below an A. In the Socratic tradition, I knew enough to know how much I did *not* know.

The belief that *people think I'm brighter than I am*—shared by a number of Quiz Kids—can lead a sensitive youngster to ask, like Claude Brenner, *Do I deserve to succeed?*, or, like Harvey Dytch, *Do I really want to?* Some of us, like Claude, are still striving upward ("Life is one constant competition"); others, like Harvey, have turned their backs on the race.

Some simply are unwilling to pay the price entailed in aiming at the pinnacle. Lon Lunde—while he enjoys competitive games—declines to compete professionally. He prefers a contented home life and plenty of time to spend with his children or to compose saxophone sonatas in his basement. A greater degree of prestige and material success would mean nothing to him and might cramp his style.

Jack Lucal, the priest, abjures fame and glory, choosing selfless service. Vanessa Brown found stardom empty and oppressive; she sought deeper and more lasting satisfactions in marriage, political involvement, writing, and broadcasting. Even Harve Bennett now deems the pursuit of excellence—meeting his own inner standards—''all there is.''

As Dick Williams points out, there has been a radical change in the way some Americans define success. In the early 1950s, when I was in college, the generally accepted goals were a home, a car, and $10,000 a year. But many of us who grew up in the rigid forties and fifties have shifted from external to internal values and a new awareness of the range of choices available to human beings. David Riesman's concept of autonomy and Abraham Maslow's philosophy of self-actualization have become, for some of us, more attractive alternatives than status-seeking. Maslow spoke of such things as self-knowledge, intrinsic motivation, spontaneity, joy, and devotion to a task or cause—not polishing apples, bucking for promotion, and getting to the top.

Thus (as Dick says) if one asks the question ''Did the Quiz Kids fulfill their potential?'', one first must define what is meant by potential. And that definition, to be meaningful, can come only from the individual concerned. The key is not *what* one does but *why,* and by whose choice. Pat Conlon, the struggling actor, found the courage in his thirties to do what he most wants to do, and he is willing to pay the price in material sacrifice. How can we judge his success except in his own terms?

The special question of women's choices has come to the fore since Quiz Kid days. Each of the prominent Quiz Kid women struggled with the issue somewhat differently, though all of us are broadly in sympathy with feminist thinking. Margaret, Joan, and Vanessa—like a majority of the other female Quiz Kids in their age group—built full-time careers at a time when few women did. Joan, as a lounge performer, felt marriage would interfere with her career. She married late and retired early, giving up the chance for parenthood in the process—a choice that Lon Lunde, a male in the same occupation, did not feel compelled to make. Margaret, despite polio, managed to ''do it all,'' and in fact has become her family's chief breadwinner. Vanessa, pushed into an early, successful acting career not entirely of her own choosing, found in her second marriage and maternity a chance to step back and assess what she herself wants to do with the rest of her life.

Naomi and I—the two ''cute little girls''—followed patterns perhaps more characteristically feminine than did the older three. As young adults, we both drifted into life decisions that we failed to realize would severely limit our options; and while Naomi worked full time throughout marriage and I did not, we both spent a number of years in second-rate jobs due to inertia and what we saw as the need to compromise with family responsibilities.

My story probably is fairly typical of the middle-class woman of my generation who married young and fell into motherhood without having made a clear-cut career commitment. But, laboring under the Quiz-Kids-induced delusion that I would continue to be an exception, I assumed I would be able to pick up where I had left off and arrive at a distinguished career some day. Two decades later, I found that catching up was not so easy.

As the youngest of the five Quiz Kid girls whose portraits have been drawn here, Naomi—influenced by the women's movement—represents most closely the metamorphosis from "good little girl" to self-assertive person. Her rebellion against doing what she was "supposed to do" led her from a constrictive marriage and what started as a stopgap academic job into divorce and now the business world. While her embrace of material success seems to reflect society's current pendulum swing, she views her new venture from a feminist perspective—as an opportunity to seek the financial rewards denied to women who are steered into traditional fields like teaching.

For many of us Quiz Kids, both males and females, the evolution toward autonomy has not been a simple process; and the road to "success," however defined and to whatever extent attained, has been neither short nor straight. Our efforts as performers were bent toward pleasing others. As children, we found out we were bright, as Claude puts it, "from getting high marks and being shoved forward." For Vanessa, being a Quiz Kid confirmed that she was smart; being a hit in *Seven Year Itch* told her she was funny.

Of course, praise, attention and approval can help build a sense of self-worth—the most essential prerequisite for success and happiness. Healthy, enjoyable competition and the incentive of a tangible prize can spur the development of gifts and talents. Recitals and contests have their place. But recognition can become an end in itself, prompting a child to strive for outside affirmation and obscuring inner purpose. Thus Harve Bennett's need for applause kept him "frozen in childhood" for years.

The effort to become ourselves has been complicated, for some of us, by our ambivalence about having stood out. Being tagged a "superbrain" was often a real drawback—though not for Harve, who had the personality and athletic prowess to carry it off. For Claude (and probably more so, for Joel) the after-effects of such labelling were deep and painful. Pat, on the other hand, now feels he draws strength for his present nonconformist lifestyle from having been tested in the crucible of social isolation. But Naomi believes the energy she put into chasing popularity and sloughing off the Quiz Kid stamp sidetracked her from pursuing intellectual challenge.

Today, despite greater toleration of individuality, some teachers and students report that there still is a stigma attached to being intellectually gifted, resulting in the temptation to underachieve. The captain of the football team is cheered, the star of the school play is applauded, but the brilliant youngster who has not learned to "hide" or be "nice" may be made to feel out of step.

Dr. Diane H. Schetky, a psychiatrist with the Yale University Child Study Center, writing in *G/C/T*, a journal for parents and teachers of gifted, creative and talented children, cites a gifted eleven-year-old who seemed perversely pleased that he was doing poorly in art. He told his parents, "Other kids expect too much from you and resent you if you are a superman, that's why it's good to be terrible at something."

Because gifted children often are regarded as misfits, ex-Quiz Kid Marjorie Bruce Runnion points out, their self-confidence often suffers. A list of typical characteristics of 3,800 gifted San Diego school children, compiled by Associate Superintendent Richmond Barbour, included such items as "the need to appear average" and "the feeling that they are different—maybe even inferior."

The need to appear average was a bind we Quiz Kids were placed in. We were expected to be not only abnormally brilliant but brilliantly normal. Some of us might have had an easier time or accomplished more if we hadn't been trying to be all things to all people.

"Children need help in learning to live with the anxiety that being different may cause," says Laurel Crandus, teacher of the gifted in Woodridge, Illinois. "To make them fit in may be to destroy their specialness."

Gifted youngsters draw reassurance, as well as stimulation, from contact with others like themselves. In special classes, clubs, private schools or camps, they can enjoy common interests without softpedaling abilities. For some of us—if only sporadically—"Quiz Kids" helped fill that need. But children in those inhibited days did not readily share feelings; one tended to assume, as Claude did, that *this is happening only to me.*

Ultimately, each human being is alone, and the gifted child, especially, may be acutely aware of that. Parents can help, ex-Quiz Kid Janet Ahern Martin suggests, by making the child feel "special" rather than different. "A child who is exceptional in any way," says Janet, "should be encouraged to accept it as nothing to be embarrassed about or particularly proud of—it just simply is.''

Probably the question we ex-Quiz Kids are most often asked is, ''Would you want your child to be one?'' The implied question is, ''Considering everything, are you glad you were?'' For the vast majority of us, the answer to that is yes, though for some a qualified yes. It was an exciting adventure that opened new vistas. Many of us—even those who participated only briefly—gained self-assurance and poise. A few, notably Hollywood dialect coach Bob Easton, feel the program changed their lives.

Most of those (like me) who knew some discomfort have come to regard our Quiz Kid past in a more positive light—Joel being the glaring exception. Having done something so out-of-the-ordinary was enriching —an ''early high,'' as Sally Wilhelm Fullerton puts it. In dwelling on the perils of such an experience, I have not meant to minimize the almost self-evident profits, but only to point out that an awareness of the former can help maximize the latter.

Very few of us feel we were unfairly exploited, as Gerard Darrow apparently did. Exploitation can be a two-way street. We were used (kindly) to make the show succeed. But we, in turn, had a rare opportunity we could use to our advantage, and on the whole, most of us did. As Harve Bennett says, ''It's not the experience that makes you what you are, it's what you do with it.'' In any event, Harve adds, ''Regret is an act of self-destruction.'' Even Harvey Dytch, whose feelings are much more mixed, says, ''I am what I am because it happened that way.''

So, would we want our children to be Quiz Kids? Most of us say yes, though several offer sensible caveats: ''If they wanted to,'' or ''It would depend on the child.'' Some of us, while not sorry, on balance, about our own experience, would not want to risk it for our young; as Dick Williams points out, there are safer avenues open to children these days.

The hazards of being a Quiz Kid affected mainly those of us whose public exposure was long, frequent, and intense. The way each of us came out depended largely on our age, our family and school circumstances, our reasons for being on the show, and our personalities.

Those of us who became national figures at a very early age and were subjected to a constant barrage of attention—Joel and Gerard in particular had the most difficulty. The social penalties often were exacerbated by our being younger, smaller, and less physically coordinated than our classmates. The problem became most severe during adolescence, when identity formation and peer relationships become all-important and gifted youngsters typically experience anxiety about social acceptance. The way each of us handled our situation depended, in the final analysis, upon the personal baggage we carried to it. No doubt some of us were hyper-sensitive; I'm sure I was.

Those who already were in high school when they started, like Jack Lucal and Margaret Merrick, found it easier to keep their perspective and shrug off the inevitable teasing. ("Ribbing is good for Quiz Kids," Betty Swanson once said. "It ensures their not acquiring the tendencies some-times ascribed to them.")

Parental attitudes made a difference, too. Jack's, Margaret's and Betty's parents took the whole thing lightly; so did Jack, Margaret, and Betty. ("I do feel," says Betty, "that my mother fantasized that the Quiz Kid show was the first step in 'My Brilliant Career.' This led to conflict when I opted for marriage, but I believe in later life she was proud of my accomplishments.")

Despite the producers' attempt to steer clear of stage parents, some families tended to get carried away. Sometimes a father would serve as ballast for an ego-involved mother. Most of us, and our siblings, came out all right. That it could have been otherwise, given less solid familial structures and more fragile personal ones, is evident from Gerard's example. With little Janet Ahern, efforts to keep her unspoiled un-wittingly translated into a mixed message. "My parents," she says, "bent over backwards so that I wouldn't be impressed with myself, and yet I could tell *they* were impressed."

Janet was propelled into the public eye, as both a Quiz Kid and a model, despite her desire for a more normal childhood. Another reluctant Quiz Kid was Louis E. Sissman, who for many years before his death penned the "Innocent Bystander" column for the *Atlantic Monthly*. Sissman once wrote a piece on his single appearance as the Detroit contest winner:

> . . . for a long time now, American children have been treated as
> extensions of their parents' and teachers' frustrated drives for
> power and glory, as little guided missiles programmed to rise
> meteorically and burst dazzlingly above the faces of the crowd. . . .
> I, like many of these children—the child stars, the infant tap
> dancers, the tiny, tail-coated piano prodigies—had discovered that
> the way to an adult's heart, and the perquisites that flowed there-
> from, was through the exercise of my trick intellect.

. . . When it became apparent to my parents and teachers that I was glibber than most in parroting things back, I was not quietly encouraged, as I might have been in Europe, to study deeply for a serious scholarly career—or a serious artistic one. Instead, being in America, I was loudly encouraged, not to say coerced, to become a competition winner. . . .

Sissman said his ''grueling'' episode of ''being bright for money'' had ''fostered an unalterable belief in the sanctity of the child and his own wishes for himself.'' Although I do not share his acerbic view of the Quiz Kid experience, I'll second his ''vote for children's lib.'' The fact that I was able to decide, with my parents' support, to cut out the touring when it became a social liability was an important step toward self-assertion and probably toned down my adolescent troubles. (Today, though, I confess to a twinge of regret about all the trips I missed!)

Psychologist Gerald E. Gruen, among others, has stressed that a child who has a sense of control over his or her own life has a greater chance for future success. But often it is not easy for well-meaning mothers and fathers to perceive what their children really want, nor for children to realize their power to choose. Far less so in those days. Self-determination for the junior citizen was a radical idea in that time of economic and social constraint, when, as Dick Williams recalls, hardly anyone had the perspective to do much questioning—we simply accepted what was. Coming home from a tour of duty in the Orient, Dick observed how cold the winters are in the American north: ''Winter did not seem cold in my childhood; it was just winter.''

Clara Williams, incidentally, is the one Quiz Kid mother who admitted to second thoughts. Looking back, she recognizes the hurdles her shy son faced at school and wonders whether her spending so much time on the road with him was fair to his brother. ''But,'' she says, ''Dick enjoyed it, and you get into a thing, and the momentum carries you on.''

Having been on both ends of the parent-child connection, I well know the fallibility of judgment and the failures of communication. Neither parent nor child can foresee the ultimate effects of any experience. But one thing I have learned: we parents should search our souls to make sure our true motives for putting Susie or Mark onstage or into a contest or a gifted program, or for urging them to apply to Harvard rather than State U., arise from the child's own inclinations and best interests, not our own. And then, have the flexibility to change course if we see that we have erred.

As has been said, it is sometimes as hard to be a parent of a gifted child as it is to be a gifted child. I asked the former Quiz Kids (many of whom have been both) to give their advice to parents of today's gifted children. (See inset.) The themes repeated again and again were, "Encourage, stimulate, educate and expose, but *don't push*. Give them love, discipline, approval and attention. Accept them for themselves, not just for their gifts and accomplishments." And finally, "Relax! And let the children do the same."

It is almost a truism today that gifts need nurturing; genius will *not* always out, and rarely does untended talent reach full fruition. Yet there is danger that a parent conscious of the responsibility for stewarding a child's precious endowment may become overly involved in the child's life, as I did with my musical son.

Ex-Quiz Kid Dick Frisbie speaks of having seen many children of bright parents pushed into "utter rejection of their parents' values" and sometimes into painful lives. "I think my wife and I probably started out pushing too hard," admits Dick, the father of eight. "We even wrote a book about it, God help us (*The Do-It-Yourself Parent*), but we learned to back off and let them find their own way, which they have done."

Parents walk a fine line between encouraging and pushing, between "staying out of a child's way" and neglecting the child's needs, between giving merited praise and making praise the point of the endeavor, between helping a child set realistic expectations and letting the parent's expectations control. There is a difference between helping a child search for answers and looking them up yourself, between sharing interests and dictating them, between instilling and drilling. There is a difference between forcing a youngster to practice an instrument and insisting on reasonably regular practice as a condition of taking lessons. There is a difference between concern and cross-examination, between advising on a college choice and making that choice.

Children have their own lives to live (as do parents) and their own mistakes to learn from. Parents, no matter how lovingly, cannot do it for them. As Carol N. Nathan, editor of *Dialogue*, has written, "When parents say that all they want is for their child to be happy or successful or contented, they should be sure they know how the child defines happiness, success, contentment. Those definitions may be very different from theirs." Sometimes an "underachiever" actually is a child who has channeled productive energy in directions different from those the parents or teacher might choose.

Here are excerpts from the advice the ex-Quiz Kids offer to parents of gifted children:

Harvey Dytch: Let your children do what they want to do. Don't typecast them as "Johnny the little scientist" or "Martha the ballerina."

Peggy Bangert Thompson: Avoid criticism and bestow a lot of praise. Don't be too demanding of obedience.

Virginia Booze Klages: Keep them challenged for *their* satisfaction.

Anneke de Bruyn Overseth: Don't single them out.

Richard A. Freeman: Spend time with them. Money and presents do not make up for company and conversation.

Marie Gleason Vonder Heide: Provide multiple opportunities, but don't push. Offer a cafeteria, not a stomach tube.

Dr. Judith Graham: Give them plenty of time to be kids; keep them pretty close to their social peers; fill the home with books.

Dr. C. David Jenkins: Accept them joyfully as they are. Don't treat them as "unusual" or "great."

Julia Marwick Rainer: Watch out for boredom in school—I am an expert in writing backward and reading books hidden in textbooks.

Eloise Matthies Niwa: Don't agonize too much . . . Do what seems right at the moment, and don't punish yourself if it isn't. Develop your child's special gift or interest to the fullest with the *best* teacher, tutor or coach you can find, not just the best in your neighborhood. Seek the best advice regarding these.

William Fleming McHugh: Realize that the gifts are the child's, not the parents'. Don't become ego-involved in how the youngster uses the gifts.

Rev. Mark Mullin: Help them set realistic goals that are challenging but not beyond reach.

Peter M. Reich: Make sure there's time for baseball and swimming and loafing.

C. Harker Rhodes: Be sensitive, serve as an example, and above all, listen. When a child is expected to have something worthwhile to say, the child will try to meet the expectation.

Betty Swanson Upjohn: Read widely to your children, expose them to the wonders of the world. Do not expect them to conform.

Lois Piske Parks: Offer opportunities for independence.

Parents' desire to boost their offspring into promising futures can take bizarre forms. Some parents, using gaily colored flash cards, are teaching infants to read before the babes even can talk. The question is, to what purpose? And whose? I am all for encouraging a child to read who shows real readiness and interest; there is nothing magic about age six. But an infant?

The late Benjamin Fine, noted education writer and headmaster of Sands Point Country Day School for the gifted, wrote in his book, *Stretching Their Minds*: "The parent who pushes and prods can squeeze creativity and curiosity out of the child . . . . It will not truly matter, when your youngster is thirty years old, whether he learned to read at four, five, or seven. It will matter whether he learned that reading is a source of delight, information, knowledge, strength."

Although many Quiz Kids did learn to read before kindergarten, James Watson, the future Nobel Laureate, was not among them. Yet by ten, Watson was reading himself to sleep with the World Almanac. Another Quiz Kid, Warren Cavior, was the only first-grader in his class who could not spell his name; at eleven, he startled his camp counselor by reading Marx and Engels.

Raising a gifted child should be a rich experience but not a heavy one. A parent can provide food for the child's natural curiosity and exposure to the best our culture has to offer: books, music, museums. But a youngster does not need to be overloaded with "educational" toys and supervised constantly to make sure time is being used "constructively." A child *does* need freedom to explore the wonders of nature or just to daydream or "goof around."

As my sister, Bunny Duskin Shuch, points out, a gifted child is first of all a child and needs the same loving, disciplined nurture as any other. "Try to understand their special needs," says Bunny, "but expect them to contribute to family life. Even a gifted child can take out the garbage." Gifted children need guidance to develop a sense of responsibility for the use of their gifts and an appreciation and respect for those who are less gifted. As ex-Quiz Kid DiAnne Mathre Thomas says, "A superior intellect does not necessarily guarantee a superior human being."

Every child, it has been said, is in some way gifted—each has some special ability. Margaret Merrick Scheffelin, speaking from experience as an educator as well as a parent, suggests that watching what a child likes to do may be the best clue to undiscovered talents.

Parents of intellectually gifted children, in an effort to "accentuate the positive," sometimes emphasize mental development exclusively and overlook the importance of the physical side—for girls as well as boys. My discovery of tennis in midlife provided more than just fun; it gave me a new kind of self-esteem, a sense of wholeness, and an understanding of what goes into playing the game of life that I never could have gotten from books. A child who cannot or does not want to compete athletically may enjoy noncompetitive games.

One important thing parents can do is to place a child in the most appropriate educational setting available and then—without undue hovering—remain in close enough touch to make sure the child's unique needs are met. Even with the welcome proliferation of options, there often is no ideal solution. Parents should seek the best advice but ultimately must go with their own and the child's instincts. One youngster may thrive in a highly competitive situation; another, like Harvey Dytch, may not. Enrichment may be best for one, homogeneous grouping for another, a special program or private school for a third, tutoring for a fourth, acceleration for a fifth. But more important than format is the content and quality of instruction. Most crucial are a teacher's sensitivity to special needs, respect for independent thinking, and ability to keep gifted minds challenged. As some of us Quiz Kids can attest, a memorable teacher is worth more than the best curriculum guide.

In view of my own experience and that of some of the other Quiz Kids, I would be very cautious about grade skipping, especially in the early years when the child cannot make an informed judgment and when the rate of physical and social maturation cannot always be foreseen. Having skipped made things more difficult for some of us Quiz Kids who were small, immature, and unathletic. To be labelled a size sixteen mind in a size six body when everybody was size ten could be highly uncomfortable, especially as puberty approached.

On the other hand, a child who skips in the middle grades may have trouble reestablishing good peer relationships, as happened with Harve and Dick. When my younger daughter was in seventh grade and still ''learning'' basic grammar she had known for years, she regretted that we had not skipped her earlier, but she decided not to accelerate at that point because it would have meant leaving her friends.

The balance between intellectual and social considerations is a delicate one to strike, and there are likely to be costs either way. It is possible that had I entered the University of Chicago at fourteen, I might have had a brilliant academic career. It is also possible that I might have ended up as what Dr. Bruno Bettelheim has called a ''savant idiot,'' erudite but socially and emotionally immature.

I must add, however, that what seemed the wisest course in 1948 might not necessarily be so today, when lockstep learning is breaking down and college entrants as young as eleven and twelve are becoming more common. Radical acceleration is being practiced with apparent success through Professor Julian Stanley's Study of Mathematically Precocious Youth at Johns Hopkins University. Math is a field in which time lost may never be regained; according to Stanley, the splendid reasoner who vegetates at twelve may fail to develop the capacity for fast-paced thinking and may wind up unfulfilled at forty or fifty. To be accepted for the Johns Hopkins program, youngsters must be reasonably well-adjusted and must themselves be eager to do advanced work. The youths are counseled to determine the best approach for each—whether a special class, tutoring, or early college entrance.

Experiments with the blurring or elimination of age segregation, such as the ungraded school, may hold promise for resolving the gifted child's educational-social dilemma. Prototypes of ungraded learning existed in the one-room school and the pioneer family, in which children of all ages worked side by side at lessons of varying levels of difficulty.

Ultimately, if Alvin Toffler is right, the advent of the computer age may again make the home the focal point of both work and education. Already some parents, unable to find learning situations suited to their children's needs, are turning to home schooling—an alternative that apparently was satisfactory for Joan Bishop, though her special fondness for her Quiz Kid associates does suggest that these relationships filled a lack for her.

Professor Bloom, in his study of how top achievers developed, has found that the home (especially in the early childhood years) exerted a far more positive influence than the school—as was true with most of us Quiz Kids. Bloom's study points up the advantages of informal, personalized, one-to-one learning and of support and guidance from parents tuned in to their children's progress.

Whatever the dangers of overattachment that Harve Bennett spoke of, we Quiz Kids gained immeasurably from the extraordinary efforts of parents (particularly mothers) who were not too busy to invest themselves generously in enriching our childhood. They passed on to us a treasured heritage: the joy of learning for its own sake, not merely as a means of getting into the "right" college or earning x dollars a year.

In some ways, schools today are better than the ones we attended, and youngsters have more opportunities and advantages. They are being taught to analyze and imagine, not just to memorize and repeat.

Although it is fashionable to lament the impact of television, this techno-
logical tool—if properly used, within wise limits—can add a dimension
not available from the printed page. Many of the young people I see in my
suburban community seem more self-confident, sophisticated, and
articulate than I was at their age. Ex-Quiz Kid Ann Bokman Akers, who
helps run New Orleans' "Quiz Bowl," finds that the good students she
works with—coming from sixty-four high schools—are brighter, more
alert, better informed, and broader in their interests and activities than
was true in our generation.

On the other hand, there is often a lack of depth. In this age of special-
ization and vocational emphasis, those of us who cherish the value of a
liberal education are in danger of becoming a lonely-hearts club. Renaissance Man is being replaced by Computer Person, with a galaxy of
information available at the push of a button.

The democratization of education, once believed to be the means to
extend the blessings of enlightenment to all citizens, has resulted in a
turning away from the classical learning that many of us Quiz Kids began
absorbing at our parents' knees—the great works like the Bible and
Shakespeare that, as columnist George Will has written, served a "uni-
fying, civilizing function," forming the basis for shared communal values
and ideals. For us, the classics were not merely a source of rote answers
for a quiz show but beloved companions that, as we grew older, repaid
more serious examination.

Susanne Murphy, coordinator of the elementary gifted programs in
Clinton, Connecticut, has made a well-reasoned plea for a return to
classical studies:

> In the bad old days of standard academic programming and re-
> quired courses, Latin was a routinely prescribed component of many
> curricula. The justification for this, long after Latin had ceased to
> be a *lingua franca* for the internationally educated community, was
> that Latin exercised the brain. . . . just as the skeletal muscles were
> trained in physical routines. The problem with this outlook, of
> course, is that it denigrates the *matter* of the lessons. . . . *What*
> was studied became as unimportant as the sit-up. . . . It became
> quite easy for the critics of the sixties, then, to attack *irrelevant*
> curriculum requirements. Educators who suspected that memor-
> izing the Gettysburg Address might be meaningfully different from
> memorizing Mark Rudd's remarks on the president of Yale were
> unable to justify their position. . . . We felt that we could teach the
> same skills in more relevant ways by changing the materials so

that they would be more in keeping with the modern world. For a variety of reasons, the attempt failed. . . . Yes, we want to teach the gifted "creative thinking," but they also need to think creatively *about something,* and that something can just as well be the classically valuable subject matter. . . Particularly to the gifted do we owe the opportunity to master the traditional basic curriculum, since they can conquer it and still have time and energy to deal creatively and analytically with it.
 —"Programming for the Academically Gifted: The
 Hard Day's Night Model," *G/C/T,* March/April, 1980

Some teachers of the gifted are finding that the classics can speak to to-day's youth in profound ways. Dramatizing *Julius Caesar,* Laurel Crandus' students in suburban Woodridge, Illinois grapple with such un-dying themes as loyalty, friendship, patriotism, power, and persuasion. As a Junior Great Books leader, I have seen a group of gifted black eighth graders (in an inner city school that physically has changed not one iota from the dreary institutions I remember) become so engrossed in the ethical issues raised by *Antigone* that they could hardly wait to come back for more.

This is not to advocate the elimination of curricular variety and choice. Rather, it is to affirm that the lessons of the past are still worth learning. As Claude Brenner, the Quiz Kid who started as an aeronautical engineer and became president of his own energy consulting firm, advises: "Your career can take you anywhere. Educate yourself as a whole human being."

What is uniquely human is the ability to build tomorrow's achieve-ments on yesterday's experience. We impoverish our youth if we allow them to grow up unacquainted with their heritage. Young and old alike need a solid foundation from which to view the passing parade on our television and computer screens.

The increasingly rapid changes of the post-Quiz Kid decades have left us, as a society, uncertain of our moorings. Excitement about the expansion of human possibilities mingles with nostalgia for the time when it seemed that the human mind could comprehend everything worth knowing, and a radio program that celebrated knowledge—albeit for commercial purpose—could command a prime time national audience.

That was an era when Roby Hickok, the Quiz Kids' assistant director, could write that Quizmaster Joe Kelly turned the shade of a bedsheet, and everyone knew exactly what color she was talking about. We Quiz Kids (like our less conspicuous contemporaries) had to learn, as we matured, to deal with a more and more complex world.

It remains to be seen just what sort of future today's gifted children will face and what they will do with their potential. We cannot guard them from every peril; we can offer them the gift of our experience and hope that they will profit from it. But the dream, the risk, and the prize are theirs. In foiling their dragons and pursuing their golden fleece, they may be aided by sage advice and talismans, but ultimately they must depend on their own wits and inner strength.

Appendix

The following ex-Quiz Kids contributed to this book through interviews, questionnaires, and/or letters:

Ralph E. Adler—Computer programmer/analyst, Schaumburg, Illinois

Janet Ahern Martin—Substitute teacher, Troy, Michigan

Marguerite (Peggy) Bangert Thompson—English teacher, Wright College; Chicago, Illinois

Harve Bennett—Executive producer, Paramount Pictures; Los Angeles, California

Dean L. Berry—Lawyer, Squire, Sanders & Dempsey; Cleveland, Ohio

Shirley Bersadsky Goldman—Real estate broker, New Orleans, Louisiana

Joan Bishop Barber—Pianist and singer (retired), housewife; New York, New York

Dr. Joseph Bogen—Neurosurgeon, New Hope Pain Center; Alhambra, California

Ann Bokman Akers—Housewife, television writer, biochemist; New Orleans, Louisiana

Virginia Booze Klages—Housewife, Columbus, Ohio

Claude Brenner—President, Commonwealth Energy Group; Winchester, Massachusetts

Sheilah Brenner Lang—President, Lang Dental Manufacturing Co.; Chicago, Illinois

Vanessa Brown—Actress, writer, producer; Los Angeles, California

Marjorie Bruce Runnion—Writer; editorial researcher, *People* Magazine; New York, New York

Warren J. Cavior—Corporate and financial public relations consultant; New York, New York

Kenneth Childers—Architect (semi-retired); Las Vegas, Nevada

Patrick Conlon—Actor, director; New York, New York

Sheila Conlon—Producer; Chicago, Illinois

Naomi Cooks Mann—Proprietor, Think Big! (art boutique); San Francisco, California

George Cooks—Manufacturer's representative, consultant; Northbrook, Illinois

Anneke de Bruyn Overseth—Director of Development & External Relations, University of Michigan School of Business Administration

Bunny Duskin Shuch—Social worker; Phoenix, Arizona

Harvey Dytch—Computer programmer, Chicago Lying-In Hospital

Gail Dytch Schaffner—Housewife, Highland Park, Illinois

Robert Easton—Dialect coach, actor, author; Pasadena, California

Sydel Finfer Silverman Wolf—Professor of Anthropology, City University of New York Graduate School

Ruel Fischmann—Writer-producer; Los Angeles, California

Ruth Fisher Henoch—Housewife, college English teacher; Potomac, Maryland

Richard A. Freeman—Stockbroker, assistant branch manager, Bear, Stearns and Company; Atlanta, Georgia

David Freifelder—Professor of Biochemistry, author, University of California, San Diego

Richard Frisbie—Communications consultant, author; Chicago, Illinois

Marie Gleason Vonder Heide—Housewife; Chicago, Illinois

Dr. Judith Graham—Physician, counselor; Seattle, Washington

Dr. Arthur W. Haelig—Physician; Ocean Springs, Mississippi

Robert W. Haller—Attorney-at-law; Fort Wayne, Indiana

Lois Hesse Niemann—Computer Science instructor; Colorado State University

Jonathan Jackson—Advertising executive, Ogilvy & Mather; New York, New York

Dr. C. David Jenkins—Director of Sociomedical Sciences, University of Texas, Medical Branch, Galveston, Texas

Lois Myna Karpf—Word processor, statistical typist; Chicago, Illinois

Joel Kupperman—Professor of Philosophy, University of Connecticut

Richard Lieb—Composer-arranger; Briarcliff Manor, New York

Brenda Liebling Goldberg—Law student; Houston, Texas

Rochelle Liebling Kahan—Pianist, lawyer; Houston, Texas

Rev. John Lucal, S.J.—Jesuit priest, International Labour Office; Geneva, Switzerland

Lawson C. (Lon) Lunde—Pianist, composer; Des Plaines, Illinois

Julia Marwick Rainer—Proprietor, The Book Mark; Northfield, Illinois

DiAnne Mathre Thomas—Housewife; DeKalb, Illinois

Eloise Matthies Niwa—Pianist, teacher, De Paul University; Chicago, Illinois

Mary Clare McHugh Sanders—Housewife; Rolling Meadows, Illinois

William McHugh—Federal government administrator; San Francisco, California

Margaret Merrick Scheffelin—Consultant, Program Evaluation & Research, California Department of Education; Sacramento, California

Joan Moy Smith—Elementary school reading specialist; Naperville, Illinois

Rev. Mark H. Mullin—Headmaster, St. Albans School; Washington, D.C.

Michael M. Mullin—Professor of Biological Oceanography, University of California; San Diego

David Nasatir—Professor of Sociology, California State University; Dominguez Hills

Noreen Novick Cornfield—Associate professor of sociology, Barat College; Lake Forest, Illinois

Lois Piske Parks—Assistant manager, laundry equipment export business; Highland Park, Illinois

Peter M. Reich—Aviation-military writer, *Phoenix Gazette*; Phoenix, Arizona

Arthur Reinwald—Lawyer; Hoddick, Reinwald, O'Connor & Marrack Honolulu, Hawaii

Virginia Rhoads Kingland—Housewife; Lake Mills, Iowa

C. Harker Rhodes, Jr.—Lawyer; Sonnenschein, Carlin, Nath & Rosenthal; Chicago, Illinois

Daryce Richman—Studio singer, actress, pianist; Los Angeles, California

Marlene Richman—Piano teacher; Van Nuys, California

John P. Rooney—Law professor, Michigan State University

Barbara Scott Huszagh—Social worker; Wheaton, Illinois

Harry L. Sebel, Jr.—Financial consultant; Dallas, Texas

Dr. Richard E. Sedlack—Staff physician, Mayo Clinic; Rochester, Minnesota

Paul E. Sigmund—Professor of Politics, Princeton University

Elinor Smith Miller—Chairman, Division of Arts and Letters, St. Mary's College of Maryland

David Smothers—Senior editor, United Press International; Chicago, Illinois

Alan Stamm—Lawyer; Long & Levit; Los Angeles, California

Betty Swanson Upjohn—Real estate investment, public relations; Kalamazoo, Michigan

Joanna Tyrny Noncek—Hospital supervisor; Barrington, Illinois

Verne W. Vance, Jr.—Lawyer; Foley, Hoag and Elliot; Boston, Massachusetts

Frank P. VanderPloeg—Lawyer; Hopkins & Sutter; Chicago, Illinois

Charles F. Vihon—Bankruptcy law consultant; Stamford, Connecticut

James D. Watson—Molecular biologist & director, Cold Spring Harbor Laboratory; New York

Ronald Weintrob—Certified public accountant (retired); Chicago, Illinois

Sally Wilhelm Fullerton—Teacher-coordinator of alternative school; Hastings, Michigan

Richard Williams—Deputy U.S. Consul-General; Hong Kong

Nancy Wong Nelson—Theology student; Princeton, New Jersey

Rev. Ronald Youngblood—Professor of Old Testament, Bethel Seminary West; San Diego, California

Too late to tabulate:

Nancy McCleery Mein—History teacher, St. Andrews School; Middletown, Delaware

Bob Senescu—Trumpet player, music supervisor, ABC-TV; Los Angeles, California